MOTIVATION AND SELF-REGULATION IN SPORT AND EXERCISE

The ability to effectively use one's thoughts, emotions and motivation to enhance performance and well-being is one of the most important skills in sport and exercise contexts. *Motivation and Self-Regulation in Sport and Exercise* explores the theories, research and processes that underpin these self-regulatory and motivational processes. A deeper understanding of motivation and self-regulation has far-reaching implications, from helping individuals to begin an active lifestyle, to seasoned athletes looking for a competitive edge. For the first time, the globally leading researchers in this research field come together to provide their unique, cutting-edge insight into how to exercise or perform more effectively. In doing so, the book provides new insight into established theories of motivation and self-regulation, but also breaks new ground by inspecting lesser-known or emerging paradigms.

This book is intended for all scholars interested in self-regulation and motivation, from undergraduate students to experienced researchers, as well as practicing sport and exercise psychologists, coaches and athletes.

Chris Englert is an Assistant Professor in the department for Educational Psychology at the University of Bern, Switzerland.

Ian M. Taylor is a Senior Lecturer in Psychology in the School of Sport, Exercise and Health Sciences at Loughborough University, UK.

MOTIVATION AND SELF-REGULATION IN SPORT AND EXERCISE

Edited by
Chris Englert and
Ian M. Taylor

Routledge
Taylor & Francis Group
NEW YORK AND LONDON

First published 2021
by Routledge
52 Vanderbilt Avenue, New York, NY 10017

and by Routledge
2 Park Square, Milton Park, Abingdon, Oxon, OX14 4RN

Routledge is an imprint of the Taylor & Francis Group, an informa business

Library of Congress Cataloging-in-Publication Data
A catalog record for this title has been requested

ISBN: 978-0-367-43316-1 (hbk)
ISBN: 978-0-367-43314-7 (pbk)
ISBN: 978-1-003-17669-5 (ebk)

Typeset in Bembo
by codeMantra

CONTENTS

FIGURES

TABLES

CONTRIBUTORS

Catherine J. Berman Center for Advanced Hindsight, Duke University, US

Maik Bieleke Department of Cognitive Psychology, University of Vienna, Austria

Ralf Brand Sport and Exercise Psychology, University of Potsdam, Germany

Denver M. Y. Brown Department of Family Medicine, McMaster University, Canada

Panteleimon Ekkekakis Department of Kinesiology, Iowa State University, US

Chris Englert Department of Educational Sciences, University of Bern, Switzerland

Jeffrey D. Graham Ontario Tech University, Faculty of Health Sciences, Canada

Stina Grant School of Exercise Science, Physical and Health Education, University of Victoria, Canada

Martin S. Hagger Department of Psychological Sciences, Health Psychology, University of California, Merced

Andrew P. Hill School of Science, Technology, and Health, York St John University, UK

Anna Hirsch Department of Sport Sciences, Sport Psychology, University of Konstanz, Germany

Henry La School of Exercise Science, Physical and Health Education, University of Victoria, Canada

Samuele Marcora University of Bologna, Italy

Susette A. Moyers Psychological Sciences, Health Psychology, University of California, US

Ross M. Murray Kinesiology and Physical Education, University of Toronto, Canada

Julia D. O'Brien Behavior Change, WW (formerly Weight Watchers) and Duke University, US

Alison Quinlan School of Exercise Science, Physical and Health Education, University of Victoria, Canada

Ryan E. Rhodes School of Exercise Science, Physical and Health Education, University of Victoria, Canada

Catherine M. Sabiston Kinesiology and Physical Education, University of Toronto, Canada

Amitai Shenhav Department of Cognitive, Linguistic, and Psychological Sciences, Brown University, US

Ian M. Taylor School of Sport, Exercise, and Health Sciences, Loughborough University, UK

Madison F. Vani Kinesiology and Physical Education, University of Toronto, Canada

Jeroen Van Cutsem Royal Military Academy Brussel, Belgium

Wanja Wolff Department of Sport Sciences, Sport Psychology, University of Konstanz, Germany

Zachary Zenko Department of Kinesiology, California State University, Bakersfield, US

1

INTRODUCTION TO MOTIVATION AND SELF-REGULATION IN SPORT AND EXERCISE

Chris Englert and Ian M. Taylor

Introduction

Motivation and self-regulation are two of the most important psychological aspects in sport and exercise settings. An athlete or exerciser who is optimally motivated and possesses the necessary self-regulatory resources and skills is not only more likely to persistently strive toward goal achievement, but is also likely to psychologically and physically thrive during his or her endeavors. Given this significance, self-regulation and motivation are two key concepts in sport and exercise research, with a cursory internet search revealing over 18,000 publications on self-regulation and over 21,000 publications on motivation since 2000. The main goal of this textbook is to provide a single source of information that highlights the importance of motivational and self-regulatory processes in sport and exercise contexts. The chapters provide a comprehensive overview of recent theoretical developments in the field and discuss possible approaches to improve motivational and self-regulatory processes, which, in turn, can influence sport and exercise performance, engagement, and well-being. While this textbook is not an exhaustive compendium of the different theoretical perspectives that describe motivation and self-regulation, the chapters represent state-of-the-art developments that build on, or provide counterpoints to, more historically grounded theories of motivation and self-regulation. The aim of this opening chapter is to introduce the terms motivation and self-regulation and their relationship. Each concept will be described, and a brief history of the construct's development will contextualize the structure and content of the remaining chapters in the textbook.

Motivation in Sport and Exercise

Motivation is at the core of human psychology and essential to understanding all human behavior. It is unsurprising, therefore, that motivation plays a central role in participation, performance, and well-being in sport and exercise contexts. The proliferation of theoretical perspectives each provides a unique definition of motivation; however, motivation can be broadly described as the forces that drive and direct behavior (Dweck, 2017). These forces range from basic physiological needs, such as thirst and hunger, to materialistic desires, such as trophies and prizes. In between exists a range of explicit and implicit motives that can be approach-oriented, such as the seeking of pleasure or value, or avoidance-oriented, such as the desire to prevent guilt or anxiety (Elliot, 1997). Due to this vast array of potential motives, there is often little empirical value in asking "what motivates?" because there are infinite specific phenomena that can energize or forestall action. In the same way as stressors are only one facet of the broader stress process (Fletcher & Arnold, 2017), motivational stimuli are one component of broader motivational processes that explain how intrapsychic mechanisms shape human thought and behavior. Several chapters in this book use these motivational processes to describe and explain diverse phenomena, such as exercise participation, consequences of engagement in exercise and sport, and persistence in endurance sport contexts. Sport and exercise settings represent ideal scenarios to examine human motivation because the full range of motivational processes can be observed, from the young child excited but nervous about participating in sport for the first time, to the sedentary adult with negative attitudes to exercise, to the elite athlete striving for a competitive advantage.

Although motivation drives behavior, it does not mean that motivation can be comprehensively assessed through behavior alone. Doing so would fail to capture the complexities of human motivation. For example, two young sport participants may similarly engage in basketball sessions with identical attendance and physical intensity during matches. A naïve conclusion would be that the two participants were identically motivated. But this scenario does not tell us that one child might be anxious about attending and believed that she would be letting her mother down if she did not attend. In contrast, the second attendee may love basketball and cannot wait to attend the coaching sessions. As these examples imply, motivation has significant consequences beyond behavior; our affect and cognition are also the products of motivational processes. This is particularly important to consider because sport and exercise contexts can often emphasize behavioral outcomes, such as performing well or working hard in the gym, at the expense of psychological consequences.

The investigation of motivation in sport and exercise has a considerable history. Norman Triplett's (1898) social facilitation experiment investigated how the presence of others could motivate superior performance. However, the late 1970s witnessed a growth in motivation as an important topic in sport and exercise settings, largely due to the birth of the *Journal of Sport Psychology* (later the *Journal of Sport and Exercise Psychology*). Several theories were being developed in psychology, such as attribution theory (Weiner, 1974) and self-efficacy theory (Bandura, 1977), which were applied to sport and exercise settings (Roberts & Pascuzzi, 1979; Weinberg, Gould, & Jackson, 1979). The subsequent decades saw the growth of many important motivation theories for sport and exercise psychology. Three theories stand out from the crowd and still hold much influence today: Achievement goal theory (Duda & Nicholls, 1992), self-determination theory (Deci & Ryan, 1985), and the theory of planned behavior (Ajzen, 1991).

Achievement goal theory has been largely investigated in sport contexts, particularly youth sport participation. The theory focuses on the need to demonstrate competence by emphasizing self-referenced improvement or possessing a *task-goal orientation* (e.g. "am I better than I was?") versus normatively referenced improvement or possessing an *ego-goal orientation* (e.g. "am I better than others?"; Duda, 1992). A task-goal orientation typically leads to favorable cognitive, affective, and behavioral outcomes, whereas an ego-orientation enhances the risk of negative outcomes, especially when perceived competence is low

(Nicholls, 1989). Over the years, this dual goal orientation approach has been gradually expanded to 2 × 2 (Elliot & McGregor, 2001), and 3 × 2 frameworks (Elliot, Murayama, & Pekrun, 2011). This latest incarnation includes task-, ego-, and social-goal orientations, with each dimension containing an approach or avoidance motivational valence. The approach versus avoidance distinction may be particularly important for sport performance, compared to the task versus ego distinction (Van Yperen, Blaga, & Postmes, 2014). However, these extensions to the original dual goal orientation approach have been criticized and suggested to be unwarranted (Midgley, Kaplan, & Middleton, 2001; Roberts & Nerstad, 2020).

Self-determination theory is commonly described as a theory of motivation, but perhaps more accurately should be described as a meta-theory that adopts a motivational perspective to cover much broader phenomena, including personality, development, and well-being. A central component of the theory is that individuals possess fundamental needs for autonomy (the experience of volition and internal locus of causality), competence (the experience of effectiveness), and relatedness (the experience of socio-emotional connectedness; Ryan & Deci, 2017). Consistent satisfaction of these three psychological needs facilitates several adaptive growth and developmental processes, including (i) a tendency to engage in activities for intrinsically motivated reasons, (ii) effective integration into one's sense of self of activities that are not inherently intrinsically motivating (Ryan & Deci, 2000), and (iii) the development of an autonomous causality orientation, in which individuals seek out activities that provide opportunities for psychological need satisfaction (Hagger & Hamilton, 2020). Overall, these three psychological needs are deemed essential for psychological and physical well-being (Vansteenkiste & Ryan, 2013) and the growth tendencies have been shown to facilitate a myriad of positive outcomes in sport and exercise contexts (Taylor, 2015; Teixeira; Carraça, Markland, Silva & Ryan, 2012).

The theory of planned behavior describes how favorable personal attitudes, social norms, and perceived control over behavioral execution are the necessary ingredients for developing an intention to act, which then energizes engagement in the focal behavior (Ajzen, 1991). Perceived behavioral control also moderates the relationship between intentions and behavior (Fishbein & Ajzen, 2010). Meta-analysis of the theory in exercise contexts generally supports these relationships (Hausenblas, Carron, & Mack, 1997). Nonetheless, this theory has evolved into the reasoned action approach, which separates attitudes, subjective norms, and behavioral control into two subcomponents each (experiential and instrumental attitudes, injunctive and descriptive norms, capacity and autonomy control beliefs; Fishbein & Ajzen, 2010). This more detailed specification has been shown to be useful in health contexts (McEachan et al., 2016). The theory of planned behavior has been largely used to explain behavior in exercise and health contexts; however, constructs from the theory have been shown to be helpful in predicting doping intentions and behavior in sport (Ntoumanis, Ng, Barkoukis, & Backhouse, 2014).

The popularity of these theories continued in the 1990s and 2000s. As Chapters 3 and 4 in this book detail, this was the era of cognitivism, in which reflective, conscious processes were at the heart of motivation research. Textbooks on motivation were published that provided a compendium of insights into motivation from a cognitivist perspective (Hagger & Chatzisarantis, 2007; Roberts & Treasure, 2012). However, we are currently witnessing an increase in critical perspectives and investigation into new areas of motivation. In recent times, the theory of planned behavior, in particular, has attracted criticism (Sniehotta,

Presseau, & Araújo-Soares, 2014). One of the most interesting criticisms is the gap between intention and behavior. That is, why do people who hold an intention to engage in an activity commonly fail to do so (Orbell & Sheeran, 1998)? This question is the foundation for several chapters in this book.

Other criticisms of the theory of planned behavior, which can also be aimed at many other motivation theories, include the failure to account for automatic influences on behavior (Sheeran, Gollwitzer, & Bargh, 2013) and the role of emotions in the motivational process (Conner, Godin, Sheeran, & Germain, 2013). Especially in performance settings, emotion has been viewed as the enemy of effective performance and athletes have been encouraged to regulate emotion to such an extent that emotion becomes devalued. In exercise contexts, affect has also been neglected in favor of cognitive processes (Brand & Ekkekakis, 2019). Yet, one of the most basic principles of motivation is that individuals typically veer toward activities that they find pleasurable and away from activities that they do not (Epstein, 2013). This tenet has not received sufficient attention in motivational models in sport and exercise, but there is a growing trend to rectify this issue. Rather than viewing emotion as the enemy of goal-driven rational choices or performance, we are beginning to see emotion as a fully integrated component of adaptive motivational processes (Inzlicht, Werner, Briskin, & Robert, 2021). These related limitations represent further stimuli for several chapters in this book.

The Relationship between Motivation and Self-Regulation in Sport and Exercise

One of the most important consequences of motivation in sport and exercise contexts is that it provides the foundation for the initiation and maintenance of self-regulation strategies. As such, motivation and self-regulation can be viewed as complementary processes that are inextricably linked. For example, the Rubicon model of action phases was one of the first comprehensive theoretical models which included motivational as well as self-regulatory process to explain goal-directed behavior (Gollwitzer, 1990; Heckhausen & Gollwitzer, 1987). The Rubicon is a river in northern Italy and legend has it that Julius Cesar contemplated for days whether he and his army should cross it, as he was well aware that the crossing would lead to a civil war. In the end, Cesar crossed the Rubicon which led to his famous words, *alea iacta est* or "the die has been cast" (Heckhausen, Gollwitzer, & Weinert, 1987). The model broadly assumes that motivational processes support the formation of intentions (i.e. goal setting) at which the individual crosses the hypothetical "Rubicon" and self-regulatory processes (i.e. volitional processes) are initiated to persistently pursue these goals (i.e. goal striving), especially in the presence of tempting alternative behaviors or currently experienced barriers (e.g. increased levels of fatigue; Achtziger & Gollwitzer, 2009, 2010; Kuhl & Beckmann, 1994). In a similar fashion, the Health Action Process Approach (HAPA; Schwarzer, 2008; Schwarzer, Lippke, & Luszczynska, 2011) also stresses the importance of motivational processes, which support intention formation, and volitional processes, which enable one to strive for these intentions (see also Luszczynska & Schwarzer, 2003). The HAPA and Rubicon model of action phases, as well as related models, are explained in more detail in Chapter 12 of this book.

Self-Regulation in Sport and Exercise

Self-regulation is one of the most important predictors of goal achievement (Baumeister & Heatherton, 1996; Carver & Scheier, 1998) and takes center stage of psychological research (Duckworth & Seligman, 2017). Self-regulation describes the ability to volitionally control or alter predominant impulses and response tendencies to achieve future benefits (Baumeister, Heatherton, & Tice, 1994). For example, an athlete has to regulate current thoughts or emotions in a given situation in order to secure future benefits (Englert, 2016, 2017). While the first studies on self-regulation and volition have been conducted in the early 20th century by Narcissus Ach (1935), self-regulation as well as related, overlapping psychological constructs (e.g. delay of gratification, willpower) have only been extensively studied since the 1970s. Social cognitive theory was one of the first psychological models which stressed the importance of cognitive processes like goal-monitoring and self-regulation to achieve a desired end-state (Bandura, 1977). Since then, many self-regulation models have been developed to explain self-regulatory behaviors (for an overview, see De Ridder & De Wit, 2006). All these models agree that self-regulatory processes enable us to resist immediate gratifications and to instead keep striving for more desirable and oftentimes delayed gratifications (Hagger, 2010). In general, research has reliably shown that individuals who are more adept at regulating their impulses are more likely to achieve their long-term goals (De Ridder, Lensvelt-Mulders, Finkenauer, Stok, & Baumeister, 2012; Tangney, Baumeister, & Boone, 2004). On the contrary, lower self-regulatory abilities are associated with several maladaptive behaviors (e.g. procrastination, substance abuse) and lower academic as well as sports-related achievement (Tangney et al., 2004).

In one of the earliest studies on self-regulation – often referred to as the Marshmallow Test – children were informed that they could either receive an immediate reward (i.e. a delicious piece of candy) or a delayed reward (i.e. two delicious pieces of candy; Mischel, 1961). This situation created a *goal conflict*, as most children were aware that delaying immediate gratification would subsequently lead to a larger but delayed gratification. To deal with this goal conflict and to keep striving for the long-term reward, the children applied different types of self-regulatory strategies (e.g. distraction). The results from numerous longitudinal studies revealed that being able to resist the immediate reward was related to several positive health-related and academic outcomes several years later (Davis, Patte, Curtis, & Reid, 2010; Mischel, Shoda, & Rodriguez, 1989; Schlam, Wilson, Shoda, Mischel, & Ayduk, 2013). These early results demonstrated the importance of self-regulation for a successful and healthy life (for a critical discussion, see Watts, Duncan, & Quan, 2018; see also Duckworth, Tsukayama, & Kirby, 2013).

Self-regulation has also been extensively studied in sport and exercise contexts, which is hardly surprising as there are several potential goal conflicts in these domains which need to be solved in order to achieve a desirable long-term goal (Englert, 2016, 2017; Hagger, Wood, Stiff, & Chatzisarantis, 2009). Imagine a recreational athlete who wants to participate in a marathon which takes place in three months. The athlete has to practice on a regular basis; however, there might be several temptations along the way: On an evening where he originally wanted to go for a 2-hour run, there is a match involving his favorite football team on TV which he would like to see. In this situation, two goals collide, leading to a goal conflict. If he wants to follow his long-term goal of running the marathon, he has to resist the short-term goal of watching the match, even though striving for the short-term goal would lead to immediate gratification (Englert & Rummel, 2016).

Over the years, two different lines of research on self-regulation in sport and exercise developed, with one line coming from the field of sport psychology and the other line coming from the field of physiology. Sport and exercise psychologists primarily adopted a resource-based approach assuming that there is only a limited amount of self-regulatory willpower which can become temporarily depleted (i.e. *ego depletion*; Englert, 2016). Physiologists have argued that lapses in self-regulation are caused by states of mental fatigue (Marcora, Staiano, & Manning, 2009). Even though both theoretical approaches assume that primary self-regulatory acts can potentially impair subsequent performance, they interestingly have mostly evolved in isolation from each other. One of the major differences between both research approaches is that ego depletion researchers assume that states of ego depletion can be induced after having worked on relatively short primary self-regulatory tasks (i.e. less than five minutes; Englert, 2016, 2017). In contrast, it is postulated that states of mental fatigue can only be induced if the primary self-regulatory task lasted at least 30 minutes (Pageaux, Marcora, & Lepers, 2013; Van Cutsem et al., 2017). As will be shown in this book, these different lines of inquiry are now being integrated to advance our knowledge of self-regulation in sport and exercise.

So why is it that for some individuals it does not seem to be challenging to resist these urges, while for others it is a constant internal battle to work out on a regular basis? What are the underlying mechanisms of self-regulatory behaviors and how can self-regulation be improved? These are just some of the core questions which will be addressed in this book.

Chapter Overview

Broadly speaking, this book consists of two main sections each focusing on motivation or self-regulation; however, many describe their interactive influence on human cognition, affect, and behavior. Each of the chapters has been written by leading researchers from around the world.

Chapter 2 describes the multi-process action control model, which illuminates many processes and strategies that have the potential to bridge the intention-behavior gap in planned physical activity contexts. In addition, the chapter addresses the issue of failing to turn the initiation of physical activity behavior into sustained adherence. Chapter 3 critically evaluates the dominant empirical paradigms in exercise psychology. After a historical analysis of the cognitive traditions of exercise psychology, the chapter calls for a change in direction by describing the affective-reflective model of physical activity and exercise. A central component of this framework suggests that (dis)pleasure and basic affective states greatly shape our decision making in exercise contexts. Following on from this same tenet, Chapter 4 describes and evaluates behavioral economic approaches to exercise motivation and engagement. This chapter also discusses how to take advantage of several heuristics (i.e. systematic biases that aid decision making) to redesign environments and build a motivational toolkit to enhance physical activity and exercise behavior.

Like the preceding chapters, Chapter 5 also focuses on emotion but in a significantly different context. The chapter contains a review and analysis of how body-related self-conscious emotions act as motivational and self-regulatory processes in sport and exercise contexts. This chapter explains how body image, social physique anxiety, and many other emotions can not only drive (dis)engagement in sport and exercise, but also shape well-being within those contexts. Chapter 6 investigates a potential dark side of sport and exercise motivation, namely perfectionism. Perfectionism has been studied for an extensive period and many existing reviews exist. Hence, rather than simply describe the theories of perfectionism, the chapter attempts to debunk several myths about perfectionism that have infiltrated empirical and lay communications. Finally, Chapter 7 shifts focus to motivational processes in endurance performance settings. The theory provides a counterpoint to existing models of endurance that insufficiently recognize the role of motivation for optimal performance. This chapter describes how motivational states can underscore self-regulatory processes that have a key role in endurance. As a result, it represents an example of how motivation and self-regulation interact.

Chapters 8–12 emphasize the importance of self-regulatory processes during sport and exercise performance. First, Chapter 8 introduces the strength model of self-control, which assumes that there is only a limited amount of self-regulatory strength which enables us to regulate our impulses and urges. Hence, the model assumes that if a first task places self-regulatory demands on an individual, then performance in a subsequent self-regulation task will be impaired as one's self-regulatory resources had been depleted in the foregoing task. In Chapter 9, Graham and Brown discuss the differences and similarities between ego depletion and mental fatigue. They also present meta-analytical evidence suggesting that performing an initial cognitively demanding task leads to subsequent performance impairments across a broad range of aerobic and resistance-based tasks that require prolonged effort regulation (Brown et al., 2020; Giboin & Wolff, 2019). In Chapter 10, Van Cutsem and Marcora report an update on research on the effects of mental fatigue on sports performance. Furthermore, potential strategies to reduce mental fatigue and its negative effects on sports performance are discussed. In Chapter 11, the neuronal mechanisms underlying self-regulatory behaviors will be discussed as Wolff and colleagues aim at introducing neuroscientific approaches to self-regulatory control in sports. Findings on cortical activity during self-regulated sports performance as well as psychometric tools to assess cortical activity during sports are presented. In Chapter 12, Moyers and Hagger integrate motivational and self-regulatory processes of goal setting and goal striving to describe how planning and implementation intentions, also called "if-then plans," can be valuable strategies to improve self-regulatory performance during sport and exercise.

Finally, the focus of Chapter 13 is to draw out common features within the preceding chapters and to provide an outlook on potential future research endeavors. Many of the chapters represent new thinking and different approaches to the study of motivation and self-regulation; therefore, they raise as many questions as answers in the search for optimal motivation and self-regulation. As such, we hope that these chapters motivate scientific curiosity and stimulate new ideas and avenues of investigation.

2

ENACTING PHYSICAL ACTIVITY INTENTION

A Multi-Process Action Control Approach

Ryan E. Rhodes, Henry La, Alison Quinlan, and Stina Grant

Introduction

Chronic diseases, such as heart disease, diabetes, and cancer, now comprise the leading causes of death in all high-income countries (World Health Organization, 2018). Mental health conditions, such as depression and anxiety, also have large lifetime incidences across the world (GBD 2017 Disease and Injury Incidence and Prevalence Collaborators, 2018; Ritchie & Roser, 2020). Furthermore, the personal, social, and economic impacts of these diseases and conditions are enormous and involve low quality of life, workplace absenteeism, familial distress, and high costs for treatment (Mascie-Taylor & Karim, 2003; Walker, 2007). Most chronic conditions have complex etiologies that involve environmental, genetic, and behavioral antecedents (Kujala, 2011; Mulle & Vaccarino, 2013). Physical inactivity is one of the most important factors attributed to most of these chronic conditions (Lee et al., 2012; Rhodes, Bredin, Janssen, Warburton, & Bauman, 2017; Warburton & Bredin, 2017). Specifically, 150 minutes or more of moderate to vigorous intensity physical activity (PA) is linked to reduced odds of over 25 chronic health conditions with relative risk reduction between 20% and 40% (Arem et al., 2015; Rhodes et al., 2017; Warburton & Bredin, 2017). Unfortunately, many people do not engage in this recommended level of PA on a regular basis (Hallal et al., 2012). For example, globally in 2016, 27.5% of adults aged 18 years and over were considered insufficiently physically active (Guthold, Stevens, Riley, & Bull, 2018). In high-income countries, this increased to 36.8% of adults who were considered insufficiently active. Clearly, moderate-to-vigorous physical activity (MVPA) promotion efforts are needed.

Theoretical understanding of the determinants behind PA has been a line of research inquiry for over half a century, based on the premise that a sound understanding of PA determinants will aid in intervention success by targeting key variables (Rhodes, McEwan, & Rebar, 2019). Theories represent an organization of structure, function, and common nomenclature to critical variables under study (Michie, West, Campbell, Brown, & Gainforth, 2014). While debate about the utility of various theoretical approaches has been growing (Brand & Ekkekakis, 2018; Dalgetty, Miller, & Dombrowski, 2019; Gourlan et al., 2016;

Hagger & Weed, 2019; McEwan et al., 2019; Rhodes, McEwan, et al., 2019; Sniehotta, Presseau, & Araújo-Soares, 2014), the dominant approach to understanding PA has been through the social cognitive tradition (Conner & Norman, 2015; Rhodes & Nasuti, 2011). Theories from this tradition have unique aspects; yet, almost all suggest that expectations of the outcomes from behavioral action and the perception of one's capability to perform the behavior affect the formation of intentions; these intentions, in turn, impact behavior (Rebar & Rhodes, in press; Rhodes, McEwan, et al., 2019).

Social cognitive approaches to understanding PA have been useful. Approaches such as the theory of planned behavior (Ajzen, 1991; Fishbein & Ajzen, 2010) and social cognitive theory (Bandura, 1998), for example, explain roughly 25% of the variance in PA and do support the tenets of these models noted above (McEachan, Conner, Taylor, & Lawton, 2011; Young, Plotnikoff, Collins, Callister, & Morgan, 2014). Furthermore, these approaches have produced small changes in PA through interventions (Gourlan et al., 2016; McEwan et al., 2019; Murray et al., 2018; Rhodes, Boudreau, Weman Josefsson, & Ivarsson, in press; Rhodes et al., 2017).

Despite the utility of these social cognitive approaches, there is certainly room for improvement in theoretical fidelity and PA promotion effectiveness. One of the most common criticisms is the modest association between intention and behavior, when intention is considered the critical proximal determinant of behavior (Sheeran & Webb, 2016; Sniehotta, 2009). To be clear, the relationship between intention and PA is substantial, and one of the largest known predictors of behavior (Rhodes et al., 2017). Still, there are several streams of research that demonstrate a sizeable "intention-behavior gap" which highlights the insufficiency of social cognitive approaches to understanding PA. For example, experimental manipulations that increase PA intention (d = 0.45 or r = 0.22) result in much lower, and clinically less meaningful increases in PA (d = 0.15 or r = 0.075) (Rhodes & Dickau, 2012). A meta-analysis of the dichotomization (e.g. those who intended to engage in regular PA but did not follow through, those who did not intend to engage in PA and subsequently followed through with no PA) of the intention and PA relationship around public health guidelines also showed that 48% of intenders failed to follow through with PA (Rhodes & de Bruijn, 2013a). This finding is similar across various activities such as resistance training (Vallerand, Rhodes, Walker, & Courneya, 2016), dog walking (Rhodes & Lim, 2016), and parental support of child MVPA (Rhodes, Spence, et al., 2016). By contrast, the intention-behavior gap is magnified for those who are beginning PA (66%) compared to those who are continuing PA (29%) (Rhodes & Plotnikoff, 2006) and when accelerometry is used as the PA measure compared to self-report (62%–79%) (Rhodes, Quinlan, Naylor, Warburton, & Blanchard, 2020). Perhaps most important is the lowered practical value of theories that place intention as the proximal antecedent of health behavior. It is extremely common for inactive participants in PA interventions to report to the trial with high intentions at baseline, a tautological implication of volunteering in the first place (Rhodes & Rebar, 2017).

Based on this information, the purpose of this chapter is to overview evidence for the predictors of intention-behavior discordance in PA, as well as to outline critical mechanisms and behavior change techniques to reduce the intention-behavior gap. This overview is addressed through the lens and tenets of Multi-Process Action Control (M-PAC; Rhodes, 2017), which is one of several theoretical frameworks designed to address the intention-behavior gap (Rhodes & Yao, 2015). It should be acknowledged that intentional PA is only one form of MVPA that can be accumulated to achieve health benefits (Sallis et al., 2006).

Spontaneous PA (unplanned activities) and PA performed as a more incidental means of achieving other directives (e.g. shopping, commuting) are behaviors unlikely to be explained by the approaches outlined in this chapter. Furthermore, intentional PA is based on the assumption that an individual is choosing to perform or not perform PA compared to other possible alternative actions. PA that is constrained by a lack of choice (Ng et al., 2012) or considerable social inequalities (Schüz, Brick, Wilding, & Conner, 2020) is not applicable to M-PAC.

Intention-Behavior Discordance: What Is Happening?

The history of the intention concept offers some explanation as to why the intention-behavior gap has risen in prominence (Heckhausen, 2007). Intention has a double-barreled meaning that can include (i) a decision to enact a target behavior (self-instruction) and/or (ii) the determination to enact that decision (see Rhodes & Rebar, 2017 for a detailed overview). These two constructs were identified early in theoretical research, with operationalization of two phases that comprised (1) intention formation and (2) the subsequent volitional effort needed to translate the intention (Ach, 1905). However, intention was streamlined to a single working construct by Lewin (1951), who suggested that the separation of the volitional effort component of intention from the formation component of intention was a rarity under most circumstances. This streamlined intention construct is the one generally used in many social cognitive approaches that emerged in the 1960s through the 1980s (Fishbein & Ajzen, 1975; Rogers, 1983).

Despite the wide-ranging use of theories that considered a streamlined intention construct as the proximal determinant of behavior, there were still several noteworthy exceptions that revived the potential differentiation between an aim and the effort enacted to achieve that aim. For example, Leventhal, Singer, and Jones (1965) found that people who enacted specific volitional plans to get tetanus shots were more likely to follow through with attitudes/intentions. Kuhl (1984) formally labeled the phase of translating intentions into behavior as action control, and offered a series of constructs that may be essential for this purpose. This model was followed by theoretical approaches that recommended a specific focus on action control in various forms (Bagozzi, 1992; Freund & Baltes, 2002; Heckhausen & Gollwitzer, 1987; Prochaska & DiClemente, 1982; Schwarzer, 1992; Weinstein, 1988). Overall, action control models that attempt to understand how intentions are translated into behavior in order to foster effective interventions are a viable and important area of future PA research (Rhodes & Yao, 2015).

Of course, effective action control models will be predicated on a sound understanding of why the intention-behavior gap is occurring and not just a mere conceptualization of intention formation and action control phases. Figure 2.1 provides a conceptual diagram for intention-behavior discordance in PA, based on M-PAC which highlights strategic challenges and automatic tendencies as the most likely determinants.

Strategic Challenges: Strategic challenges comprise determinants that prohibit the long-term execution of intention-behavior relations. In a sense, these are failures that may be visible from a distance, and present from the initial formation of the intention. Two critical strategic failures are outlined in Figure 2.1: Outcome vs. behavioral goal confusion and failure to consider multiple goals.

Confusion between outcome and behavioral goals from the formation of an intention to the enacting sequence is likely most understandable through New Year's resolutions. Every

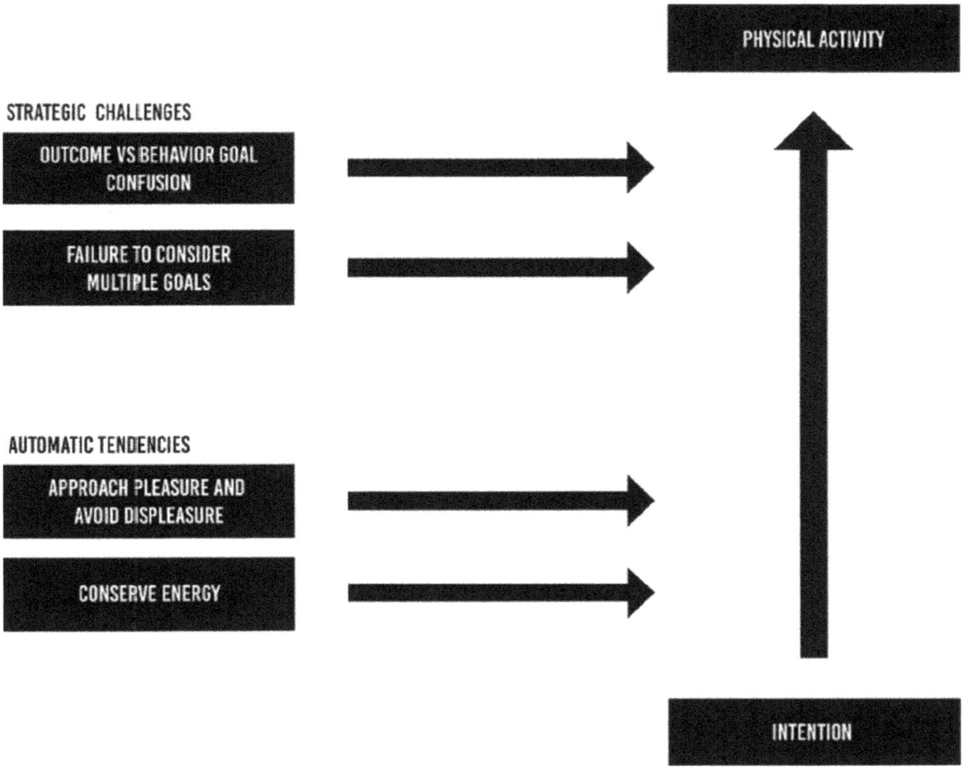

FIGURE 2.1 Influences on physical activity intention-behavior discordance.

January 1st, people from around the world set new intentions toward health and prosocial behaviors. An increase in PA is among the most prevalent of these resolutions (Statistica, 2020; The Telegraph, 2017; Time Magazine, 2012). Yet, the intention to engage in PA is almost inevitably linked to the desired long-term outcomes of PA, such as weight control, health, and fitness (Symons Downs & Hausenblas, 2005). The intention is rarely linked to the performance of PA itself, in most circumstances. This is an enormous strategic error in intention development which is well-established in theories of goal formation (Locke & Latham, 2006) and behavior change techniques (Michie et al., 2013). This is also a critical error in PA action control, given the behavioral cost (i.e. time and effort) that is required from regular PA to achieve these outcomes (Rhodes & Nigg, 2011). The importance of the experience itself to sustained PA has been well-established (Kwasnicka, Dombrowski, White, & Sniehotta, 2016; Rhodes, Fiala, & Conner, 2009; Teixeira, Carraça, Markland, Silva, & Ryan, 2012) and the importance of behavioral experience is also established in the action control sequence. For example, Keer, Conner, Van den Putte, and Neijens (2013) showed that intentions founded on experiential attitudes (i.e. the behavioral experience) about PA were far better predictors of behavior compared to intentions founded on instrumental attitudes (i.e. the outcomes derived from the behavior). In a review of ten studies on the topic, strong experiential/affective attitude predicted successful translation of PA intentions in 90% of the studies, while strong instrumental attitudes were inconsequential to action control (10% of studies) (Rhodes & de Bruijn, 2013b). Taken together, the evidence suggests that intentions to engage in PA formed on the basis of long-term benefits are likely to fail compared to those less common individuals who form intentions based on the behavioral experience itself.

Another key strategic challenge contributing to PA intention-behavior discordance is the failure to consider the multiple goals one is trying to achieve. A focus on one specific goal is likely to under-estimate complex goal-directed actions (Little, 1983) because intentions for one behavior will affect the subsequent resources to perform other behaviors (Orehek & Vazeou-Nieuwenhuis, 2013; Rachlin, Kagel, & Battalio, 1980). Indeed, juggling multiple goals is one of the prime reasons for why new intentions are forgotten during the action control phase (Sheeran & Webb, 2016). Failure to consider one's other goals in context may also contribute to unrealistic, fanciful intentions, which are far less likely to be fulfilled (Avishai, Conner, & Sheeran, 2019). Further, PA goals that compete for time and resources (i.e. goal conflict) increase the intention-behavior gap, compared to goals that can be mutually achieved with the same actions (goal facilitation) (Rhodes, Quinlan, & Mistry, 2016). Because we typically possess multiple goals, prioritizing one intention over another becomes an important strategic factor during action control (Freund & Baltes, 2002). A failure to prioritize PA intention has been linked to increased intention-behavior discordance (Conner et al., 2016). Overall, the evidence strongly indicates that lack of consideration of one's multiple intentions will increase failure in action control.

Automatic Tendencies: While a failure to consider key strategic factors clearly disrupts intention and behavior correspondence (Sheeran & Webb, 2016), action control can also be affected by more impulsive, situational, or abrupt determining factors. These determinants have been categorized in Figure 2.1 as automatic tendencies to indicate that there is some predictability in how these factors may lower action control (i.e. tendencies); yet, the cause of these interruptions is less salient to one's awareness and less a consequence of reflective expectations during the intention formation process (Melnikoff & Bargh, 2018; Sheeran, Gollwitzer, & Bargh, 2013).

The first critical determinant is based on the premise that people have a basic underlying tendency to approach experiences that are pleasant and avoid experiences that are unpleasant (Cabanac, 1992). This assumption has been substantiated in PA research because the affective response during a bout of PA is a reliable predictor of future PA (Rhodes & Kates, 2015). Several research teams theorize that much of this relationship may affect behavior below reflective awareness, or at least preceding cognitive reflection (Brand & Ekkekakis, 2018; Conroy & Berry, 2017; Strobach, Englert, Jekauc, & Pfeffer, 2020; Williams & Evans, 2014; see also Chapters 3 and 4, this volume). This implies that negative experiences during PA may be acting as an underlying restraining force that counteracts positive reflective factors like positive intentions (Brand & Cheval, 2019; Rhodes & Gray, 2018). This effect is likely exaggerated when it interacts with incidental affect on a given day (Rhodes & Gray, 2018). For example, Maher et al. (2017) found that positive affect at any given time resulted in more successful odds of translating PA intentions into behavior compared to negative affect using ecological momentary assessment methods. Incidental negative affect in the form of daily stressors and displeasure is also a reliable predictor of physical inactivity (Almeida et al., 2020; Dunton, 2017), and much of this effect is likely through the disruption of intention-behavior relations (Rhodes & Gray, 2018). Some of this effect may be mediated through experiential/affective attitudes, which represent proxy expectations of how one expects to feel about the PA experience (Baumeister, Vohs, DeWall, & Zhang, 2007; Rhodes et al., 2009; Williams, Rhodes, & Conner, 2019). To support this notion, Rhodes and Kates (2015) found a large correlation between affective attitude and prior affective response to PA. Still, our ability to engage in affective forecasting is not particularly accurate (Gilbert & Ebert, 2002), so it seems unlikely that all incidental affect and the underlying stimuli associated with an affective response will be completely accounted for through experiential/affective attitudes. Overall, there is likely a basic tendency for us to avoid PA, and thus disrupt action control, in situations where we have had unpleasant past experiences or negative incidental affect.

The second tendency noted in Figure 2.1 is the underlying nature to conserve energy. This tenet comes from evolutionary psychobiology (Lieberman, 2015) and is elucidated in the theory of energetic cost minimization (Brand & Cheval, 2019; Cheval et al., 2018). Human beings have an underlying tendency to minimize metabolic costs which stems from an evolutionary survival necessity. From an action control perspective, this would suggest that fulfilling PA intentions that do not involve necessity (e.g. exercise) are likely to be met with an underlying avoidance tendency, because it represents unnecessary energetic cost (Cheval, Sarrazin, Isoard-Gautheur, Radel, & Friese, 2016). Research has supported this premise by showing that sedentary behaviors require less cognitive resources to enact than PA (Cheval, Sarrazin, & Pelletier, 2014) and studies comparing dietary behavior and PA have demonstrated human tendencies to load, rather than expend energy (Epstein & Saelens, 2000). Overall, there seems a likelihood that fulfilling PA intentions will experience some underlying resistance due to a basic human approach-avoidance tendency to minimize energetic cost.

Translating Intentions into Physical Activity: Application of M-PAC

M-PAC (Rhodes, 2017; Rhodes & de Bruijn, 2013b; Rhodes & Yao, 2015) constructs have been overviewed in past reviews and while the schematic has been expressed in different ways, the main tenets of the approach have remained constant among these different writings. Overall, M-PAC suggests a layered approach to behavior change that involves three interlocking, yet progressive processes. Reflective processes are predominately determinants of intention formation, regulatory processes are generally determinants of action control during behavioral adoption, and reflexive processes are determinants of more sustained action control. The three processes subsequently co-determine a sustained PA pattern.

Intention Formation

Reflective processes represent the consciously deliberated expectations of performing a behavior that culminate in the formation of an intention. These are entirely based on the substantive research from the social cognitive tradition (Bandura, 1998; Fishbein & Ajzen, 2010) and manifest in the variables of instrumental attitude (evaluation of the expected benefits from performing PA), affective judgments/affective attitude (evaluation of the expected pleasure and satisfaction from performing PA), perceived capability (evaluation of one's ability to perform PA, circumscribed from motivation), and perceived opportunity (evaluation of the perceived chances and circumstances to perform PA, circumscribed from motivation). Intention in M-PAC is viewed as a decisional construct and not the strength of conviction necessarily underlying that decision (Rhodes & Rebar, 2017). Thus, a defining difference of M-PAC compared to many intention models is the acknowledgment that some reflective constructs, in particular affective judgments and perceived opportunity, may also be post-intentional determinants of action control. In the case of affective judgments, for example, M-PAC suggests that the levels required to form a decision will be lower than the levels required to enact that decision because affective judgments act as a proxy for the approach-avoidance tendencies of the individual as well as the behavioral vs. outcome focus of the intention (see section above). Overall, however, reflective processes are well-established in PA social cognition models (McEachan et al., 2011; McEachan et al., 2016) and have no novel characterization in M-PAC. This chapter will focus more on the other two processes of M-PAC.

Adoption of Action Control

Regulatory processes represent the tactics that are employed to manage action control. Specifically, these constructs do not involve any motives or reasons for behavioral engagement; they are instead a series of behavioral, affective, and cognitive tactics to assist an individual in the selection of the intention over other possible options and to provide counter-measures against basic tendencies that may thwart the execution of the PA intention. These are entirely consistent with the constructs of most action control theories (Rhodes & Yao, 2015) but are broadly defined to include planning, monitoring, contracting, self-reward, emotion regulation, distraction, and restructuring the environment (social, built). They have been described and detailed in many leading models of goal pursuit (Bagozzi, 1992; Bandura, 1986; Carver & Scheier, 1982; Karoly, 1992; Locke & Latham, 2006). In M-PAC, however, there are some specifics that may be unique to the conceptualizations in some other approaches.

M-PAC conceptualizes regulation processes as a formative construct (Petter, Straub, & Rai, 2007), where the volume of different tactics is a better determinant than any one or two specific tactics. This is akin to a person who has more tools in their tool belt being more capable of keeping to intentions, compared to any one specific tool. The conceptualization is informed by analyses that support a general index over any specific tactic in past research on PA action control (Rhodes & Plotnikoff, 2006; Rhodes, Plotnikoff, & Courneya, 2008; Rhodes, Spence, et al., 2016), as well as meta-analyses of these tactics (as behavior change techniques) that show the advantages of a cluster of tactics in explaining behavior change over any specific tactic (Greaves et al., 2011; Michie, Abraham, Whittington, McAteer, & Gupta, 2009). We also note in M-PAC that these may be a natural consequence of intention formation (i.e. spontaneous behavioral regulation), or modified via outside intervention based on past research (Allan, Sniehotta, & Johnston, 2013; Carraro & Gaudreau, 2013). Specifically, some people may engage in these regulation processes right after intention formation without a need for external intervention. Others, by contrast, may require skills intervention to assist in how these tactics can be used to stick to PA intentions and enact counter-measures against basic approach-avoidance tendencies (Rhodes, Grant, & De Bruijn, 2020).

Another difference in the conceptualization of regulation processes in M-PAC over some other models of action control is how they work. Figure 2.2 details three paths for how regulation processes may work upon PA action control. Path 1 is as a moderator of intention-behavior relations (Heckhausen & Gollwitzer, 1987; Kuhl, 1984). Specifically, regulation processes assist in the selection of the intention and act as counter-measures against deselection (Sheeran & Webb, 2016). They assist by preventing forgetfulness, raising the priority

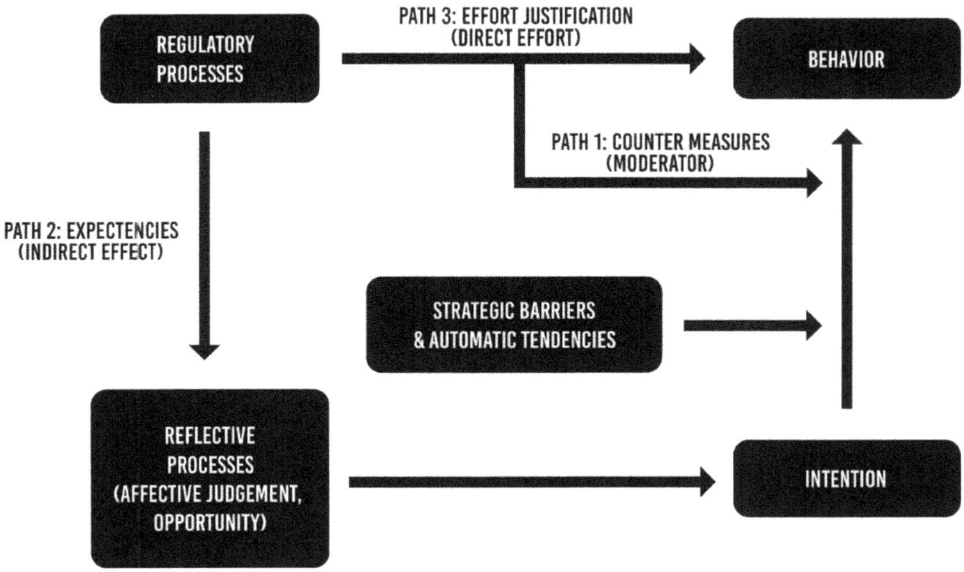

FIGURE 2.2 Schematic explaining the effect of regulatory processes on action control.

of the intention over others, and having strategies in place to counter energy conservation and displeasure avoidance tendencies. Path 2 represents the effect that regulatory processes may have on intention via re-setting expectations and thus making the intention pragmatic (Avishai et al., 2019; Locke & Latham, 1990, 2006). Making plans and facilitating conditions to enable a positive behavioral experience should facilitate reflective processes to focus intentions on behavioral experiences rather than behavioral outcomes and thus improve the stability of the intention (Keer et al., 2013; Rhodes & Gray, 2018). Finally, path 3 represents the effect that behavioral regulation can have on PA as a motive unto itself (Prochaska & Di-Clemente, 1982; Schwarzer, 2008). This effort justification effect (Festinger, 1957) has been shown in prior PA research where regulation processes, such as planning, have an effect on behavior even after controlling for intention (Carraro & Gaudreau, 2013; Zhang, Zhang, Schwarzer, & Hagger, 2019).

Sustaining Action Control

Reflexive processes in M-PAC are those constructs that develop as a consequence of repeated action over time and action control from cues (Rhodes, 2017). Indeed, we conceive that regulatory processes provide a kind of glue that allows PA action control to continue long enough for reflexive processes to develop and subsequently determine the sustainability, or maintenance, of the PA action control. M-PAC includes two key reflexive constructs: Habit and identity.

Habit is a process by which a behavior is influenced by learned cue-behavior associations (Gardner, 2015). Ostensibly, the cue stimuli provide a drive toward the enactment of behavior independent of a reflective reason for enacting the behavior. Prior PA research has supported the premise that consistency of practice, with similar cues, for PA that is considered somewhat pleasant, results in habit formation (Kaushal & Rhodes, 2015). The exact time-frame for the length of this habit formation process is poorly understood but current estimates suggest that it may occur between six weeks and two months if these conditions of consistency, cues, and pleasant affect are in place (Kaushal & Rhodes, 2015; Lally, van Jaarsveld, Potts, & Wardle, 2009).

Action control habits are based on the premise that complex behaviors, such as PA, do not comprise an all-or-nothing habit response (Gardner, Phillips, & Judah, 2016; Gardner, Rebar, & Lally, 2019; Kaushal, Rhodes, Meldrum, & Spence, 2017; Phillips & Gardner, 2016). PA is such a complicated behavioral process that it does not fully make sense that the entire sequencing could be automated (Hagger et al., 2016; Rhodes & Rebar, 2018). While any number of micro-sequences in PA could be habituated, Phillips and Gardner (2016) have suggested that it may be pragmatic to think of two key phases in habit formation: Instigation and execution. Instigation represents the selection process of a behavior, while execution represents the enactment of that behavior. In action control circumstances, habit is therefore more akin to the instigation habit, where there is a cue-based selection response toward enactment of an intended behavior (Rebar, Rhodes, & Gardner, 2019; Rhodes & Rebar, 2018). In essence, habit in M-PAC assists primarily in creating a tunnel vision toward enacting the intention and thus shields from automatic tendencies that may constrain PA intention translation (see Figure 2.3, path 1). This is not to say that habits cannot assist in PA execution or additional PA behaviors beyond the initial intention (see Figure 2.3, path 2), but the primary expected determination of habits in M-PAC is through the instigation path as a form of selection bias toward intended action.

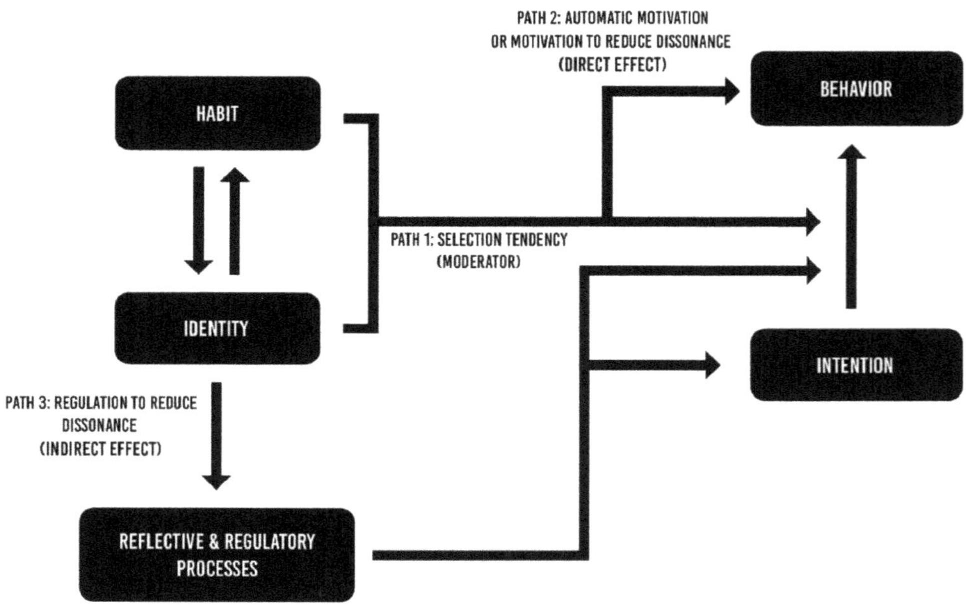

FIGURE 2.3 Schematic explaining the effect of reflexive processes on action control.

Identity is a component of a multi-dimensional self-concept, hierarchically organized by how one categorizes themselves in a given role (Burke, 2006). The formation of identity is not entirely understood or agreed upon but M-PAC follows prior theoretical work that suggests past behavioral (Bem, 1972) and habit (Verplanken & Sui, 2019) experiences based on reflections of the amount of investment (time, effort, resources), ability/agency, and social comparators (Burke & Stets, 2009; Kendzierski, Furr, & Schiavoni, 1998; Kendzierski & Morganstein, 2009; West, 2009) regarding the behavior (including investment in regulation processes) are critical antecedents. Identity, in turn, activates reflexively on behavior from triggers (environmental, social, individual) that challenge one's identity standard with the current observed behavioral practice. This dissonance between the identity standard and observed behavior results in negative affect and produces motivation to reduce the discrepancy (Stryker & Burke, 2000). It has been suggested that identity thus acts as a reflexive self-regulating behavioral system (Burke, 2006).

Identity in the role of action control may have three paths of influence (see Figure 2.3). The primary path (Figure 2.3, path 1) is likely a selection bias that assists in the enactment of planned PA. Essentially, those with a PA identity are probably more attuned to seize opportunities to be active and thus fulfill their intentions. This is supported by research that shows those with PA identities are able to discern PA words and images faster than those without such identities (see Rhodes, Kaushal, & Quinlan, 2016 for a review). Thus, identity acts as a kind of automatic tunnel vision toward action control. The next path is the role identity may play back into the regulatory processes system (see Figure 2.3, path 3). The motivation produced to reduce identity standard and observed behavior discordance is likely focused upon bolstering regulatory processes to fulfill PA intentions. This has been established in prior mediation analyses (Strachan, Brawley, Spink, Sweet, & Perras, 2015); yet, it is also apparent in how self-regulation is described as a central component of a PA identity (Strachan, Perras, Forneris, & Stadig, 2017). Identity may also augment PA through more impulsive motivation independent of action control and regulatory processes (see Figure 2.3, path 2) (Rise, Sheeran, & Hukkelberg, 2010), but the primary expected effect of identity on PA in M-PAC is through the selection bias and regulatory processes paths.

Evidence of M-PAC and Physical Activity

A search was conducted in a unified database in March 2020 with no restriction for year of publication. Boolean operators were employed for search terms, including three groups of terms relating to M-PAC (and the relevant processes), PA, and action control. Articles were screened for eligibility by title and abstract, after which manual cross-referencing was conducted. Studies were retained if they included four or more M-PAC constructs and action control. Our review resulted in 26 original data sets and 30 papers that had used either a full M-PAC approach or a variant with at least 75% of the variables present in the analysis. All the studies have been conducted in either North America (k = 20) or Europe (k = 6) and most of these studies have focused on MVPA as the dependent variable (k = 19). The methods employed have been a relatively equal mix of cross-sectional (k = 9), longitudinal (k = 10), and experimental designs (k = 7), and the populations sampled were also diverse, including university students, older adults, parents of young children, workplace samples, and cancer survivors.

Combining the observational data (k = 19), we present a breakdown of the studies by M-PAC construct in terms of their multivariate prediction of action control and their respective effect size. For reflective processes, instrumental attitude was only a significant predictor in one of 15 tests, with effect sizes in the trivial to small range (Cohen, 1992). By contrast, affective attitude was a significant positive predictor of action control in 10 of 13 tests, with the majority of effect sizes in the small to medium range (Cohen, 1992). Most studies used a composite perceived behavioral control construct, rather than a sub-division of perceived capability and opportunity, respectively. Nine of 15 tests showed that perceived control positively predicted action control with considerable heterogeneity of effect sizes ranging from trivial to large (Cohen, 1992). There is clear evidence to support the M-PAC tenet that affective judgments are a predictor of action control within the model. There is some support that perceptions of behavioral control may also be a predictor of action control, but the finding has considerable heterogeneity.

Regulation processes was a significant predictor of action control in 10 of 13 studies. Effect sizes ranged from large to trivial (Cohen, 1992) with 7 of 12 in the small effect size range (one study did not provide an effect size). The evidence, overall, supports the focus on self-regulation tactics in action control theories generally (Rhodes & Yao, 2015), and M-PAC specifically. Two studies distinguished the effects of regulation processes on action control adoption and maintenance, defined as participants who had not been active according to public health guidelines for the prior six months to those who had been active at public health guidelines (Rhodes & Plotnikoff, 2006; Rhodes, Plotnikoff, & Courneya, 2008). These studies showed that regulation processes predicted action control adoption (d = 0.38 and d = 0.43) more than maintenance (d = 0.25 and d = 0.16). Thus, there is preliminary support for the placement of regulation processes at the adoption-level of the M-PAC, compared to maintenance.

Finally, both identity (seven of seven tests) and habit (eight of nine tests) were reliable predictors of action control. Habit showed effect sizes in the small to large range (Cohen, 1992); yet, the majority were small effect sizes (five of eight available effect sizes). Identity showed effect sizes in the trivial to medium-sized range (Cohen, 1992), with three of seven in the medium range. Taken together, these findings support M-PAC's inclusion of these reflexive constructs to understand action control. Unfortunately, no study distinguished these relationships across adoption and maintenance participant groups, so there is no available evidence to substantiate the action control "maintenance" tenet of M-PAC at present.

M-PAC is based on the conception that reflexive, regulatory, and reflective constructs provide multivariate influences on a pattern of PA action control. Eight tests of this tenet were possible with the current data. Five (Bassett-Gunter, Tanna, Arbour-Nicitopoulos, Rhodes & Leo, 2020; Rhodes, Berry, et al., 2019; Rhodes & Lim, 2016; Rhodes, Nasuti, & Fiala, 2012; Vallerand et al., 2016) of these tests supported significant independent contributions of each process, with the remaining three tests showing reflexive constructs as key determinants (Grant, Juba, Quinlan, & Rhodes, 2018; Rhodes et al., 2020; Wienert, Kuhlmann, Storm, Reinwand, & Lippke, 2019). Thus, the current evidence supports the proposed multivariate structure of M-PAC and the inclusion of its reflexive constructs in particular, which are relatively unique to the approach compared to other action control theories (Rhodes & Yao, 2015), absent in social cognitive theories (Fishbein et al., 2001), yet a mainstay in dual-process models (Sheeran et al., 2013).

Experimental applications of M-PAC have been sparse, compared to observational examinations. Two of the seven studies have been feasibility studies (Husband, Wharf Higgins, & Rhodes, 2019; Lim, Wharf Higgins, & Rhodes, in press), and three others are noted as preliminary studies (Rhodes, Naylor, & McKay, 2010; Tanna, Arbour-Nicitopoulos, Rhodes, & Bassett-Gunter, 2017; Vallerand, Rhodes, Walker, & Courneya, 2018). Six of the seven studies (Husband et al., 2019; Kaushal, Rhodes, Spence, & Meldrum, 2017; Lim et al., in press; Rhodes, Naylor, Blanchard, Quinlan, & Warburton, 2019; Rhodes et al., 2010; Vallerand et al., 2018), however, showed significant evidence of behavior change across time, employing behavior change techniques aligned with M-PAC. All these studies showed changes from baseline in M-PAC target constructs as a result of these behavior change techniques. Three of the studies were focused on regulatory processes (Rhodes, Naylor, et al., 2019; Rhodes et al. 2010; Tanna et al., 2017), one was focused on identity (Husband et al., 2019), one was focused on habit (Kaushal, Rhodes, Spence, et al., 2017), and the others included a multi-component M-PAC intervention (Lim et al., in press; Vallerand et al., 2018). Overall, there is preliminary evidence that M-PAC constructs are changeable and that these changes may result in subsequent PA change. There is no evidence yet as to whether specific behavior change targeting of identity and habit, beyond targeting regulation processes, is effective.

Summary

Many forms of regular PA are goal-directed; yet, the gap between the decision to act and behavioral enactment is often considerable. M-PAC is one of several theoretical approaches created to promote greater success in translating intentions into behavior (Rhodes & Yao, 2015). In this chapter, we overviewed the theoretical lens behind M-PAC, suggesting that intention-behavior discordance is likely occurring from both strategic challenges in goal pursuit and automatic tendencies that, all things being equal, restrain PA intention follow through. In particular, the critical role of regulatory processes and the eventual role of reflexive processes were highlighted with theorizing on the likely pathways of impact on action control. Finally, the efficacy of the M-PAC framework was reviewed, showing that observational studies generally support the proposed structure. Experimental application of M-PAC is preliminary but early evidence was also generally supportive that M-PAC constructs can be modified and collectively and independently change PA. Still, the M-PAC framework requires more testing of its temporal relationship among key constructs from adoption to sustainability of PA. A higher volume of studies in different contexts is also needed to validate the initial findings, and modification (either addition and/or subtraction) of core constructs may be prudent as more evidence becomes available.

3

EXERCISE MOTIVATION FROM A POST-COGNITIVIST PERSPECTIVE

Affective-Reflective Theory

Panteleimon Ekkekakis and Ralf Brand

Introduction

The promotion of exercise and physical activity has proven to be one of the greatest unmet challenges in the chronicles of public health (De Souto Barreto, 2013, 2015; Du et al., 2019; Guthold, Stevens, Riley, & Bull, 2018; Hagger & Weed, 2019; Pratt, Ramirez Varela, Salvo, Kohl, & Ding, 2020). No intervention approach to date has been reliably shown to change exercise and physical activity behavior in a meaningful and sustainable manner in any setting (lifestyle or clinical) and in any age group (Howlett, Trivedi, Troop, & Chater, 2019; Love, Adams, & van Sluijs, 2019; Murray et al., 2017; Patnode, Evans, Senger, Redmond, & Lin, 2017; Sims, Scarborough, & Foster, 2015; Zubala et al., 2017). Estimates from meta-analyses place the efficacy of interventions within the "small" range at the conclusion of the intervention period (with standardized mean differences ranging between 0.20 and 0.30), progressively diminishing over the course of follow-up. Moreover, there are indications that standardized mean differences between 0.20 and 0.30 overestimate the true effect of interventions because effect sizes tend to be larger for trials with smaller sample sizes, shorter intervention durations (fewer than 14 weeks), and lower methodological quality scores (Bernard et al., 2017).

To put figures between 0.20 and 0.30 into perspective, the magnitude of the so-called "question-behavior" or "mere measurement" effect (i.e. the change in behavior observed in control groups, presumably as a result of merely responding to questionnaires inquiring about a behavior) is also estimated to be in the same range in the case of physical activity (i.e. 0.20 to 0.22; Miles, Rodrigues, Sniehotta, & French, 2020; Rodrigues, O'Brien, French, Glidewell, & Sniehotta, 2015; Wilding et al., 2016). Importantly, not only is there no apparent difference in behavior-change efficacy between different psychological theories (Gourlan et al., 2016) but even whether or not any theory is identified as having served as the basis of an intervention does not appear to make a difference (McEwan, Beauchamp et al., 2019). At present, there is no reliable evidence that changing a specific psychological mediator or implementing the constructs comprising any particular psychological theory can meaningfully change exercise or physical activity behavior (Murray et al., 2018; Rhodes,

Boudreau, Weman Josefsson, & Ivarsson, in press). In other words, after the first 50 years of research, the psychological mechanisms underlying exercise and physical activity behavior change remain largely unknown, leaving public health practitioners and exercise professionals without evidence-based intervention guidelines of proven efficacy and effectiveness. In this chapter, we address the conceptual limitations of past research on the promotion of exercise and physical activity, and outline the basic postulates of the Affective-Reflective Theory (ART) of exercise and physical inactivity.

Conceptual Limitations of Previous Approaches

The persistent failure to produce intervention approaches that can reliably increase exercise and physical activity behavior has exposed weaknesses or limitations in the armamentarium of behavior-change methods traditionally used in public health. Critical reviewers have pointed out that, while varied terminologies used in different theories may give a semblance of conceptual plurality, closer inspection reveals that the conceptual overlap between central constructs across different theories is "striking" (Sheeran, Klein, & Rothman, 2017, p. 581; also see Gainforth, West, & Michie, 2015; Weinstein, 1993).

The reason for this overlap is that major theories of health behavior change were all developed during the same historical period, starting in the 1950s, when psychology became enthralled by the "cognitive revolution" (Baars, 1986; Simon, 1991). Miller (2003) characterized the cognitive revolution as a "counter-revolution" (p. 141) to the first revolution in the history of psychology, namely behaviorism. The cognitive revolution was prompted by the realization that "if scientific psychology were to succeed, mentalistic concepts would have to integrate and explain the behavioral data" (Miller, 2003, p. 142). In the years of cognitivism, psychologists felt the freedom to devise a limitless number of explanatory constructs and use them in building hypothetical models of the mental processes underlying human behavior that resembled logical rules of inference, decision trees, and computer algorithms (Bandura, 1991; Carver & Scheier, 1982; Kuhl, 1986). Exercise psychology first emerged in the late 1960s and early 1970s, precisely the period when behaviorism lost its place as the dominant paradigm in psychology and was replaced by the new and exciting cognitivist perspective (Spear, 2007). Since that time, cognitivism has been the only paradigm that has influenced how exercise psychologists theorize and conduct research.

Starting with the Health Belief Model (Maiman & Becker, 1974; Rosenstock, 1974b), theories of health behavior explicitly or implicitly endorsed the fundamental assumption that the central force driving health behavior is the inherent human desire to attain or maintain a positive state of health (i.e. expressed as a desire to lower the susceptibility to disease or reduce the severity of any negative consequences of disease on lifestyle and well-being). Moreover, the idea that the motivation to undertake a health behavior is a function of the expectancy (i.e. the subjectively estimated probability) that the behavior will result in the desired positive state of health became the conceptual backbone of all subsequent health behavior theories. This expectancy could depend on additional subjective estimations, such as estimations that the behavior in question will be feasible and efficacious in light of perceived barriers or costs. Subsequent theories elaborated upon this basic framework, either by introducing additional explanatory constructs, such as self-efficacy (i.e. the perceived ability to overcome the perceived barriers; Bandura, 2004) or social norms (i.e. the perceived likelihood that important others will approve and/or support the health behavior, thereby lowering the perceived costs; Ajzen & Fishbein, 2005), or by renaming existing constructs, such as referring to the perceived susceptibility to disease as risk perception (Schwarzer, 2008). As Lee (1998) observed: "The argument is basically the same in each case. A variety of component variables arise from a variety of classes of experiences and combine in some way to produce a single cognition that has a direct effect on behavior" (p. 9).

What was not directly or immediately addressed in the process of proposing and elaborating theories of health behavior are the underlying – and tacitly endorsed – assumptions about the nature of the human mind. Theories such as the social-cognitive theory (Bandura, 2004), the theories of reasoned action and planned behavior (Ajzen & Manstead, 2007), the transtheoretical model (Prochaska & Marcus, 1994), and self-determination theory (Teixeira, Carraça, Markland, Silva, & Ryan, 2012) are based on the common assumption that motivation rests upon a foundation of beliefs, cognitive appraisals, and rational inferential analyses of data, driven by the principle of maximizing self-interest (for a detailed analysis, see Ekkekakis & Zenko, 2016). This fundamental assumption is most evident in the "reasoned action framework" that formed the basis of the theories of reasoned action and planned behavior. According to Fishbein and Ajzen (1975):

> The totality of a person's beliefs serves as the informational base that ultimately determines his attitudes, intentions, and behaviors. Our approach thus views man as an essentially rational organism, who uses the information at his disposal to make judgments, form evaluations, and arrive at decisions.
>
> *(p. 14; sexist language retained from the original)*

Similarly, in social-cognitive theory, human decision making is described as a constant process of collecting and analyzing information, using these data to make probabilistic predictions about the future consequences of possible courses of action or inaction, and then using the results of these calculations as the basis for deciding how to behave:

> A major function of thought is to enable people to predict the occurrence of events and to create the means for exercising control over those that affect their daily lives. Many activities involve inferential judgments about conditional relations between events in probabilistic environments. Discernment of predictive rules requires cognitive processing of multidimensional information that contains many ambiguities and uncertainties. In ferreting out predictive rules, people must draw on their state of knowledge to generate hypotheses about predictive factors, to weight and integrate them into composite rules, to test their judgments against outcome information, and to remember which notions they had tested and how well they had worked.
>
> *(Bandura, 1989, p. 1176)*

According to this view, the lack of exercise or physical activity can only be described as an *irrational* behavioral choice in light of the widely recognized health benefits associated with these behaviors. From the perspective of cognitivist theories, seemingly irrational behavioral choices, such as abstaining from exercise, can only be attributed to faulty (e.g. inaccurate, incomplete) information. Therefore, a typical behavior-change intervention aims to address such deficits by providing correct, complete, and compellingly presented information. For example, in the reasoned action framework, it is recognized that "beliefs need not be veridical; they may be inaccurate, biased, or even irrational" (Ajzen & Fishbein, 2005, p. 193). Ajzen (2011) emphasized that it is a misinterpretation to think that the theory of planned behavior "posits an impassionate, rational actor who reviews all available information in an unbiased fashion to arrive at a behavioral decision" or that "behavioral, normative and control beliefs are formed in a rational, unbiased fashion or that they accurately represent reality" (p. 1116). However, importantly, the culprit for any deviations from rationality is not the architecture of the human mind itself but rather deficiencies in the information that served as the basis for the problematic beliefs: "this information is often inaccurate and incomplete; it may rest on faulty or irrational premises, be biased by self-serving motives, by fear, anger and other emotions, or otherwise fail to reflect reality" (p. 1116). Therefore, the purpose of interventions is to lay an appropriate "cognitive foundation from which attitudes, perceived social norms, and perceptions of control - and ultimately intentions - [will] follow in a reasonable and consistent fashion" (Ajzen & Fishbein, 2005, pp. 193–194). The explanation for seemingly irrational behaviors within social-cognitive theory is similar:

> To say that people base many of their actions on thought does not necessarily mean they are always objectively rational. Rationality depends on reasoning skills which are not always well developed or used effectively. Even if people know how to reason logically, they make faulty judgments when they base their inferences on inadequate information or fail to consider the full consequences of different choices. Moreover, they often misread events in ways that give rise to faulty conceptions about themselves and the world around them. When they act on their misconceptions, which appear subjectively rational given their errant basis, such persons are viewed by others as behaving in an unreasoning, if not downright foolish, manner. Thought can thus be a source of human failing and distress as well as human accomplishment.
>
> *(Bandura, 1986, p. 19)*

Based on these theoretical premises, the standard public-health approach for changing health behaviors is described as the "rational educational" model, the fundamental assumption of which is that "people are basically rational, and their behavior driven by logically derived principles… people need to be given factually correct information and then they will probably make a sensible decision" (Weare, 2002, p. 107). While this assumption has served as the foundation of public-health campaigns that can be credited with substantial successes even in domains that remain beyond the reach of legal mandates (e.g. sensitizing some smokers to the harmful effects of nicotine, convincing many people to adopt safer sexual practices), it is now increasingly questioned by medical and public-health researchers (Corrigan, Powell, & Michaels, 2015; Corrigan, Rüsch, BenZeev, & Sher, 2014; Rice, 2013; Roberto & Kawachi, 2016). According to Mogler et al. (2013), although "interventions implicitly assume a classical model of patients as rationally self-interested agents," in reality "patients may not always be the rational actors that we imagine" (p. 711). These authors warned that "even when patients have learned how to control a disease, they may find regimens to be time consuming or unpleasant, or may be distracted from the task of disease control by competing demands" (p. 712). Researchers in physical activity epidemiology are now inevitably arriving at the same conclusion. Commenting on the standard approach of promoting physical activity on the basis of the promise of long-term health, the Lancet

Physical Activity Series Working Group acknowledged that "the traditional public health approach based on evidence and exhortation has - to some extent - been unsuccessful so far" (Hallal et al., 2012, p. 254).

Disregarding the Uniqueness of Exercise and Physical Activity

Consider the typical format and contents of a physical-activity promotion counseling session. During such sessions, counselor and client typically meet at an office setting, are seated, and exchange ideas through verbal communication. While the style of interactions may vary (e.g. being more or less directive in nature), the agenda typically consists of efforts on the part of the counselor to modify cognitive appraisals theorized to underlie motivation (e.g. bolstering self-efficacy via verbal persuasion, cultivating instrumental attitudes through education about the health benefits of physical activity or the risks associated with chronic diseases, identifying potential sources of social support, reframing environmental and other perceived barriers, setting goals, encouraging self-monitoring).

At this point, this intervention approach has become entrenched (e.g. it is what is typically taught in textbooks; Nigg, 2014). However, the same approach could be applied to any behavior; neither the theoretical models nor the intervention techniques take the uniqueness of exercise and physical activity into account. This approach is also reflected in investigations conducted over the past several decades, in which exercise and physical activity were among long lists of other health-related behaviors, including alcohol abuse, smoking, speeding, brushing and flossing teeth, consuming fruits and vegetables, using sunscreen, and conducting preventive self-examinations (Lawton, Conner, & McEachan, 2009). For example, in the question "On how many days in the past four weeks have you binge drunk?" researchers would simply replace "binge drunk" with "exercised." Evidently, this extensively employed approach to deciphering the motivational underpinnings of exercise and physical activity was based on the assumption that these behaviors are all motivated by essentially the same underlying psychological processes as any other health-related behavior. However, according to data from four large national surveys, self-reported exercise shares no variance with smoking and a healthy diet (Newsom, McFarland, Kaplan, Huguet, & Zani, 2005; Ufholz & Harlow, 2017). Moreover, seemingly paradoxically, the relationship between alcohol use and physical activity appears to be positive (Dodge, Clarke, & Dwan, 2017). Even more interestingly, when faced with a serious chronic-disease diagnosis, such as coronary heart disease, diabetes, cancer, stroke, or lung disease, people tend to reduce their smoking and slightly curtail their alcohol use, but rarely consider increasing their physical activity; in fact, they tend to avoid it even more than they did before the diagnosis (Newsom et al., 2012; Williams, Steptoe, & Wardle, 2013).

As Rhodes and Nigg (2011) have argued, physical activity is unlike other health behaviors because

> it should be repeated several times a week across a lifetime, requires considerable time commitment in each bout, places the body in an aversive body state out of homeostasis, requires environmental supports, produces variable affective responses that are dependent on the load and temporal aspects of the act, and can be achieved via disparate modes (arguably, each a unique behavior).
>
> *(p. 117)*

Thus, these authors concluded that "there is adequate, if not overwhelming, evidence to suggest that unique theories of [physical activity] should be pursued" (Rhodes & Nigg, 2011, p. 114).

Disregarding the Affective Consequences of Exercise and Physical Activity

The observation that the potential motivational implications of the affective aspects of exercise and physical activity have been generally overlooked is not new. For example, in one of the earliest reviews of the correlates and determinants of exercise and physical activity, Dishman, Sallis, and Orenstein (1985) noted that, arguably, what may provide the initial thrust to get people active may be the awareness and the value placed on the health benefits but what will keep them active over time – or not – is whether they reliably derive pleasure and enjoyment from the experience: "Knowledge of and belief in the health benefits of physical activity may motivate initial involvement, but feelings of enjoyment and well-being seem to be stronger motives for continued participation" (p. 162). Along the same lines, Dishman (2003) later pointed out that although

> physical activity arguably offers more opportunities for pleasure than do most other health-related behaviors (compared to brushing, flossing, buckling up, and seeing the doctor, for example), we, ironically, have learned very little about intrinsic reinforcements (e.g., enjoyment of physical activity) for continued participation.
>
> *(p. 46)*

These early remarks about the role of pleasure and displeasure have since been supported by the findings of qualitative studies, in which respondents were given the opportunity to report what was important to them, as opposed to having to respond to questionnaires assessing constructs from the predominant cognitivist theories. In a review of this literature, Allender, Cowburn, and Foster (2006) noted that "fun, enjoyment and social support for aspects of identity were reported more often as predictors of participation and non-participation than perceived health benefits" (p. 832). The same conclusion was reached from interviews conducted with adults with disabilities (Smith & Wightman, in press).

The neglect of the motivational implications of pleasure, displeasure, and other affective factors may seem peculiar or perhaps indefensible, but it is not something that is unique to exercise psychology or to the study of exercise and physical activity. It is a phenomenon that demonstrates the powerful influence that paradigms can have in restricting thinking within scientific fields (Ekkekakis, 2017; Ekkekakis & Zenko, 2016). Authors have criticized this gap in theorizing in several other fields for years. In building his case for the "bounded" nature of human rationality in decision making, Simon (1983) argued that "in order to have anything like a complete theory of human rationality, we have to understand what role emotion plays in it" (p. 29). He later identified this issue as an "area that needs to be pursued vigorously in the next thirty years," pointing out that "human beings have emotions and we have motivations, in addition to our thoughts" and adding that "the connections between the cognitive system and the motivational systems have been explored only a little in this new cognitive revolution" (Simon, 1991, p. 52). Inspired by Simon, Bettman (1993) lambasted the dominant models of consumer choice for being "overbearingly cognitive; like the tin man in the Wizard of Oz, these models have no heart" (p. 8). Similarly, Loewenstein

(1996) contended that "disjunctions between perceived self-interest and behavior" (of which the avoidance of exercise and physical activity would be a prime example) can be explained by "the action of visceral factors," including "moods and emotions, and physical pain" (p. 272). According to Loewenstein, "the defining characteristics of visceral factors are, first, a direct hedonic impact (which is usually negative), and second, an effect on the relative desirability of different goods and actions" (p. 272). As a result, provided that these hedonically charged visceral factors reach "sufficient levels of intensity," they can "cause people to behave contrary to their own long-term self-interest, often with full awareness that they are doing so" (pp. 272–273).

Much of Loewenstein's (1996) discussion seems directly relevant to exercise and physical activity, and even several of his examples refer directly to physical tasks, such as sports, and physical sensations, such as fatigue. He claimed that "much behavior is non-volitional or only partly volitional - even in situations characterized by substantial deliberation" (p. 289). This scenario is strongly reminiscent of the intention-behavior gap observed with exercise and physical activity. For example, in a survey of 356 overweight or obese women and men who had been unsuccessful at weight maintenance, Miller and Eggert (1992) found that 82% of them identified discontinuing exercise as a major reason for their failure. Strikingly, although only 29% reported having done any exercise in the past three months, 98% of the men and 97% of the women indicated that they would be willing to exercise for up to 50 minutes per day, on five to six days per week, if accepted into a new weight loss program. Loewenstein's (1996) proposal that, despite substantial deliberation, people may act nonvolitionally against their own self-interest due to the action of visceral factors could provide a clue that may help explain these seemingly contradictory self-reports.

Loewenstein (1996) wrote that the "treatment of motivation and effort" (p. 287) is one area in which cognitivist models of decision making fall short because such models assume "no qualitative distinction between choosing, say one car over another, or 'deciding' to pick up one's pace in the last mile of a marathon; both are simply decisions" (p. 287). He noted that, from the perspective of cognitivist models, an observer may be mystified by the fact that Olympic speed-skaters "failed to maintain their pace in the face of such overwhelming incentives" (p. 287). So, Loewenstein reminded those perplexed by such phenomena that physical effort produces "an aversive sensation referred to as fatigue or, at higher levels, exhaustion" (p. 287). He then suggested that "like other visceral factors, fatigue and exhaustion are directly aversive, and alter the desirability of different activities; most prominently, they decrease the desirability of further increments of effort" (p. 287). If considered in conjunction with evidence that exercise is perceived as substantially more effortful and unpleasant by individuals with excess body mass (Ekkekakis, Vazou, Bixby, & Georgiadis, 2016; Ekkekakis, Zenko, & Werstein, 2018), these suggestions offer testable hypotheses about the causes of the remarkable discrepancy between perceived benefits, attitudes, and intentions toward exercise and physical activity on the one hand, and the absence of sustained positive behavior change on the other.

Affective-Reflective Theory of Exercise and Physical Inactivity

Kuhn (1962/1996) warned that one of the detrimental effects of paradigms is that they tend to bring about not only "considerable resistance to paradigm change" but also an "immense restriction of the scientist's vision" that eventually leads to science becoming "increasingly rigid" (p. 64). When an old paradigm starts to reveal "anomalies" (i.e. cases of lack of paradigm-nature fit) that are acknowledged by a "critical mass" of scientists, the paradigm will reach a point of "crisis," and alternative viewpoints will begin to emerge. Based on recurring patterns in the history of science, Kuhn argued that "the transition from a paradigm in crisis to a new one from which a new tradition of normal science can emerge is far from a cumulative process" (p. 84). Instead, such transitions tend to instigate dramatic shifts in how problems are conceptualized and studied. A paradigmatic transition is usually

> a reconstruction of the field from new fundamentals, a reconstruction that changes some of the field's most elementary theoretical generalizations as well as many of its paradigm methods and applications… When the transition is complete, the profession will have changed its view of the field, its methods, and its goals.
>
> *(p. 85)*

Kuhn identified several indicators that a research field is undergoing a transition from "normal" to "extraordinary" research: (a) A "proliferation of competing articulations," (b) a "willingness to try anything," (c) "expression of explicit discontent," and (d) a "recourse to philosophy and to debate over fundamentals" (p. 91).

Arguably, all these indications are currently evident in research investigating the processes that motivate exercise, physical activity, and sedentary behavior. After an extended period of theoretical stagnation, there has been a sudden proliferation of competing theoretical proposals that are, for the first time, specific to these behaviors. Some of these represent syntheses of elements from cognitivist models (Hagger & Chatzisarantis, 2014; Rhodes, 2017), whereas others represent deviations from the cognitivist tradition, with the common denominator of incorporating, in various ways, affect as a motivational construct (Brand & Ekkekakis, 2018; Cheval et al., 2018; Conroy & Berry, 2017; Edwards, Addoh, Herod, Rhodes, & Loprinzi, 2017; Strobach, Englert, Jekauc, & Pfeffer, 2020; Williams & Bohlen, 2019; Williams & Evans, 2014). Indications of a willingness to introduce investigative approaches that are unfamiliar to most researchers, and may even strike some as "unorthodox" or "farfetched" (i.e. what Kuhn called a "willingness to try anything"), can be found in innovative attempts to extract motivational implications from sources such as components of the electroencephalogram (Cheval et al., 2018), heart rate variability (Schinkoeth, Weymar, & Brand, 2019), or facial microexpressions (Brand & Ulrich, 2019). "Expressions of explicit discontent," both about the narrow theoretical scope of cognitivist motivational theories (Brand & Cheval, 2019; Ekkekakis, 2017) and about the persistent failure to increase the rates of exercise and physical activity participation (De Souto Barreto, 2013, 2015; Du et al., 2019; Guthold at al., 2018; Hagger & Weed, 2019; Pratt et al., 2020), are rising. Finally, there are growing signs of a "recourse to philosophy and to debate over fundamentals," with researchers within the field of exercise psychology, for the first time, citing literatures outside of the psychological "mainstream" and discussing fundamental issues such as the limits of human rationality (Ekkekakis, 2017; Ekkekakis & Zenko, 2016; Williams & Bohlen, 2019).

Affective-Reflective Theory: Conceptual Antecedents

The ART of exercise and physical inactivity (Brand & Ekkekakis, 2018; Ekkekakis & Brand, 2019) is a dual-process model specifically developed to conceptualize the psychological mechanisms underlying the behaviors of exercise and physical inactivity. The theory was based on the fundamental assumption that understanding the bases of these behaviors will require a "quantum leap" in theorizing, a dramatic expansion of the current theoretical perspective, overcoming paradigmatic barriers and taking advantage of the accumulated knowledge of a much broader swath of psychological concepts than those provided by cognitivist theories. Because some of the concepts incorporated into the ART are not discussed often in the exercise psychology literature, we outline seven of them below.

Bounded Rationality

First, contrary to fundamental postulates underpinning cognitivist models regarding the nature of human contemplative, inferential, and decision-making processes, the ART borrowed from **behavioral economics** the idea that human rationality is limited. The notion of "bounded rationality" was proposed by Simon (1983), who defined the term as follows (readers should contrast this description of human cognitive processes to those by Ajzen and Bandura earlier):

> Bounded rationality is simply the idea that the choices people make are determined not only by some consistent overall goal and the properties of the external world, but also by the knowledge that decision makers do and don't have of the world, their ability or inability to evoke that knowledge when it is relevant, to work out the consequences of their actions, to conjure up possible courses of action, to cope with uncertainty (including uncertainty deriving from the possible responses of other actors), and to adjudicate among their many competing wants. Rationality is bounded because these abilities are severely limited. Consequently, rational behavior in the real world is as much determined by the "inner environment" of people's minds, both their memory contents and their processes, as by the "outer environment" of the world on which they act, and which acts on them.
>
> *(Simon, 2000, p. 25)*

The deviations of human judgments and decisions from strict standards of rationality can be demonstrated through several procedures, and such demonstrations have also been performed within the context of exercise behavior (Zenko, Ekkekakis, & Kavetsos, 2016). Also from the field of behavioral economics, the ART adopted the notion of behavioral heuristics, namely the idea that people resort to simplified "shortcuts" or "rules of thumb" when confronted with problems that challenge their bounded rationality, such as when decisions exceed their knowledge (Dunning, 2011) or numerical ability (Gigerenzer, Gaissmaier, Kurz-Milcke, Schwartz, & Woloshin, 2007; Reyna, Nelson, Han, & Dieckmann, 2009). Of particular importance within the ART is the affect heuristic (Finucane, Alhakami, Slovic, & Johnson, 2000; Slovic, Finucane, Peters, & MacGregor, 2002a, 2002b), which has been characterized as "probably the most important development in the study of judgment heuristics in the past few decades" (Kahneman, 2003a, p. 710). According to the affect heuristic, affect, besides being "a powerful motivator of behavior," "facilitates information integration in judgments and decisions, guides reason, and gives priorities among multiple goals" (Finucane, Peters, & Slovic, 2003, p. 341). A basic idea behind the affect heuristic is that "representations of objects and events in people's minds are tagged to varying degrees with affect" and then, in the process of making a judgment or decision, "people consult or refer to an 'affect pool' containing all the positive and negative tags consciously or unconsciously associated with the representations" (Slovic et al., 2002b, p. 400). Affect qualifies as a "mental shortcut" or "heuristic" because accessing

> an overall, readily available affective impression can be far easier - more efficient - than weighing the pros and cons or retrieving from memory many relevant examples, especially when the required judgment or decision is complex or mental resources are limited.
>
> *(p. 400)*

Opposing Forces

Second, the ART has borrowed certain constructs from Lewin's (1935, 1951a) **field theory**, which was an effort to reconcile the pressure of his time to express psychological constructs in mathematical and physical terms with the necessity of invoking concepts not easily amenable to such representations. In field theory, psychological (motivational) concepts are represented as a physical vector or a "force" resulting in a "tendency to locomotion" (movement from one location to another, either physically or psychologically). Forces can be induced by "values" (i.e. the positive or negative valence attached to different activities). A "goal" or "positive valence" is a force field in which all forces point toward the same region. Conversely, "aversion" is a force field in which the distribution of forces points away from a region. Of particular interest to ART is Lewin's concept of a "conflict," which refers to a situation in which two or more force fields overlap: "Conflict is defined psychologically as the opposition of approximately equally strong field forces" (Lewin, 1935, p. 88). Certain constellations of force fields may result in "equilibrium" or the absence of "locomotion." These are situations in which an individual "faces something that has simultaneously both a positive and a negative valence," such as, for example, when a child wants to climb a tree but is afraid, or in general situations in which "the attainment of the goal is impeded by some barrier" (p. 89):

> After the child has run against the barrier several times and perhaps hurt himself, or had the wounding experience of failure, the barrier itself acquires a negative valence. Beside the positive, there comes into existence a negative vector, and we have [a] conflict situation. The negative vector usually increases gradually in strength and finally becomes stronger than the positive... In such situations the withdrawal is at first almost always merely temporary. The child turns away, only to return after a while for another try at the barrier. A final and permanent withdrawal usually occurs only after several temporary withdrawals, the duration of which increases until finally the child does not return.
>
> *(pp. 89–90)*

The concept of opposite but equally strong field forces resulting in "conflict" and absence of "locomotion" (i.e. either psychological or physical indolence) can be applied to health behaviors in general (Hofmann, Friese, & Wiers, 2008) and to the phenomenon of physical inactivity in particular (Bluemke, Brand, Schweizer, & Kahlert, 2010). Like the example of the child who wants to climb a tree but is afraid, many adults may wish to be physically active (e.g. because the idea of good health is highly valued) but may remain inactive due to an equal but opposing force (e.g. because the idea of "physical activity" has acquired negative valence, perhaps through "the wounding experience of failure," as per Lewin, 1935, p. 89, or a history of physical or emotional trauma associated with physical activity). Consider, for example, the case of individuals with knee osteoarthritis or low-back pain. These individuals are routinely advised to be physically active and presented with compelling evidence about the beneficial effects of regular activity on their condition. However, physical activity participation rates among these clinical populations are even lower than the overall rate, presumably due to what clinical practitioners have termed "kinesiophobia," the tacit knowledge that a bout of physical activity will transiently exacerbate their pain (Luque-Suarez, Martinez-Calderon, & Falla, 2019). The idea that affective reactions may "diverge" from or "conflict" with the cognitive evaluation of a situation is at the core of the "risk-as-feelings" hypothesis, which was proposed to explain behaviors, like the lack of physical activity, that are contrary to self-interest and contrary to what one knows to be the optimal course of action (Loewenstein, Weber, Hsee, & Welch, 2001).

Law of Effect

Third, the ART incorporates the basic **behaviorist principle** of learning called the "law of effect" (Thorndike, 1911) and its evolution into contemporary associationism (Dickinson, 2012). According to the law of effect, when a behavior is consistently paired with pleasure, it becomes more likely to be repeated, whereas, if it is consistently paired with displeasure, it becomes more likely to be avoided:

> Of several responses made to the same situation, those which are accompanied or closely followed by satisfaction to the animal will, other things being equal, be more firmly connected with the situation, so that, when it recurs, they will be more likely to recur; those which are accompanied or closely followed by discomfort to the animal will, other things being equal, have their connections with that situation weakened, so that, when it recurs, they will be less likely to occur. The greater the satisfaction or discomfort, the greater the strengthening or weakening of the bond.
>
> *(Thorndike, 1911, p. 244)*

The basic idea at the core of the law of effect has received preliminary empirical support in the context of physical activity. Studies examining the relationship between experiences of pleasure or displeasure associated with exercise or physical activity and subsequent physical activity behavior were not undertaken for several decades because the prevailing assumption was that such experiences were almost universally positive. This presumed lack of variability in affective responses was incompatible with the observed variation in adherence and dropout. Expressing this view, Morgan and O'Connor (1988) characterized the rationale for investigating the linkage between pleasure and behavior as "intuitively defensible" but nevertheless argued that "such a view is simplistic" and thus "it is probably not necessary" (p. 116) to design studies to look further into the matter.

Despite the slow start and the fact that methodological "best practices" continue to evolve, there is now evidence that (a) exercise and physical activity can result in both negative and positive affective responses (Ekkekakis, Parfitt, & Petruzzello, 2011), (b) there can be substantial interindividual variability in affective responses even to the same level of exercise intensity, and (c) affective responses can predict physical activity, both concurrently and prospectively (Ekkekakis & Dafermos, 2012; Rhodes & Kates, 2015). Moreover, personally relevant, culturally framed, body-related, self-conscious emotions, such as guilt, shame, and pride (Castonguay, Pila, Wrosch, & Sabiston, 2015; Sabiston et al., 2010), as well as social physique anxiety (Sabiston, Pila, Pinsonnault-Bilodeau, & Cox, 2014), also exhibit interindividual variability and have been found to be related to physical activity participation.

Declarative versus Habit Memory

Fourth, the ART incorporates the idea of **multiple memory systems**, as demonstrated in the field of cognitive neuroscience (Squire, 2004). These memory systems are functionally and neuroanatomically distinct but also constantly interacting. Of particular relevance to the ART is the distinction between "declarative" or "cognitive" memory (i.e. memory about facts, places, or events), subserved primarily by the hippocampus, and the broad and heterogenous category of "nondeclarative" or "habit" memory (i.e. memory about stimulus-response associations), subserved primarily by the dorsolateral striatum (Gasbarri, Pompili, Packard, & Tomaz, 2014). The so-called "habit memory" is acquired through multiple repetitions of stimulus-response pairings, including the association of stimuli with affective or emotional responses (Packard, Goodman, & Ressler, 2018; Smith & DeCoster, 2000). These stimulus-response bonds tend to develop outside of conscious awareness and to become rigid. Thus, a habit memory may be expressed through behavioral choices made without simultaneous conscious memory content. Both cognitive and habit memories operate constantly, building multiple, parallel views of the world. However, although they can function cooperatively, these memory systems may also function independently and even competitively, as demonstrated in animal research and studies of patients with focal brain lesions (Packard & Goodman, 2013; Poldrack & Packard, 2003; White, Packard, & McDonald, 2013).

One domain in which the idea of competition between memory systems for control of behavior has found fertile ground is the study of addiction, with researchers theorizing that the transition from recreational substance use to addiction requires a shift from cognitive to habit memory (Hogarth, Balleine, Corbit, & Killcross, 2013). This shift toward inflexible, habitual drug-seeking behavior has been shown to be facilitated under conditions of chronic and acute stress, and reflects both the relative strengthening of the role of habit memory and the relative weakening of cognitive control and flexibility (Schwabe & Wolf, 2013; Wirz, Bogdanov, & Schwabe, 2018). For example, the choice between a chocolate cake (rated highly from a hedonic standpoint but less favorably from a cognitive standpoint) and a fruit salad (with the converse ratings) shifts in favor of the immediate reward and against the option that offers the promise of a future positive outcome when the information-processing capacity is compromised (e.g. by stress, competing considerations, time pressure, or limited knowledge; see Shiv & Fedorikhin, 1999, 2002; Shiv, Fedorikhin, & Nowlis, 2005).

Within the ART, a central concept is the associative pairing (or "tagging") of exercise or physical activity experiences with either a positive or negative affective valence. Following similar uses in behavioral economics (Kahneman, Ritov, & Schkade, 1999), affective psychology (Feldman Barrett, 2006), and affective neuroscience (Ochsner, Silvers, & Buhle,

2012; Small et al., 2003; Zorrilla & Koob, 2013), this process is termed "affective valuation." In accordance with the concept of "habit memory," the process of affective valuation is theorized to take place outside of conscious awareness through repeated, pleasant or unpleasant, experiences that individuals derive from exercise and physical activity (whether these were the result of valenced bodily sensations, such as bliss or exhaustion, or associated with complex and culturally framed emotions, such as pride or embarrassment). One of the conceptual forerunners of the notion of affective valuation is the bio-informational theory of emotional imagery proposed by Lang (1979). He theorized that images are subject to "multiple coding," an idea analogous to multiple memory systems. Besides propositional elements (what, where, when), Lang suggested that associationist networks also include response elements that may encompass coded motor patterns, postural adjustments, verbal responses, behavioral acts, affective expressions, and patterns of somatovisceral arousal. He further claimed that behavior-change attempts tend to fail when they focus on "the verbal response propositions" but overlook the "motor and visceral response propositions" (p. 510).

Primacy of Affect

Fifth, the ART has borrowed from early **affective psychology** the idea of the primacy and automaticity of affective reactions to stimuli (Zajonc, 1980, 1984; Zajonc & Markus, 1982). At the turn of the 20th century, Wundt (1907) first theorized that memories of the affective responses associated with ideas are stored, retrieved, and processed separately from the ideas themselves. Moreover, he speculated that the recollection of the affective experiences associated with ideas typically precedes the recollection of the ideas themselves, writing that "the special affective tone of the forgotten idea" enters conscious awareness first, "although the idea itself still remains in the background of consciousness" (pp. 243–244). In his description, the "affective elements" will "begin to force themselves energetically into the fixation-point of consciousness before anything is perceived of the ideational elements" (p. 243).

Much later, Zajonc (1980, 1984) resurrected this idea. After clarifying that he focused only on "feelings" that are "involved in the general quality of behavior that underlies the approach-avoidance distinction" (Zajonc, 1980, p. 152) and not on complex emotions like anger, guilt, or shame, he argued that, although "to be sure, the early affective reaction is gross and vague," it nonetheless has the ability "of influencing the ensuing cognitive process to a significant degree" (p. 154). This suggestion, which was considered controversial if not absurd at the time, subsequently amassed considerable empirical support, including studies showing that the subliminal presentation of angry or happy faces can influence subsequent preferences for neutral stimuli (Murphy & Zajonc, 1993) and even overt behavior such as drinking (Winkielman & Berridge, 2004; Winkielman, Berridge, & Wilbarger, 2005). Subsequent neuroimaging investigations provided further substantiation by identifying dissociable neural pathways underlying the elicitation of affective and autonomic responses during preattentive, preconscious, and predeliberative stages of processing (Critchley et al., 2000; McFadyen, Mermillod, Mattingley, Halász, & Garrido, 2017; Méndez-Bértolo et al., 2016; Morris, Öhman, & Dolan, 1999; Sato, Kochiyama, Minemoto, Sawada, & Fushiki, 2019).

Like Lang (1979), Zajonc argued that these phenomena can be explained by the formation of associations in memory linking ideas or past experiences with their attendant affective responses, as well as their associated "motor tendencies and other somatic manifestations" (Zajonc & Markus, 1982, p. 129). Echoing Lang (1979), Zajonc and Markus (1982) wrote that interventions targeting cognitions (e.g. educational campaigns, advice, counseling) should be supplemented with approaches aiming to change the affective experience and the associated action tendencies:

> While preferences have cognitive correlates, they may become functionally autonomous of these cognitive correlates and persist merely by virtue of the behavioral tendencies that have become their expressions. Once they are autonomous, behavioral tendencies that represent attitudes and preferences are hard to change, particularly if only cognitive means are to be employed. A simple communication is seldom sufficient to change a well-established behavioral habit. Methods are needed that can reach habitual behavior and motor output.
>
> *(p. 129)*

While the ART incorporates the idea of automatic activation (Bargh, 1994; Bargh & Chartrand, 1999; Fazio, 1995, 2001) of valenced associations upon the mere exposure to a stimulus-concept such as "exercise," we deliberately avoid the use of the terms *evaluation* and *attitude* in order to avoid the cognitivist connotations that these terms have acquired. Specifically, we wanted to avoid any inferences that either the process of assigning a positive or negative valence to an object necessarily required a cognitive appraisal or the type of memory involved in this process is declarative (e.g. "I believe that exercise is good for the following reasons"). We have opted instead for the term *valuation*, which is unburdened by such connotations and has already been used in other fields to refer to associative learning.

Affective and Somatic Markers

Sixth, the ART adopted from **neurology** the concept of the somatic marker (Bechara, Damasio, & Damasio, 2000; Damasio, 1994, 1996). According to Damasio (1994), somatic markers are "a special instance of feelings," which "have been connected by learning to predicted future outcomes of certain scenarios" (p. 174). When a positive somatic marker is juxtaposed to a certain future outcome, "it becomes a beacon of incentive" (p. 174). Conversely:

> When the choice of option X, which leads to bad outcome Y, is followed by punishment and thus painful body states, the somatic marker system acquires the hidden, dispositional representation of this experience-driven, noninherited arbitrary connection. Reexposure of the organism to option X, or thoughts about outcome Y, will now have the power to reenact the painful body state and thus serve as an automated reminder of bad consequences to come.
>
> *(p. 180)*

The idea of somatic markers emerged from studies of neurological patients with focal lesions in parts of the brain implicated in the encoding and elicitation of affective responses. These patients have intact cognitive abilities but exhibit severe deficits in decision making; they can methodically enumerate the pros and cons of various options but evidently cannot apply this information in reaching efficient and appropriate decisions:

> Deprived of this emotional signal, these patients rely on a reasoned cost-benefit analysis of numerous and often conflicting options involving both immediate and future

> consequences. The impairment degrades the speed of deliberation (e.g., choosing between two brands of cereal may take a patient a very long time because of endless reasoned analyses of the pros and cons of each brand), and also degrades the adequacy of the choice, i.e., patients may choose disadvantageously.
>
> *(Bechara & Damasio, 2005, p. 339)*

The concept of the somatic marker has been applied to the study of addiction (Verdejo-García & Bechara, 2009). In this context, authors have proposed that, when an individual experiences an addictive substance, the substance acts as a *primary inducer* of a particular, presumably rewarding, somatic state or "marker" associated with that substance (i.e. a particular affective response and an attendant configuration of brain chemistry, autonomic activity, and neuroendocrine function). Subsequently, when the individual perceives a cue that is linked through experience to the addictive substance (e.g. encounters a picture of a lighter or a needle), the cue acts as a *secondary inducer* that reactivates the somatic marker associated with the substance, albeit in a fainter form, thereby triggering the urge to seek and reexperience the substance. Theorists proposed that individuals with a propensity for addiction may be characterized by one or both of the following dysfunctions: (a) Hyperactivity of their impulsive system, resulting in an exaggerated representation of the rewarding effect of the addictive substance, and/or (b) hypoactivity of their reflective system, resulting in the discounting or underestimation of the long-term consequences of a given action. This theoretical rationale can also be applied to physical inactivity. For example, if an individual has experienced episodes of physical activity that were accompanied by an unpleasant or aversive somatic state (e.g. exhaustion, breathlessness, pain, embarrassment), subsequent encounters with related cues (e.g. a reminder to go back to the gym) would reactivate a more faint version of the associated somatic marker (e.g. a sudden sense of reduced energy, muscular weakness, or a "knot" in the stomach), as well as the attendant urge to avoid it.

Dual-Process Models

Seventh, the ART belongs to the long tradition of **dual-process models** that have arisen in several domains of psychology, including the study of perception (Norman, 2002), cognition (Evans & Stanovich, 2013; Reber, 1993; Sloman, 1996), social cognition (Deutsch, 2017; Deutsch & Strack, 2010; Gawronski & Bodenhausen, 2006; Gawronski, Brannon, & Bodenhausen, 2017; Strack & Deutsch, 2004, 2015), neural development (Casey & Jones, 2010; Shulman et al., 2016), decision making (Alós-Ferrer & Strack, 2014; Dhar & Gorlin, 2013), emotion (Buck, 1999; Rolls, 2007), personality (Epstein, 1991, 1994, 2013), and consciousness (Damasio, 2000; Edelman, 2003; Toates, 2006). In general, despite often vexing differences in terminology, dual-process models postulate that the architecture of the human mind comprises two main types of processes (Epstein, 1994, 2013; Evans, 2008; Evans & Stanovich, 2013).

One, termed Type-1 (Evans & Stanovich, 2013), is characterized by automaticity (i.e. is activated unintentionally, quickly, and efficiently, requires minimal involvement of cognitive resources, operates effortlessly, mostly outside of conscious awareness, and mostly beyond deliberate control), relies on nonpropositional associative memories, and does not involve language. Type-1 processes access behavioral actions through "compulsions," and cue-triggered "impulses" or "urges" (e.g. to eat when hungry, to drink when thirsty, to consume drugs or alcohol when addicted; see Berridge, Ho, Richard, & DiFeliceantonio, 2010; Berridge & Robinson, 2016), as well as through unintentional approach-avoidance postural changes (e.g. posterior sway when confronted with a threatening stimulus; see Eerland, Guadalupe, Franken, & Zwaan, 2012; Lelard, Stins, & Mouras, 2019) and associated patterns of electromyographic activity. For example, when negotiating a potentially painful bodily posture, patients with chronic pain exhibit reduced activity of the agonist and increased activity of the antagonist muscles, a pattern theorized to reflect an instinctive "guarding" response (Geisser, Haig, Wallbom, & Wiggert, 2004; Lund, Donga, Widmer, & Stohler, 1991; Sterling, Jull, & Wright, 2001; Watson, Booker, & Main, 1997). The second type of processes, termed Type-2 (Evans & Stanovich, 2013), are reflective, controlled, analytical, dependent on language and propositional memory, relatively effortful and slow, and reliant upon the availability of cognitive resources. Type-2 processes access behavioral actions through behavioral plans.

Affective-Reflective Theory: Basic Postulates

Unlike models that distinguish between "fast" and "slow" modes of cognition or between "cold" and "hot" cognition, the ART is more closely affiliated with models in which affective processes are explicitly identified as constituting the core of Type-1 processes. While other models also explicitly emphasize the role of affect within Type-1 processes, the labels used to refer to these processes vary widely: *Experiential* versus *rational* or *cognitive* (Epstein, 1994, 2013; Epstein & Pacini, 1999), *experiential* versus *analytic* (Slovic et al., 2002a), *affective* versus *analytical* (Peters & Slovic, 2000), *impulsive-associative* versus *reflective-propositional* (Deutsch, 2017), and *intuitive* versus *deliberate* (Dhar & Gorlin, 2013). As in the cognitive-experiential self-theory by Epstein (2013), the ART assumes that "without affect there would be no associative learning and therefore no experiential system" (p. 95) or what we have termed the "affective" class of processes. We also concur with Epstein (2013) that "the primary motive" of this "experiential" system (or our "affective" processes) is to "operate according to the hedonic principle" (p. 95), namely the pursuit of pleasure and the avoidance of displeasure.

It is important to point out that identifying one of the two types of processes in the ART as explicitly *affective* in nature renders certain criticisms leveled against other dual-process models inapplicable. The main argument that transcends critical analyses of dual-process models is that the postulated duality reflects merely convenience or simplification, whereas the supposed distinct processes represent the two ends of a single continuum (a "unimodel"), namely different degrees of cognitive processing, or different levels of "reasoning" or "judgment" (Grayot, 2020; Keren & Schul, 2009; Kruglanski & Gigerenzer, 2011; Melnikoff & Bargh, 2018; Osman, 2004). In contradistinction, in the ART, a case can be made for "affective" and "reflective" processes, which, despite being functionally integrated and in constant interaction, are also functionally and neuroanatomically distinguishable. Affective neuroscience has progressed beyond earlier notions of distinct evolutionary "layers" of paleomammalian ("limbic") and neomammalian cortex (MacLean, 1970) and simplified models of cortical-subcortical interactions (Pessoa, 2008) to more contemporary ideas, such as the "neural reference space for core affect" (Feldman Barrett & Bliss-Moreau, 2009; Feldman Barrett, Mesquita, Ochsner, & Gross, 2007) and "integrated functional systems" (Pessoa, 2017) that combine both cortical and subcortical (or "traditionally" affective) areas into integrated dynamic networks. Nevertheless, although it has become evident that multiple prefrontal cortical areas are involved in affective processes, it is also clear that the overlap between brain areas involved in core affect and reflective cognition is only partial and, therefore, unlikely to conform to a "unimodel."

The ART also departs from certain postulates of other dual-process models that emphasize the central role of affect within Type-1 processes. For example, according to the reflective-impulsive model (Strack & Deutsch, 2004), while core affect is at the center of the impulsive system and is encoded via associative processes, "complex emotions" fall under the rubric of the reflective system and engage propositional processes (Deutsch, 2017, p. 56). In the ART, although emotions require cognitive appraisals, affect still forms the main experiential and motivational core of emotions (Feldman Barrett, 2006; Russell, 2003). Therefore, whether core affect is experienced in a "free-floating" form or embedded within complex emotions, we theorize that it would engage associative memory processes in what is termed *affective valuation* or *affective learning* (Feldman Barrett & Bliss-Moreau, 2009).

In terms of the differentiation between "parallel-competitive" models, such as the reflective-impulsive model of Strack and Deutsch (2004), which posits a competition between the two systems for control over behavior, and "default-interventionist" models (Evans, 2008), the ART belongs to the latter, in the tradition of Zajonc (1980, 1984) and the associative-propositional evaluation model of Gawronski and Bodenhausen (2006, 2014). While the ART posits that both the affective and the reflective processes are constantly operating and interacting, it is particularly concerned with moments of "situated decisions," namely common everyday situations in which individuals are faced with physical activity-versus-inactivity dilemmas, such as: "After a long day of work, you have just arrived at home and you feel tired. However, you planned to go work-out tonight" (Brand & Schweizer, 2015). In such situations, the fast, efficient, and cognitive resource-independent affective processes are theorized to respond first, with the evocation in consciousness of a positively or negatively valenced somato-affective reaction (the "somatic marker" according to Damasio, or the "affective gut response" according to Gawronski and Bodenhausen) congruent with the previously formed affective valuation of the concept of "physical activity" (or "exercise" or "bodily movement") in conjunction with the affective valuation of the idea of physical rest. The reflective processes, which will be engaged quickly thereafter, will likely contemplate the dilemma in terms of pros and cons. However, in doing so, reflective processes will be called upon to validate or override the already formed urge generated by the preceding affective processes.

This chain of events presents two possible scenarios, namely congruence and incongruence of the physical vectors or "forces" generated by the affective and reflective processes. It is possible, for example, that (a) the idea of "exercise" has registered in associative memory with a positive affective valuation, as a result of years of pleasant and enjoyable past experiences, and (b) the reflective evaluation of "exercise" is also positive, based on information stored in declarative memory (e.g. I know exercise is greatly beneficial for my health). Or, conversely, the affective and reflective processes may converge toward inactivity (e.g. if "exercise" has been associated with a negative affective valuation and a negative or even an indifferent expectation of possible short- or long-term benefits). In these scenarios, both force vectors would point in the same behavioral direction and behavioral predictions would be straightforward. However, of greater interest to interventionists would be the – presumably common – scenario in which the affective and reflective processes would be incongruent, resulting in conflicting physical vectors. Of the two possibilities (i.e. positive affective valuation combined with negative reflective evaluation, and vice versa), presumably the more common scenario would involve a positive reflective evaluation (e.g. appreciation of the likelihood and the value of the potential health benefits, adequate self-efficacy for at least some forms of activity, expectation of social support and encouragement from at least some important others) combined with a negative affective valuation for physical activity, probably in conjunction with a positive or neutral affective valuation for sedentary alternatives (e.g. media consumption, television viewing). In this scenario, echoing similar predictions by Lang (1979) and Zajonc and Markus (1982), the ART predicts that the long-term outcome will be a tendency toward sedentary behavior. The reflective processes may override the urge to remain sedentary but this is likely only if the affective valuation is not overpoweringly negative and the cognitive resources are not compromised by stress, time pressure, limited knowledge, or other agents that can diminish self-control (Schwabe & Wolf, 2013; Shiv et al., 2005; Wirz et al., 2018).

The ART contains no specific postulates about the nature of reflective processes involved in regulating exercise, physical activity, and sedentary behavior. It seems reasonable to concede that the constructs postulated in cognitivist theories to date possess some – albeit evidently limited – degree of explanatory power. Accordingly, it is also acknowledged that part of the intervention approach to motivate exercise and physical activity should consist of talking sessions aimed at building an appropriate informational basis to support behavior change.

The advance that the ART brings consists of reintroducing affective processes to the motivational collage and, by doing so, reassigning the valenced experience of exercise, physical activity, and sedentary behavior a central role in shaping motivation. The theory postulates that the role of affect in behavior is not merely indirect (e.g. to "bias" cognitive appraisals or to prioritize the recollection of certain memories over others). Instead, the ART posits that affective processes constantly interact with reflective processes in dynamically shaping behavior.

Practical Examples

Implicit in the fundamental postulates of the ART is the assumption that, for many or perhaps most people, the ideas of "exercise" and "physical activity" have been associated with displeasure. This speculation would be consistent with the observation that the promotion of pleasure and enjoyment has not traditionally been among the primary aims of most sport, exercise, or physical activity programs. The field of sport and exercise science has been mainly preoccupied with the maximization of performance, physical fitness, and health outcomes.

For example, during the developmental period that brackets the dramatic childhood-to-adolescence decrease in physical activity, school physical education programs have prioritized the promotion of fundamental motor and sport skills, along with efforts to prevent childhood obesity. Prominent among initiatives aimed at preventing obesity have been government-mandated programs of fitness testing, in which the results (intended to be kept confidential) are clearly visible to peers. Although the potential aversive effects of these widespread practices for long-term motivation have been highlighted periodically in the literature by authors approaching the subject from the perspective of developmental and educational psychology, these isolated voices have not prompted substantial change in practice. However, emerging empirical evidence suggests that negative emotions arising from physical education experiences (Simonton & Garn, 2020) and subsequent memories of enjoyment (or lack thereof) associated with physical education (Ladwig, Vazou, & Ekkekakis, 2018) may have implications for physical activity or inactivity. Similarly, while the pursuit of "fun" is the leading reason for participating in organized youth sport, the absence of "fun" and related reasons (perceptions of low competence, high pressure from parental expectations) is the leading reason for dropout (Crane & Temple, 2015).

In adulthood, a major challenge is the unprecedented in human history combination of increased body mass (more than 1.00 kg/m^2 per decade from 1975 to 2014; NCD Risk Factor Collaboration, 2016) and reduced cardiorespiratory fitness (1.6% per decade from 1967 to 2016; Lamoureux et al., 2019). Higher body mass is a robust predictor of reduced physical activity participation, a phenomenon that may be mediated by diminished pleasure and enjoyment (Ekkekakis et al., 2016). Evidence suggests that higher body mass may reduce the pleasure of exercise and physical activity through a variety of mechanisms, including feelings of dyspnea or breathlessness, joint pain, thermoregulatory difficulties, self-presentational concerns, perceptions of antiobesity bias, dysfunctional beliefs, and violated weight-loss expectations (Ekkekakis, Zenko, et al., 2018). At the same time, exercise science has been promoting the transfer from the domain of high-level competitive athletics to the domain of public health of a model of training (i.e. high-intensity interval training) that explicitly promises that any gains in cardiometabolic health will incur the cost of "a little pain" (Gibala & McGee, 2008). Perhaps predictably, in a group of individuals with overweight or obesity, a 12-month program of high-intensity interval training (i.e. intervals at 80%–90% of peak aerobic capacity intermingled with periods of active recovery) resulted in a two-minute per week reduction of accelerometer-assessed moderate-to-vigorous physical activity at the twelfth month assessment compared to their (below-guidelines) baseline. However, individuals assigned to moderate-intensity continuous exercise (i.e. 45%–55% of peak aerobic capacity) still averaged 62 minutes more moderate-to-vigorous physical activity per week at the twelfth-month assessment compared to baseline (Jung et al., 2020).

Implications for Professional Practice

Given the current state of professional practice in exercise science and public health, if intervention approaches were to transition from the current "rational educational" model to a model based on the ART, global professional practice norms would change in a radical way. Exercise prescription guidelines would be based on a tripartite rationale that, besides the maximization of health and fitness gains and the minimization of injury risk, would also take into consideration the promotion of pleasure and enjoyment (Ekkekakis et al., 2011). Public health physical activity recommendations and promotion campaigns would highlight the potential for immediate affective benefits (e.g. pleasure, perceived energy, mood regulation, stress management) over long-term health adaptations (Smith & Wightman, in press; Williamson, Baker, Mutrie, Niven, & Kelly, 2020). Motivational consultations with individual participants would acquire a second component besides the traditional (seated) counseling sessions that involve the exchange of information; exercise and public health professionals would also intervene during the exercise or physical activity experiences, helping to tailor aspects of the activity itself, as well as the physical, sensory, and social environment, to promote pleasure and enjoyment.

Future Directions

The ART is a new theory, so the systematic testing of its postulates is at its early stages. At this point, there is supporting evidence for certain key predictions. First, while this research is still at a nascent stage and the standards of methodological "best practices" are still evolving (Ekkekakis, Zenko, Ladwig, & Hartman, 2018), early studies suggest that ratings of affective valence obtained during a bout of exercise show modest but significant associations with self-reported and device-assessed physical activity, both concurrently and prospectively (Ekkekakis & Dafermos, 2012; Rhodes & Kates, 2015). Second, various measures presumed to tap automatic processes also show modest but significant and consistent associations with both self-reported and device-based assessments of physical activity, accounting for additive (i.e. nonoverlapping) variance, beyond the variance accounted for by self-report measures of motivational constructs (Chevance, Bernard, Chamberland, & Rebar, 2019; Schinkoeth & Antoniewicz, 2017). Third, measures of explicit evaluations of exercise or physical activity (such as self-reported attitudes) and measures presumed to reflect automatic associations of these concepts are not necessarily concordant. The discrepancies between these categories of measures may carry important implications for behavior, such as accounting for parts of the difference between ideal and actual exercise frequencies (Brand & Antoniewicz, 2016) or dropout from an exercise program (Berry, Rodgers, Divine, & Hall, 2018).

From a theoretical standpoint, a crucial missing piece of the puzzle is the establishment of a causal link between affective experiences associated with exercise or physical activity and performance in tests presumed to reflect automatic (or "implicit") processes (Zenko & Ekkekakis, 2019a). However, progress is being made on this front, with evidence suggesting that differences in psychophysiological indices (Schinkoeth et al., 2019) or behavioral expressions (Brand & Ulrich, 2019) that are theorized to reflect affective processes can distinguish between individuals with different levels of physical activity participation.

From an applied standpoint, a great unmet challenge is the development and testing of interventions that can robustly and reliably improve the affective experience of exercise and physical activity across diverse groups of participants (Ekkekakis, Hartman, & Ladwig, 2020). This is a prerequisite before pragmatic randomized controlled trials can be conducted to examine whether improved affective experiences can ultimately lead to increased and sustained exercise and physical activity participation (Ekkekakis, Zenko, et al., 2018). At present, some (Antoniewicz & Brand, 2016a; Markland, Hall, Duncan, & Simatovic, 2015), though not all (Chevance, Berry, Boiché, & Heraud, 2019), proof-of-concept studies have shown that short-term evaluative conditioning or associative learning interventions (i.e. repeatedly pairing the concept of exercise with visual depictions or mental images of pleasure) can change performance on tests presumed to assess automatic associations and even improve exercise-related behaviors in the short term (e.g. choice of exercise intensity). However, as has also been demonstrated in contexts other than exercise (Forscher et al., 2019), such procedures are primarily of theoretical interest, and have limited practical implications for changing behavior.

In summary, we have established the urgent need for theorizing in the field of exercise psychology to advance beyond the cognitivist paradigm, taking advantage of a broader array of conceptual tools. To this end, we summarized the conceptual antecedents and basic postulates of the ART of exercise and physical inactivity, a domain-specific dual-process theory that, besides reflective processes such as cognitive appraisals, places renewed emphasis on the role of affective processes in regulating behavior. Considering that a model of professional practice based on the ART could radically alter the way that exercise and physical activity are being promoted on a global scale, we welcome and encourage the testing of ART-derived hypotheses.

4

HEURISTICS, BIASES, AND BOUNDED RATIONALITY

A Dual-Process and Behavioral-Science Approach to Exercise Initiation and Maintenance

Zachary Zenko, Catherine J. Berman, and Julia D. O'Brien

Physical Activity and Exercise Behavior: Current Status

Participation in regular physical activity is associated with overwhelmingly positive outcomes. A comprehensive review of the benefits of an active lifestyle is beyond the scope of this chapter. Nonetheless, someone considering adopting an active lifestyle can expect reductions in risk of cardiovascular disease (Myers, 2003), cancer (Kushi et al., 2012), Alzheimer's disease and dementia (Larson et al., 2006), falling (Arnold, Sran, & Harrison, 2008), and depression (Craft & Perna, 2004), among many diverse positive outcomes of physical activity and exercise. Further, people adopting an active lifestyle can expect increases in quality of life (Gill et al., 2013). Exercise has been called a "polypill" because of its multiple benefits and low likelihood of adverse effects (Fiuza-Luces, Garateachea, Berger, & Lucia, 2013). From a cost-benefit perspective, the benefits of physical activity and exercise outweigh the potential risks for the majority of the population, and the decision to adopt an active lifestyle appears simple and straightforward. Unfortunately, relying on changing knowledge is insufficient for changing physical activity and exercise behavior (Morrow, Krzewinski-Malone, Jackson, Bungum, & FitzGerald, 2004).

Are Adults Meeting the Physical Activity Recommendations?

According to the latest guidelines from the U.S. Department of Health and Human Services and from the Physical Activity Guidelines Advisory committee, adults should engage in at least 150 minutes of moderate-intensity aerobic physical activity per week, or 75 minutes of aerobic vigorous-intensity physical activity, or an equivalent combination of both moderate- and vigorous-intensity aerobic activities (Physical Activity Guidelines Advisory Committee, 2018). Further, adults are recommended to engage in muscle-strengthening activities on at least two days per week. What proportion of adults meets these guidelines? The answer to this question can be complicated.

Estimates of physical activity behavior depend on whether the measurements are self-report or device-based methods, which can have limited agreement (Lines et al., 2020).

Self-report methods may overestimate physical activity behavior, in comparison to device-based measurements (e.g. accelerometers) (Nelson, Taylor, & Vella, 2019). More importantly, estimates depend on the physical activity guidelines used and the processing of data; within the same dataset, estimates can range from 3.4% to 95.6% meeting physical activity guidelines (Zenko, Willis, & White, 2019). Taken together, it is difficult to use estimates of physical activity behavior to definitively describe current levels of activity.

That said, we are unfortunately confident that the population level of physical activity behavior is much too low, especially when considering both aerobic activity and muscle-strengthening activity (Bennie, De Crocker, Teychenne, Brown, & Biddle, 2019). If cardiorespiratory fitness can be used as a proxy to estimate physical activity behavior, there is evidence of a decreasing trend since the 1980s (Tomkinson, Lang, & Tremblay, 2019) and 1960s (Lamoureux et al., 2019). Within large cohorts (e.g. 640 adolescents, followed for 12 years into early adulthood), physical activity has been shown to decline by 24% (Kwan, Cairney, Faulkner, & Pullenayegum, 2012; also see Lagestad, van den Tillaar, & Mamen, 2018; and Kimm et al., 2000). Physical inactivity has been called a "pandemic" (Kohl et al., 2012).

In short, it seems reasonable to suggest that the population is insufficiently active, even in the absence of precise estimates. Moreover, despite increasing evidence of the benefits of an active lifestyle, we are not aware of evidence of meaningful increases in physical activity behavior; insufficient physical activity appears to be stable (Guthold, Stevens, Riley, & Bull, 2018). We do not suggest that behavioral-science solutions – the focus of this chapter – will perfectly correct the "pandemic." However, we do suggest that behavioral-science solutions warrant further attention and research and may help meaningfully move the needle on physical inactivity. This point is essential to clarify early because some people may tend to overestimate the effectiveness of novel intervention strategies based on interesting new areas (e.g. behavioral economics or behavioral science). It is equally necessary to recognize that a single panacea for physical inactivity is unlikely, but even a 10% increase in physical activity can have profound impacts on public health and wellness (Lee et al., 2012).

Are People Trying to Become Physically Active?

By all indications, the lack of exercise and physical activity behavior is not due to lack of interest. Analysis of Google trends data indicates that the search term "exercise" frequently peaks in the United States and worldwide around January, a pattern that has been documented since 2004 (Google Trends, 2020). Yet, despite individuals' widespread interest in physical activity, this motivation rarely translates to consistent exercise behavior. Researchers investigating adherence to fitness center usage in an unsupervised setting have described discouraging data. Sperandei, Viera, and Reis (2016) analyzed records of 5,240 members of a fitness center, tracking the first 12 months since joining. More than half (63%) ceased attending the fitness center within three months, and just 4% were continuing for one year. Importantly, an intention is an insufficient marker of behavior change; the high rates of inactivity in the population do not appear to be caused by a lack of initial interest or intention.

Still, many theories regularly applied to explain volitional exercise behavior continue to include intentions as a predictor of behavior (e.g. "I will exercise tomorrow morning"). The theory of planned behavior, for example, is one of the most popular theories applied to the context of exercise (Ekkekakis & Zenko, 2016). Although "the theory assumes that intentions are the most important determinant of behavior" (Webb & Sheeran, 2006, p. 250), meta-analytic evidence indicates that changing intentions do not always lead to changing behavior (Webb & Sheeran, 2006). The gulf between intentions and actions is known as the intention-behavior gap (Rhodes & Dickau, 2012; see also Chapter 2, this volume); this gap is often so large that the "relationship between intention and behavior ... may be below meaningful/practical value" (Rhodes & Dickau, 2012, p. 724).

Comparing Contrasting Theoretical Approaches to Physical Activity and Exercise Behavior

Traditionally, theories of exercise behavior have common origins in cognitivism. Sharing overlapping assumptions, these theories postulate that humans act following a rational, cost-benefit analysis of information (Ekkekakis & Zenko, 2016; see also Chapter 3, this volume). These theories "have one core attribution in common, stemming from the origins of cognitive theorizing in psychology: They all emphasize the importance of imagined end states (behaviors or goals)" (Brand & Cheval, 2019, p. 2). Examples include the social cognitive theory (Bandura, 1986), theory of reasoned action (Fishbein & Ajzen, 1975) and its successor, theory of planned behavior (Ajzen, 1991), self-determination theory (Deci & Ryan, 1980, 1985), and the transtheoretical model (Prochaska & Marcus, 1994). Ekkekakis and Zenko (2016) summarized the common assumptions:

> [The assumptions of cognitivist models of behavior] imply that human beings possess the capacity to collect and retain all pertinent information, that their behaviors result from the informational input in a rational and predictable manner, and that there is no alternative pathway that determines behavior besides the theorized (algorithmic and data-bound) cognitive processes. A further implication is that, if the behavioral output is undesirable (i.e., suboptimal in promoting self-interest), this can be corrected by feeding the system with additional, more accurate, or more compelling data. In other words, the theories assume that, to change physical activity and/or exercise behavior (or any type of behavior for that matter), more information should be provided and subjected to rational cognitive evaluation.
>
> *(p. 395)*

These theories, and others with similar assumptions, provide a starting point for practitioners and interventionists interested in changing behavior. Each theoretical framework identifies constructs of interest for explaining behavior and targets for behavior change. It is worth noting that these theories have received support and have shown some promise in the context of exercise promotion (e.g. self-determination theory: Edmunds, Ntoumanis, & Duda, 2006, 2008; Silva et al., 2010; Teixeira, Carraça, Markland, Silva, & Ryan, 2012; social cognitive theory: Amaya & Petosa, 2012; Hallam & Petosa, 2004; theory of planned behavior: Bryan & Rocheleau, 2002; Courneya & Friedenreich, 1999; Parrot, Tennant, Olejnik, & Poudevigne, 2008; transtheoretical model: Romain et al., 2018).

However, the assumption of rationality also has noteworthy limitations. In the context of exercise, where the benefits of an active lifestyle outweigh the potential risks, it seems that this assumption is not supported. The provision of information does not always change behavior, even when we have intentions to change. Further, evidence of the effectiveness of interventions to change physical activity leaves much to be desired. A meta-meta-analysis by Ekkekakis and Zenko (2016) found that these interventions had a "small" effect size (Cohen's $d = 0.26$) on average. The limitations of the rationality assumption and the "rational-educational model" will not be the primary focus of this chapter, as these limitations have been elaborated elsewhere (Ekkekakis, 2017; Ekkekakis & Zenko, 2016; see also Chapter 3, this volume).

Dual-Process Theories

We do not adopt the philosophy that each of the cognitivist theories should be discounted or ignored. Instead, we advocate for a postcognitivist, *dual-process* approach. These approaches assume that both (a) automatic or heuristic processes (known as "Type 1" processes) and (b) deliberate or controlled processes (known as "Type 2" processes) are involved in the decision-making process and influence behavior. Although many terms have been used to describe these distinct processes, including System 1 and System 2 (Kahneman, 2011), the terms Type 1 and Type 2 processes are used here (Evans & Stanovich, 2013; Stanovich & Toplak, 2012). The adoption of a dual-process approach means that – *in addition* to Type 2 processes – the influence of Type 1 processes is recognized (also see Ekkekakis & Zenko, 2016).

Importantly, several properties have been described as "typical correlates" of Type 1 processes (e.g. automatic, relatively fast, implicit, evolutionarily old, relatively undemanding of cognitive capacity) and Type 2 processes (e.g. controlled, relatively slow, explicit, evolutionarily recent, capacity demanding; see Table 4.1 in Stanovich and Toplak, 2012). Stanovich and Toplak (2012) suggest that the "defining feature of Type 1 processing is its autonomy—the execution of Type 1 processes is *mandatory* when their triggering stimuli are encountered, *and they are not dependent on input from high-level control systems*" (p. 8, emphasis added), while the defining feature of Type 2 processes is cognitive decoupling that allows hypothetical reasoning (also see Pennycook, Neys, Evans, Stanovich, & Thompson, 2018). Thus, Type 1 processes are assumed to result in the default behavioral response *unless overridden* by the effortful, more deliberate, and controlled Type 2 processes (Evans & Stanovich, 2013). Further, because Type 1 processes occur automatically and operate as the default, Type 1 processes are theorized to influence Type 2 processes and can often result in heuristic or cognitive bias in decision making (Kahneman, 2011). The terms "heuristics and biases" are sometimes used in this chapter because these sometimes automatic or heuristic processes occur rapidly and *bias* subsequent rational, deliberate, controlled processes (Kahneman, 2011).

Applied to the context of physical activity or exercise, this dual-process theorizing suggests that unless Type 1 processes result in a physical activity (or unless more cognitively demanding and effortful Type 2 processes override Type 1 processes), sedentary behavior will likely persist. Further, it is likely that Type 1 processes usually favor sedentary or physically inactive alternatives (Brand & Cheval, 2019; Cheval et al., 2018).

Chapter Roadmap

The link between dual-process theorizing and behavioral-science approaches may not be self-evident. In the remaining parts of this chapter, we describe bounded rationality to illustrate how many behavioral-science principles are derived from dual-process frameworks. We then illustrate examples of bounded rationality and heuristic processes, highlighting the affect heuristic (Finucane, Alhakami, Slovic, & Johnson, 2000; Slovic, Finucane, Peters, MacGregor, 2007; Table 4.1) as a crucial example that has received particular attention in the context of physical activity and exercise promotion. The discussion of the affect heuristic is camped with the Affective-Reflective Theory (Brand & Ekkekakis, 2018; see also Chapter 3, this volume), given theoretical overlaps between this theory and the affect heuristic. Next, we elaborate additional behavioral-science research in the context of physical activity and exercise. Finally, we conclude with an overview of potential strategies for changing physical activity and exercise behavior from the perspective of a behavioral designer.

Dual-Process Theories and Behavioral-Science Approaches

Behavioral-science and behavioral-economic approaches respond to the limitations of deliberative information provision on human decision making, given its susceptibility to the influence of heuristics and biases (Kahneman, 2003). By eschewing information provision and instead focusing on other psychological and contextual decision-making processes, behavioral scientists implicitly or explicitly adopt dual-process frameworks. Behavioral-science interventions, then, achieve at least one of the following: (a) Target Type 1 processes, or (b) recognize that Type 2 processes can be influenced by heuristics and biases. Thus, behavioral science adopts the perspective that humans operate using "bounded rationality," rather than perfectly rational decision-making processes (Simon, 1979). The concept of *bounded rationality* suggests that humans do not necessarily behave *irrationally*, but instead operate in ways that do not maximize utility or in ways that operate with unlimited information-processing capacity; "thus, the term 'bounded rationality' can be interpreted to mean rational choice under computational constraints" (Lee, 2011, p. 511).

For an example in the exercise context, consider the following. From a cognitivist perspective, a rational exerciser would have the same preference among a choice set (e.g. 30 minutes of moderate-intensity exercise vs. 20 minutes of vigorous-intensity exercise), regardless of the presence of irrelevant or less attractive options or "decoys" (e.g. *90 minutes* of moderate-intensity exercise). Perhaps the preference ratio for the 30-minute session vs. the 20-minute session is 2:1; that is, for every person choosing the 20-minute session, two people choose the 30-minute session. One would not expect this ratio to change if a third, decoy alternative was added. This assumption is known as the constant-ratio rule (Latty & Beekman, 2011). However, in practice, and supporting the concept of "bounded rationality," the presence of the decoy effect suggests that irrelevant, alternative exercise options can influence decision making, even when the added exercise option is designed to be unappealing and avoided.

Zenko, Ekkekakis, and Kavetsos (2016) illustrated this phenomenon by asking one group of participants to choose between two options, namely a target option of 30 minutes of exercise at a moderate intensity or an alternative option of 20 minutes at a vigorous intensity. A second group was asked to choose between these two options, as well as an additional decoy option. The third, decoy option was 90 minutes of exercise at a moderate intensity. The decoy option was meant to increase the appeal of the target option because it was similar to the target option in the dimension of intensity (both moderate), but inferior in the dimension of duration (90 minutes, rather than 30 minutes). Therefore, the presence of the decoy was designed to highlight the shorter duration but same intensity of the target option. When the decoy option was present, participants were 58% more likely to choose the target option compared to the 20-minute alternative, which violated the constant-ratio rule. In this example, decisions changed because of a biasing effect of heuristic processes, not because of the provision of relevant additional information, which violates the assumption of rationality. Applied to the exercise context, it may be possible for a personal trainer to increase the appeal of a target personal training program by juxtaposing it with a particularly unappealing decoy that was never intended to be prescribed in the first place (for an additional example, see Zenko, Ekkekakis, & Kavetsos, 2016).

A list of heuristics and biases and their potential applications for physical activity promotion are presented in Table 4.1; some of these examples are untested in the context of physical activity and exercise and all of them warrant further investigation. Moreover, Hathaway and Fedewa (2017) described several strategies for applying these principles to new clients in a fitness center setting. Many of the strategies suggested by Hathaway and Fedewa (2017) do not rely on the provision of additional information about the benefits of exercise, which supports our perspective that researchers or practitioners adopting behavioral-science approaches implicitly or explicitly adopt a dual-process framework. These strategies frequently either avoid targeting Type 2 processes or recognize the "bounded nature" and limitations of the rationality assumption, as well as the susceptibility to heuristics and biases. For instance, a person who prepares for the next day by gathering exercise clothes and a gym bag before bed because they know – despite good goals and intentions – that they will be less likely to gather their exercise items the next morning recognizes the limitations of the rationality assumption, at least implicitly.

To provide an example, "commitment contracts" represent a behavioral-science intervention technique that applies dual-process principles. Hathaway and Fedewa (2017) considered using commitment contracts to help exercisers become more likely to follow through with intentions of exercising. For example, an exerciser may sign a contract between themselves and an accountability partner to keep the exerciser honest (sometimes called an accountabilibuddy). The exerciser may commit to exercising five times per week for six months. If they succeed, the accountabilibuddy may donate to a charity that the exerciser supports. If the exerciser fails, they donate to a political cause that they would rather not support. Potential contingent outcomes are nearly limitless. At the beginning of an exercise program, a new client has demonstrated their intentions to exercise by signing up for the exercise program. However, it may be possible that commitment contracts and other commitment devices can enhance adherence to these intentions, perhaps especially when self-control resources are low (Hofmann, Friese, & Wiers, 2008) and the likelihood of being influenced by Type 1 processes is higher. This hypothesis is supported by empirical data (Royer, Stehr, & Sydnor, 2015). In a longitudinal study using a website for commitment contracts (https://www.stickk.com/), participants were randomly assigned to either 8-, 12-, or 20-week commitment contracts that could have been modified by the participants (Bhattacharya, Garber, & Goldhaber-Fiebert, 2015). *Default* options, or the options that will be followed unless a decision maker actively chooses an alternative, appear to be influential in shaping the commitment contracts. The researchers found that the default duration of the commitment contract influenced commitment duration; longer duration defaults resulted in increased duration of commitment. Even though the participants *could* modify this choice by engaging in Type 2 processes, the default option was still influential.

TABLE 4.1 Example Heuristic Influences on Decision Making and Behavior

Heuristics and Biases	*Summary*	*Examples of Possible Applications to Physical Activity and Exercise Contexts*	*Key Conceptual Reading(s)*
Affect Heuristic	Our immediate affective reaction toward a stimulus shapes judgment and decisions about the stimulus.	Creating positive affective associations with exercise should result in more exercise behavior. See text for elaboration, especially related to Affective-Reflective Theory (Brand & Ekkekakis, 2018).	Brand and Ekkekakis (2018) Finucane et al. (2000) Slovic et al. (2007)
Delay Discounting and Preference for Immediate Rewards	The value of a reward decreases as it is moved further into the future; people often prefer smaller immediate rewards or gratification over larger but delayed rewards or gratification (e.g. spending money now vs. spending money in retirement, after years of investment).	Focus on immediate benefits of physical activity, including pleasure, enjoyment, and increased energy.	Ainslie (1975) Frederick, Loewenstein, and O'Donoghue (2002)
Duration Neglect and the Peak-End Rule	Our memory of an experience is disproportionately impacted by the most intense moment of an experience and the final moment of an experience.	Ensure that the most intense moment of exercise and the final moment of exercise are pleasant. For more on its application and generalizability to the exercise context, see Hargreaves & Stych, 2013.	Fredrickson & Kahneman (1993) Hargreaves and Stych (2013) Kahneman, Fredrickson, Schreiber, and Redelmeier (1993)
Friction and Defaults	Decisions and behaviors often follow the "path of least resistance," making us susceptible to being influenced by the default choice options.	At orientation in a workplace, set the default expectation that 1:00 pm is the post-lunch time for exercise, allowing participants to opt-out of exercise, rather than expecting them to opt-in. Allow new fitness center members to sign up with minimal information and paperwork (and no startup fee).	Johnson and Goldstein (2013)

(*Continued*)

Heuristics and Biases	*Summary*	*Examples of Possible Applications to Physical Activity and Exercise Contexts*	*Key Conceptual Reading(s)*
Framing and Loss Aversion	The context or mental model of a decision changes how we perceive it.	Choose the framing of exercise-related messages (e.g. "If you exercise, you will reduce your risk of cardiovascular disease" vs. "If you don't exercise, you will increase your risk of cardiovascular disease") carefully, as they may have different impacts on behavior. Positive frames are more likely to be effective than negative frames (Williamson, Baker, Mutrie, Niven, & Kelly, 2020)	Kahneman and Tversky (1979, 1992) Soman (2004) Williamson, Baker, Mutrie, Niven, & Kelly (2020)
Self-Control Processes	Acting on the earlier stages of the self-control process (e.g. situation selection or modification) may be more effective than acting on the later stages (i.e. preventing vs. interrupting a self-control lapse).	Plan to exercise prior to work or school, anticipating that feelings of energy and desire to exercise may be lower at the end of the day.	Duckworth et al. (2016) Gross and Thompson (2007)
Slope or Trend Effects	Our memory of an experience is disproportionately impacted by how pleasant or unpleasant an experience becomes over time.	Create exercise sessions that become progressively more pleasant and enjoyable, perhaps by decreasing intensity throughout an exercise session, perhaps especially among nonathletic populations (for more, see Hutchinson, Zenko, Santich, & Dalton, 2020; Stuntz, Grosshans, Boghosian, Brendel, & Williamson 2020; Zenko, Ekkekakis, & Ariely, 2016).	Ariely and Carmon (2000) Hutchinson et al. (2020) Stuntz et al. (2020) Zenko et al. (2016)

The researchers also found that commitment contracts increased the likelihood of success in achieving goals (Bhattacharya et al., 2015). In short, people with good intentions to exercise can consider increasing the likelihood of achieving their goals by signing up for an exercise class in advance, when self-control is high and temptation for sedentary alternatives is low (Duckworth, Gendler, and Gross, 2016; see Table 4.1, Process Model of Self-Control).

Dual-Process Approaches in the Context of Physical Activity and Exercise: The Affect Heuristic

The affect heuristic (Finucane et al., 2000; Slovic et al., 2007; see Table 4.1) has received particular attention in the context of physical activity and exercise promotion and it is closely aligned with behavioral-science principles. The affect heuristic allows people to efficiently make judgments and decisions by relying on the initial affective reaction to a stimulus. This idea is supported by the concept that affective reactions are the first reactions to stimuli, occurring prior to complex cognitive appraisals (Zajonc, 1980).

> All of the images in people's minds are tagged or marked to varying degrees with affect. The affect pool contains all the positive and negative markers associated (consciously or unconsciously) with the images. The intensity of the markers varies with the images. People consult or "sense" the affect pool in the process of making judgments... Using an overall, readily available affective impression can be easier and more efficient than weighing the pros and cons of various reasons or retrieving relevant examples from memory, especially when the required judgment or decision is complex or mental resources are limited.
>
> *(Slovic, Finucane, Peters, & MacGregor, 2002a, p. 332)*

The affect heuristic is conceptually similar to the somatic marker hypothesis (Damasio, 1994). Like the affect heuristic, "somatic markers probably increase the accuracy and efficiency of the decision process" (Damasio, 1994, p, 173). Experiences become "marked" as positive or negative through learning and are predictive of positive or negative future outcomes. Somatic markers can consciously or unconsciously influence complex decision making.

The affect heuristic, which can occur independently of more effortful cognitive appraisals, operates as a Type 1 process, whereas the cognitive appraisals that occur slower and can endorse or override the initial affect heuristic response function as a Type 2 process. If a person has an immediate positive affective reaction associated with an exercise-related stimulus (e.g. the choice to exercise), then exercise behavior would be expected. In contrast, if the immediate affective reaction evoked by the exercise-related stimulus is negative, then the likelihood of engaging in exercise would be expected to decrease. Although the affect heuristic increases the efficiency of decision making (Slovic et al., 2002a), it should be clear that this can lead to suboptimal behaviors if the affective heuristic reaction encourages short-term behaviors and immediate gratifications that are at the expense of long-term goals, interests, and maximum benefits. The affect heuristic may be even more influential on decision-making processes and ultimately behavior when self-control or "mental resources" are low (Finucane et al., 2000), suggesting that reliance on the heuristic partly depends on situational factors (e.g. being tired or fatigued) or individual factors (e.g. executive functioning, trait self-control; see also Strobach, Englert, Jekauc, & Pfeffer, 2020).

The Affective-Reflective Theory of physical inactivity and exercise (Brand & Ekkekakis, 2018; see also Chapter 3, this volume) shares overlap with the affect heuristic and somatic marker hypothesis and is a promising dual-process theory for explaining and promoting physical activity and exercise. The theory assumes that exercise-related stimuli (e.g. a thought about exercise, an exercise-related image, a cue to exercise, a memory of an exercise session) trigger automatic associations related to exercise and a valenced (positive/negative) automatic affective valuation. The elicitation of the automatic associations and automatic affective valuation is rapid, not mediated by cognitive appraisal, and is the result of Type 1 processing. These initial reactions appear to occur without input from high-level cognitive control systems, which is a defining element of Type 1 processes (Stanovich & Toplak, 2012). Similarly, the Physical Activity Adoption and Maintenance model (PAAM model; Strobach et al., 2020) emphasizes the role of automatic, affective heuristic reactions. These affective reactions are categorized as implicit processes that arise spontaneously and do not depend on deliberation. Taken together, both the Affective-Reflective Theory and the PAAM emphasize the influence of an automatic, heuristic, affective reaction on physical activity behavior.

According to Brand and Ekkekakis (2018), the automatic affective valuation may be based on repeated positive or negative affective experiences with exercise (also see Conroy & Berry, 2017; Ekkekakis, 2017; Ekkekakis & Dafermos, 2012; Ekkekakis & Zenko, 2016; Zenko & Ekkekakis, 2019b). Maximizing the pleasure and enjoyment of physical activity and exercise would theoretically result in positive automatic associations and a positive automatic affective valuation.[1] This Type 1 process results in an action impulse that, if positive, would increase likelihood of exercise behavior. However, if the affective valuation is negative, then physical activity would be less likely. Following the concept that the Type 1 process is the default process (Evans & Stanovich, 2013), Brand and Ekkekakis (2018) suggested that the "fast and effortless automatic affective valuation is the default-response upon which the slower, controlled response is based. The automatic affective valuation can be rejected as a basis for the reflective evaluation or can 'color' the subsequent controlled process" (p. 54). The Type 2 process – characterized by slower, more effortful reflection and cognitive appraisal – can endorse or override the Type 1 action impulse.

For example, triggered by an exercise-related stimulus (e.g. seeing a calendar reminder to exercise), an action impulse can be based on negative automatic associations and negative automatic affective valuations of exercise. This action impulse would be expected to decrease the likelihood of following through with the exercise plans. However, the slower Type 2 processes may strongly favor exercise (e.g. "I previously made this commitment and do not want to fail" or "I know that exercise is healthy and that I will feel accomplished if I achieve my goal of exercising"). In this example, the person might override the immediately negative reaction triggered by the exercise-related stimulus (seeing the calendar reminder) and follow through with the original intentions to exercise. In support of Affective-Reflective Theory and PAAM, mounting evidence suggests automatic associations are correlated with or predictive of motivational variables (e.g. attitudes, intentions to exercise) and behavioral outcomes, such as self-reported exercise behavior and device-based estimates of physical activity (Antoniewicz & Brand, 2014; 2016b; Banting, Dimmock, & Lay, 2009; Berry, 2006; Bluemke, Brand, Schweizer, & Kahlert, 2010; Brand & Antoniewicz, 2016; Brand & Schweizer, 2015; Calitri, Lowe, Eves, & Bennett, 2009; Cheval et al., 2020; Cheval, Sarrazin, Isoard-Gautheur, Radel, & Friese, 2015; Chevance, Caudroit, Romain, & Boiché, 2017; Chevance et al., 2018; Conroy, Hyde, Doerksen, & Ribeiro, 2010; Hyde, Doerksen, Ribeiro, & Conroy, 2010; Hyde, Elavsky, Doerksen, & Conroy, 2012; Eves, Scott, Hoppé, & French, 2007; Rebar, Ram, & Conroy, 2015; for reviews, see Chevance, Bernard, Chamberland, & Rebar, 2019 and Schinkoeth & Antoniewicz, 2017).

Brand and Ekkekakis (2018) theorized that the rapid action impulse will be more likely to shape behavior when sufficient self-regulatory resources are not available; if self-control resources are high, then Type 2 processes become more influential on behavior (see Chapters 8 and 9, this volume). Similarly, Strobach et al. (2020) theorized that executive functions and trait self-regulation are moderators of the relation between intentions and behavior. According to Strobach et al. (2020), Type 2 influences on behavior will be more likely if self-regulatory abilities are high. The importance of self-control and self-regulatory processes – a focus of this volume – is well-documented. Self-control and self-regulatory processes are implicated in smoking cessation (Feng, 2005), healthy lifestyles and lifestyle medicine more broadly (Faries, 2016), and the avoidance of temptation in the first place such that the need to overcome temptation is less frequent (Hofmann, Baumeister, Förster, & Vohs, 2012). In the context of exercise, self-control resources also predict exercise behavior, especially among people with low trait self-control (Englert & Rummel, 2016; Schöndube, Bertrams, Sudeck, & Fuchs, 2017). Self-control has also been implicated in the gap between exercise intentions and exercise behavior (Pfeffer, Englert, & Mueller-Alcazar, 2019). Habits – theorized to be influenced by some Type 1, automatic processes – have also been shown to predict exercise behavior especially when (Type 2) intentions for activity are weak (Rebar, Elavsky, Maher, Doerksen, & Conroy, 2014). Overall, the moderating role of self-control, theorized by Brand and Ekkekakis (2018) and Strobach et al. (2020) to determine the level of Type 2 influence on physical activity and exercise behavior, appears to be well-supported.

Thus, capacity for self-control should be maximized (Brand & Cheval, 2019), and situations in which limited self-control resources exist should be anticipated so that appropriate strategies for reducing lapses in self-control may be implemented (e.g. using commitment devices, appropriate situation selection; see Table 4.1). However, it should also be recognized that these strategies may not always be possible. It would therefore be beneficial to anticipate situations in which Type 1 processes become more dominant influences on behavior. Taken together, people interested in promoting physical activity and exercise should focus on increasing the likelihood that automatic associations and automatic affective valuations favor an active lifestyle, rather than sedentary behavior. Possible approaches to modify automatic associations and automatic affective valuations might include evaluative conditioning, approach-avoidance retraining, attentional bias modification (Brand & Cheval, 2019), as well maximizing the pleasure experienced during exercise (Brand & Ekkekakis, 2018; Ekkekakis & Dafermos, 2012; Ekkekakis, 2017; Ekkekakis & Zenko, 2016; Rhodes & Kates, 2015). Some of these approaches are discussed later in this chapter.

Additional Behavioral-Science Approaches to Promote Physical Activity and Exercise

Other intervention strategies that follow what can be called a behavioral-science approach may go beyond the affect heuristic. As mentioned earlier, the perspective adopted here suggests that behavioral-science approaches may target Type 1 processes, recognize the limitations of Type 2 processes, or both. The research focusing on the promotion of physical activity and exercise in this area is broad and often adopts intervention strategies that have been successful in other domains (e.g. finance, medication adherence, other health behaviors). It is often of mixed quality and results, providing ample opportunity for future investigators, interventionists, and practitioners.

In the context of exercise initiation and maintenance, there have been several valuable discussions (Shuval et al., 2017; Zimmerman, 2009) and interesting findings in recent years. Shuval and colleagues (2017), for instance, provide strategies for counseling primary care patients about physical activity and exercise. The guidance offered acknowledges the existence of some heuristics and biases – including "present time bias" and the "status quo bias." Present time bias refers to the preference for immediate gratification rather than delayed, potentially larger rewards (also see Delay Discounting and Preference for Immediate Rewards; Table 4.1). Therefore, behavioral designers may consider emphasizing immediate rewards (e.g. more energy after a walk) rather than long-term outcomes (e.g. reduced risk of cardiovascular disease). The status quo bias refers to the tendency for people to opt for the default-response option (also see Friction and Defaults; Table 4.1). Specific examples of advice provided by Shuval and colleagues (2017) include "changing the status quo from sedentary to more active" and increasing the salience of information that is likely already available to the patients, such as "the connections between patients' behavioral changes and health outcomes" (p. 237). Zimmerman (2009) highlights social norming, habit formation, and framing as potentially valuable behavioral-science approaches. Norming refers to emphasizing the popularity or frequency of a behavior done by a large group of people, if true (e.g. "60% of your coworkers make time to exercise regularly"). Habit formation refers to making physical activity a more regular part of a routine so that engaging in activity requires less effort. Norming and habit formation are discussed in greater detail later. Framing refers to the idea that information may be more or less influential based on how it is presented. For example, Williamson et al. (2020) noted that messages designed to promote physical activity should focus on gains rather than losses (e.g. "exercise will make you feel good"), and highlight short-term outcomes (also see Framing and Loss Aversion; Table 4.1).

Choice architecture refers to the environment that influences the choices of a decision maker; choice architects can "nudge" people to behave in certain ways by altering the environment to increase or decrease the likelihood of choices without force (Thaler, Sunstein, & Balz, 2013). Systematic reviews of "nudge" and choice architecture interventions have now been conducted. Forberger, Reisch, Kampfmann, and Zeeb (2019) classified 35 studies based on the type of choice architecture category and technique used. For example, a strategy for changing decision structure involved "changing choice defaults." This strategy might include prompting choices with default options or using point-of-decision prompts, which characterized the majority of interventions (27 of 35) and generally had positive effects. Other choice architecture categories included "decision information" (e.g. providing information about social norms) and "decision assistance" (e.g. using commitment contracts and providing reminders). Most of the studies included used point-of-decision prompts and focused on changing behavior of individuals or small groups of individuals (i.e. micro-level interventions). The authors highlighted existing gaps in the literature, including the need for additional research that explores other nudge and choice architecture interventions, as well as the need for community-, organization-, institutional-, and societal-level interventions (i.e. meso- and macro-levels). The scoping review by Forberger and colleagues (2019) provides a roadmap for researchers interested in advancing the understanding of behavioral-science approaches in the physical activity and exercise context.

Landais and colleagues (2020) performed a systematic review of choice architecture interventions on physical activity behavior, sedentary behavior, intentions, and health outcomes. In addition, they assessed the study quality of the included interventions. Overall, 88 studies and 84 articles were included in the review and synthesized in a rather impressive table that readers are encouraged to examine further (the article is open access). The authors concluded that prompting (e.g. using point-of-decision prompts to encourage stair use) is effective, but they could not make strong conclusions about other choice architecture interventions (i.e. social influence, feedback, anchoring, default change). Finally, the authors concluded that more research using experimental design, long-term follow-up, and more objective outcome measurement is needed. Together, the systematic reviews by Forberger and colleagues (2019) and Landais and colleagues (2020) preliminarily indicate promise of interventions targeting choice architecture for the promotion of physical activity and reduction of sedentary behavior. Both reviews provide directions to future researchers interested in advancing the literature.

Changing Physical Activity and Exercise Behavior: Perspectives of a Behavioral Designer

The behavioral biases and heuristics described in this chapter attest to an important lesson in behavioral science: Much of our behavior is influenced by automatic, Type 1 processes related to affective, social, and contextual factors, not just Type 2 processes such as goal setting, intentions, and cost-benefit analyses. Setting goals is rarely sufficient for successful, long-term behavior change. Fortunately, we can attempt to use principles and concepts from behavioral science to change physical activity and exercise behavior. Below are suggestions for behavior-change interventions and initiatives. Some of these suggestions are theory-based and based on well-researched behavioral-science principles but are not yet sufficiently evidence-based as interventions to promote physical activity and exercise. In true dual-process fashion, the approaches consider the importance of influencing *both* Type 1 and Type 2 processes to promote activity. These suggestions warrant formal empirical investigation and efficacy and effectiveness trials. Therefore, researchers interested in a research agenda focused on dual-process interventions or theorizing may consider building on some of the suggestions below.

Prioritizing Pleasure and Enjoyment to Promote Activity

According to hedonic theory, pleasurable behaviors are most likely to be repeated (Ekkekakis & Dafermos, 2012). Mounting evidence suggests that pleasure plays a role in exercise behavior. Evidence from a systematic review indicates that the pleasure experienced during exercise predicts future exercise behavior, even despite the "relatively negligible" relation between affect and intentions (Rhodes & Kates, 2015). Numerous strategies can be employed to increase pleasure and enjoyment in the exercise domain.

Changing the Affective Responses to Exercise

Extensive research focusing on enhancing the pleasure experienced during exercise exists, and this literature is growing rapidly. Currently, the evidence indicates that experienced pleasure during exercise – more than post-exercise pleasure experienced following the cessation of exercise – is related to future behavior (Rhodes & Kates, 2015). Affective responses during exercise can be captured with the moment-to-moment assessments of pleasure or displeasure. Allowing participants to self-select exercise intensity (Ekkekakis, 2009;

Williams et al., 2015; 2016), using music (Hutchinson et al., 2018; Hutchinson & O'Neil, 2020), prescribing exercise that "feels good" (Hamlyn-Williams, Tempest, Coombs, & Parfitt, 2015; Parfitt, Alrumh, & Rowlands, 2012), and prescribing exercise that is below the ventilatory threshold (e.g. Ekkekakis, Parfitt, & Petruzzello, 2011) are among the strategies that can be used to increase pleasure experienced during exercise, or at least help prevent declines in pleasure. As discussed earlier, repeated pleasant exercise experiences are theorized to contribute to Type 1 automatic associations and automatic affective valuations that would favor future physical activity and exercise behavior (Brand & Ekkekakis, 2018; Conroy & Berry, 2017; Ekkekakis, 2017; Ekkekakis & Dafermos, 2012; Ekkekakis & Zenko, 2016; Zenko & Ekkekakis, 2019b).

In contrast to post-exercise pleasure (e.g. momentary ratings of pleasure recorded in the moments following exercise), measuring the affective responses associated with the "remembered utility" and "predicted utility" of an experience might also be motivationally relevant (Kahneman, Wakker, & Sarin, 1997). Rather than asking participants to respond to questions about how they feel in the moments following the end of an exercise bout (e.g. "how do you feel right now?"), this might be done by asking participants to respond to measures *about* the exercise by assessing enjoyment of a recently completed exercise session, remembered pleasure of the exercise session (e.g. "how did you feel during the exercise bout?"), or forecasted pleasure about future exercise sessions (e.g. "how will you feel if you repeat this exercise bout again?"). In addition to using the strategies described above for increasing pleasure experienced during exercise, early evidence indicates that promising strategies for increasing enjoyment, remembered pleasure, and predicted pleasure include (a) ensuring that the final moment of exercise is pleasant and (b) ensuring that exercise becomes progressively more pleasant, perhaps by continually decreasing intensity (see "Duration Neglect and the Peak-End Rule" and "Slope or Trend Effects" described in Table 4.1; Ekkekakis & Dafermos, 2012; Hargreaves & Stych, 2013; Hutchinson et al., 2020; Zenko et al., 2016; Zenko & Ekkekakis, 2019a; but see Stuntz et al., 2020, who observed how the sense of accomplishment acts as an important mediator between exertion and feeling states in athletic populations).

Changing Automatic Associations with Exercise Using Conditioning and Retraining Procedures

Based on the literature on the affect heuristic (Finucane et al., 2000, Slovic et al., 2002a, 2007) and Affective-Reflective Theory (Brand & Ekkekakis, 2018; see also Chapter 3, this volume), changing automatic associations to favor physical activity and exercise is theorized to result in greater activity behavior. In addition to making the experience of exercise more pleasant, it may be possible to change automatic associations using nonexercise procedures (Brand & Cheval, 2019). Empirical evidence suggests that automatic associations can be made more positive using conditioning and approach-avoidance retraining procedures (Antoniewicz & Brand, 2016a; Cheval et al., 2016), which may also result in increased physical activity (Cheval et al., 2016). Cheval and colleagues (2016), for instance, randomized 115 participants to be retrained to either (a) approach physical activity and avoid sedentary behavior, (b) approach sedentary behavior and avoid physical activity, or (c) approach and avoid physical activity and sedentary behavior equally. The retraining consisted of a computerized task in which participants were tasked with moving an on-screen representation of a human, called a "manikin." Depending on the randomization, participants were trained to "approach" or "avoid" physical activity or sedentary behavior by moving the manikin toward or away from pictures representing physical activity (e.g. images showing figures cycling, running, swimming) or sedentary behavior (e.g. playing video games, laying on the couch, reading). Cheval and colleagues (2016) concluded that retraining participants to approach physical activity and avoid sedentary behavior resulted in more time on an exercise task. Like participation in pleasant exercise sessions, conditioning and approach-avoidance retraining may represent an additional strategy for changing Type 1 processes to favor physical activity. This may be especially useful for people who cannot exercise (e.g. due to injury) or will not exercise (e.g. due to an intense feeling of dread or anxiety toward exercise) and are therefore not likely to gain exposure to positive experiences with actual exercise sessions. According to Cheval et al. (2016), the results need to be replicated using more extensive retraining procedures and more externally valid measurement procedures (e.g. accelerometers in a free-living environment). For now, conditioning and retraining is promising but warrants further investigation.

Targeting Affective Forecasts about Exercise

Recognizing the tendency for people to engage in Delay Discounting, or the tendency to value smaller, immediate rewards over larger, long-term rewards (see Table 4.1), Segar, Eccles, and Richardson (2011) suggested that promoters of physical activity and exercise should emphasize immediate outcomes of exercise because they may be more compelling than long-term rewards (e.g. disease prevention). Immediate outcomes recommended include benefits to daily living, and often include affective components (e.g. stress reduction, increased vitality). Interestingly, although focusing on immediate outcomes (e.g. exercising for fun) has been shown to relate to more exercise behavior, the majority of people seem to intuit that delayed outcomes (e.g. better health) would be more motivating, indicating that focusing on immediate outcomes might be a useful target for intervention (Woolley & Fishbach, 2016). Focusing on the immediate affective benefits can also increase intrinsic motivation and satisfaction of the need for autonomy (Segar, Taber, Patrick, Thai, & Oh, 2017).

Affective forecasts or affective expectations are predictions about the pleasure or displeasure that will be experienced in the future. Targeting affective forecasts about physical activity and exercise has theoretical support (Kahneman et al., 1997) and preliminary empirical support for increasing exercise intentions. For example, Helfer, Elhai, and Geers (2015) focused on manipulating forecasts about post-exercise affect, in part because post-exercise affect is less likely to be negative than affective responses during exercise and because expectations about post-exercise affect may be more malleable. The researchers manipulated affective forecasts by providing a very brief description about recent research on the effects of exercise and positive feelings (e.g. happiness, personal satisfaction, increased self-esteem). Results indicated that the manipulation of affective forecasts improved post-exercise affect and intentions to exercise. More research is needed to determine the effects of affective forecast manipulations on long-term exercise behavior. Further, researchers should determine whether manipulating forecasts about affect experienced during exercise is more or less effective than interventions on post-exercise affective forecasts.

Pairing Exercise with Pleasure: Temptation Bundling

When affective responses to, and forecasts about, exercise are unpleasant, bundling the option of exercise with a pleasant reward or activity appears to be a promising strategy. Milkman, Minson, and Volpp (2014) cleverly tested the immediate pairing of extrinsic rewards with exercise behavior by using what they called "temptation bundling": Pairing a tempting "want" behavior (listening to a favorite audiobook) with a "should" behavior (exercising). In the full treatment condition, participants were given access to a listening device with four audiobooks that they chose – but that they could only indulge in while they visited a fitness center. In a second (intermediate) treatment condition, participants were also treated to four audiobooks of choice, but they could access the audiobooks at any time from their personal devices. These intermediate participants were encouraged to create a personal rule whereby they only allowed themselves to listen to these books while exercising. In a control condition, participants were given gift cards to a bookstore equivalent to the value of four audiobooks.

Milkman and colleagues (2014) found that temptation bundling was particularly effective at encouraging fitness center visits in the short term. Compared to the control group, fitness center visits increased by 51% (0.48 visits/week) and 29% (0.27 visits/week) for the full and intermediate treatment participants, respectively, in the first week of the experiments. The effects of the full treatment were statistically significant, although the effects of the intermediate treatment were not. Behavioral designers could apply these findings on temptation bundling to other enjoyable activities, besides audiobooks. Fitness centers can (and some already do) offer WiFi, treadmills with television screens, and Netflix access. People can easily create their own versions of temptation bundling for temptations that are especially appealing to them, such as listening to their podcasts or audiobooks.

These ideas should be interpreted with an important caveat: The impacts of extrinsic rewards may decline over time because people tend to habituate to them after repeated exposure. In the temptation bundling study (Milkman et al., 2014), the efficacy of the treatment conditions steadily declined over the course of nine weeks, especially after a holiday period in the study (i.e. a routine disruption). Thus, people who try temptation bundling may need to devise additional ways to sustain their exercise behavior over the long term, perhaps by also deploying some of the other behavioral strategies described in the rest of the chapter.

Redesigning the Physical World: Creating Opportunities for Physical Activity

The physical world plays a large role in governing our exercise behavior. Given that habits are cued by environments, those who want to improve exercise adherence should alter their environments to change their physical activity and sedentary behavior. Individuals and groups can leverage small, daily opportunities to exercise by building cues that encourage physical activities and disrupting (or adding friction to) cues that lead to sedentary behavior. For example, individuals can consider altering their work commute to increase opportunities for exercise on the way home by driving by parks and fitness centers.

Redesigning Homes and Interactions with Personal Devices to Promote Activity

The typical household is designed to maximize comfort and rest, which reinforces sedentary behavior. Soft living room seating, for example, surrounds the television screen in many living rooms and makes the experience of being sedentary and comfortable more salient. Tempting and engaging content can be accessed with the click of a button in seconds. Our homes and digital environments are essentially engineered to reduce the friction of watching television or using social media and have the side effect of increasing opportunities for sedentary behavior. Negative correlates and effects of increasing screen time have been studied extensively (Stiglic & Viner, 2019, Tamana et al., 2019), including negative associations between screen time and moderate-to-vigorous physical inactivity (Serrano-Sanchez et al., 2011).

One strategy to decrease activities associated with sedentary behavior is to leverage the principle of friction, or making an undesirable behavior more difficult by adding barriers to it (see Table 4.1). For instance, friction can be added to activities such as watching television or using computers or phones, behaviors we tend to do when we're sitting or lying down. We may be less likely to reach for our phones, computers, or television remotes if using these devices became more cumbersome. For instance, we could add friction by keeping these devices out of sight, unplugged, or even locked away. We could also add friction to tempting streaming services or social media by logging out every time we use them so that logging in would be more cumbersome (especially if logging in requires a complex password).

Further, we might also add friction by creating automatic interruption points. Internet apps (such as the Google Chrome extension called StayFocusd) allow users to predetermine how much time they want to allow themselves on specific websites, and they automatically time out of these websites after that amount of time has elapsed. By predetermining the time allowed on specific websites, people use self-control resources when self-control resources are high (e.g. when feeling rested and while setting goals for the week) to help prevent undesired behaviors when self-control resources are low (e.g. aimlessly browsing websites after an exhausting day). This practice is sometimes called a Ulysses pact or contract, after the Latin variant of Odysseus (Burcher, 2013). It is similar to the idea of commitment contracts and strategies for self-control (Duckworth et al., 2016), such that people can make decisions in advance to help their future selves behave more optimally or avoid anticipated temptation, "like Odysseus tying himself to the mast to avoid the tempting song of the sirens" (Ashraf, Karlan, & Yin, 2006, p. 636). For television use, automated outlet timers could be installed so that after a predetermined amount of time (30 minutes, for instance), the television would turn off. These interruptions create "decision points" during which people must consciously decide whether to continue with a sedentary behavior, rather than defaulting to continued sitting. Requiring the user to make the deliberate decision to continue being sedentary would prompt them to engage in a Type 2 process, which, for a person with the goal of becoming more active, may tend to favor physical activity or exercise (for relevant reviews, see Kaushal & Rhodes, 2014; Maitland, Stratton, Foster, Braham, & Rosenberg, 2013).

Redesigning Occupational Spaces to Promote Activity

Given that most people spend the majority of their lives working, the workplace may also be an important context that can be redesigned to encourage physical activity. For example, architects might consider making stairs much easier to find and more visually appealing to encourage their use. Interior designers might consider installing bicycle racks to make cycling easier or limiting the number of trash and recycling bins on an office floor to ensure that people must walk into another room to use them.

Sit-stand desks might also be used to encourage standing as a default behavior. Sit-stand desks on their own have been shown to reduce sitting time at work by an average of 100 minutes per day over short-term follow-up (up to three months) and 57 minutes per day over the medium-term follow-up (3–12 months), even in the absence of informational interventions or counseling (Shrestha et al., 2018). These effects can be further amplified by setting sit-stand desks into a "stand" position as a default, as Venema, Kroese, and Ridder (2018) demonstrated in a study examining sedentary behavior in the workplace. To create a default standing behavior, researchers set the desks to a "stand" position at the beginning of the intervention period and placed a sign on top of desks encouraging employees to set their desks to standing height when they left their desks or the office. Researchers found that the intervention nudging stand-ups led to a significant increase in stand-up rates of office workers from 1.82% at baseline to 13.3% during the two-week intervention period. Furthermore, these effects persisted two months later, leading to an overall 7.78% increase in standing rates overall. Workplaces could also leverage the power of social norms by indicating that physical activity is a typical (or at least not uncommon) behavior. As one example, the installation of an office bicycle rack might not only facilitate parking bicycles in the office more easily, it might also make the behavior of cycling more visible to others in the office, which could increase perceptions that cycling or being active is a norm. Creating an environment in which physical activity is perceived as a social norm may contribute to an active lifestyle (Okun et al., 2003; for a scoping review, see Kim, Dunn, Rellinger, Robertson-Wilson, & Eys, 2017).

Behavioral designers can also create visible reminders of these social norms. Signs can be placed around the office to remind people that being active is a norm. For instance, Burger and Shelton (2011) tested the impact of placing signs outside elevator doors communicating different messages about physical activity in three-story buildings on a university campus. One sign (the treatment condition) emphasized that most (90% of) people in the building use the stairs, and the other sign (the control condition) simply stated that taking the stairs is a good method for increasing physical activity. The no-sign condition did not involve posting any signs outside the elevator. The researchers observed people's behavior in these buildings and compared the effects of the signs across a period of three weeks, namely (a) a baseline period when no signs were posted, (b) a second week in which a sign was posted at each of the elevators used in the study, and (c) a third week in which the signs were removed. The frequency of elevator use (compared to stair use) decreased by 46% in the norm condition between the first and second weeks, whereas no significant effects were found in the informational control condition or in the no-sign condition. Lower rates of elevator usage continued in the third week, after the sign was removed. Thus, creating visible reminders of norms strategically placed in locations to interrupt sedentary behavior may be one way of encouraging physical activity. However, with repeated exposure to the signs, people may be likely to habituate to them and stop responding to consistent messaging. Therefore, behavioral designers should consider creative ways to keep attention and reduce habituation to these point-of-decision prompts.

Further, collaborative health reminders (i.e. reminders that intervene on entire groups of people together) may also be a way to leverage the physical environment to enhance physical activity cues (see O'Leary, Tanghe, Pratt, & Ralston, 2018). For example, rather than reminding a person to act independently, a group of colleagues may receive a reminder to meet for group physical activity later in the day. Another example may involve a health coach providing a reminder about exercise goals to their client, as well as a small support network. These reminders may reinforce norms because everyone responds to the cue together. These types of collaborative interventions may have the added benefit of reducing awkward feelings. Rather than being the only one responding to a reminder to walk or stand in a meeting, it may be less awkward and more socially acceptable if everyone does it together. We can reasonably expect that people will be more likely to be active in workplace if they are not the only ones combining board meetings with physical activity (e.g. walking around the community instead of sitting at a conference table).

Redesigning Urban Environments and Public Spaces to Promote Activity

The urban design, topography, and geography of a city impact the daily physical activity behaviors of residents. Especially in the absence of time or access to safe and affordable fitness facilities, everyday surroundings govern how people move through their environments and the extent to which people can incorporate physical activity as part of their routines. Public works projects, including (a) sidewalks, (b) designated bicycle lanes and paved bicycle paths, and (c) trails that make physical activity easier, safer, accessible, more visually appealing, and enjoyable are important interventions for increasing physical activity. The availability of designated bicycle lanes, for example, is associated with greater commuting by bicycle, independently of climate, socioeconomic factors, cost of gasoline, public transportation, and cycling safety (Buehler & Pucher, 2012). In areas where cycling and public transportation are feasible, it may be worth slowly reducing the number of parking spaces available to increase walking and other accessible, active modes of transportation. In this example, the sedentary option of driving would still be available, but the added friction would encourage the physically active alternatives (see Table 4.1). Further, friction to engage in physical activity may be reduced by increasing the automaticity and habitual nature of physical activity and reducing the need to rely as much on Type 2 processes to engage in exercise. Importantly, to address what is perhaps a common misconception about "habit," one should not expect to suddenly find themselves in the middle of an exercise session with no conscious recollection of how they started to exercise (Phillips, 2019). As Hagger (2020) explains, "[habit] does not mean that behavior becomes entirely controlled non-consciously, rather that some aspects of performing the behavior have become less reliant or dependent on conscious, deliberative control with control shifting toward non-conscious, automatic processes" (p. 2). Therefore, making exercise more habitual would reduce the need to regularly engage in as much effortful Type 2 processing and, according to Affective-Reflective Theory (Brand & Ekkekakis, 2018), would reduce the need to rely on self-control resources to carry out the exercise behavior.

Planning for Lapses in Self-Control

In addition to the strategies discussed above, people should recognize that lapses in self-control or self-regulatory processes are normal. Exercisers should anticipate failures to follow through with exercise intentions. Along with commitment devices and Ulysses contracts (described earlier), exercisers, interventionists, and practitioners can consider using implementation intentions that specify "when, where, and how" one will carry out intentions, which may take the form of if-then plans designed to manage lapses in self-control and self-regulatory processes (Gollwitzer, 1999; see also Chapter 12, this volume). For example, an exerciser might use the following if-then statement to address derailed exercise plans: "If the rain prevents me from exercising outside as originally intended, then I will watch an exercise video and exercise indoors instead." The use of implementation intentions in interventions has improved activity behavior (Milne, Orbell, & Sheeran, 2002; Robinson, Bisson, Hughes, Ebert, & Lachman, 2019).

Exercisers, interventionists, and practitioners should be ready to acknowledge that "failure" is only temporary, lapses in self-control can be anticipated and overcome (also see Duckworth, Milkman, & Laibson, 2018), and that each passing day (or week, or month, or year) represents a new beginning and a new opportunity to improve upon past behaviors. These new beginnings are known as temporal landmarks. Dai, Milkman, and Riis (2014) noted that fitness center visits increase following temporal landmarks (e.g. the start of a new week, the start of a new month, the start of a new semester) that demarcate the passage of time and create "new mental accounting periods" and "relegate past imperfections to a previous period" (p. 2563). Dai and colleagues (2014, 2015) suggest that "fresh starts" can be used to allow people to overcome past experiences with failure. Attempts at motivating people to adopt new goals may be more effective around these temporal landmarks (Dai et al., 2015). Relatedly, people interested in promoting exercise initiation and maintenance should be aware of the tendency of some to completely abandon goals after initial experiences with failure – a tendency known as the "what the hell effect" (Zemack-Reguar, Corus, & Brinberg, 2010). Perhaps fresh starts can be leveraged to help people overcome this tendency and understand that no matter how many times they experience lapses in self-control, the next day provides an opportunity for a fresh start.

Conclusions and Future Directions for Dual-Process Theorists and Behavioral-Science Approaches to Exercise Initiation and Maintenance

In this chapter, we have contrasted the paradigm that has traditionally dominated exercise psychology with more recent, dual-process theorizing. We have also discussed how behavioral-science approaches relate to dual-process theorizing because these approaches either target Type 1 processes, anticipate that Type 2 processes are susceptible to heuristics and biases, or both. We presented examples of heuristic processes and potential application to exercise promotion, paying special attention to the affect heuristic. Then, we highlighted how the affect heuristic plays a role in a recently proposed and promising dual-process theories of physical activity and exercise behavior, namely the Affective-Reflective Theory of physical inactivity (Brand & Ekkekakis, 2018) and the PAAM model (Strobach et al., 2020. We highlighted several recent discussions and systematic reviews on the application of some behavioral-science approaches to the context of exercise initiation and maintenance, illustrating ample opportunity and need for further research.

Finally, we finished by offering suggestions for promoting exercise from the perspective of a behavioral designer. Table 4.2 provides a summary of "points of interest" that researchers and practitioners might consider. These points of interest should be considered from a dual-process and behavioral-science perspective. Although the list of example target or outcome variables presented in Table 4.2 is not comprehensive, we hope that it provides a starting point for further investigation and intervention. The long-term effects of dual-process

TABLE 4.2 Points of Interest for Exercise Initiation and Maintenance from a Dual-Process and Behavioral-Economic Perspective

Point of Interest	*Examples Target or Outcome Variables*	*Relation to Other Points of Interest*
Type 1 Processes	choice architecture, automatic associations, automatic affective valuations, heuristics and biases	Type 1 processes occur rapidly and bias subsequent Type 2 processes but can be overridden by Type 2 processes. Type 1 processes can increase efficiency of decision making. Theoretically, Type 1 processes may be more related to physical activity or sedentary behavior than exercise behavior, because the purposeful nature of exercise behavior may require more Type 2 processing for initiation.
Type 2 Processes	attitudes, beliefs, anticipated costs and benefits, self-efficacy, perceptions of autonomy, relatedness, and competence, social norms	Type 2 processes occur more slowly than Type 1 processes and are often biased by Type 1 processes. Type 2 processes can either endorse or override Type 1 processes; the tendency is to endorse Type 1 processes. Since people operate with "bounded rationality," Type 2 processes may be targets of behavioral-science interventions (e.g. choice architecture may be targeted to change social norms, framing may be used to change anticipated costs and benefits, see Forberger et al., 2019).
Individual and Situational Factors	self-control, executive functioning, impulsivity, tendency to rely on Type 1 or Type 2 processes, habit strength, time pressure, distraction, stress, arousal, cognitive load	Individual differences in self-control, executive functioning, and impulsivity moderate the influence of Type 1 or Type 2 processes on behavior. For example, individuals with greater self-control and executive functioning, less impulsivity, and greater tendency to rely on Type 2 processes (measured with e.g. the Cognitive Reflection Test, Frederick, 2005) may be more likely to override Type 1 processes. People with greater habit strength for exercise may be less dependent on Type 2 processes to successfully carry out complex exercise behaviors. Situational factors, (e.g. time pressure, distraction, high stress) may increase susceptibility to Type 1 processes.

interventions on behavioral outcomes must be tested. Future researchers should ensure that they assess and account for (a) mediating variables between intervention strategies and behavioral outcomes and (b) moderating personality characteristics or situational variables.

Note

1 This theory forms much of the basis for our suggestion to prioritize pleasure and enjoyment of exercise, discussed later.

5

BODY-RELATED SELF-CONSCIOUS EMOTIONS IN SPORT AND EXERCISE

A Self-Regulation Perspective

Catherine M. Sabiston, Madison F. Vani, and Ross M. Murray

Introduction

Body image is an important construct to examine in sport and exercise contexts because it is an intrapersonal self-regulatory factor in behavior change and participation intentions, retention, and drop-out (Sabiston, Pila, Vani, & Thogersen-Ntoumani, 2019; Teixeira et al., 2015). Furthermore, the self-regulation of behavior is thought to mitigate or perpetuate body image concerns. As will be outlined in this book chapter, the bi-directional relationship between sport and exercise behaviors and body image is a self-regulatory process that is primarily influenced by body-related self-conscious emotions.

Body Image

There is a long history of the study of body image in sport and exercise psychology (Bane & McAuley, 1998). Generally, body image is described as a factor motivating, limiting, or preventing sport and exercise behaviors, a factor impacting experiences in sport and exercise, and an outcome associated with sport and exercise behaviors.

Appearance and Function Facets

In sport and exercise contexts, body image is generally focused on what the body can do (i.e. function and fitness) and what the body looks like (i.e. appearance and weight). It is important to distinguish the function and appearance of the body because an individual's cognitions, perceptions, and affect linked to these two facets may be different. The study of body image has been historically focused on appearance facets, and predominantly cognitions and perceptions of the way the body looks have bi-directional associations with sport and exercise experiences and behaviors (Sabiston et al., 2019). Specifically, one's level of satisfaction with, and descriptions of, appearance may limit involvement in sport and exercise or may motivate greater engagement and participation. Conversely, appearance changes can result from exercise and sport participation. Nonetheless, appearance is often evaluated less favorably than function, with girls and women reporting particularly prominent distinctions between what the body can do and how it looks (Abbott & Barber, 2011; Gusella, Clark, & van Roosmalen, 2004). Furthermore, sport and exercise participation may offer greater opportunities for changes in the functional facet of the body compared to the appearance facet. For example, girls who participate in sport are more likely to focus on body function opposed to body appearance (Slater & Tiggeman 2012) and more likely to report more favorable perceptions of their bodies' functioning compared to non-participants (Abbott & Barber, 2011). Additionally, there is some evidence that the function of the body in sport and exercise settings may protect against potential adverse consequences associated with the appearance facet of the body (Vani, deJonge, Pila, Solomon-Krakus, & Sabiston, 2020). Specifically, some adolescent girls who had high perceptions of sport competence and skill (i.e. function) reported being less likely to disengage from sport due to high negative evaluations of their appearance. However, other adolescent girls reported that negative evaluations of their appearance negatively affected their perceptions of competence (Vani, Pila, deJonge et al., 2020). Attention on the body's appearance is also proposed to limit resources for skill execution, ultimately hindering performance outcomes (Cox et al., 2020). Given the collective findings, the ways that appearance and function facets of the body intersect and interact require more research attention. There is little doubt that sport and exercise are the key contexts to study the implications of function and appearance facets of body image.

General (Thompson, Heinberg, Altabe, & Tantleff-Dunn, 1999) and sport-specific (Petrie & Greenleaf, 2012) sociocultural models draw from an overarching heuristic linking body image appearance and function and sport and exercise behaviors. Specifically, there are societal ideals of appearance (informed by cultures, stereotypes, and biases) and function (often informed by sport type and position or exercise goals and workout type). It is recognized that sport and exercise environments encourage heightened focus on body appearance and function and develop body ideals through sanctioned or socially encouraged weight goals and limits, judging criteria that reward certain body types, stereotypes about what certain athlete bodies should look like for the type of sport and position played, and performance demands (Bratland-Sanda & Sundgot-Borgen, 2013; Petrie & Greenleaf, 2012). The ideals are transmitted through a variety of ways (e.g. coaches, trainers, parents and other family members, peers, media) and are internalized. This internalization process includes consideration of the importance of body function and appearance to the individual's sense of self, identity, and goals. Aligning with the degree of internalization and importance, individuals' perceptions of being similar to (or discordant with) these societal ideals for both appearance and function will lead to overall positive (or negative) outcomes that include cognitions, perceptions, emotions, and behaviors. This heuristic can be used to understand the links among sport and exercise environments and behaviors and body image facets of appearance and function.

Body Image as a Multidimensional Construct

Body image function and appearance can be further described as a multidimensional construct with core domains related to cognitions, perceptions, and affect that influence behaviors like participation in sport and exercise. The cognitive domain of body image refers to individuals' positive and negative thoughts, beliefs, and evaluations of their body appearance and function. Sport and exercise participation are associated with positive thoughts and appraisal of one's body, and more generally, body appreciation is associated with improved well-being (Avalos, Tylka, & Wood-Barcalow, 2005). Nonetheless, the comparative, social, and judgment-based natures of many sport and exercise contexts are also common ways that participation can foster the development of negative thoughts and evaluations of the body (Sabiston et al., 2019; Vani, Pila, deJonge et al., 2020).

The perceptual domain of body image refers to the mental representation that individuals hold pertinent to their own body function and appearance. A mental representation is typically conceptualized as the accuracy in evaluation between perceived and actual body characteristics. Researchers have found that there can be incongruence between the way individuals perceive their body and their actual body characteristics (Kagawa et al., 2007), with perceptions of body characteristics being a better predictor of body image than actual body characteristics (Martin Ginis, McEwan, Josse, & Phillips, 2012). Further, societal influences often encourage individuals to adopt an "ideal" body image. Discrepancies between actual body image and ideal body image are a motivator in regulating sport and exercise behaviors aimed at reducing the discrepancy (Anton, Perri, & Riley, 2000). Motivation to improve appearance through sport or exercise has been associated with negative outcomes, including more negative overall body image, whereas motivation to improve functional aspects of the body through sport and exercise has been associated with more positive outcomes (Homan & Tylka, 2014).

The affective domain of body image refers to the emotions that individuals experience in relation to one's body function and appearance. Social physique anxiety has been studied extensively as a common body image emotion in the sport and exercise contexts (Sabiston, Pila, Pinsonnault-Bilodeau, & Cox, 2014). Also, more recent research has focused on other specific emotions that individuals experience pertaining to body image. These self-conscious emotions include body-related guilt, shame, hubristic and authentic pride, envy, and embarrassment (Castonguay, Sabiston, Kowalski, & Wilson, 2015; Castonguay, Sabiston, Crocker, & Mack, 2014). The majority of this chapter focuses on body-related self-conscious emotions and the relationships with sport and exercise perceptions, beliefs, and behaviors. In spite of the many similarities between the factors that influence experiences of social physique anxiety and body-related self-conscious emotions, sport and exercise psychology researchers have maintained a distinct study of these emotions. We recommend subsuming the study of social physique anxiety within the understanding of body-related self-conscious emotions to broaden the scope and implications of body image affect. However, here they are presented as distinct affective constructs to maintain the historical way they have been studied.

Social Physique Anxiety

Social physique anxiety is a widely studied, negatively valenced emotion, defined as the anxiety a person experiences as a result of perceived or actual judgments from others (Hart, Leary, & Rejeski, 1989). For example, an adolescent may worry that teammates are judging their physical ability or an individual may express a concern that others at the gym are judging their body shape. Rooted in social anxiety, self-presentation, and body image affect literature, social physique anxiety is often experienced in social settings that highlight the physique and ability of individuals (Crombie, Brunet, & Sabiston, 2011; Sabiston, Pila, Pinsonnault-Bilodeau, & Cox, 2014). Given these features, it is not surprising that social physique anxiety is frequently experienced in sport and exercise contexts. This emotion is not often studied under the umbrella of self-conscious emotions; yet, the social evaluative, judgment-based, and self-reflective nature of the emotion suggests that there is an underlying self-consciousness to the experience of social physique anxiety.

Unlike other body-related self-conscious emotions whereby research is in its infancy, there has been tremendous focus on social physique anxiety – from the environmental and social elicitors to the antecedents and outcomes (Sabiston et al., 2014). In particular, social physique anxiety is heightened when individuals exercise in front of a mirror or when they view videos that display physique-salient instructors (Martin Ginis, Jung, & Gauvin, 2003; Martin Ginis, Prapavessis, & Haase, 2008). A desire to become more muscular (Brunet, Sabiston, Dorsch, & McCreary, 2010), changing in front of others in locker rooms (Ladwig, Vazou, & Ekkekakis, 2018), and wearing mandatory uniforms in physical education classes (Sabiston, Sedgwick, Crocker, Kowalski, & Mack, 2007) also elicit greater social physique anxiety. Interpersonal factors are also linked to social physique anxiety as those who feel accepted and like they belong in their peer group experience lower social physique anxiety in physical education class (Cox, Ullrich-French, & Sabiston, 2013). However, mothers of adolescents (Sabiston et al., 2007) and teachers and coaches who emphasize appearance (Krane, Waldron, Stiles-Shipley, & Michalenok, 2001) trigger social physique anxiety in adolescents and young adults. Furthermore, older adolescents and young adults report experiencing greater social physique anxiety around peers compared to around parents (Brunet & Sabiston, 2011). These antecedents highlight the fear of evaluation in sport and exercise settings that is inherent to social physique anxiety. Although specific aspects of sport and exercise may increase social physique anxiety, there is some evidence to show that engaging in sport and exercise may reduce this emotion. For example, Gammage and colleagues demonstrate that engagement in one resistance exercise class or yoga class reduced social physique anxiety, with yoga having a larger effect on this affective state (Gammage, Drouin, & Lamarche, 2016).

Social physique anxiety has been associated with a number of negative outcomes, including reduced perceptions of competence and enjoyment, symptoms of disordered eating, depression and competitive anxiety, and behavioral avoidance (see Sabiston et al., 2014). For example, in a cross-sectional survey with high school students, individuals who were more externally motivated (i.e. engaged in physical activity for external reasons such as avoiding punishment) for physical education and had higher social physique anxiety reported lower effort and enjoyment in physical education and lower physical activity overall compared to those who endorsed lower external motivation (Cox, Ullrich-French, & Sabiston, 2013). Furthermore, individuals who experience social physique anxiety tend to avoid scenarios where their body may be on display, such as in sport or exercise contexts (Pila, Solomon-Krakus, Egelton, & Sabiston, 2017). For example, adolescents primarily used behavioral avoidance to manage experiences of social physique anxiety in physical activity settings (Kowalski, Mack, Crocker, Niefer, & Fleming, 2006). Repeated experiences of social physique anxiety are negatively associated with physical activity in adolescence and adulthood (Sabiston et al., 2014). And so, experiencing social physique anxiety is likely to negatively impact sport and exercise behavior.

Body-Related Self-Conscious Emotions

Research on self-conscious emotions is often guided by the process model (Tracy & Robins, 2004). Consistent with the process model, self-conscious emotions (e.g. shame, guilt, pride, envy, embarrassment) must involve a self-evaluative process, wherein individuals' emotions are impacted through their thought processes and evaluations of themselves. This is in contrast to basic emotions which often do not involve a self-reflective process. Self-reflective processes are vital to the experience of self-conscious emotions, where individuals must focus their attention on representations of themselves in order to engage in self-evaluation (Tangney & Tracy, 2012). Furthermore, the self-conscious emotions can be distinguished by state-level experiences and a proneness to experience them. State level refers to an emotion felt in response to a specific event or behavior. For example, an individual who feels guilty about skipping a workout might experience state guilt. In comparison, proneness is an emotional disposition which refers to the likelihood that an individual will experience the emotion. For example, a person who generally experiences body-related guilt.

Each self-conscious emotion can shape individuals' experiences within sport and exercise, and equally these body-related emotions can be influenced by such behaviors. Specific to body image emotions, the majority of empirical investigations have focused on body-related shame (Castonguay et al., 2014; Pila et al., 2016; Sabiston et al., 2010) and guilt (Calogero & Pina, 2011; Pila et al., 2016; Sabiston et al., 2010). There is early evidence indicating the importance of understanding body-related envy (Pila, Stamiris, Castonguay, & Sabiston, 2014) and body-related embarrassment (Vani, Pila, deJonge et al. 2020). Body-related pride, the only positively appraised self-conscious emotion, has also been explored as an important emotion linked to sport and exercise experiences (Castonguay, Gilchrist, Mack, & Sabiston, 2013; Gilchrist & Sabiston, 2018; Mack, Kouali, Gilchrist, & Sabiston, 2015).

Body-Related Shame

Shame is an emotion individuals feel when they perceive a flaw in their underlying sense of self, often one they believe is visible to others. Individuals who experience shame often feel worthless and desire to hide and be unseen; they perceive or fear a loss of social status while failing to meet internal standards for oneself (Lewis, 2008). Shame is an extremely negative and painful emotion that can often arise as a result of self-perceptions pertinent to body image.

Drawing from general non-specific experiences of shame, body-related shame may be experienced both internally and externally. External body-related shame is likely to occur in social settings such as exercise and sport where the body is on display, and the experience of external shame may elicit feelings similar to social physique anxiety (Hart, Leary, & Rejeski, 1989). As the name implies, internal body-related shame is an intrapersonal devaluation of the body appearance and/or function with negative cognitive patterns characterized by perceptions of worthlessness. To date, researchers have rarely disentangled the two types of body-related shame that may have unique relevance to sport and exercise experiences. Specifically, Gilbert (2007) highlights that internal and external shame are conceptually unique with some individuals experiencing external shame but no internal shame. However, research on body-related shame has typically focused on the internal shame individuals experience due to failure to meet societal standards pertinent to body shape, size, and function (Sabiston et al., 2010). Social physique anxiety may be a closely related construct for body-related external shame, and more work is needed to generally explore the distinct antecedents and outcomes.

Body-related shame is theorized to result from causal attributions tied to perceptions of controllability (i.e. whether the cause can be influenced by the individual) and stability (i.e. whether the cause will or will not change over time) and leads to many poor cognitive and behavioral outcomes (Tracy & Robins, 2004). In early work testing these attributions in response to a hypothetical scenario created to elicit negative body-related emotions, Crocker and colleagues reported that body-related shame was predicted by less controllability and more globality (i.e. whether the cause affects a wide or narrow range of situations with which the person encounters) attributions, but in contradiction to theory, not stability (Crocker et al., 2014). Other common predictors of external body-related shame are proposed to be similar to those outlined for social physique anxiety (e.g. environmental considerations that heighten awareness on the body, such as mirrors, social comparisons, and evaluative contexts; as well as social factors such as the presence of others who may judge one's appearance and function). Common predictors of internal body-related shame may include physical self-discrepancies (Brunet, Sabiston, Castonguay, Ferguson, & Bessette, 2012; Morin, Scalas, & Marsh, 2015; Woodman & Hemmings, 2008), objectification (Fredrickson & Harrison, 2005; Slater & Tiggemann, 2011), and body surveillance (Calogero & Pina, 2011). In a recent study of over 500 adolescent girl athletes, body surveillance (i.e. regular monitoring of one's own appearance and attractiveness) was a unique significant predictor of the experience of body-related shame and related to changes in body-related shame over three years (Sabiston et al., 2020). In this study, the researchers measured body-related shame using the Body Appearance Self-Conscious Emotions Scale (Castonguay et al., 2014) that operationalizes shame consistent with an internal experience.

There are many psychosocial outcomes associated with body-related shame, with the most studied being depression symptoms and self-esteem (Bessenoff & Snow, 2006; Brunet, Pila, Solomon-Krakus, Sabiston, & O'Loughlin, 2019; Pila, Sabiston, Brunet, Castonguay, & O'Loughlin, 2015). External and internal body-related shame may also lead to avoidance or disengagement from sport and exercise (Pearl, Puhl, & Dovidio, 2014). Further, body-related shame can result in reports of higher external and lower internalized exercise regulations and low exercise behavior engagement (Castonguay, Pila, Wrosch, & Sabiston, 2015; Sabiston et al., 2010). Moreover, body-related shame has been associated with sport outcomes. For example, among adolescent girl athletes, body-related shame about appearance and function was significantly negatively associated with sport enjoyment and commitment, and positively associated with competitive sport anxiety, over three years (Pila et al., 2020). These associations were consistent at the within-person and between-person levels – suggesting that girls reported poorer sport experiences when they experienced higher body-related shame compared to other athletes, as well as when their body-related shame was higher than usual.

Body-Related Guilt

The self-regulation functions of body-related guilt relate to the conflict and alignment of behavior with standards. Body-related guilt is a negative affective experience that is evoked when an individual's physical appearance and/or function are not aligned with personal or societal standards, and this motivates reparatory behavior. Unlike shame, body-related guilt can sometimes be perceived as an adaptive emotion as it can facilitate reparative behaviors such as exercise with subsequent adaptive consequences (Gino & Pierce, 2009). However, guilt can also be maladaptive, and is often accompanied with feelings of shame (Tangney & Tracy, 2012), albeit guilt is typically less painful than shame.

Theoretically, guilt is elicited by specific and unstable attributions related to behavior (e.g. "I shouldn't have skipped soccer practice"; Tracy & Robins, 2004). In preliminary research focused on state body-related guilt, these attributions were opposite to expected, with body-related guilt predicated on more stable and global attributions (Crocker et al., 2014). Lower perceptions of physical self-concept were also associated with higher reports of body-related guilt. In a longitudinal study among adolescent girl athletes, body surveillance was also identified as a key predictor of body-related guilt (Sabiston et al., 2020). Furthermore, key distinguishing factors associated with body-related guilt include gender (women are more likely to experience the emotion compared to men), older age, and higher weight status (Pila et al., 2016). One's tendency to experience body-related guilt may also depend on exercise history, self-description, or identity, such that certain behaviors may counter exercise (e.g. drinking too much alcohol or eating poorly) and heighten negative emotional experiences, but this proposition requires further study.

There is evidence that body-related guilt leads to higher reports of exercise for men and women (Castonguay et al., 2015; Sabiston et al., 2010). Specifically, guilt without shame leads to higher levels of self-determined motivation, which, in turn, predicts increased exercise. However, this guilt may stem from maladaptive behaviors such as overeating (Mond & Calogero, 2009) or monitoring one's behavior on a fitness tracker or by exergaming (Ledger & McCaffrey, 2014; O'Loughlin, Sabiston, Dugas, & O'Loughlin, 2015). Another reason individuals may increase exercise is in response to body-related guilt for not prescribing to societal norms of attractiveness and body shape generally (e.g. thinness for women, muscularity for men) and in exercise or sport (e.g. muscular, tall, athletic). Exercise with the goal of reaching potentially unattainable body characteristics is not adaptive. Therefore, although body-related guilt has been associated with increases in exercise behaviors, appearance-motivated health behaviors are often associated with maladaptive health outcomes (Vartanian, Wharton, & Green, 2012). Indeed, body-related guilt associated with appearance is more likely to be detrimental to individuals' physical and mental health compared to guilt associated with fitness or function of the body (Calogero & Pina, 2011).

In youth sport, both appearance and function body-related guilt were associated with poorer sport experiences, including lower reports of enjoyment and commitment and higher competitive anxiety over three years (Pila et al., 2020). Nonetheless, function-based emotions were stronger predictors of the poorer sport experiences and remained significant in models when appearance-based emotions were also included. Based on these findings, reduced body-related guilt about one's function (measured as fitness) should be targeted among youth girl athletes with an aim of keeping more girls interested and engaged in sport. Furthermore, it is likely that adolescent boys may also report body-related guilt that may influence sport experiences. Given the long-standing perception that function and fitness are more important to boys' sense of selves compared to appearance for girls, research efforts are needed to test the body-related emotions and sport and exercise outcomes in boys. Overall, research on body image among boys and men is under-developed compared to efforts aimed at understanding body image among girls and women.

Body-Related Envy

Individuals often feel body-related envy when they desire the characteristics that others possess. Because envy is typically viewed as an undesirable emotion, it can also elicit feelings of shame (Smith, 2009). Further, envy is perhaps one of the only self-conscious emotions that can lead to adverse effects on others through potentially malicious acts. Body-related envy is typically categorized into two different types. Individuals who feel envy might experience a more benign form associated with feelings of inferiority and admiration of body-related attributes without negative feelings targeting the individual who possesses the object or attribute (Pila et al., 2014). For example, an individual who admires their favorite athlete's physique and wishes to possess a similar physique would be considered to have benign envy. In contrast, there is a more malicious form of envy which is typically associated with feelings of hostility and ill-will (Pila et al., 2014). For example, an athlete wishes harm or injury on another athlete who has desirable physical characteristics or skills. As can be seen in these examples, malicious envy is more maladaptive, and individuals often perceive an injustice accompanied with feelings of resentment and hostility. Individuals who experience malicious envy often do not acknowledge these feelings and sometimes are not consciously aware of the envious feelings. Researchers typically focus on more malicious forms of envy due to its maladaptive consequences and sometimes severe implications such as attempts to thwart others' achievements and enjoyment in others' failures. These feelings of body-related envy have significant implications within sport and exercise contexts and have been implicated as reasons for sport drop-out in a qualitative report (Vani, Pila, deJonge et al., 2020).

According to social comparison approaches, individuals have a propensity to strive for self-enhancement, and through this, people typically engage in upward social comparisons. This is particularly relevant for appearance as the body is almost always observable in social situations (Thøgersen-Ntoumani, Dodos, Chatzisarantis, & Ntoumanis, 2017). For example, when interacting with others, individuals might not know an individual's health status; however, their physical appearance is more often on display. In sport and exercise settings, individuals are expected or required to wear uniforms and exercise attire that are revealing and not individualized or tailored to the athletes' attributes. Further, locker rooms also provide a setting in which individuals can intentionally or unintentionally engage in body-related comparisons with teammates. Indeed, researchers have found that upward comparisons with individuals who are familiar, as opposed to strangers, are more meaningful (Pila et al., 2014). Therefore, body-related envy is a particularly worthwhile emotion to study in the sport and exercise contexts.

Self-regulation and motivation partially account for whether benign or malicious body-related envy is experienced and the subsequent outcomes that emerge from the emotion of envy. Individuals who experience benign envy are often inspired and motivated to improve, such as engaging in sport or exercise pursuits (Pila et al., 2014). In this way, benign body-related envy is considered an approach motivation. In contrast, malicious forms of envy do not lead to approach motivation and are more likely associated with maladaptive forms of behavior change such as external motivation, and thus less likely sustained exercise behaviors. More research is needed to understand the behavioral impact of envy; however, body-related envy likely plays a key role in regulating behaviors in sport and exercise settings.

Body-Related Embarrassment

Body-related embarrassment is a negatively valenced self-conscious emotion that is experienced following an individual's perception of a public violation of social standards regarding physical appearance or function. Embarrassment can occur through stable, uncontrollable, and global attributions (e.g. receiving a negative comment about one's body) or through unstable, controllable, and specific attributions (e.g. exposure of a part of the body in the change room). This body-related emotion most often occurs in social contexts in the presence of others, and to a lesser degree in anticipation of public exposure (Vani, Pila, Willson, & Sabiston, 2020). In fact, body-related embarrassment is considered the most social of the self-conscious emotions (Robbins & Parlavecchio, 2006).

Body-related embarrassment is a unique construct that can be distinguished from body-related shame, guilt, and social physique anxiety. Unpublished data from a cross-sectional study of emotions, motivation, and health behavior among 320 adolescents and young adults identified that these emotions are moderately to strongly correlated (*r*s = 0.50–0.72; Vani, Willson, Pila, & Sabiston, 2018). Indeed, emotions often co-occur and can be difficult to tease apart (Ekman & Cordaro, 2011); yet, these emotions (shame, guilt, embarrassment) have unique antecedents and outcomes and can be discretely described. Body-related embarrassment is often described similarly to external shame (outward-facing version of shame) and some measures of body-related shame and guilt use items of embarrassment (e.g. "the appearance of my body is embarrassing for me in front of others"; Conradt et al., 2007). Yet, embarrassment has been phenomenologically and quantitatively demonstrated as distinct from shame and guilt. Body-related embarrassment is not linked to an inferior global self (shame) and occurs in public, contrasting with guilt and shame emotions that can occur publicly and privately (Beer & Keltner, 2004; Vani, Pila, Willson et al., 2020). Distinctly, social physique anxiety is elicited from a fear of negative evaluation, while body-related embarrassment occurs in response to social convention violations. Further, body-related embarrassment is more transient when compared to body-related shame, guilt, and social physique anxiety (Beer & Keltner, 2004; Tangney, Miller, Flicker, & Barlow, 1996).

In sport and exercise contexts, empirical investigations of body-related embarrassment are limited. Global embarrassment (i.e. embarrassment not contextualized to the body) is often reported in sport and exercise contexts and frequently acts as a barrier to activity engagement (Lascar et al., 2014; McHugh et al., 2008; More, Phillips, & Eisenberg Colman, 2019; Sabiston et al., 2007; Toft & Uhrenfeldt, 2015). For example, global embarrassment hindered adults' exercise behaviors due to low confidence, embarrassment about body image, fear of failure, and negative comments from others (Lascar et al., 2014; Toft & Uhrenfeldt, 2015). Furthermore, in a study of young girls' perceptions of barriers for participating in physical activity, 9% of girls directly linked their barriers to embarrassment (Grieser et al., 2006). And so, embarrassment contextualized to the body may be prevalent within sport and exercise settings. In a narrative study among older adolescents and young adults, about half of the participants described experiencing body-related embarrassment in sport and exercise contexts (e.g. sports, gym; Vani et al., 2020). These contexts included both aesthetic (e.g. dance) and non-aesthetic (e.g. basketball) activities, suggesting that body-related embarrassment is not only experienced in sport and exercise settings that emphasize public displays of the body but is also reported in non-aesthetic contexts.

Antecedents for experiencing body-related embarrassment in sport and exercise settings include fearing appearance evaluation (e.g. public weighing and body fat assessments in gym class), body talk and weight commentary (e.g. being teased for body weight in gym class), sport-related mistakes (e.g. missing a catch in football), accidents occurring in public (e.g. falling on the ice during hockey), and upward body comparisons (e.g. perceiving others as more muscular in the gym; Vani et al., 2020). These eliciting experiences have been reported by men and women in a variety of active settings, outlining the prevalent opportunity for experiencing body-related embarrassment in sport and exercise.

Prolonged feelings of body-contextualized embarrassment may lead to maladaptive outcomes, including timidity and passivity (Keltner & Buswell, 1997), which may impact sport performance and participation. There is a paucity of research describing the outcomes of body-related embarrassment in sport and exercise settings. Within the limited research, Vani and colleagues (2020) demonstrated that among older adolescents and young adults, body-related embarrassment elicited affective, cognitive, and behavioral outcomes. Given the complexity of emotions and that more than one emotion can be elicited from the same event (Ekman & Cordaro, 2011), body-related embarrassment may also co-occur with other affective states such as sadness. In fact, it is suggested that basic emotions (e.g. sadness) are used to conceal self-conscious emotions (e.g. body-related embarrassment) that are difficult to experience as they may damage one's sense of self (Gilbert, 2003).

In addition to emotional outcomes, young people also described hiding or covering up their bodies to avoid public displays of the body, withdrawing oneself from activity altogether, feeling motivated to participate in exercise or to lose weight, and experiencing physiological reactions such as blushing or feeling hot (Vani et al., 2020). Body-related embarrassing experiences that motivate exercise are likely rooted in external motivation and therefore may only motivate short-term change and can be harmful to physical and mental health (Assor, Vansteenkiste, & Kaplan, 2009; Ingledew & Markland, 2008). Furthermore, using avoidance behaviors to manage feelings of body-related embarrassment may impact future sport and exercise experiences and participation (Cash, Santos, & Williams, 2005). In fact, unpublished data from a cross-sectional study among adolescents and young adults demonstrated a small significant negative relationship between body-related embarrassment and exercise frequency for men and women (Vani et al., 2018). Therefore, the outcomes of body-related embarrassment may lead to negative consequences for sport and exercise experiences and behavior. Furthermore, there are currently no known measures of body-related embarrassment and no distinction between embarrassment tied to appearance versus function.

Body-Related Pride

In relation to body image, pride is a positive self-conscious emotion that individuals feel about their fitness or appearance (Gilchrist, Pila, Castonguay, Sabiston, & Mack, 2018; Tracy & Robins, 2004). Pride can play an influential role in facilitating and sustaining motivation that is often required when engaging in adaptive behaviors such as sport and exercise. For example, an individual trying to improve their fitness must consistently make the decision whether to go to the gym or watch television. The feeling of pride is an important self-regulation emotion for individuals to consistently forgo short-term pleasurable experiences (e.g. watching television) to attain long-term reward through commitment and effort (e.g. improved fitness).

Pride can be experienced pertaining to body-related appearance or function, and also as a state or disposition. Also, there may be two facets of pride that are labeled hubristic and authentic pride. Hubristic pride is derived from perceptions of superiority through downward comparisons between oneself and others. In contrast, individuals feel authentic pride from the satisfaction and achievement through their own effort and hard work (Castonguay et al., 2013). Individuals' explanations for why they present with certain body-related function and appearance characteristics (i.e. their attributions) are believed to elicit the different facets of pride (Castonguay et al., 2013; Tracy & Robins, 2004). Feelings of hubristic pride are derived from attributions that are relatively uncontrollable and stable across time. For example, individuals who believe they are in good shape because they have a fast metabolism (something which people do not have a lot of control over and is unlikely to change much across time) are more likely to feel hubristic pride. In comparison, someone who attributes their fitness to causes that are controllable and unstable (e.g. the effort they put in at the gym over the past three months) is likely to feel authentic pride.

Theoretically, the distinction between hubristic and authentic pride is reasonable (Tracy & Robins, 2007). However, body-related authentic and hubristic pride may be more conceptually similar compared to general experiences of pride. Castonguay and colleagues examined experiences of body-related pride and noted a similar pattern of relationships between the two facets (Castonguay et al., 2014, 2016). High correlations (r = 0.70 and above) have been reported between body-related hubristic and authentic pride among youth athletes (Pila et al., 2020; Sabiston et al., 2020). Furthermore, there is some evidence that the measurement of hubristic pride is limited, and the existence of hubristic pride as a distinct facet of pride has been questioned (Holbrook, Piazza, & Fessler, 2014). These trends need to be further explored in the context of body image. It is important to note that the two facets of body-related pride have been measured with scales developed to overcome challenges associated with the measurement of hubristic pride (Castonguay et al., 2014, 2016), and this is promising for maintaining a distinction with body-related authentic pride.

Similar to the other self-conscious emotions we have presented, the process model of self-conscious emotions (Tracy & Robins, 2004) also provides a theoretical framework for understanding antecedents of authentic and hubristic pride. Specifically, feelings of pride arise when an individual evaluates the actual self (i.e. how they currently appear) as congruent with the ideal self (i.e. how they would ideally like to appear). Greater congruence between actual and ideal self-perceptions of fitness (function) has been associated with greater anticipated authentic pride among young adults (Gilchrist, Sabiston, & Kowalski, 2018). Greater congruence between actual weight and ideal weight has been associated with greater authentic pride among adult females (Castonguay, Brunet, Ferguson, & Sabiston, 2012). Furthermore, the congruence between actual and ideal perceptions of muscularity and thinness was significantly associated with hubristic and authentic pride in male adults (Mackowiak, Lucibello, Gilchrist, & Sabiston, 2019). Taken together, congruence in actual and ideal self-perceptions of weight, function, muscularity, and thinness contributes to feelings of pride, suggesting interventions that promote actual and ideal self-perception congruence may be important for fostering positive emotional experiences.

Pride is associated with favorable health-related behaviors. Specifically, Gilchrist and colleagues (2018) found that both hubristic and authentic pride in one's function were positively associated with higher levels of moderate-to-vigorous physical activity (MVPA). Appearance-related hubristic and authentic pride, however, were not related to MVPA, indicating that pride pertinent to function and fitness might be a stronger predictor of physical activity than pride pertinent to appearance (Gilchrist, Pila, et al., 2018). Mack and colleagues also found a positive association between functional facets of authentic and hubristic pride and engagement in MVPA (Mack et al., 2015). These results suggest that experiences of body-related hubristic and authentic pride about function are associated with engagement in physical activity. Pila and colleagues (2020) found similar associations between body-related authentic and hubristic pride and positive sport experiences over time among girl athletes. Function-related pride was a stronger predictor of sport enjoyment and commitment compared to appearance-related pride, and these associations held over time. The implications of this research suggest the beneficial effects of promoting feelings of pride pertinent to the functioning of the self and the effort one directs to improving physical function, as opposed to focusing on one's appearance. Self-regulatory processes focused on function over appearance are important when linking sport and exercise behaviors and positive body image emotions.

Mechanisms Linking Body-Related Self-Conscious Emotions and Sport and Exercise Experiences

The associations among body-related self-conscious emotions and sport and exercise perceptions, beliefs, and participation behaviors have been presented in the respective sections describing each emotion. Surprisingly, there are limited theoretical perspectives used to guide these associations and researchers often draw on overarching theories of motivation (e.g. self-determination theory; Ryan & Deci, 2017), self-concept (e.g. exercise and self-esteem model; Sonstroem & Harlow, 1994), objectification (Fredrickson & Roberts, 1997), broaden and build (Fredrickson, 2004), process model of self-conscious emotions (Tracy & Robins, 2004), and self-discrepancy (Higgins et al., 1987) to make sense of the way body-related emotions relate to sport and exercise experiences, and the way sport and exercise experiences influence body-related emotions. It is beyond the scope of this chapter to review these theories, and further discussion of theory in self-conscious emotion research and practice has been reviewed elsewhere (Sabiston, Pila, & Gilchrist, 2020).

Notwithstanding the underlying model or framework used, and as highlighted throughout this chapter, it is important to note that the regulatory processes are distinct when explaining the directional relationships between self-conscious emotions and sport and exercise. To manage negatively valenced body-related emotions, individuals often use cognitive strategies or behaviors that include avoidance and/or concealment (e.g. not going to practice or the gym; wearing loose-fitting clothing), compensatory (e.g. exercising longer or with greater intensity to "make up" for poor eating choices), and checking and monitoring (e.g. constant awareness of the body while competing or exercising). As a collective, these strategies include using sport and exercise as negative reinforcement to enable the individual to temporarily regulate the discomfort tied to social physique anxiety, shame, guilt, envy, and embarrassment emotions.

Sport and exercise behaviors can also be used as proactive, purposeful self-regulatory behaviors to control negative body-related emotions and enhance positive body-related emotions. When the focus is on management of emotions specifically focused on appearance, these self-regulatory behaviors may be deemed maladaptive, whereas the management of emotions focused on function through the use of sport and exercise behaviors is considered more adaptive. Yet, little is known about the interaction between appearance and function, and positive and negative, body-related emotions and the links to adaptive and maladaptive outcomes.

Figure 5.1 brings together the associations between many of the self-regulatory factors linked to body-related self-conscious emotions and sport and exercise based on the research findings presented in this chapter. The direct and proximal associations are illustrated, with consideration that there are many indirect and more distal associations among the constructs that have been introduced in this chapter. In brief, the paths in Figure 5.1 illustrate a circular pattern in which self-conscious emotions inform attitudes, beliefs, and motives for sport and exercise, which foster or preclude engagement in sport and exercise. Participation in sport and exercise informs congruency or degree of self-discrepancy on body appearance and function, which are often internalized into the self-concept. The internalization and importance of body appearance and function then inform individuals' attributions/explanations for exercise and sport-related events (i.e. controllability, stability, and globality), which then relate to the experience of unique self-conscious emotions.

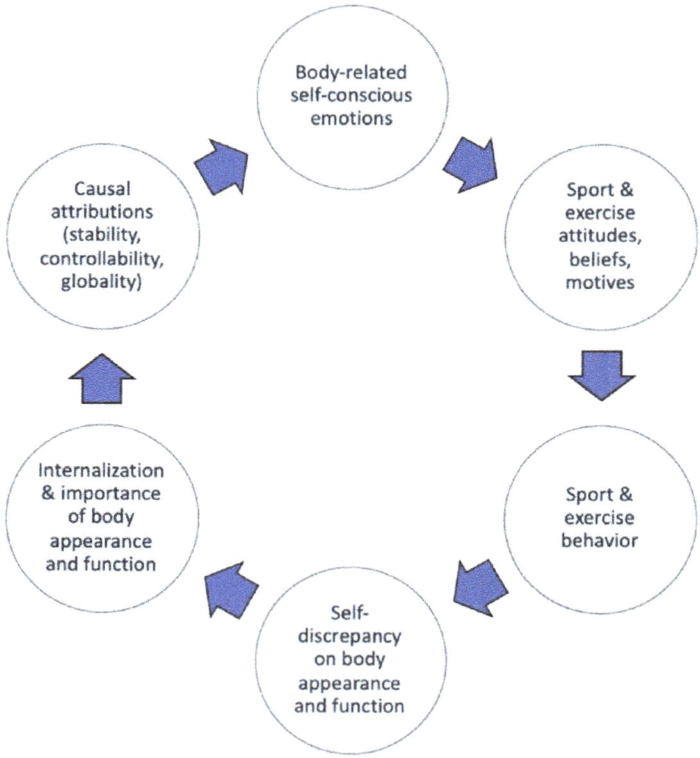

FIGURE 5.1 Proposed associations between self-regulatory factors, body-related self-conscious emotions, and sport and exercise behavior.

Future Considerations

In addition to the gaps and possible areas of future research already outlined throughout this chapter, there are two directions to study self-conscious emotions that have rarely been explored as body image emotions. These include an exploration of anticipated emotions and the study of group-based emotions.

Anticipated and Experienced Emotions

In this chapter, we have presented a number of considerations for the experience of body-related self-conscious emotions, including the positive and negative valence, state and trait/proneness, and appearance and function facets. These emotions can also be described as experienced/felt (i.e. in the moment emotion) or anticipated (i.e. a future experience of the emotion); however, there is very little work exploring anticipated emotions.

Anticipated emotions have been predominantly framed around negative emotions. For example, Gilchrist and colleagues found a negative association between physical self-concept (i.e. a cognitive indicator of functional body image) and anticipated body-related shame among young adult women but not men (Gilchrist, Solomon-Krakus, Pila, Crocker, & Sabiston, 2020). Physical self-concept was not associated with anticipated body-related guilt, although men reported anticipating more guilt compared to women. These findings demonstrate potential uniqueness among the anticipation of shame and guilt emotions. When linked to behavior, anticipated emotions have been mostly studied with psychological and behavioral indices of eating disorders (e.g. body size misperception, caloric consumption, fear of weight gain). For example, Troop's program of research has articulated the important and unique distinction between experienced and anticipated body shame with relevance to disordered eating (Troop, 2016; Troop & Redshaw, 2012). In this work, even if an individual does not currently experience shame about their weight, self-regulation and behavioral modification may occur to avoid the onset of shame in the future. Drawing on this work, the anticipation of negative emotions may also be motivational or discouraging for exercise or sport participation (Gilchrist, Conroy, & Sabiston, 2018; Gilchrist & Sabiston, 2018; Gilchrist, Sabiston, et al., 2018; Gilchrist et al., 2020). Furthermore, the association between anticipated authentic and hubristic pride and engagement in MVPA has been reported among young adults (Gilchrist & Sabiston, 2018). In this study, intentions significantly mediated the association between anticipated authentic and hubristic pride and MVPA. These recent findings focused on anticipated positive emotions suggest that targeting anticipated hedonic outcomes of MVPA may be valuable in interventions targeting exercise participation.

Overall, more work is needed to understand the implications of anticipated emotions in the self-regulation of exercise and sport behaviors. Preliminary evidence suggests that understanding distinctions between experienced and anticipated emotions, and association to behavioral outcomes, may be valuable and have implications for understanding underlying self-regulatory processes.

Group-Based Emotions

Emotions are often perceived to be an individual-based construct as they are responses to events that help individuals adapt to their environment and overcome obstacles (Lazarus,

1991). Informed by intergroup emotion theory, researchers have found that group membership can also be a powerful predictor of emotional experience and subsequent action (Mackie, Devos, & Smith, 2000). This is important considering that nearly all sport activities take place in some type of groups or teams (Evans, Eys, & Bruner, 2012). Researchers exploring emotions in the group context have approached the phenomena through group-based emotions (e.g. shame an individual feels from losing a championship) and collective emotions (e.g. pride that teammates feel when winning a championship).

Group-based emotions are dependent on an individual's membership within a group or team. These emotions typically occur in response to group events or experiences. In other words, through an individual's membership in a group, they share experiences with fellow group members, and, in turn, experience group-based emotions through these experiences (Goldenberg, Saguy, & Halperin, 2014). Group-based emotions are influenced by factors such as individuals' levels of identification with their group, their unique appraisal of events, as well as their groups' collective emotional experiences (Goldenberg et al., 2014). In contrast to group-based emotions, in which individuals' emotional responses to group-based events are assessed, collective emotions are emotions that can be measured at the group level, with all individuals in a group experiencing the same emotions to the same events. Therefore, collective emotions are emotions that group members share and experience simultaneously (Niedenthal & Brauer, 2012).

In the sport and exercise contexts, levels of group-based emotions and collective emotions are associated with important constructs pertinent to individuals' experiences in sport (e.g. team functioning, performance, communication, and coping strategies; Tamminen et al., 2016). Further, individuals' level of identification with their team (i.e. their social identity) can impact group-based emotions (Campo et al., 2019) in that participation within a team competition can lead to more positive and less negative group-based emotion. In a recent study exploring group-based self-conscious emotions among adolescent girls involved in sport, 60% reported experiencing group-based guilt, 45% reported group-based shame, 46% experienced group-based embarrassment, and 78% and 99% of the athletes reported group-based hubristic and authentic pride, respectively (Doré, Pila, Gilchrist, & Sabiston, 2020). These group-based emotions were uniquely associated with sport commitment in expected directions, whereby higher negative and lower positive group-based emotions were related to lower sport commitment. This study demonstrates possible interest in further understanding group-based emotions, and extensions of this work to explore body-related group-based self-conscious emotions.

The extent to which individuals experience body-related self-conscious emotions at an intrapersonal level might stem from, or inform, their interpersonal group-based emotions. As a broad summary, individuals who identify with a group typically experience higher negative body-related self-conscious emotions if a member of their group displays skills, appearance, or acts in a way that does not represent the identity of the group (Lickel, Schmader, Curtis, Scarnie, & Ames, 2005). Further work is needed to establish pathways linking body-related self-conscious emotions and group-based emotions in the sport and exercise contexts.

Conclusion

In summary, the bi-directional relationship between sport and exercise behaviors and body image is a self-regulatory process that is primarily influenced by body-related self-conscious emotions. The main negative body-related self-conscious emotions often relate to behavioral disengagement, avoidance, and apathy, whereas both hubristic and authentic pride have been associated with approach motivation, greater effort, and participation in sport and exercise. Furthermore, participation in sport and/or exercise behavior(s) has heightened negative emotions for some individuals, and enhanced the experience of positive body-related self-conscious emotions for others. The research in the area of body-related self-conscious emotions is relatively new, and predominantly informed by cross-sectional study findings. Longitudinal research has emerged linking body-related self-conscious emotions to sport outcomes among adolescents, and this recent evidence signals for more work in this area. The interplay between negative and positive body-related self-conscious emotions is understudied, and there is no singular main model or theory to explain the links with sport and exercise. Finally, there is limited evidence of practical programs or intervention research aimed at addressing body-related self-conscious emotions. As such, there is a great opportunity to contribute to this area of research.

6

PERFECTIONISM MYTHS

Andrew P. Hill

Introduction

Sport and exercise psychology are fraught with various myths and misunderstanding. Recent studies of coaches serve to illustrate this point with many coaches holding common but incorrect beliefs about learning and the brain (Bailey, Madigan, Cope, & Nicholls, 2018). Such myths and misunderstanding have varying degrees of impact on the effectiveness of coaches and practitioners. Whereas some myths and misunderstandings will have very little impact, others will undermine the ability to work with athletes effectively and safely. With this in mind, this chapter focuses on myths surrounding perfectionism – a personality trait that is central to athlete motivation. Even though perfectionism has been studied in sport and exercise psychology for nearly 30 years, perfectionism remains misunderstood by many coaches and other practitioners. Indeed, some accounts of perfectionism are proving difficult to dispel despite being contradicted by scientific research.

The chapter discusses four common perfectionism myths. The first myth is that perfectionism pertains only to the standards that athletes have for themselves, as opposed to having other equally important defining features. The second myth is that perfectionists exist and, therefore, types of athletes who are perfectionists can be identified and studied. The third myth is that perfectionism is a personal quality that is necessary in order to be successful. The final myth is that perfectionism, or some form or type of perfectionism, can be good for your health. Here, each myth is debunked and, in doing so, a foundation is provided for those who wish to better understand perfectionism and its consequences for athlete motivation and self-regulation, performance and well-being.

Myth 1: Perfectionism Is Just about Personal Standards

The first perfectionism myth is that perfectionism pertains just to the personal standards that people have. However, perfectionism refers to more than the personal standards people have or pursue. Perfectionism includes a particular mind-set and set of beliefs that shape the way people think about the world and give meaning to personal experiences

(Ellis, 1958; Burns, 1980; Pacht, 1984). Broadly defined, perfectionism is excessively "high standards of performance *which are accompanied by tendencies for overly critical evaluations of one's own behavior*" (Frost et al. 1990, p. 450, italics in original). The latter part of the definition serves to highlight the features of perfectionism that extend beyond personal standards. The additional features manifest in various ways such as doubts, concerns, and negative reactions to imperfection, and are central to understanding the consequences of perfectionism (Gotwals, Dunn, Dunn, & Gamache, 2010; Stoeber, Otto, & Stoll, 2006). Moreover, these additional features are equally as important to defining and understanding perfectionism as personal standards (Frost et al., 1990).

Because these other features are not always considered alongside personal standards, the lines can blur between perfectionism and apparently similar personality characteristics. Research examining perfectionism and conscientiousness, in particular, serves to underscore the importance of being clear about what perfectionism is and is not (see Flett & Hewitt, 2006, 2007). In a study of junior cricketers, Hill and colleagues compared the tendency to demand perfection from oneself (self-oriented perfectionism) with a sub-facet of conscientiousness, conscientious achievement striving, in regard to relationships with other indicators of perfectionism (Hill, Hall, & Appleton, 2010). The tendency to demand perfection from oneself had a significant positive relationship with high standards, concerns, doubts, fear of failure, self-criticism, and negative reactions to imperfection. By contrast, conscientious achievement striving had a significant positive relationship with only high standards (and to a lesser degree self-criticism). Additional analyses revealed that demanding perfection from oneself includes irrational beliefs, namely, that it was important to be perfect, which explained these differences (see Campbell & Di Paula, 2002).

The problem with focusing on just personal standards is made worse by the tendency of researchers to statistically create and examine new personal standards dimensions of perfectionism that are unrelated to other dimensions of perfectionism. The technique used to do so is known as "partialling" and the new dimensions created are labeled either residualized or partialled personal standards. The merits of partialling have been debated by researchers in this area (see Hill, 2014, 2017; Stoeber & Gaudreau, 2017). In this debate, I have argued that partialled personal standards offer an inappropriate basis to make inferences about perfectionism because it no longer contains core features that overlap with other perfectionism dimensions (e.g. concerns, doubts, and negative reactions). Whether colleagues agree or not, the importance of being clear about what the exact bases of our conclusions are is illustrated by the opposing conclusions of two reviews of research examining perfectionism in sport. One, drawing heavily on findings using partialled personal standards, concluded that personal standards may be part of a healthy striving for excellence (Stoeber, 2011). The other, focusing on personal standards, concluded that they were complex and ambiguous (Hill, Mallinson-Howard, & Jowett, 2018). The latter is a more accurate account of research so far in sport psychology, in my opinion.

A related part of this myth is the notion that perfectionism pertains only to how you think and feel about yourself – demanding perfection from oneself (self-oriented perfectionism). However, one of the most important advances in our understanding of perfectionism has been to broaden the study of the trait to include beliefs about other people and the target of the perfectionistic demands. Perfectionism can include demanding that other people are perfect (other-oriented perfectionism) and believing that other people demand that you are perfect (socially prescribed perfectionism). Distinguishing between these three dimensions of perfectionism is the cornerstone of a model developed by Hewitt and Flett (1991). This model is perhaps the most popular model of perfectionism outside of sport and exercise psychology and has now been used numerous times to study perfectionism in athletes (see Hill, Mallinson-Howard, & Jowett, 2018, for a review). One thing that this research has taught us is that if we want to fully understand the consequences of perfectionism, we need to consider each of these different dimensions.

One recent example of research testing this model serves to illustrate the importance of studying perfectionism in this way. Grugan, Jowett, Mallinson-Howard, and Hall (2020) examined the relationship between the three different dimensions of perfectionism and antisocial behavior in competitive team athletes. They found that self-oriented perfectionism was not significantly related to antisocial teammate behavior and negatively related to antisocial opponent behavior. By contrast, socially prescribed perfectionism and other-oriented perfectionism were positively related to both antisocial teammate and opponent behaviors. For other-oriented perfectionism, the relationships were also mediated by angry reactions to poor teammate performance. As such, we can expect the likelihood of antisocial behavior, and underpinning triggers for that behavior, to differ depending on the dimension of perfectionism athletes exhibit. This information would be lost if we were to focus only on the tendency to demand perfection from oneself.

One final point on the myth regarding perfectionism being just about personal standards is worth making. Hill and Grugan (2019) have recently proposed that perfectionism can be conceptualized as a quality of the social environment, in addition to the individual. Specifically, we believe that different social environments can be construed as more or less perfectionistic. Perfectionistic climates are environments that promote the view that performances must be perfect and less than perfect performances are unacceptable. More perfectionistic climates include unrealistic expectations that performances should be perfect (expectation), harsh criticism when performances are not perfect (criticism), coercive behavior used to pressure perfect performance (control), recognition and appreciation based on perfect performances (conditional regard), and worry and vigilance regarding mistakes and the consequences of not performing perfectly (anxiousness). Although our research on perfectionistic climate is in its infancy, we believe that this approach offers great promise in regard to understanding perfectionism. If others agree, the study of perfectionism in sport will move even further away from focusing on just the personal standards of athletes.

Myth 2: "Perfectionists" Exist

The second perfectionism myth is that "perfectionists" exist. That is, there are types of athletes who are perfectionists and there are types of athletes who are not perfectionists. In actuality, like most personality traits, perfectionism exists in everyone (and every athlete) to some degree. This is the conclusion of research that has directly examined the structure of perfectionism. Specifically, Bromen-Fulks, Hill, and Green (2008) examined the structure of perfectionism using taxometric procedures to determine whether perfectionism is best conceptualized as taxonic (categorical) or dimensional (continuous). Taxometric procedures are used to uncover naturally occurring patterns in data and the existence of underlying taxons or classes. These procedures have been applied to a range of personality characteristics in the same way to determine their structure (see Haslam, Holland, & Kuppens, 2012). On the basis of their analyses, they argued that "…individual differences in perfectionism are reflective of a difference in degree rather than type of perfectionism experienced" (p. 488).

This means that there is no point, cut-off, or threshold on the instruments that are used to measure perfectionism that can identify an athlete who is a perfectionist or a non-perfectionist. Some athletes will have higher levels of perfectionism and other athletes will have lower levels of perfectionism. Every other athlete will be somewhere in between. Moreover, while we can impose typologies to study perfectionism, these typologies offer investigative convenience at the expense of studying perfectionism as it occurs – a difference in degree, rather than type. As such, rather than labeling athletes as "perfectionists," it is more accurate and preferable to describe them as being more or less "perfectionistic" (Hill, 2016; Hill, Madigan, Smith, Mallinson-Howard, & Donachie, 2020).

There are two important ramifications of this realization. The first ramification is that perfectionism is relevant for everyone (because everyone has it to some degree). It is not a rare quality found mainly or only in the most talented or gifted. This incorrect notion should be avoided in sport and exercise psychology (e.g., Rees et al., 2016). Essentially, to study perfectionism is to study everyone. Some of the more revealing research on perfectionism that has taken place so far in sport has focused on non-elite samples. This includes research examining moral behavior in school and community-based junior sports participants (Mallinson, Hill, & Hall, 2019), burnout in sports coaches (Tashman, Tenenbaum, & Eklund, 2010), and parental origins of perfectionism (Olsson, Hill, Madigan, & Woodley, 2020).

The notion that we should seek to identify and study perfectionism only in specific types of people, and not others, would also do little to encourage research in more general settings. Exercise, for example, is an important setting to study perfectionism. Not least because people are bombarded with images of bodily perfection and shamed if they do not conform to body ideals no matter how unrealistic they are (see Chapter 5, this volume). Initial research in this area suggests that perfectionism may tell us a great deal about the experiences of exercisers. One of the most frequently examined relationships so far has been between perfectionism and exercise dependence with higher levels of perfectionism related to greater symptomology (e.g., Hill, Robson, & Stamp, 2015). More recently, researchers have begun to examine other relationships. Notably, in one study it was found that perfectionism was related to how recreational runners coped with injuries (Jowett, Hill, Forsdyke, & Gledhill, 2018), for example.

The second ramification of the realization that perfectionists do not exist is that perfectionism is best examined using the entire continuum of scores. This is important in regard to how perfectionism is studied in sport and exercise psychology. Some models of perfectionism are typological and emphasize comparison of groups who have different mean levels of perfectionism (Tripartite Model of Perfectionism; Parker, 1997). Other models are continuum-based and empathize the examination of perfectionism across all scores (2 × 2 Model of Perfectionism; Gaudreau & Thompson, 2010). The difference between the two models is exemplified in sport by research that has examined perfectionism and burnout with some studies comparing athletes with different types of perfectionism (e.g. parent-oriented perfectionists versus doubt-oriented perfectionists; Gotwals, 2011) and others examining how dimensions of perfectionism interact across all scores to determine the level of burnout (e.g., Hill, 2013). In the absence of meaningful cut-offs and thresholds, models of perfectionism that are continuum-based are preferable to typological-based models (Hill & Madigan, 2017).

Similarly, statistical analyses that allow examination of the effects of perfectionism across the whole range of scores offer greater insight into its likely consequences.

Myth 3: Perfectionism Is Necessary To Be Successful

Perhaps the most insidious perfectionism myth is that perfectionism is necessary to be successful. This myth is partly based on the issues discussed in myth 1 and confusion between being highly perfectionistic and simply having high or exceptionally high standards. Athletes can have exceptionally high standards and not be highly perfectionistic. One of the key differences between people who have exceptionally high standards and those who are highly perfectionistic are the features of the standards themselves. Perfectionistic standards are more rigid and unrealistic, given the circumstances people find themselves in. This includes disregarding personal constraints (e.g. low ability, injury, or illness) or situational constraints (e.g. task novelty or difficulty). Because of this feature, perfectionistic standards deny people the opportunity to set goals that are optimally challenging and adjust their goals if necessary. This is something that is important for maintaining performance, motivation, and well-being over the long term (Wrosch, Scheier, & Miller, 2013) and something particularly important for talent development (Chase & DiSanti, 2017).

Another key difference between athletes who have exceptionally high standards and athletes who are highly perfectionistic is how they respond to not being perfect. People who are highly perfectionistic have harsh and strict evaluative tendencies and tend to respond to imperfection with severe criticism. The criticism is often directed toward themselves, rather than the performance, and extends beyond what most people would experience especially when underpinned by concerns regarding the expectations of others (Gilbert, Durrant, & McEwan, 2006). These harsh self-critical tendencies are a major source of performance and mental health difficulties for people who are highly perfectionistic (Dunkley, Zuroff, & Blankstein, 2006; Powers, Koestner, & Zuroff, Milyavskaya, & Gorin, 2011).

This is not to say that there are no circumstances in which higher levels of perfectionism will contribute to better performance, at least in the short term. People who are highly perfectionistic can be organized, hardworking, and dedicate considerable amounts of time and effort to performance tasks. There is evidence for this in other achievement domains such as education (e.g., Madigan, 2019). There are also a small number of studies in sport that illustrate that striving for perfection may contribute to better athletic performance (e.g., Madigan, Stoeber, Culley, Passfield, & Hill, 2018; Stoeber, Uphill, & Hotham, 2009; Stoll, Lau, & Stoeber, 2008). This includes when examining team level perfectionism and team performance (Hill, Stoeber, Brown, & Appleton, 2014). However, these effects are part of a complex set of behaviors that need to be viewed and studied holistically and over time. When perfectionism is studied in this manner, it is revealed to include a strong vulnerability to motivation, performance, and mental health issues for most people.

There is evidence of the vulnerability that underlies perfectionism in a series of studies which examined how student-athletes respond to personal and competitive failures (Hill, Hall, Duda, & Appleton, 2011; Curran & Hill, 2018; Lizmore, Dunn, Causgrove Dunn, & Hill, 2019). In the first study, we examined differences between student-athletes high and low in self-oriented perfectionism in their response to failing to meet a personally set goal on a cycle ergometer task (Hill et al., 2011). In three trials, participants set a personal target and received (false) feedback that they failed to meet their personal target. We found that failure on just one trial was enough to trigger differences in the two groups in self-reported threat, effort, and satisfaction with performance. This study provided one of the first indications in sport that perfectionism might be problematic for athletes when they encounter achievement difficulties.

In the second study, we examined the interaction between self-oriented perfectionism and socially prescribed perfectionism in determining responses to competitive failure, again, on a cycle ergometer task (Curran & Hill, 2018). Unlike in the first study, student-athletes competed against each other three times with all participants receiving (false) feedback that they had performed the worst. In this study, we found that following competitive failure, self-oriented perfectionism was related to a pronounced decrease in pride and socially prescribed perfectionism was related to a pronounced increase in shame. Both dimensions of perfectionism were related to a pronounced increase in guilt. We also found that a combination of high levels of both dimensions of perfectionism were related to higher guilt and higher shame following failure when compared to other combinations of perfectionism. The more negative response to failure associated with perfectionism therefore extends to competition with others and includes an array of emotions.

Finally, in the most recent study, we examined the interactive effects of perfectionistic strivings (a combination of perfectionism dimensions that measure personal strivings for perfection) and perfectionistic concerns (a combination of perfectionism dimensions that measure evaluative concerns and negative reactions to imperfection) on athletic performance (golf putting) following competitive failure (Lizmore et al., 2019). We found that at lower levels of perfectionistic concerns, perfectionistic strivings had a significant positive relationship with performance. However, as levels of perfectionistic concerns increased, the effect became non-significant and was eventually reversed with perfectionistic strivings having a negative effect on performance. Surprisingly, the level of perfectionistic concerns that instigated the change in effect from significant to non-significant was below the midpoint on the response scale. In other words, only a small amount of perfectionistic concerns was required in order to subvert the performance benefits of perfectionistic strivings.

Although not without limitations, these three studies provide evidence that the consequences of perfectionism are likely to be complex and problematic if the intention is to develop resilient, high-performing athletes. My view is that highly perfectionistic athletes are typically unprepared for achievement difficulties. This is because they invest their sense of self-worth heavily in their performances and curate their achievement experiences in a manner designed to protect themselves from achievement difficulties (Hill, Hall, & Appleton, 2011; Hill et al., 2011). There is evidence for this argument in studies outside of sport that have found a relationship between perfectionism and self-handicapping behaviors and procrastination that are indicative of a strong desire to avoid scenarios in which you might appear incompetent and perform less than perfectly (Kearns, Forbes, Gardiner, & Marshall, 2008; Sirois, Molnar, & Hirsch, 2017). These are hardly desirable features for anyone but particularly problematic for aspiring athletes.

What, then, should be made of the accounts of successful athletes who are identified as being perfectionistic (e.g., Gould, Moffett, & Diefenbach, 2002)? First, it is important to note that the qualitative studies from which these accounts are drawn are not intended to uncover causal relationships. Rather, studies that adopt interpretative perspectives aim to explore and better understand the lives and perspectives of the participants – a valuable goal. They tell us what athletes think may have been determining factors but cannot tell us what actually was. Second, when the focus of the discussion broadens outside of performance, qualitative accounts of perfectionism are more complex. In our own research adopting qualitative approaches, for example, successful athletes reported that the energizing aspects of perfectionism occur in tandem with an array of negative consequences, not least how athletes say they routinely sacrifice important aspects of their lives and their health in pursuit of their goals (Hill, Witcher, Gotwals, & Leyland, 2015).

There are also instances where research has found perfectionism to be higher among more-elite athletes in comparison to less-elite counterparts (e.g., Rasquinha, Dunn, & Dunn, 2014). However, there are many reasons why perfectionism may be higher in more elite samples other than being a causal factor for success or "eliteness." With its focus on competition and objectively available criteria for perfection, some sports may attract those higher in perfectionism (attraction hypothesis). It is also possible that sport whittles out those who are less perfectionistic for similar reasons (rejection hypothesis). Finally, it is also possible that sport engrains perfectionism in its participants so that the longer people remain in sport, the more perfectionistic they become (development hypothesis). We currently do not have sufficient tests of these alternative hypotheses. When weighing the evidence for and against perfectionism being a causal factor, I would argue that it is not perfectionism, per se, that distinguishes successful athletes from less successful athletes. More likely, it is that more successful athletes have not fully succumbed to the negative consequences of perfectionism that is the key difference.

Myth 4: Perfectionism Is Good For You

The final perfectionism myth is that perfectionism, or some form or type of perfectionism, can be good for your health. This is evident in the way perfectionism is labeled as functional, adaptive, or healthy (Enns, Cox, & Clara, 2002; Rhéaume et al., 2000; Stoeber & Otto, 2006). Labeling perfectionism in this way originates from outside of sport but there is now a trend toward doing so in sport psychology, too (e.g., Sarkar & Fletcher, 2014). The case against the notion of healthy perfectionists and perfectionism has been made by many researchers in this area. Some of the criticisms have been touched upon earlier. For example, if perfectionists do not exist, it is difficult to argue that healthy (or even unhealthy) perfectionists do. In addition, it is problematic to consider someone to be highly perfectionistic if they only have exceptionally high standards. On the latter point, Greenspon (2000, 2008) has been one of the strongest critics of the notion of healthy perfectionism and has argued that it is largely the result of conceptual confusion and that, essentially, there is little about healthy perfectionism that is perfectionistic. Others have made similar arguments (e.g., Flett & Hewitt, 2006; Hall, 2006; Hall, Hill, & Appleton, 2012).

In regard to research findings, the last few years have seen the publication of a large number of meta-analytical studies examining perfectionism and psychopathology that allow us to now better understand the likely consequences of being highly perfectionistic. *There is no evidence for healthy perfectionism in these studies.* Elements of perfectionism other than those that pertain to striving for perfection invariably emerge as highly problematic for mental health. There is evidence that perfectionistic concerns are related to higher levels of anxiety symptoms, bulimic symptoms, depressive symptoms, and suicidality (Kehayes, Smith, Sherry, Vidovic, & Saklofske, 2019; Smith, Vidovic, Sherry, Stewart, & Saklofske, 2018; Smith et al., 2016; Smith et al., 2018). Some of these findings are evident over time and after controlling for baseline levels of mental ill-health. When focusing on dimensions that are the best candidates for healthy perfectionism (typically personal standards and self-oriented perfectionism), no evidence can be found for any health benefits either. Like perfectionistic concerns, albeit to a smaller degree, they have positive relationships with anxiety symptoms, bulimic symptoms, depressive symptoms, and suicide ideation with an increase in anxiety and depression evident over time (Smith et al., 2016, 2018). The relationships between perfectionistic strivings and eating disorder symptoms were especially large in one meta-analysis (Limburg, Watson, Hagger, & Egan, 2017) which we know may be more prevalent among athletes than non-athletes (Sundgot-Borgen & Torstveit, 2004).

At this point, it is worth revisiting the difference between high standards and perfectionistic standards and the revealing findings of one particular study. Blasberg, Hewitt, Flett, Sherry, and Chen (2016) distributed different versions of the same questionnaires designed to measure perfectionism. The versions were altered, so the items referred to either high standards or perfectionistic standards (e.g. "I have *high standards* for my performance at work or at school" versus "I have *perfectionistic standards* for my performance at work or at school"). They then examined levels of these variables and their relationship with various outcomes among three samples of university students. There were two key findings. First, students reported higher levels of high standards than perfectionistic standards (i.e. it is more common to have high standards than perfectionistic standards). Second, perfectionistic standards predicted greater depressive symptoms, lower self-esteem, and lower life satisfaction, whereas high standards predicted lower depressive symptoms (or did not predict them at all), higher self-esteem and higher life satisfaction. Whether standards are perfectionistic or just high, again, clearly matters for mental health.

There is also a smaller but growing amount of research that implicates perfectionism in the development of physical ill-health and research that illustrates higher levels of perfectionism are related to difficultly living with chronic illness or disability. In regard to being a predictor of ill-health, there is evidence for perfectionism being related to headaches and insomnia, for example (Bottos & Dewey, 2004; de Azevedo et al., 2009). In regard to adjustment difficulties to illness, this includes fibromyalgia, Crohn's disease, and coronary artery disease (Molnar, Flett, Sadeva, & Colautti, 2012; Flett, Baricza, Gupta, Hewitt, & Endler, 2011; Dunkley et al., 2012). We have found this ourselves in our own work examining psychosocial adaptation to spinal cord injury (Read, Hill, Jowett, & Astill, 2019). There is great potential in examining similar issues in athletes such as susceptibility to illness and how athletes cope with injuries and life after sport which for many athletes involves living with debilitating long-term health conditions (e.g. osteoarthritis; Shepard, Banks & Ryan, 2003).

Research examining the relationship between perfectionism and mental and physical health in sport is among the most important areas of future work. In time, this work will firmly debunk the healthy perfectionist myth. However, for now, we will need to draw on existing evidence outside of sport. In doing so, it is quite clear that perfectionism is related to poorer mental health and physical health, even dimensions of perfectionism that are typically considered more desirable. With this in mind, we need to be aware that by propagating the healthy perfectionism myth, we may inadvertently place athletes at risk to these outcomes. While we wait for research in sport to take place, or until compelling evidence can be provided that perfectionism does not have a detrimental effect on the mental and physical health of athletes, a more conservative and cautious approach is required when labeling and discussing perfectionism in sport and exercise psychology.

Concluding Remarks

This chapter debunked a series of common perfectionism myths. Perfectionism was revealed to include more than just personal standards and exist in every athlete to some degree. It was also shown how perfectionism can contribute to better athletic performance on some occasions but also be problematic in various other ways. Motivationally, perfectionism is exceedingly complex. In some instances, it may energize the intense pursuit of goal-directed behavior and better athletic performance. However, there is also evidence that an aversion to mistakes and competitive failure provides the basis for motivation and performance difficulties. Importantly, perfectionism is far from healthy with a large amount of research suggesting that higher levels of perfectionism will place athletes at greater risk to mental and physical health issues.

Will the myths surrounding perfectionism be fully dispelled? Myths can be challenged, subjected to empirical scrutiny, and their flaws exposed. However, unfortunately, myths can be stubborn and difficult to eliminate. Even formal training and education seems unable to eliminate some myths completely (see Macdonald, Germine, Anderson, Christodoulou, & McGrath, 2017). Current misunderstanding of perfectionism in sport and exercise psychology may reflect a deeper-rooted set of beliefs. Specifically, it appears to be accepted wisdom in sport that exceptional feats of performance require great personal sacrifice and suffering, and that sacrifice and suffering are a price that must be paid for success. While people continue to believe that this is the case, it will be difficult to convince those in sport that perfectionism is problematic and should be discouraged among athletes who are aiming to reach its highest levels.

7

A MOTIVATIONAL MODEL OF ENDURANCE AND PERSISTENCE

Ian M. Taylor

Introduction

Motivation has been a hot topic in sport and exercise psychology for many decades. The first issue of the *Journal of Sport Psychology* contained an article concerning commitment to running (Carmack & Martans, 1979), and subsequent decades witnessed the rise of self-determination theory, achievement goal theory, and several other motivation frameworks applied to sport and exercise contexts (Vallerand & Reid, 1984; Duda & Nicholls, 1992). This attention has led to an understanding of how motivation can energize physical activity and exercise engagement (Edmunds, Ntoumanis, & Duda, 2008; Fenton, Duda, & Barrett, 2016) or prevent lapses in exercise behavior and dropout (Murphy & Taylor, 2019; Sarrazin, Vallerand, Guillet, Pelletier, & Cury, 2002). It is also possible to identify different qualities of motivation that facilitate well-being and those that hinder it (Gunnell, Crocker, Mack, Wilson, & Zumbo, 2014). However, the same level of understanding cannot be observed in the motivation and self-regulation to persist during acts of endurance. Numerous human feats, such as athletic pursuits, military operations, and even survival in perilous circumstances, necessitate the capacity to endure (Jaworski, Jensen, Niederberger, Congalton, & Kelly, 2015; Wolff, Bieleke, & Schüler, 2019). Whether it be quitting entirely or fractionally reducing effort, failure to endure leads to varying undesirable consequences, from losing a race to extreme danger. However, there remains a lack of understanding about the motivational factors that lead to superior endurance performance.

The aim of this chapter is to take a step toward filling this void by presenting a novel model of motivational processes that occur during acts of endurance. Endurance is defined as the ability to continue doing something painful or difficult for a period without giving up. This definition can be applied to many sporting and non-sporting scenarios. In the same way, the model described here does not only apply to 'endurance' classified events, such as the 10,000m track and field event. The model is generalizable to any athletic scenario in which the individual is required to physically persist in the face of psychological and physiological difficulties. Underpinned by this definition, the first section of the chapter provides context by considering some existing perspectives on human endurance that have been developed largely within physiology. This overview is used to demonstrate that motivational processes have been discounted as an important factor during endurance activities in some of these models. Other viewpoints consider motivational processes to varying degrees, and so differences and similarities with the model described in this chapter are presented. The second section draws on generalizable principles and empirical evidence to illustrate the critical motivational dynamics of competing desires and goals that occur *during* acts of endurance performance. Subsequently, it is proposed that these dynamics are influenced by an optimal motivational basis *prior* to the endurance act. This optimal state reflects elevated concordance between one's core values and the act of endurance. In combination, these motivational components explain effective persistence and endurance. Throughout the chapter, evidence is provided in support of this perspective, with areas highlighted where direct evidence is lacking. The chapter concludes by outlining potential future research avenues and unanswered questions.

Why Do We Need a Motivational Perspective?

Physiologists have pioneered the investigation of optimal conditions for, or limits of, human endurance. For example, the maximum limits of energy expenditure over prolonged periods have been estimated based on data from a variety of human endurance events (Thurber et al., 2019). This attention has led to significant understanding of the biological factors that regulate human endurance (St Clair Gibson, Swart, & Tucker, 2018). An overemphasis of single scientific perspectives, however, can lead to somewhat distorted conclusions, such as the view that task failure (i.e. the point at which a participant is unwilling or unable to continue a physical task) during severe intensities of effort is a wholly physical process with no deliberative decision making involved (Burnley & Jones, 2018). This inference is based on data showing that muscular neural activity does not decline despite mechanical forces doing so during repeated leg contractions (Burnley, Vanhatalo, & Jones, 2012) or during cycling (Chidnok et al., 2013). These data are suggested to imply that physiologically based task failure has occurred before a psychologically based decision to terminate (Burnley & Jones, 2018). Other viewpoints are less extreme about the insignificance of motivation or deliberative decision making, but nonetheless propose single biological systems as 'the key' to resisting fatigue (e.g. the pulmonary system; Amann, 2012).

In contrast to these prevailing views of endurance performance, it is proposed that task failure (i.e. complete cessation) and pacing decisions (i.e. modifying work rate) are purposeful judgments based on a variety of increasingly persuasive psycho-physiological factors. Afferent signals, including those associated with physical exertion, are affectively charged in the insula cortex area of the brain (Critchley & Harrison, 2013). These labels are integrated and form a consciously accessible representation of overall homeostatic condition (Craig, 2003). The primary function of this signal is to motivate action (Critchley & Garfinkel, 2017). Thus, interoceptive neural networks convey motivationally important information about bodily functioning and departures from homeostasis (Craig, 2003). If disengagement from endurance activities contains no deliberative judgment, the affect associated with the underlying physiology has no purpose and no reason to have evolved.

Convincingly, this functional anatomical perspective is consistent with cognitive theories of motivation suggesting that affect is a signal of discrepancy between input (e.g. current physiological state) and reference value (e.g. homeostasis; Carver, 2006). For example, affective responses to exercise are increasingly negatively valenced at intensities above the level at which lactate begins to accumulate in the blood (Ekkekakis, Parfitt, & Petruzello, 2011). Once this affective indicator occupies deliberative (i.e. conscious) attention, it gains access to a wide range of systems that control cognition and behavior (Baars & Franklin, 2003). The more resources occupied, the more influence on decision making in favor of a desire to desist (Hofmann & Van Dillen, 2012; Kavanagh, Andrade, & May, 2005). It is plausible that this process could break down at severe intensities of activity, although no evidence for this idea exists. Rather, afferent signals will manifest as formidable motivation because they are viewed as urgent challenges to homeostasis (Craig, 2003). These psychosomatic signals dominate working memory capacity (Hutchinson & Tenenbaum, 2007) to such an extent that task failure becomes almost certain. This process may even seem out of one's control in the same way as lashing out in anger is often viewed. Nonetheless, it is still motivated behavior. In sum, desisting from any endurance act is a combination of physiological processes and deliberative motivation.

Not all models of human endurance overlook psychological components. The integrated governor model proposes that competition between psychological factors and physiological homeostatic drives regulates human capability (St Clair Gibson et al., 2018). In this model, perception of effort is a signal of physiological homeostatic disturbance; therefore, disengagement occurs when effort required exceeds motivation. The psychobiological model draws a similar conclusion, as well as subscribes to the view that deliberative thinking is a central component of task failure (Marcora & Staiano, 2010). Nonetheless, the role of afferent feedback from heart, lungs, and muscles is viewed as independent of perceived effort, and so its role in regulating performance is dismissed (Marcora, 2009, 2010). Indeed, classic work has shown that changes in physiological parameters, such as heart rate and VO2, do not necessarily lead to changes in perceived effort (Davies & Sargeant, 1979; Kamon, Pandolf, & Cafarelli, 1974).

However, it is not the physiological cues that should be dismissed. It is the overemphasis on perceived effort as the motivational basis of endurance that is problematic. Afferent signals have been rejected because they have affective properties, whereas effort is affectively neutral (Marcora, 2009). The properties of effort are not disputed here, but it is precisely the affective properties of physiological cues that make them motivationally salient and central predictors of task disengagement (see Chapter 3, this volume). A focus on effort and a dismissal of affect does not offer a comprehensive description of motivation. The proposed model, therefore, represents a significant challenge to existing views on endurance and a potential step-change in the understanding of human capacity.

It is unlikely that a single physiological parameter causes alterations in motivational phenomena (Hampson, St Clair Gibson, Lambert, & Noakes, 2001). Instead, converging evidence indicates that the brain integrates individual afferents into a collective sensory indicator of homeostatic balance (Critchley & Harrison, 2013). For example, neurons that receive input from different visceral organs all lie in proximity in the nucleus of solitary tract, suggesting early integration of these individual afferent indicators into a composite signal (Paton, Li & Kasparov, 1999). These and other afferents are translated into a one-dimensional hedonic motivational state (Ramirez & Cabanac, 2003). This view has two major implications. First, one must consider the collective emergent properties of these biological pathways; no single individual component causes motivational sensations. Second, the manifestation of the collective afferent signals as a motivational signal is one-dimensional and must consider affective components.

The Motivational Dynamics during Physical Endurance

Based on the above, it is proposed that during endurance activities, the physiological cues and their affective sensations culminate in a one-dimensional motivational state. This can be described as the proximally satisfying (or immediately relieving) desire to restore homeostasis, which cognitively develops to become a temptation to disengage entirely or reduce effort. In other words, humans do not typically attend to homeostasis *per se* but do consider actions to achieve it. It should not go unnoticed at this point that work that has been conducted by neuroanatomists to explain how afferent signals manifest as emotion converge on similar ideas held by psychologists investigating motivational desires. For example, appetitive triggers, such as a deviation from homeostasis during exercise, can be differentiated from the subsequent cognitive elaboration that typically follows (Kavanagh et al., 2005). Scientific efforts in understanding self-regulation also consider a desire to begin as an internal need state, which is processed relatively automatically but then emerges within working memory and cognitively reprocessed (Hofmann & Van Dillen, 2012; Kotabe & Hoffmann, 2015).

In motivation regulation systems the desire is only one pillar of motivation which competes against a distal, deliberative goal. In an endurance activity, the goal could be to win, reach a destination, not embarrass oneself, run a marathon in under two hours, or one of countless others. The specific content of the goal may have worth regarding certain psychological phenomena, such as the long-term durability or fragility of the goal. However, the content of the goal is less important when considering individual endurance bouts, and it is very likely to be idiosyncratic. More important is the motivational magnitude assigned to the goal. In other words, in any single endurance activity, it is not what motivates but how much it motivates. The goal operates as a reference value in a feedback loop, and is compared to the current situation, state, or behavior (Carver, 2006). For example, if the goal is to run a marathon in two hours, this will be compared to inputs from within (e.g. physiological state) and external to the individual (e.g. completed distance) and corrective behavior initiated as necessary (e.g. modify pacing strategy). However, the desire to return to homeostasis or, more specifically, its cognitive manifestation as a temptation to reduce effort represents an incompatible violation of goal pursuit; hence, a desire-goal conflict occurs (Kotabe & Hoffman, 2015).

Desire-goal conflicts are a function of (a) the relative magnitude of the desire and the higher order goal, and (b) the incompatibility between the two (Kotabe & Hofmann, 2015). This desire-goal conflict underpins motivational and self-regulatory decisions during endurance endeavors (Taylor, Boat, & Murphy, 2018) and represents a parsimonious framework that explains how affectively laden proximal desires compete with more deliberative long-term goals to predict endurance. Identification of a desire-goal conflict stimulates the behavioral inhibition system (Gray, 1994) to initiate negative affect (Kurzban, Duckworth, Kable, & Myers, 2013). In endurance situations, this is the recognition that the desire to relieve performance-related discomfort is conflicting with optimal performance. This identification phase initiates subsequent inhibitive responses or behavioral modifications to attempt to resolve the conflict (Tooby, Cosmides, Sell, Lieberman, & Sznycer, 2008). But when the perceived value of the temptation is sufficiently large to override the benefits of persisting, the most consequential modification occurs, namely maximal effort is forsaken (Botvinick & Braver, 2015).

Desire-goal conflicts are a focal point in many life dilemmas, such as healthy versus indulgent food, exercise versus watching TV, and revision versus scrolling through social media (Hofmann, Baumeister, Förster, & Vohs, 2012). In these scenarios, the process of resisting an immediately satisfying desire is associated with increasing negative affect (Saunders & Inzlicht, 2016). This affect is adaptive because without it there would be no signal that goals are at risk of being unfulfilled (Inzlicht & Legault, 2014). This increasingly distressing episode is the primary reason why it becomes progressively harder to resist temptation. However, the objective characteristics of the temptation do not typically change to become harder to resist (e.g. the ingredients of a tempting cake do not change to become more seducing). In contrast, endurance acts are unique because the consequences of resisting the temptation to reduce effort leads to exponential increases in many components of energy metabolism (e.g. lactate concentration, core temperature, heart rate, respiratory frequency). As previously described, these sensations are associated with increasing levels of negative affect (Ekkekakis et al., 2011). Hence, this dynamic state provides a compounding reason to succumb to the temptation, over and above the incremental negative affect associated with the desire-goal conflict itself. In other words, resisting the proximal desire to reduce effort in endurance contexts has a somewhat masochistic component that is absent in other desire-goal scenarios. It is perhaps for this reason that the desire-goal conflict is so salient during feats of endurance performance (Brandstätter & Schüler, 2013). This complex psycho-physiological dynamic is unique and simply applying what we know about the desire-goal conflict in other scenarios may not stand up to scrutiny in endurance contexts. Moreover, the negative affect typically associated with desire-goal conflicts provides negative reinforcement and motivates avoidance of similar scenarios or to alter goals. Many endurance performers, such as athletes and the military, do not have this option available because endurance scenarios are a necessary part of their vocation that cannot be avoided.

The Motivational Antecedent of Desire-Goal Conflicts

Thus far, the focus has been on *in-task* motivational components. In addition, *pre-task* motivational states can direct attentional resources to specific elements of the desire-goal dilemma, and subsequently explain variation in endurance performance. Several existing models of motivation, self-control, or endurance define motivation as the magnitude of effort one is prepared to use on the task (Richter, Gendolla, & Wright, 2016; Marcora, 2010) or to resolve the desire-goal conflict (Kotabe & Hofmann, 2015). In contrast, the present theory aligns with multiple theoretical frameworks to converge on the idea that one's sense of self is a robust and effective motivational foundation of behavior. As such, the extent that the act of enduring is assimilated with the performer's identity can lead to predictable patterns of desire-goal conflict and, therefore, performance.

Over a century ago, William James described how the 'I' perceives the 'Me' as a collection of hypothetical traits and personal experiences (James, 1892/1963). This idea has evolved into the proposal that humans develop knowledge about themselves from tangible personal experiences, but this knowledge is ultimately condensed into broader semantic trait categories (McAdams, 2013). For example, an individual may conclude that they are 'resilient' based on a series of perceived experiences in which they have prevailed despite obstructing circumstances. Over time, these labels persist without requiring access to the individual episodes. Indeed, individuals unable to access episodic memory through injury or neural damage are still able to accurately describe their dispositional characteristics (Klein & Lax, 2010). By adulthood, these semantic labels shape immediate behavior (the self as an 'actor'), future goals, and personal values (the self as an 'agent'), and help integrate past, present, and future selves (the self as an 'author'; McAdams, 2013). The semantic labels that are self-attributed, therefore, represent tremendously powerful motivators of behavior, including acts of endurance performance.

Abstract definitions of identity and sense of self have been developed into more mechanistic theories of motivation. One of the primary reasons for this advancement is the idea that identity-related goals, or 'be' goals, are superordinate compared to other goals, such as goals aimed at 'doing' or 'having'. As such, identity-based goals are often the most valued and durable goals individuals possess (Carver & Scheier, 1998). It is possible to dedicate resources to other types of motives, such as tangible rewards and titles, but they will typically fail when competing against goals that allow individuals to express their true self. The identity-value model, for example, focuses on identity as a vital motivational input of self-control processes (Berkman, Livingston, & Kahn, 2017). The central hypothesis of this model is that identity-relevant behaviors have enhanced value (compared to self-irrelevant behaviors) and, therefore, they are heavily weighted in self-control dilemmas, compared to alternative immediately satisfying behaviors (Berkman, Livingston et al., 2017). In exercise contexts, an individual self-labeled with a 'healthy' identity may assign greater value to taking the stairs compared to taking the less effortful escalator. Thus, all things being equal, the healthy person will be more inclined to take the stairs. The identity-value model is based on complementary areas of research. Social psychologists propose that ascribing greater value to identity-relevant behaviors has the benefit of buffering the self from threats (Sherman & Cohen, 2006) and maintaining self-worth (Crocker & Wolfe, 2001). Neuroscientists have identified that self-related information processing and value computations are related because they both occur in similar areas of the brain, most notably the ventromedial prefrontal cortex (Kim & Johnson, 2015). The enhanced value of identity-relevant tasks leads to greater self-regulation during goal pursuit. For example, performance on a self-regulation task is improved when participants are convinced that the task reflects their own willpower (Magen & Gross, 2007).

A second theory integrating sense of self and motivation is self-determination theory, particularly the sub-theory organismic integration theory (Ryan & Deci, 2017). This perspective concerns the basic human process of internalization, that is, the extent an externally energized activity is assimilated into one's sense of self (Deci, Eghrari, Patrick, & Leone, 1994). Externally regulated activities can be partially transformed into actions that are acknowledged as obligatory but without alignment to one's identity (i.e. introjection; Ryan & Brown, 2003). Alternatively, the act can be aligned with an aspect of one's core sense of self (identification) or, ideally, fully assimilated with all components of the self (integration; Ryan & Deci, 2017). To describe this view with previously used terminology, internalization refers to the extent that individuals' semantic self-labels are attached to the endurance activity. For example, one can pursue a feat of endurance because one's social networks are impressed with the ability to endure, without necessarily subscribing any personal meaning to it (introjection). However, one can engage in an endurance act because it has personal meaning and reflects a 'resilient' character (identification). Finally, demonstrating the ability to endure could be an expression of one's 'dedicated', 'resilient', 'talented', 'athletic' self (integration). All three degrees of internalization can be highly motivating; however, it is identified and especially integrated regulation, collectively termed autonomous motivation, which are associated with high-quality engagement. In the health domain, for example, all three motivational regulations are associated with higher levels of healthy behavior; however, only autonomous forms of motivation were concurrently associated with well-being (Ng et al., 2012). In sport, autonomous motivation has been associated with superior performance (Gillet, Vallerand, Amoura, & Baldes, 2010) and lower symptoms of athlete burnout (Jowett, Hill, Hall, & Curran, 2013). Alternative frameworks adopt a different lexicon to describe autonomous motivation (e.g. 'want to' motivation and self-concordant goal pursuit), but nonetheless view this type of motivation as an optimal driver of well-being and behavior (Sheldon & Elliot, 1999; Werner & Milyavskaya, 2019).

This identity-relevant, autonomously motivated state is critical to endurance and persistence because it triggers important processes with consequences for the desire-goal dilemma. When autonomously motivated, the desire to reduce effort will be incompatible with one's superordinate identity-driven values. This cognitive dissonance is psychologically uncomfortable (Harmon-Jones & Mills, 2019). To necessarily remedy this discord a lower motivational value is assigned to the proximal desire to reduce effort. The ongoing motivational decision to maintain optimal goal pursuit versus reduce effort is, therefore, weighed in favor of the former. This leads to a greater propensity to persist during physically intense activities. It is not suggested that autonomously motivated individuals possess higher self-control and are able to more effectively resist the desire, as this would use considerable resources and be unsustainable over time (Baumeister, 2014; see also Chapter 9, this volume). Instead, autonomous individuals find it easier to resist because the motivational value of the desire is lower. In the same way, autonomous motivation leads to lower attraction to immediately tempting desires that digress from healthy eating and personal life goals, rather than by increasing self-control (Milyavskaya, Inzlicht, Hope, & Koestner, 2015).

Supplementary to the inhibitory effects on the desire to reduce effort, autonomous integration between core values and the endurance act is also proposed to magnify the value of the distal endurance goal during the activity. In this autonomous motivational state, there is concordance between identity and goal; hence, dissonance-based psychological discomfort is absent. The performance goal is positioned at a superordinate level in the motivational systems hierarchy, because it reflects a broad abstract principle of 'being' (Carver & Scheier, 2000). For example, the same endurance goal would be better labeled as an abstract expression of the self (e.g. 'a demonstration of my ability to endure'), than a concrete behavioral act (e.g. 'cycle as long as possible'). A self-concordant goal is activated more efficiently, easier to pursue, and requires less effort (Werner, Milyavskaya, Foxen-Craft, & Koestner, 2016). This allows for greater dedication of cognitive resources toward goal pursuit, which, in turn, leads to greater performance (Ntoumanis et al., 2014). The dual impact of autonomous motivation on the desire to reduce effort and performance goal is proposed to be largely independent, although not mutually exclusive. For example, the activation of the distal valued goal is likely to lead to decreases in proximal temptation-related stimuli (Fishbach & Shah, 2006).

Autonomous motivation is proposed to impact endurance task engagement in a third, albeit distal, way. During endurance tasks, there will be setbacks or disruptions to goal pursuit. This impediment could be an external factor, such as an increase in task difficulty due to the pace in a race suddenly increasing. Autonomously motivated individuals tend to cope and respond better to this type of setback. For example, during an increasingly difficult cycling task, autonomous motivation positively predicted task persistence indirectly via task-based coping (e.g. focusing on optimal effort) and challenge appraisals (viewing the task as a challenge; Ntoumanis et al., 2014). Disruptions may also manifest internally, such as a disturbance to self-regulatory processes. Endurance athletes may err from optimal self-regulation by focusing on negative factors such as fatigue, pain, and discomfort or decreasing pace during an endurance trial (Whitehead et al., 2018). Once more, autonomously motivated individuals are disposed to respond better to these internal self-regulation obstructions. Individuals with a tendency toward autonomous motivation exhibit enhanced brain sensitivity (i.e. error-related negativity) to self-regulation failures (Legault & Inzlicht, 2013). Error-related negativity is observed through electroencephalography (EEG) and is likely generated in the anterior cingulate cortex (Dehaene, Posner, & Tucker, 1994) to signify inconsistency between intended and actual responses (Holroyd & Coles, 2002). This greater sensitivity allows for correction and improved performance. Also using EEG, psychological need fulfillment, which is a precursive ingredient for autonomous motivation, has been shown to enhance participants' responsivity and processing of events that challenge decision making (Di Domenico, Le, Liu, Ayaz, & Fournier, 2016).

At a more conscious level of analysis, autonomously motivated individuals typically perceive self-regulation disruptions as lower threats to self and adaptively respond to such disruptions (Hodgins & Knee, 2002), even if disruptions are attributed internally (Hodgins, 2008). For example, in imagined predicaments that led to a reprimand, autonomous individuals were less defensive and more willing to apologize when mildly or moderately reproached, compared to controlled motivation participants (Hodgins & Liebeskind, 2003). Applying these principles to endurance activities, autonomous motivation is expected to facilitate greater response to self-regulatory and behavioral errors, which subsequently enables more efficient and effective performance.

Initial Direct Evidence of the Motivational Model

In the section above, several working hypotheses have been presented concerning the different components of pre-task and in-task motivation and how they influence the ability to endure. It is assumed that some motivational principles are generalizable across contexts, for example, we see no reason why autonomous motivation biases attentional processes in other domains but not in the endurance domain. Nonetheless, the evidence presented so far has been indirect and a direct assessment of these predictions has been absent from the discussion. This omission is rectified below.

To better understand the motivational dynamics outlined in this chapter and displayed in Figure 7.1, two studies involved participants engaging in a ten-minute self-paced cycling trial (Taylor, Smith, & Hunte, 2020). In the first study, participants were required to complete an increasingly difficult fitness test to establish the maximum power output they could sustain before voluntary exhaustion. Then, in the principal phase of the experiment, participants were required to maintain an unrealistically high intensity (90% of their maximum power output obtained in the preliminary test). If participants were to fall below the threshold, they were to continue cycling at a self-selected intensity, with the overall goal to try and cycle as far as possible. In line with goal setting experiments (Landers, Bauer, & Callan, 2017), the relevance of the goal was enhanced by instructing participants that their performance would be entered onto a leaderboard alongside other participants and they

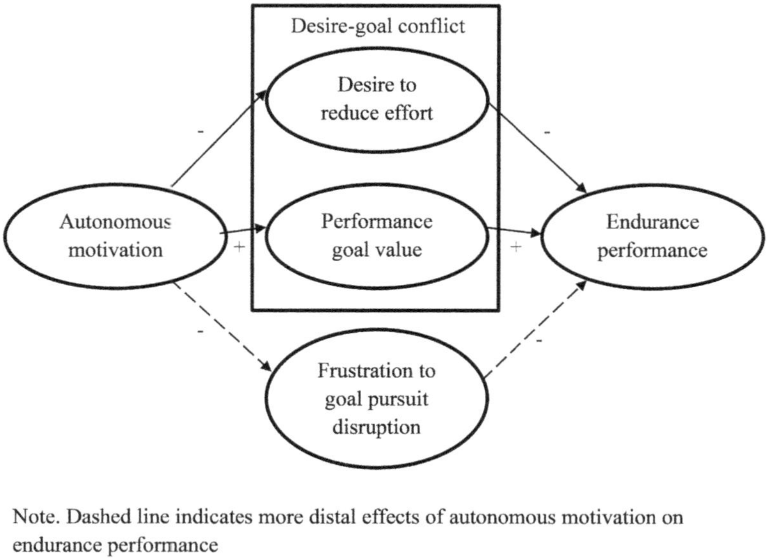

FIGURE 7.1 A motivation process model of endurance performance.

were requested to set a target position on the leaderboard. Participants' temptation to reduce effort and goal value was measured every minute throughout the cycling task.

The motivational trajectories of the temptation to reduce effort and the competing performance goal were observed to be non-linear. Specifically, the temptation to reduce effort followed a cubic trend, in which the temptation increased rapidly in early phases, stabilized somewhat in the mid-section, and accelerated again as the end of the trial approached. This trajectory is coherent with the power output curve typically observed in self-paced endurance tests (Jeukendrup, Hopkins, Aragón-Vargas, & Hulston, 2008), which implies at least a synchronized, if not causal, relationship with objective effort and associated physiological consequences. In contrast, the motivational importance of the goal was shown to decrease across the trial, but this decline decelerated across the trial. This implies that a motivational crisis (Brandstätter & Schüler, 2013) can occur in the early stages of high-intensity endurance activity. Indeed, motivational episodes that occur during early phases of endurance trials may have important consequences for later stages (Boat, Taylor, & Hulston, 2017). This implies that the investigation of task failure or end performance should consider the preceding motivational dynamics. In combination, the patterns of the temptation to reduce effort and the value of the distal goal echo broader principles outlined in previous work. That is, competing goals and desires are dynamic during broad decision-making processes (Berkman, Livingston et al., 2017; Johnson & Ratcliff, 2014), as well as more specific fatiguing tasks (St Clair Gibson et al., 2018).

Of course, these patterns mean little if they cannot explain variation in endurance performance. In Taylor and colleagues' (2020) first cycling study, the rate of increase in temptation to reduce effort was consistent across participants, irrespective of performance. What was able to distinguish between high and low performances was the temptation at the beginning of the trial. Poorer performers began the task with a higher temptation to reduce effort. This finding implies that poorer performers possessed anticipatory motivation prejudiced toward hedonic desires, such as discomfort avoidance, rather than relatively distal goals (Braver, 2012). This tendency toward short-term protective mechanisms may be the cognitive underpinning of a greater temptation to reduce effort, altering the start point of the inevitable increase in temptation to reduce effort, rather than the rate at which the temptation manifests.

The same study revealed a different pattern regarding the value of the performance goal. High and low performers reported similar goal importance at the beginning of the trial; however, high performers maintained goal value (or at least slowed the reduction in goal value) more effectively than lower performers. On the one hand, the greater reduction in goal value for poorer performers could be viewed as self-worth protection if performance is perceived to be going awry. The relatively low importance of the goal (doing well on a leader board) may have also led to greater fragility in goal pursuit in low performers. Indeed, cognitive disengagement can have benefits when the goal is perceived to be out of reach (Wrosch, Scheier, Miller, Schulz, & Carver, 2003). On the other hand, high performers may be more effective in mobilizing goal-driven reactive attentional processes in the face of increasing interference from hedonistic homeostatic desires (Jacoby, Kelley, & McElree, 1999).

The predictive worth of temptation and goal value was also observed in the second of the two cycling studies (Taylor et al., 2020, Study 2). Rather than continual assessment of temptation and goal value, the second study measured temptation and goal value at the midpoint of the trial. After controlling for pre-task autonomous motivation, greater temptation to reduce effort was associated with lower endurance performance and the importance of the performance goal positively predicted performance. Thus, two studies provide evidence that the competing temptation to reduce effort and value of performance goal help explain endurance performance.

The hypothesis that autonomously motivated participants would report lower temptation to reduce effort and higher goal value during endurance activity was also evidenced in both studies. Study 1 additionally demonstrated that temptation to reduce effort increased at a reduced rate during the trial in autonomously motivated individuals, compared to low-autonomous individuals. During a high-intensity activity, attention is dominated by psycho-physiological sensations (Hutchinson & Tenenbaum, 2007). It is unlikely that autonomous individuals possess a superior ability to actively ignore the incremental development of these sensations, because doing so would require considerable cognitive resources (Maranges & Baumeister, 2016). This conclusion would misalign with the view that autonomous goal pursuit is relatively effortless (Ryan & Deci, 2017) and not underpinned by increased self-control strength (Milyavskaya et al., 2015). More likely, autonomously motivated individuals evaluate the uncomfortable sensations as a necessary aspect of completing the objective; therefore, they are less tempted to reduce effort and modify the sensations. Non-autonomous individuals do not make this connection between the sensations and goal. Not only does this view align with self-determination theory, but structural perspectives of motivation propose a fusion of action (e.g. managing sensations) and goal (e.g. to complete the objective) to be necessary for optimal persistence (Kruglanski et al., 2018).

Autonomously motivated individuals also reported the performance goal to be more important, compared to participants lower in autonomous motivation. This was expected, given that correspondence between identity-based values and the endurance task leads to the performance goal being highly valued (Carver & Scheier, 2000). Despite autonomous goals being easier to pursue (Werner et al., 2016), the rate of decline in goal importance across the trial was consistent for autonomous and non-autonomous participants. That is, integration between core motivational values and endurance activity impacts on initial appraisals of goal importance, rather than disturbing goal dynamics during performance. Preemptive motivational processes may be predisposed toward distal valued goals in autonomously motivated individuals (Braver, 2012).

In the second cycling study, the level of intensity that participants were required to sustain was unexpectedly increased halfway through the trial, and degree of frustration with this disruption to goal pursuit was measured. Evidence was found for the hypothesis that autonomously motivated participants responded with less frustration following disruptions to goal pursuit (Taylor et al., 2020; Study 2). This mechanism may exert a less direct impact upon performance in comparison to the temptation to reduce effort and the performance goal. Nonetheless, emotional regulation is an important competency during performance at high physical intensity (McCormick, Meijen, Anstiss & Massey, 2018). That said, due to the measure of frustration occurring at the end of the cycling task in the study by Taylor and colleagues, it cannot be ruled out that a poor performance outcome led to enhanced frustration, rather than underlying autonomous motivation. A more precise measure of frustration toward a specific event is required in future work.

Further Developing and Testing the Motivational Model

In the preceding sections, a new model of motivational processes during endurance performance has been proposed (see also Figure 7.1). The model builds on several other theoretical perspectives of motivation, self-control, endurance, and fatigue. Direct evidence from two studies (Taylor et al., 2020) builds upon generalizable principles of motivation and evidence from a variety of scientific disciplines. It is hoped that the framework articulated in this chapter stimulates theorizing and empirical examination that will afford a greater understanding of endurance and persistence. With this aim in mind, some potential lines of investigation are proposed below.

From a broad perspective, there are other models of human endurance that have not yet been compared to the present framework but could provide additional insight into the human capacity to endure. The present model considers how autonomous motivation diverts attentional resources away from the desire to reduce effort and toward goal pursuit. Existing models focused on attentional processes, therefore, have significant potential to develop our understanding. For example, a metacognitive framework of attentional focus (Brick, MacIntyre, & Campbell, 2016) may help identify precisely how autonomously motivated individuals manage the dual reflective and proactive attentional resources during endurance tasks. It is possible that autonomously motivated athletes possess better metacognitive skills (i.e. planning, monitoring, and evaluating goal pursuit; Brick, MacIntyre, & Campbell, 2015), relative to non-autonomous athletes. For example, implementation intentions can downplay the positive affect associated with giving in to temptation (Hofmann, Deutsch, Lancaster, & Banaji, 2010) and therefore may explain why autonomous motivation was associated with lower temptation at the beginning of endurance tasks.

In the present model, affect is proposed to cognitively manifest as a desire to reduce effort, but affect does not play a central role in the model itself. In contrast, Venhorst, Micklewright, and Noakes (2017) propose a three-dimensional model of exercise regulation, in which core affect also plays a central role in triggering approach and avoidance motivational tendencies. Venhorst and colleagues also describe action crises, in which athletes are caught in a dilemma between goal pursuit and disengagement (Brandstätter & Schüler, 2013). Evidently, this theory shares several common features with the model presented in this chapter, and amalgamating insights from both frameworks to develop experiments would be fruitful. The physiological underpinning of affective states and how this impacts the desire-goal conflict also represents an exciting avenue for future endeavor. Specifically, the relationship between temptation and goal value and underlying metabolic parameters, such as levels of blood lactate accumulation, is underexplored. These physiological cues could plausibly act as motivational inputs to the desire-goal conflict. The interface of motivation and metabolism and other physiological sub-disciplines is only just beginning to be explored but could be particularly interesting for other psychobiological models of endurance and fatigue (St Clair Gibson et al., 2018).

One theory deserves special attention because it has significant implications for explaining how the desire-goal conflict can be manipulated to enhance human endurance. Outside of endurance contexts, the most effective strategy to resist a desire is to avoid it and circumvent a desire-goal conflict. If you don't want to eat candy, don't go near the candy shop. This tactic does not apply to endurance because it is impossible to succeed in this scenario without some discomfort and urge for homeostasis, hence a desire-goal conflict is inevitable. Yet, it may be possible to delay or lower the desire-goal conflict through means-end fusion (Kruglanski et al., 2018). Means-end fusion typically refers to blending a behavioral act, such as exercising, with an end-goal, such as getting fit. The act of dieting to reach the goal of losing weight would be another common example. However, the focal activity could also be the cognitive process of handling the desire to reduce effort. In endurance contexts, the act of resisting the temptation to reduce effort could be fused with the goal of optimal performance. In other words, perceiving optimal performance and resisting temptation as integrated parts of the same entity would lead to a lower conflict between the two and greater persistence.

Means-end fusion has four antecedents. First, *repeated coupling* of action and goal is necessary. Based on the Gestalt principle of common fate (Campbell, 1958), if an athlete repeatedly experiences the act of resisting the temptation leading to successful completion of the objective, this will lead to fusion of act and objective and greater persistence. How this process is facilitated by, or interacts with, autonomous motivation is currently unknown. Autonomously motivated athletes could simply engage with endurance activity to a greater extent, and so the repeated coupling process is expediated. Repeated coupling could naturally occur with experience, given the appropriate environmental supports. Hence, a reverse process may occur in which successfully coupling activity and goal may enhance competence, a necessary precursor to autonomous motivation (Ryan & Deci, 2017).

Activity-goal fusion can be also be facilitated through a *unique bond* between activity and goal. In other words, there exists a perception that the only way to achieve the goal of optimal performance is through the cognitive act of resisting the temptation to reduce effort. Other options, such as strategy and tactics to outwit opponents, are viewed as inadequate or futile. Sports with limited interaction with opponents, such as pursuit track cycling and rowing, may be particularly acquiescent to this process. When participants were asked to generate two options for achieving a goal, they reported experiencing less positive affect and less commitment pursuing the goal, compared to when one option was generated

(Fishbach, Shah, & Kruglanski, 2004, Study 1). At first glance, this may seem to conflict with autonomous motivation, which is sometimes viewed to be underpinned by choice (Cordova & Lepper, 1996). Nonetheless, choice may not be as important for autonomous regulation as an internal locus of causality and volition (Reeve, Nix, & Hamm, 2003). One can be autonomously motivated without choice if there exists an unpressured willingness to engage. Teasing out the compatibility between volition and uniqueness is an interesting avenue for future research.

The Gestalt idea of *proximity* (Helson, 1933) has led to the idea that contiguity between activity completion and goal attainment also creates fusion and persistence (Kruglanski et al., 2018). In three studies, when individuals perceived benefits of a task as immediate, compared to delayed, they reported the activity as more enjoyable, interesting, and fun (Woolley & Fishbach, 2017). These affects are prototypical responses to intrinsic motivation (Ryan & Deci, 2017) and people persist longer when they hold such sentiment toward the activity (Jõesaar, Hein, & Hagger, 2011). Woolley and Fishbach's fourth study confirmed this assumption by demonstrating that children read for longer when rewards were immediate, as opposed to delayed rewards. Receiving an immediate signal (i.e. knowledge of successful performance) that resisting the desire to reduce effort has helped achieve the goal may have benefits for the development of autonomous motivation, compared to receiving delayed feedback.

The final antecedent of fusion is *similarity*, taken from the Gestalt principle that alike components convey the existence of a relationship between them, creating a perception that they are unified (Campbell, 1958). When participants possessed a goal of improving performance on a computer game, they were more interested when the game was described as a game of skill, compared to when it was described as a fantasy game. This implies that the similarity between activity (game of skill) and goal (enhanced performance) increased interest, relative to dissimilar activity (playing a fantasy game; Sansone, Sachau, & Weir, 1989). Semantically describing cognitive processes in line with performance goal may have similar consequences for the capacity to endure (e.g. the activity of cognitive endurance and the goal of physical endurance). Overall, means-end fusion can delay or modify the desire-goal conflict so that persistence is optimized. This can potentially be facilitated by, and facilitate, autonomous motivation in a mutual relationship. The combining of these two motivational perspectives uncovers a vast number of options for further investigation.

Complementing these broader theoretical suggestions, more specific work building on the foundations laid by Taylor and colleagues (2020) is needed. For instance, the measures employed to measure temptation and goal value were based on previous examinations of desire strength using a single item (Hofmann et al., 2012), albeit with increased response options to maximize sensitivity to change over the endurance trials. To a degree, the study validates the measures because they are associated with other variables in theoretically expected ways (i.e. nomological validity). However, it is acknowledged that future validation of these temptation and goal measures is required. Other methods could also be employed. For example, greater theta-wave activity in the brain represents a neural manifestation of attempts to persist toward a goal (i.e. to endure) at the expense of natural tendencies (i.e. desire to reduce effort; Cavanagh & Frank, 2014). Thus, EEG, which has been successfully employed in endurance contexts (Enders et al., 2016), could measure theta-wave activity in the midfrontal cortex area of the brain as an indicator of desire-goal *conflict*, which would complement measurements of desire and goal *value*. There is limited foundation for assuming that the desire-goal conflict at low absolute levels of value (e.g. a score of two versus three on an arbitrary scale) would function similarly as the same degree of conflict at high levels (e.g. eight versus nine). EEG would also enable comparison of desire-goal conflict at basic levels of human functioning versus overt processes and be employed in exploratory work to identify yet unknown patterns of neural activity during desire-goal dilemmas.

The observed patterns in the desire to reduce effort and performance goal may seem like opposing sides of the same coin (as one rises, the other one declines). However, this relationship is improbable in other circumstances when the value of both motivational components is considerable, such as life-threatening survival situations or the final of a global competition. There is little doubt that the absolute magnitude of desire and goal value will be idiosyncratic to the task and goal under scrutiny. Nonetheless, some generalizations may be discovered about their relativity. For example, temptation may need to exceed goal value by predictable amounts to cause a reduction in physical effort or task cessation (i.e. decision thresholds; Berkman, Hutcherson et al., 2017). Alternatively, rates of change in desire may be predictable as a function of the competing goal, and vice versa. The temptation to reduce effort may increase more rapidly when the outcome goal is low.

To further examine the generalizability of desire-goal value patterns, other endurance scenarios should be examined. In the two cycling studies (Taylor et al., 2020), a discrete task with a known endpoint was used. What if the individual is required to persist for an unknown time? Unknown task durations may lead to the adoption of more conservative approaches (Baumeister, Vohs, & Tice, 2007), hence, lower desires to reduce effort may also occur. Alternatively, unknown task characteristics could lead to greater evaluation of threat and self-protection forming the basis of higher desires and lower goal value, or a lower required desire for task disengagement. Lower intensity scenarios would lead to participants not exerting effort at suitable intensities to cross physiological thresholds (i.e. lactate threshold and critical power). As a result, the desire to reduce effort may be underpinned to a greater extent by boredom and the appeal of alternative activities, rather than affectively labeled physiological cues. Time-to-exhaustion tests, where participants continue to work until they can no longer continue, may also impact the generalizability of trends. These differences in task characteristics should not be viewed only as methodological considerations, but also interesting conceptual avenues to analyze desire and goal patterns.

The third mechanism presumed to be facilitated by autonomous motivation was lower frustration in response to setbacks. The implication is that this response could also enhance endurance performance, however, frustration was measured after the trial by Taylor et al. (2020). This design defect prevented tests of indirect effects because the mediator (frustration) was measured after the outcome (performance). Moreover, the focus of participants' frustration may not have been the disruption to goal pursuit, but the performance itself. Hence, the relationship could be the reverse as to what is hypothesized in this chapter. Future work should examine frustration or other responses (such as anger, focus, and flow) to self-regulatory setbacks during the endurance trial.

The field of endurance science would be helped by more precise distinguishing between different types of activity. There do seem important differences between activities where performance is largely governed by neuromuscular or biomechanical factors (e.g. repeated quadricep leg extensions) versus those dominated by aerobic sensations (e.g. endurance cycling or running). Perceptions of pain may play a differing role in these activities, with a greater role possibly in the former type of activity. Different types of disengagement may also be an interesting avenue. Burnley and Jones (2017) refer to task failure as 'the point at which a participant is unwilling or unable to continue a physical task' (p. 1). It may be worth distinguishing between willingness and ability to continue as, from a motivational perspective, these significantly differ in their underlying mechanisms. To some extent, this is a motivational scientist joining a party when not invited. This existing definition is acceptable if researchers wish to examine the point at which activity ceases, as many people do. It is not adequate, however, if the desire is to explain why people stop. The present model considers the moment of task cessation to be determined by a preceding process, rather than any single moment in time. Definitions that emphasize a point in time may inadvertently shine the light on motivational factors only at that point. This makes it difficult to appropriately separate the absolute limit of physiological capability and motivational decision making because of their temporal proximity at severe intensities of activity.

Equally, there may be worthwhile distinctions between complete disengagement (i.e. task failure) and partial disengagement (reduction in effort). The motivational model presented here has not been examined in the context of task failure, even though similar patterns are expected. If one can tolerate higher intensities during a fixed-time challenge, then one might assume that people can last longer until voluntary exhaustion. Future research needs to explicitly focus on task failure, goal failure, task behavioral disengagement, or disengagement as a coping strategy (e.g. reducing effort, lower pace).

Summary

The present chapter describes a motivational model of human endurance, in which a desire to reduce effort in order to maintain homeostasis and avoid discomfort competes against the deliberative objective of the endurance activity. The conflict between these two motivational pillars is dynamic and can explain variation in endurance performance. This perspective is distinct from other models of human endurance because (a) it considers deliberative motivation as an essential component of endurance, and (b) it embraces the role of affect as a manifestation of physiological cues in motivational decision making. The model further considers pre-task motivational states as an important foundation that desire-goal dynamics are built upon. This motivational state reflects the degree that the endurance activity is congruent with the sense of self (i.e. autonomous motivation). Emphasis is placed on this phenomenon because sense of self represents a superordinate motive in human goal systems hierarchy (Carver, 2006). Two studies are presented as initial evidence of this motivational model, but these hopefully signal the beginning of scientific scrutiny. There are several models of motivation and human endurance that emphasize different components of the capacity to endure that the present model does not. Hence, a multi-theory perspective seems worthwhile.

8

THE STRENGTH MODEL OF SELF-CONTROL

Chris Englert

Introduction

In sport and exercise contexts, it is highly important to volitionally control one's impulses in order to achieve long-term goals (Audiffren & André, 2015). Oftentimes, the satisfaction of immediate desires leads to short-term benefits, while striving for and achieving long-term goals might lead to longer-lasting satisfaction (Hagger, Wood, Stiff, & Chatzisarantis, 2009). For instance, if an athlete has the long-term goal of winning a boxing match, he or she has to work out on a regular basis. Along the way, there are several temptations, for instance, hanging out with friends, which seem tempting in a given moment and might lead to immediate pleasure (c.f. Baumeister & Heatherton, 1996). However, following these impulses might interfere with the long-term goal, consequently leading to a goal conflict. Therefore, the athlete has to resist the urge to hang out with friends, which allows him or her to work out and train, and potentially win the boxing match. However, under what circumstances can we resist temptations, desires, or impulses and under what conditions do we fail to control ourselves? In the present chapter, the focus will be on the strength model of self-control in order to explain lapses in self-control (Baumeister, Heatherton, & Tice, 1994).

The Strength Model of Self-Control

In the mid-20th century, Hull postulated that dominant response tendencies possess some sort of motivational strength, which almost forces one to follow the respective impulses (Hull, 1943). It has been suggested that if an individual wants to override the respective predominant impulses, it is necessary to invest some sort of volitional strength (Baumeister, Bratslavsky, Muraven, & Tice, 1998). Baumeister and colleagues (1998) argue that there is a central self-control strength that helps us to volitionally control ourselves. This strength energizes all acts of self-control, for instance, resisting the impulse to interrupt an exhausting task, controlling negative emotions, or selectively regulating one's attention (for an overview of tasks requiring self-control strength, see Baumeister, Vohs, & Tice, 2007). So what is self-control—which has also been referred to as self-regulation, self-discipline, willpower, effortful control, ego strength, or inhibitory control (Duckworth & Kern, 2011)? Baumeister and colleagues (2007) define self-control as "the capacity for altering one's own responses, especially to bring them into line with standards such as ideals, values, morals, and social expectations, and to support the pursuit of long-term goals" (p. 351). Based on this definition, it can be concluded that self-control processes come into play when an individual has to control a certain response he/she *wants* to display in the given moment and instead show another response that enables him or her to strive for a more meaningful long-term goal (Hagger, Wood, Stiff, & Chatzisarantis, 2010a). The problem is, however, that most of the time this alternative response will not lead to immediate gratification or reward, which makes it less attractive in the given moment and might eventually lead to lapses in self-control (Baumeister et al., 1998). The strength model of self-control differentiates between trait self-control strength and state self-control strength to explain self-control behaviors (Tangney, Baumeister, & Boone, 2004).

Trait Self-Control Strength

Some individuals are generally better at controlling their impulses than others, which can be explained by focusing on differences in their trait self-control strength (Tangney et al., 2004). For instance, some individuals might have negative attitudes toward strenuous physical exercises or simply do not like the idea of being on an indoor treadmill in a packed gym (Englert & Rummel, 2016; Pfeffer & Strobach, 2017; Schöndube, Bertrams, Sudeck, & Fuchs, 2017). In these cases, to follow the long-term goal of getting in better shape (e.g., negative emotions, negative attitudes) need to be volitionally overridden. One of the most influential studies on trait self-control strength is the so-called Marshmallow Test by Walter Mischel (even though Mischel labeled this phenomenon as *delay of gratification*; Mischel, 1961). There are several different setups of this experiment, but in its most "traditional" form, a child is seated in front of a table on which a tempting piece of candy is presented. The child is then informed that the experimenter has to leave the lab for an undisclosed amount of time and that the child can either consume the candy right away or wait until the experimenter gets back to the lab. In the latter case, the child will get two pieces of candy. Therefore, the child can choose between a smaller, immediate reward and a larger, but delayed reward. In a series of longitudinal studies, Mischel and colleagues have reliably shown that the ability to resist the candy as a child is significantly positively related to several beneficial outcomes years later (Mischel, Shoda, & Rodriguez, 1989; for a critical discussion, see Watts, Duncan, & Quan, 2018). For example, longer delay of gratification durations have been related to a healthier lifestyle (Davis, Patte, Curtis, & Reid, 2010), higher academic achievements (Evans & Rosenbaum, 2008), or a lower body mass index years later (Schlam, Wilson, Shoda, Mischel, & Ayduk, 2013). So how are delay of gratification and trait self-control strength interrelated, or are they actually capturing an identical psychological construct? Duckworth and colleagues conducted two studies to address this question and found that students' ability to delay gratification was positively related to concurrent teacher ratings (Study 1), as well as parent and caregiver ratings (Study 2), of students' general self-control abilities but not with other personality traits, intelligence, or reward-related impulses (Duckworth, Tsukayama, & Kirby, 2013). Therefore, being able to delay immediate gratification and reward seems to be closely related to trait self-control strength (see also Duckworth & Seligman, 2017).

How to Measure Trait Self-Control Strength

To investigate the relationship between trait self-control strength and sport and exercise performance, it is highly important to first apply reliable psychometric measures. According to Duckworth and Kern (2011), there are more than 100 self-report questionnaires on self-control, with most questionnaires focusing on specific behaviors and/or specific populations. Given that the strength model assumes that trait self-control strength energizes all acts of self-control—meaning that one's self-control strength is not domain-specific—the most frequently used self-report instrument of trait self-control strength is the *Brief Self-Control Scale* (BSCS), which is a short version of the 25-item *Self-Control Scale* (SCS) (Tangney et al., 2004; for a recent meta-analysis on the validity of the most frequently used self-control questionnaires, see Duckworth & Kern, 2011). The BSCS is a one-dimensional scale that consists of 13 items to be answered on five-point Likert-type scales (1—*not at all* to 5—*very much*). The BSCS has been successfully translated into several languages (Bertrams & Dickhäuser, 2009) and has been validated by numerous researchers (Finkenauer, Engels, & Baumeister, 2005; see also De Ridder, Lensvelt-Mulders, Finkenauer, Stok, & Baumeister, 2012). Furthermore, the reliability and test-retest reliability have been empirically demonstrated in two large studies by Tangney and colleagues (2004; for a critical discussion, see also Fullerton, Lane, Nevill, & Devonport, 2018).

However, Stork, Graham, Bray, and Martin Ginis (2016) argue that self-report measures can be biased by socially desirable answering (see also Fisher & Katz, 2000). Therefore, the authors suggest also administering objective measures of trait self-control strength, for instance, the isometric handgrip test (Bray, Martin Ginis, Hicks, & Woodgate, 2008; Brown & Bray, 2017a). Participants are asked to squeeze the isometric handgrip at 50% maximum voluntary contraction for as long as possible. As the task becomes more tiring and painful over time, Bray and colleagues (2008) conclude that self-control strength is necessary to inhibit the urge to stop the task prematurely. It is assumed that longer squeezing durations are indicative of higher trait self-control strength (Baumeister et al., 2007). Stork and colleagues (2016) report strong correlations between the BSCS and the isometric handgrip test, delivering support for the assumption that both measures assess trait self-control strength (for a discussion, see also Allom, Panetta, Mullan, & Hagger, 2016).

Trait Self-Control Strength and Performance

High levels of trait self-control strength are related to a wide range of behaviors. In general, it has been empirically shown that individuals with higher levels of trait self-control strength are more adept at controlling their impulses, attention, thoughts, and emotions (for a meta-analysis, see DeRidder et al., 2012). More specifically, trait self-control strength is, among others, positively related to psychological well-being and academic success (Tangney et al., 2004) and negatively related to procrastination, obesity, and substance abuse (Baumeister & Heatherton, 1996; see also Hagger et al., 2010a). As Boat and Cooper (2019) explain, high levels of trait self-control strength are beneficial to almost all aspects of behavior that contribute to a successful and healthy life. In sport and exercise, it has been reliably shown that trait self-control strength is an important predictor for several outcome measures (for an overview, see Englert, 2016, 2017). In the following sections, the focus will be on the importance of trait self-control strength in exercisers, followed by a closer look at the impact of trait self-control strength on performance in professional athletes.

Trait Self-Control Strength in Exercisers

Even though most individuals are aware of the long-term benefits of regular physical exercise and even have the intention to work out regularly, they fail to translate their intentions into actual exercise behavior (Rhodes & de Bruijn, 2013a). This gap has been termed the *intention-behavior gap* (Sheeran & Webb, 2016). Over the years, several influential models of exercise adherence have been developed, and several psychological predictors have been identified (for an overview, see Rhodes & Dickau, 2013; see also Chapters 2 and 4). In contrast to earlier theoretical models, which assumed that exercise intentions trigger exercise behavior (e.g. Theory of Planned Behavior; Ajzen, 1991; for a meta-analysis, see also Hausenblas, Carron, & Mack, 1997), there is a general agreement among researchers today that even the strongest intentions might sometimes fail and that intentions alone cannot explain behavior (Sniehotta, Presseau, & Araújo-Soares, 2014). Recently, it has been reliably shown that self-control processes (Brand & Ekkekakis, 2018; de Bruin et al., 2012) and especially trait self-control strength are significantly related to the intention-behavior gap (Englert & Rummel, 2016; Pfeffer & Strobach, 2017; Schöndube et al., 2017). As discussed in the earlier parts of this chapter, working out in the gym or going for a run on a regular basis can oftentimes be associated with negative thoughts, negative emotions, or even painful or tiring experiences that are not pleasant (Martin Ginis & Bray, 2010). To focus on the long-term benefits of regular exercise (e.g. health), it is important to inhibit the impulse of stopping the unpleasant experience prematurely (Hagger, 2010, 2014). In a study by Bertrams and Englert (2013), individuals were asked to indicate how often they intended to work out during the next two weeks. After two weeks, they reported their actual workout behavior and their trait self-control strength. As expected, the intention-behavior gap was significantly smaller in individuals with higher levels of trait self-control strength. Adding to these findings, Crescioni et al. (2011) conducted a 12-week weight loss program and found that individuals with higher levels of trait self-control ate fewer calories, worked out more, and lost more weight during the program than individuals with lower trait self-control strength levels. Ntoumanis (2014) argues that trait self-control strength is particularly important during stressful episodes. For instance, after a busy and stressful day at work, one has to suppress the desire to relax on the sofa and visit the gym instead. Gerber and colleagues (2015) found support for this assumption in a ten-month longitudinal study, as higher levels of trait self-control strength protected exercise-related intentions even in highly stressful situations (see also Englert & Rummel, 2016; Pfeffer, Englert, & Mueller-Alcazar, 2020). These findings further foster the assumption that trait self-control strength is an important predictor of health behaviors in general and specifically exercise adherence.

Trait Self-Control Strength in Professional Athletes

To become a professional athlete, individuals have to make a great deal of sacrifices, for instance, attending training sessions instead of meeting up with friends (Tedesqui & Young, 2017). It is also important to note that only a small percentage of athletes manage to achieve their dreams of becoming professional. Haugaasen and Jordet (2012) reported that only about 0.3% of the registered male soccer players worldwide attain a professional status, highlighting that youth players should not only focus on soccer training but also on their academic career. Furthermore, while aiming to become a professional athlete, there might be several setbacks along the way (e.g. injuries), meaning that it is necessary to manage negative emotions. These are just some examples of the many self-control demands that need to be handled by young athletes as the road to success oftentimes is a rocky one (Wolff, Bertrams, & Schüler, 2019). Several studies have delivered empirical evidence that trait self-control strength is an important antecedent for a professional sports career (Bartulovic, Young, & Baker, 2017). For instance, Wolff and colleagues measured trait self-control strength in German youth football players competing for a roster spot on a national talent development program and found that the players who were selected displayed higher levels of trait self-control strength than their non-selected peers (Wolff et al., 2019). In the same vein, a study comparing professional with recreational road cyclists revealed that professional road cyclists displayed higher levels of trait self-control strength (Martin et al., 2016). Toering and Jordet (2015) conducted a study with professional soccer players representing the first team of every club in the Norwegian Premier and Second Leagues. The results indicated that higher levels of trait self-control strength were positively associated with daily football practice, ample sleep at night, and football performance (i.e. players with higher trait self-control strength were more likely to have senior national team experience), while it was negatively related to watching TV, using the Internet, gaming, and being with friends. Interestingly, overall, the sample of this study had significantly higher levels of trait self-control strength than the general population. Taken together, the findings presented above suggest that trait self-control strength supports individuals in staying on track and achieving their dreams of becoming a professional athlete (Bartulovic et al., 2017). However, it is important to note that while trait self-control strength is a relatively stable personality trait, there are ways to improve self-control performance (Baumeister, Gailliot, DeWall, & Oaten, 2006). These self-control strategies will be briefly presented in the final parts of this chapter and in more detail in Chapter 12. It should also be mentioned that several researchers emphasize the importance of letting go of one's sport every once in a while and enjoying free time with family and friends (Balk & Englert, 2020; Gould, Moffett, & Diefenbach, 2002; Gustafson, Hassmèn, Kenttä, & Johansson, 2008). Otherwise, the sport itself might become less joyful and lead to a higher number of dropouts, especially in youth teams.

Ego Depletion (State Self-Control Strength)

Apart from one's general self-control skills, individuals might also differ in their level of momentarily available self-control strength (Tangney et al., 2004). Baumeister and colleagues (2007) compare self-control strength with a human muscle, which can become temporarily exhausted after having been used in a preceding task and is not immediately replenished. This state of temporary self-control strength exhaustion is called *ego depletion*. It has been demonstrated in several studies that individuals display impaired self-control performance if they had been working on another self-control task beforehand (Dang, 2018; Hagger et al., 2010b).

How to Investigate and Measure the Ego Depletion Effect

In experiments on ego depletion, researchers oftentimes apply the two-task paradigm (Muraven, Tice, & Baumeister, 1998). Participants are randomly assigned to an ego depletion condition or a control condition and start working on a similar first task (e.g. transcribing a neutral text on a separate sheet of paper; Bertrams, Englert, & Dickhäuser, 2010). The task requirements are comparable in both conditions; however, the task requires self-control strength in the ego depletion condition (i.e. omitting certain letters while transcribing the text), whereas it does not require self-control strength in the control condition (i.e. transcribing the text conventionally). Consequently, self-control strength should become temporarily exhausted in the ego depletion condition, while it should remain relatively intact in the control condition. Afterward, all participants work on an identical secondary task requiring self-control strength. It is assumed and has been empirically supported that performance in the secondary task is significantly worse for participants in the ego depletion condition compared to the control condition (Dang, 2018; Hagger et al., 2010b). A self-control task that is often used within the two-task paradigm is the Stroop task (Stroop, 1935). In the Stroop task, participants are instructed to name the font color of a series of color words as quickly and as accurately as possible. These color words are written either in the same color font as the word (e.g. "green" written in green font color; congruent trial) or in another color (e.g. "green" written in yellow font color; incongruent trial). In general, it requires more self-control strength if the color word and the font color do not match as the semantic meaning of the word needs to be ignored (Muraven et al., 1998). The Stroop task has been frequently used in sport and exercise research and is a reliable self-control task (Bray, Martin Ginis, & Woodgate, 2011; Englert & Wolff, 2015; for an overview, see also Brown et al., 2019).

To measure the level of temporarily available self-control strength, Ciarocco and colleagues developed the State Self-Control Capacity Scale (SSCCS; Ciarocco, Twenge, Muraven, & Tice, 2007), which has been successfully applied by numerous researchers (Christian & Ellis, 2011) and translated into several languages (Bertrams, Unger, & Dickhäuser, 2011). The SSCCS is a one-dimensional scale consisting of 25 items in its long version and 10 items in its short version (sample item: *"I feel exhausted"*). Each item has to be answered on a seven-point Likert-type scale in regard to how the individual feels at the moment (1—*not true* to 7—*very true*). Both the long and short versions of the SSCCS have been employed in the context of sports on several occasions and have been shown to be reliable measurements of state self-control strength (Graham, Martin Ginis, & Bray, 2017; Samuel, Englert, Zhang, & Basevitch, 2018).

Ego Depletion and Performance

In general, it has been shown that depleted individuals are, for instance, less adept at volitionally controlling their attention (Schmeichel & Baumeister, 2010), their emotions (Bertrams, Englert, Dickhäuser, & Baumeister, 2013), or their thoughts (Schmeichel, Vohs, & Baumeister, 2003). It should also be noted that, according to the strength model, each task requiring self-control strength can be used as a primary task, meaning a task to induce ego depletion (i.e. independent variable), or as a secondary task, referring to the task on which the primary task should have a carry-over effect (i.e. dependent variable). For example, the previously mentioned Stroop task has been successfully used as a primary task to induce ego depletion (Bray et al., 2008; Graham & Bray, 2015; Graham et al., 2014; Vohs, Baumeister, & Ciarocco, 2005) but also as a secondary task (Englert & Bertrams, 2014; Inzlicht & Gutsell, 2007; Richeson & Shelton, 2003). Ego depletion is also an important factor in sport and exercise contexts (for two recent meta-analyses, see Brown et al., 2019; Giboin & Wolff, 2019); hence, attention is now turned to the effects of ego depletion on endurance performance and persistence, on performance under pressure, and on impulse regulation (for an overview, see Englert, 2016, 2017).

Ego Depletion and Endurance Performance

Cyclists and runners oftentimes experience sensations of fatigue or even pain during training and competition (Millet, 2011). In order to keep going, they have to force themselves to ignore these sensations and push themselves to the limit even though their inner voice might tell them to stop (Martin Ginis & Bray, 2010). As discussed in the earlier parts of this chapter, inhibiting certain response tendencies or working persistently on rather unpleasant tasks requires self-control. Therefore, endurance athletes should be less adept at pushing themselves to their limits when they are in a state of ego depletion. This assumption has been investigated by several researchers and for several different types of endurance tasks (Giboin & Wolff, 2019). Graham and colleagues (Graham, Li, Bray, & Cairney, 2018) asked children to work on the aforementioned isometric handgrip task for as long as possible at baseline (i.e. with fully available self-control strength) and after having worked on a series of incongruent Stroop trials (i.e. in a state of ego depletion). The authors report that endurance performance significantly decreased at the second time of measurement as the children could not force themselves to keep going when ego depleted. These findings have been replicated several times in adult participants as well (Brown & Bray, 2017b; Bray et al., 2008). Furthermore, it has also been shown that individuals quit a tiring wall-sit task significantly earlier when in a state of ego depletion compared to a non-depleted state (Boat & Taylor, 2017; Zering, Brown, Graham, & Bray, 2017).

The negative effects of ego depletion on endurance performance have also been shown in whole-body endurance tasks. Englert and Wolff (2015) tested their participants at two times of measurement separated by seven days and asked them to perform an indoor cycling task. Performance and heart rate were measured at both times of measurement. At one measurement time point, participants were depleted, and at another they were not depleted via the Stroop task (order counterbalanced). The results revealed that participants' cycling performance as well as their heart rate were significantly lower when they had worked on a depleting version of the Stroop before starting the cycling task. These results are especially interesting as the same participants performed the identical task at two different times of measurement with the only difference being that at one time point they performed a five-minute incongruent version of the Stroop task, and at the other time point they worked on a five-minute congruent version of the Stroop task before starting the cycling task. Apparently, ego depletion hindered them from investing the same amount of effort (indicated by their lower heart rate; c.f. Strath et al., 2000) as under neutral conditions. Further evidence for the negative effects of ego depletion on endurance performance in a cycling task have been reported by Martin Ginis and Bray (2010) as well as Wagstaff (2014). Dorris, Power, and Kenefick (2012) also applied a within-subjects design as they asked professional rowers to perform as many sit-ups (i.e. a well-elaborated physical exercise) as possible in a state of ego depletion at one measurement time point and in a state with temporarily available self-control strength at a second time point. In line with their assumptions, participants performed a lower number of sit-ups in a state of ego depletion.

A recent meta-analysis by Giboin and Wolff (2019) reports that overall ego depletion was associated with a reduction in subsequent physical endurance performance (Effect Size [ES] = −0.506 [95% CI: −0.649, −0.369]). Additional analyses revealed that the ego depletion effect was more pronounced in subsequent tasks that applied isolation tasks (e.g. handgrip; ES = −0.719 [−0.946, −0.493]) compared to whole-body endurance tasks (e.g. cycling; ES = 0.338 [0.057, 0.621]). These findings are comparable to a recent meta-analysis by Brown and colleagues (2019). Overall, the results suggest that ego depletion is detrimental to subsequent physical endurance performance.

Ego Depletion and Performance under Pressure

Choking under pressure describes the phenomenon of athletes performing worse under high pressure conditions compared to neutral conditions (Baumeister, 1984). High pressure situations oftentimes lead to increased state anxiety levels, which, in turn, negatively affect attention and performance, primarily in fine perceptual-motor tasks (Gucciardi, Longbottom, Jackson, & Dimmock, 2010; for an overview, see also Beilock & Gray, 2007). However, the results on the anxiety-performance relationship are rather heterogeneous (Hill, Hanton, Matthews, & Fleming, 2010) as not all published papers have found evidence for a negative effect of anxiety on performance; some findings even indicate that anxiety might actually be beneficial for performance (Craft, Magyar, Becker, & Feltz, 2003). The strength model of self-control offers an intriguing explanation for these inconsistent findings (Englert & Bertrams, 2015). According to *Attention Control Theory* (ACT; Eysenck, Derakshan, Santos, & Calvo, 2007), higher levels of anxiety lead to increased distractibility as individuals tend to worry about their performance and are less adept at volitionally controlling their attention (Oudejans, Kuijpers, Kooijman, & Bakker, 2011). This increased distractibility then leads to impaired performance, especially in fine perceptual-motor tasks for which efficient attention regulation is essential (Beilock & Gray, 2007). Results from several studies applying eye-tracking devices confirmed that anxious individuals often experience difficulties regulating their attention, as indicated by a less efficient gaze behavior (Oudejans, Karamat, & Stolk, 2012; Wilson, Vine, & Wood, 2009). Eysenck and colleagues (2007) assume that anxious individuals can counteract their increased distractibility by investing additional effort, or more precisely by volitionally controlling themselves. The question is, under which conditions can we regulate ourselves and invest additional effort?

To answer this question, Englert and colleagues conducted several studies assuming that ego depletion acts as a moderator of the anxiety-performance relationship (for an overview, see Englert, 2015; Englert & Bertrams, 2015). In their studies, participants perform a perceptual-motor task under non-evaluative (i.e. neutral) conditions and are then randomly assigned to an ego depletion or a control condition. Immediately after having worked on a primary self-control task (e.g. Stroop task), anxiety is experimentally induced, and participants are instructed to again perform the same perceptual-motor task. The results reliably revealed that the typical performance drop-off from the neutral situation to the threating situation is primarily found in ego-depleted individuals but not in non-depleted individuals (Englert & Bertrams, 2012, 2013, 2015; Englert, Bertrams, Furley, & Oudejans, 2015). In one of their studies, Englert et al. measured attention regulation under pressure with an eye-tracking device (Englert, Zwemmer, Bertrams, & Oudejans, 2015). The results indicated that anxiety primarily affected dart throwing performance and gaze behavior in ego-depleted individuals, while non-depleted individuals' performance and gaze behavior did not change significantly from a neutral situation to a pressure situation. Quantitative (Shin, Kim, & Park, 2019; Yang, Park, & Shin, 2019) as well as qualitative findings (Oliver, McCarthy, & Burns, 2020) from other labs contribute additional empirical evidence that ego depletion is an important moderator of the anxiety-performance relationship. In line with Eysenck and colleagues' argumentation, individuals are generally capable of counteracting the effects of anxiety on attention and performance but only if they have sufficient levels of self-control strength.

Open Questions and Future Directions

The present chapter aimed to introduce the strength model of self-control (Baumeister et al., 1998) and highlighted its importance for the field of sport and exercise (Englert, 2016, 2017). The literature and studies presented above suggest that there is only a certain amount of self-control strength available in a given situation (Baumeister et al., 1998): If the resources are low (i.e. ego depletion), performance tends to suffer (e.g. endurance performance; Giboin & Wolff, 2019). Apart from these situational fluctuations in state self-control strength, this chapter also presented empirical evidence that individuals differ from each other in terms of their general self-control skills (i.e. trait self-control strength). Some individuals are—simply stated—better at regulating their impulses than others (Tangney et al., 2004). Beginning with the famous Marshmallow Test (Mischel, 1961), this chapter outlined the benefits of high trait self-control strength for numerous outcome measures (e.g. healthy lifestyle, regular physical activity; De Ridder et al., 2012). Several studies have highlighted the importance of considering self-control strength at both trait and state levels. For instance, in a study by Forestier and colleagues (2018), which revealed the expected positive relationship between trait self-control strength and health-related behaviors, the addition of state self-control to their statistical model more than doubled the amount of explained variance in behavior (see also Englert & Rummel, 2016). The final part of this chapter will now address the following three open questions regarding the strength model of self-control: (1) Are ego depletion and mental fatigue capturing the same psychological phenomenon? (2) How can self-control performance be improved? (3) Are there any conflicting findings regarding the ego depletion effect?

The first question regards the differences and similarities between ego depletion (Baumeister et al., 1998) and mental fatigue (Marcora, Staiano, & Manning, 2009; see also Chapter 10). According to Giboin and Wolff (2019) and Brown and colleagues (2019), there are two independent lines of research postulating that subsequent performance is impaired if individuals have previously been working on another self-control task: Research based on the strength model of self-control (Baumeister et al., 1998) and research on mental fatigue (Marcora et al., 2009). One of the most prominent models of mental fatigue is the *psychobiological model of endurance performance* (Marcora, 2009), which, similar to the strength model, postulates that states of mental fatigue are the result of prolonged exertion of self-control or mental effort. However, it is argued that the negative effects of mental fatigue on (endurance) performance are not caused by a temporary depletion of limited self-control strength but rather by an increase in the perception of effort (Marcora, 2009). This increase in perceived effort largely influences whether an individual keeps working on a strenuous endurance task, or as Giboin and Wolff (2009) stated, "perception of effort is the cardinal exercise stopper" (p. 4; see also Staiano, Bosio, Morree, Rampinini, & Marcora, 2018). In general, mental fatigue refers to a complex psychophysiological phenomenon that, on a subjective level, is associated with feelings of tiredness, lack of energy, and decreased motivation (Boksem & Tops, 2008). On a physiological level, mental fatigue is related to alterations in brain activity (Brownsberger, Edwards, Crowther, & Cottrell, 2013), while on a behavioral level, mental fatigue oftentimes leads to performance impairments (Marcora et al., 2009).

Another important difference between these two independent lines of research concerns the experimental research paradigms applied (Englert, 2016; Pattyn, Van Cutsem, Dessy, & Mairesse, 2018). Though both approaches typically adopt a two-task paradigm, the durations of the primary tasks differ significantly. In ego depletion research, the primary tasks seldom last longer than 30 minutes, whereas mental fatigue supposedly can only reliably occur if the primary task lasts at least 30 minutes (Van Cutsem et al., 2017). Interestingly, while the results of the meta-analysis by Giboin and Wolff (2019) revealed a small-to-medium effect size of ego depletion/mental fatigue on endurance performance, the duration of the primary task did not predict the magnitude of subsequent performance impairments (see also Wolff, Sieber, Bieleke, & Englert, 2019). This is in line with the meta-analysis by Brown and colleagues (2019), which also found similar negative effects of primary tasks on subsequent physical performance lasting less than 30 minutes ($g = -0.45$) and primary tasks lasting longer than 30 minutes ($g = -0.30$). However, Giboin and Wolff (2019) stress that these non-significant differences might also be attributable to the fact that the durations of the secondary tasks in mental fatigue research on average last much longer (947 ± 775 s) than those used in ego depletion research (233 ± 329 s). This is especially important since mental fatigue exerts a much stronger negative effect in longer-lasting physical endurance tasks (Van Cutsem et al., 2017; see also Pageaux, Lepers, Dietz, & Marcora, 2014). Future studies should continue to investigate the differences and similarities between ego depletion and mental fatigue. Mental fatigue will be explained in more detail in Chapter 10.

The second important issue to be discussed is if and how self-control performance can be improved (see also Chapter 12). Baumeister compares self-control strength to a human muscle, arguing that it can be increased and strengthened by applying specific training techniques (Baumeister et al., 2006). Support for this hypothesis has, for instance, been found by Muraven (2010). In his study, participants in a training condition were instructed to regularly exert self-control over a two-week period (i.e. resisting sweets and high-caloric snacks). In the control condition, participants did not take part in any specific self-control training. Self-control performance was measured at the beginning of the study and then again after two weeks. As expected, participants from the training condition significantly improved their performance, while there were no significant changes in performance for participants in the control condition. Bray, Graham, and Saville (2015) transferred the training approach to a more sport-specific setting in which participants performed a maximal incremental exercise test on a cycle ergometer (i.e. an exhausting endurance task requiring self-control strength) at the beginning of the study and then again after two weeks. During these two weeks, participants from the training condition were instructed to perform the isometric handgrip task twice a day for as long as possible, whereas the control condition did not receive any self-control training. Just as in the study by Muraven (2010), performance in the training condition improved significantly, indicating that exerting self-control on a regular basis might serve as a valuable strategy to improve self-control performance in sport and exercise (for a critical discussion, see Friese, Frankenbach, Job, & Loschelder, 2017).

Another intriguing approach to improve self-control performance is the adoption of *implementation intentions* (Gollwitzer, 1999) see also Chapter 12. An implementation intention is an "if-then plan," which specifies which behavior should be displayed in a specific situation ("If situation X occurs, then I will display behavior Y"), thus linking an anticipated situation to a goal-directed response (e.g. "If I get back from work, then I will go for a run"). In a typical experimental setup, participants are instructed to generate and write down their implementation intentions in anticipation of a situation (de Vet, Oenema, & Brug, 2011). When the situation actually occurs, the behavior gets *automatically* triggered, meaning that a conscious decision-making process is not required, making it less prone to the negative effects of ego depletion (Webb & Sheeran, 2003). Several meta-analyses provide support for the use of implementation intentions to promote physical activity, healthy nutrition, and other behaviors (Bélanger-Gravel, Godin, & Amireault, 2013).

Finally, the validity of the strength model of self-control should be discussed. Even though the findings reviewed thus far seem to deliver sound empirical evidence for the strength model of self-control, a discussion of critical, non-significant empirical findings should not be concealed. Hagger and colleagues launched a call for a Registered Replication Report (RRR) on ego depletion in 2015. In a large multi-lab preregistered study, covering 23 labs worldwide and more than 2,000 participants, the authors applied the classic two-task paradigm to investigate the ego depletion effect under strict laboratory conditions (Hagger et al., 2016). However, the results did not provide statistically significant evidence for the ego depletion effect, raising doubts regarding its validity (see also Wolff, Baumann, & Englert, 2018). Since the publication of the RRR, there has been a lively discussion on the ego depletion phenomenon (Baumeister & Vohs, 2016) as several new meta-analyses were conducted (Blázquez, Botella, & Suero, 2017; Dang, 2018), and new replication studies were initiated (Witte & Zenker, 2017). The results are rather inconclusive, and there are seemingly more open questions than answers at the moment. According to Inzlicht and Berkman (2015), some of the most pressing questions are (a) whether ego depletion is simply an aspect of mental fatigue, (b) how motivation affects ego depletion and subsequent performance, and (c) if states of ego depletion are related to changes in specific physiological variables (e.g. changes in glucose levels; Vadillo, Gold, & Osman, 2016).

Conclusion

The literature reviewed in the current chapter has shown that individuals can differ in their trait as well as their state (i.e. momentarily available) self-control strength and that lower levels of trait and state self-control strength are oftentimes related to impaired athletic performance (Brown et al., 2019; Giboin & Wolff, 2019). While the validity of the strength model of self-control has recently been challenged on an empirical level, most of the researchers agree that self-control performance cannot be maintained at all times and at all costs (Inzlicht & Schmeichel, 2012; Job, Dweck, & Walton, 2010). Especially findings from the field of sport and exercise deliver strong empirical support that self-control performance drops when individuals had to control themselves in a foregoing task (Brown et al., 2019; Giboin & Wolff, 2019). The current state of flux has led to the development of new theoretical models of self-control trying to explain lapses in self-control performance (Inzlicht & Schmeichel, 2012). The most prominent alternative models as well as a discussion of potential moderators and mediators of ego depletion will be discussed in Chapter 9.

9

UNDERSTANDING AND INTERPRETING THE EFFECTS OF PRIOR COGNITIVE EXERTION ON SELF-REGULATION OF SPORT AND EXERCISE PERFORMANCE

Jeffrey D. Graham and Denver M. Y. Brown

Introduction

Everyone knows a person who never seems to falter when it comes to sport and exercise performance. This could be the early morning riser that never skips a run, or the professional athlete that always manages to give it their all until the final buzzer. Naturally, we often wonder what it is that enables these individuals to consistently achieve their goals and perform to the best of their abilities regardless of the circumstances. Self-regulation is a key facet underlying success in many aspects of life, including sport and exercise performance (Englert, 2016; Mischel et al., 2011; Moffitt et al., 2011). But why is it that so many people fail to self-regulate their behavior in sport and exercise contexts? The cognitive demands we consistently face in society today may contribute to our struggles in this regard (Sterelny, 2007). In this chapter, we will discuss the current state of self-regulation research in relation to sport and exercise performance with an emphasis on the deleterious carryover effects of exerting cognitive effort prior to task performance.

Self-regulation broadly refers to the processes of aligning a system's current state with a desired end state or goal (Carver & Scheier, 2001). Humans regulate their thoughts, emotions, and behaviors continuously over the course of a day to maintain healthy diets, work and academic performance, and regular physical activity patterns (Hofmann et al., 2012). For example, striving to achieve a goal to exercise after work is an act of self-regulation (Buckley et al., 2014) that often requires resisting competing temptations such as watching television or hanging out with friends. Self-regulation processes are also engaged when performing various sport and exercise-based tasks, including managing feelings of pain and fatigue while running in order to achieve a desired time (Wagstaff, 2014) or ignoring distracting fans when shooting a free throw (Englert, Bertrams, Furley, & Oudejans, 2015). Thus, self-regulation is a broad process that aids in goal achievement across a diverse range of behaviors.

Self-control, however, refers to conscious, deliberate, and effortful processes that aid in the regulation of behavior toward a desired end state or goal (Baumeister et al., 2007; Inzlicht, Werner, Briskin, & Roberts, 2021). Simply stated, self-control is engaged in the self-regulation process when an event has the potential to direct our behavior out of line with our broader goals. While the terms self-regulation and self-control are often used interchangeably (Baumeister & Vohs, 2016), others have suggested that self-regulation and self-control refer to distinct processes (Inzlicht et al., 2021), with self-control often subserving self-regulation. For instance, building off the examples above, self-control would be specifically engaged when resisting temptations to watch television and hang out with friends as well as to ignore distracting fans and to cope with feelings of fatigue in order to maintain pace during a run. In these instances, and many others, self-control helps people self-regulate their behavior. As such, self-regulation and self-control are interrelated processes that allow people to achieve their goals and, ultimately, live healthier, longer, and more prosperous lives (Baumeister, Heatherton, & Tice, 1994; de Ridder, Lensvelt-Mulders, Finkenauer, Stok, & Baumeister, 2012; Mischel et al., 2011; Moffitt et al., 2011).

Given the above, we use the term self-regulation throughout this chapter as it is a broad term that encapsulates self-control processes in relation to sport and exercise performance. Indeed, the physical outcomes we review refer to acts of self-regulation whereby researchers ask participants to "*do their best*" (e.g. exercise for as long as they can, perform as many repetitions as possible, hit as many shots as possible) which requires acute acts of self-control (e.g. inhibiting pain and fatigue in order to persist, resisting the temptation to quit, managing distractions) to strive toward their overarching goal for the experimental session. Although the importance of self-regulation for achieving various adaptive physical and mental health outcomes is well understood, exerting self-regulation can be an effortful process and failures are common (Baumeister et al., 1994). This observation led to the development and refinement of several models and theories to help us understand why the prolonged exertion of self-regulation often leads to lapses in subsequent attempts to exert self-regulation across an array of behaviors, including sport and exercise performance.

In this chapter, we first review two of the most common models that have been used to understand self-regulatory processes as they relate to sport and exercise performance. We then discuss our current understanding of the effects of prior cognitive exertion on subsequent self-regulation of sport and exercise performance. The next section highlights intermediary processes that explain why sport and exercise performance is impaired following effortful cognitive exertion, in addition to factors known to mediate and moderate this relationship. Finally, we will close with briefly discussing future directions that will help improve the quality of this body of research, our knowledge about how these effects unfold in daily life, and techniques that will help us better understand the mechanisms underlying this relationship.

Models of Self-Regulation in Sport and Exercise

While research on self-regulation and self-control has garnered significant attention over the last 50 years across the broader discipline of psychology, research dedicated to understanding the importance of self-regulation for sport and exercise performance has only emerged within the last decade or so. Indeed, pioneering research within the areas of sport and exercise psychology (Bray, Martin Ginis, Hicks, & Woodgate, 2008) and exercise physiology (Marcora, Staiano, & Manning, 2009) has shown that exerting self-regulation for a brief or prolonged period of time (i.e. through a cognitive manipulation) negatively impairs subsequent physical task performance. The notion that performing a cognitive task requiring self-regulation has negative carryover effects on sport and exercise performance sparked considerable interest in this field of study (see Figures 9.1 and 9.2 and Tables 9.1a–c).[1] However, differences in the areas in which this question has been investigated – psychology/sport and exercise psychology or physiology – have led to the emergence of two distinct perspectives in which these findings are understood. Specifically, sport and exercise psychologists have generally interpreted their findings within a resource-based model which contends that performance is impaired due to a state of "ego depletion" (Englert, 2016). However, exercise physiologists have interpreted their results within a motivation-based model that argues performance is impaired due to state of "mental fatigue" (Marcora et al., 2009). Despite similarities in study designs, cognitive manipulations (including their associated symptoms), the resultant state following these manipulations (Pattyn, Van Cutsem, Dessy, & Mairesse, 2018), and tasks used to assess a variety of sport and exercise-related performance outcomes, these approaches have evolved for the most part in isolation.

Below we have provided reviews of the two models most commonly adopted to interpret findings from studies that have investigated self-regulation of sport and exercise performance following exposure to an initial task requiring effortful cognitive exertion.

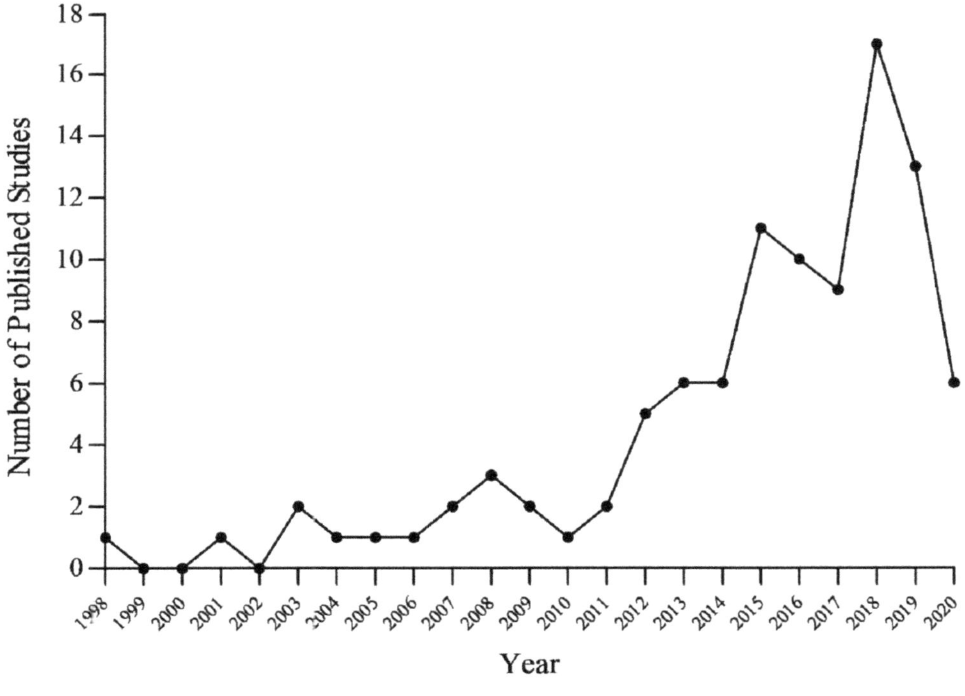

FIGURE 9.1 Cognitive exertion – physical performance publication trends (1998–2020) across all disciplines ($N = 100$), based on the Brown et al. (2020) meta-analysis and an updated search to include literature from the earliest available date up to July 2020.

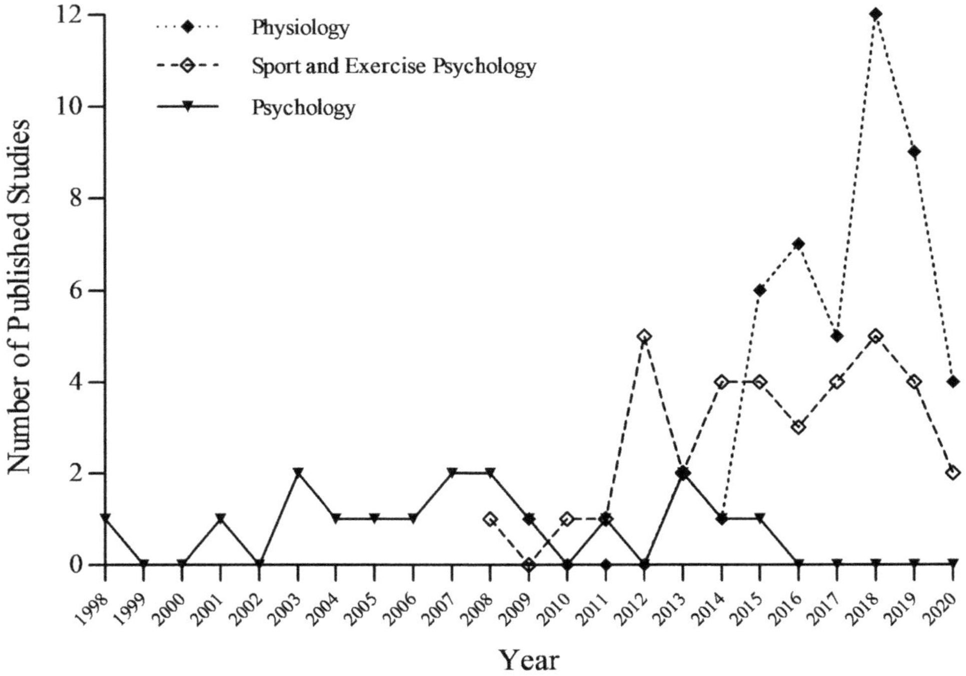

FIGURE 9.2 Cognitive exertion – physical performance publication trends (1998–2018) for physiology (N = 47), sport and exercise psychology (N = 36), and psychology (N = 17), based on the Brown et al. (2020) meta-analysis and an updated search to include literature from the earliest available date up to July 2020.

Strength Model of Self-Regulation

Self-regulation research within sport and exercise psychology has been informed largely by the strength model of self-regulation (Baumeister, Bratslavsky, Muraven, & Tice, 1998; Baumeister & Vohs, 2016). Given the observation that self-regulation failures are commonplace (Baumeister et al., 1994), Baumeister and colleagues hypothesized that our ability to use (or exert) self-regulation is based on a limited store of internal resources. That is, when self-regulation is used for a prolonged period to regulate thoughts, emotions, or behaviors, it depletes this internal reserve of resources leaving less resources available for subsequent acts of self-regulation. Baumeister and colleagues introduced the term *ego depletion* to describe the altered psychophysiological state that is brought on following the prolonged exertion of self-regulation. Ego depletion refers to "a temporary reduction in the self's capacity or willingness to engage in volitional action (including controlling the environment, controlling the self, making choices, and initiating action) caused by exercise of volition" (Baumeister et al., 1998, p. 1253). Therefore, when people are in a state of ego depletion, self-regulation failures are theoretically more likely to occur.

Ego depletion has been commonly studied using either a dual-task paradigm that requires participants to perform two tasks in succession or a multiple-task paradigm that requires participants to perform three (or more) tasks in succession. In the dual-task paradigm, participants in the control condition perform an initial task that requires

TABLE 9.1A Studies Published in Physiology Journals by Year (N = 46)

Year	*2009*	*2010*	*2011*	*2012*	*2013*	*2014*
Author(s)	(Marcora et al., 2009)				(Brownsberger et al., 2013) (Pageaux et al., 2013)	(Pageaux et al., 2014)
Total	1	0	0	0	2	1
Year	*2015*	*2016*	*2017*	*2018*	*2019*	*2020*
Author(s)	(Duncan et al., 2015) (Martin et al., 2015) (Pageaux et al., 2015) (Shortz et al., 2015) (Smith et al., 2015)	(Azevedo et al., 2016) (Badin et al., 2016) (Head et al., 2016) (Martin et al., 2016) (Smith, Zeuwts, et al., 2016) (Smith, Coutts, et al., 2016, Study 1) (Smith, Coutts, et al., 2016, Study 2)	(Head et al., 2017) (Le Mansec et al., 2018) (Otani et al., 2017) (Shortz & Mehta, 2017) (Veness et al., 2017)	(Coutinho et al., 2018) (Filipas et al., 2018) (Kunrath et al., 2018) (Moreira et al., 2018) (Penna, Filho, Campos, et al., 2018) (Penna, Filho, Wanner, et al., 2018) (Pires et al., 2018) (Roussey et al., 2018) (Salam et al., 2018) (Slimani et al., 2018) (Silva-Cavalcante et al., 2018) (Vrijkotte et al., 2018)	(Clark et al., 2019) (Filipas et al., 2019) (Fortes et al., 2019) (Franco-Alvarenga et al., 2019) (Gantois et al., 2019) (Holgado et al., 2019) (Le Mansec et al., 2019) (Martin et al., 2019) (Van Cutsem et al., 2019)	(Kosack et al., 2020) (Kunrath et al., 2020) (Lopes et al., 2020) (Van Cutsem et al., 2020)
Total	5	7	5	12	9	4

little (or no) self-regulation to perform (e.g. freely able to eat candy), whereas participants in the experimental condition perform a harder version of the task that requires a higher degree of self-regulation to perform (e.g. resisting the temptation to eat candy) and thus, induces a state of ego depletion (Baumeister et al., 1998). Following the initial task, all participants then perform a task that requires a high degree of self-regulation

TABLE 9.1B Studies Published in Sport and Exercise Psychology Journals by Year (N = 36)

Year	*2008*	*2009*	*2010*	*2011*	*2012*	*2013*	*2014*
Author(s)	(Bray et al., 2008)		(Martin Ginis & Bray, 2010)	(Bray et al., 2011)	(Dorris et al., 2012, Experiment 1) (Dorris et al., 2012, Experiment 2) (Englert & Bertrams, 2012, Study 1) (Englert & Bertrams, 2012, Study 2) (Graham & Bray, 2012)	(Bray et al., 2013) (McEwan et al., 2013)	(Englert & Bertrams, 2014) (Graham, Sonne, et al., 2014) (MacMahon et al., 2014) (Wagstaff, 2014)
Total	1	0	1	1	5	2	4

Year	*2015*	*2016*	*2017*	*2018*	*2019*	*2020*
Author(s)	(Englert & Wolff, 2015) (Englert, Bertrams, et al., 2015) (Englert, Persaud, et al., 2015) (Graham & Bray, 2015)	(Schücker & MacMahon, 2016, Study 1) (Schücker & MacMahon, 2016, Study 2) (Zering et al., 2017)	(Boat & Taylor, 2017) (Boat et al., 2017) (Brown & Bray, 2017a) (Graham et al., 2017)	(Brown & Bray, 2019b)★ (Boat et al., 2018) (Englert et al., 2018) (Graham et al., 2018) (Stocker Englert, & Seiler, 2019)★	(Brown & Bray, 2019a) (Harris & Bray, 2019) (MacMahon et al., 2019) (Shin et al., 2019)	(Shaabani et al., 2020) (Stocker et al., 2020)
Total	4	3	4	5	4	2

★ = studies originally published online in 2018, but officially published in a journal issue released in 2019

to perform (e.g. trying to solve an impossible maze or puzzle) and the performance on this task serves as the outcome measure of self-regulation. If self-regulation is based on a limited amount of resources, Baumeister and colleagues (1998) assumed that participants in the experimental condition would perform worse on the second task when compared to participants in the control condition as they had less self-regulatory resources to draw upon due to expending them on the first task.

In an illustrative example of the multiple-task paradigm (Muraven, Tice, & Baumeister, 1998, Study 1), all participants completed an initial physical endurance task that required

TABLE 9.1C Studies Published in General Psychology Journals by Year (N = 17)

Year	*1998*	*1999*	*2000*	*2001*	*2002*	*2003*	*2004*	*2005*	*2006*	*2007*	*2008*
Author(s)	(Muraven et al., 1998, Study 1)			(Ciarocco et al., 2001)		(Seeley & Gardner, 2003, Study 1) (Seeley & Gardner, 2003, Study 2)	(Murtagh & Todd, 2004, Study 1)	(Vohs et al., 2005, Study 2)	(Finkel et al., 2006, Study 4)	(Alberts et al., 2007, Study 1) (Alberts et al., 2007, Study 2)	(Alberts et al., 2008) (Tyler & Burns, 2008, Experiment 1)
Total	1	0	0	1	0	2	1	1	1	2	2

Year	*2009*	*2010*	*2011*	*2012*	*2013*	*2014*	*2015*	*2016*	*2017*	*2018*	*2019*	*2020*
Author(s)	(Tyler & Burns, 2009, Experiment 2)		(Alberts et al., 2011)		(Hagger et al., 2013, Study 1) (Hagger et al., 2013, Study 2)	(Xu et al., 2014)	(Yusainy & Lawrence, 2015)					
Total	1	0	1	0	2	1	1	0	0	0	0	0

Note: Studies taken from the Brown et al. (2020) meta-analysis that included literature from the earliest available date up to September 2018. Based on the Brown et al. (2020) eligibility criteria and search terms, an updated search was conducted to include literature up to July 2020.

participants to hold a wad of paper between the handles of a spring-loaded handgrip exerciser (i.e. by squeezing the handles tightly) for as long as possible. All the participants then watched a documentary for 3 minutes. Participants in the control condition were simply instructed to watch the movie. Participants in one experimental condition were instructed to increase their emotional response to the movie as much as possible, whereas those in a second experimental condition were told to decrease (or suppress) their emotional response to the movie as much as possible. Following the movie, all the participants performed another endurance handgrip task and the change in the time they were able to persist holding the handgrip served as the outcome measure of self-regulation. Participants in the experimental conditions were hypothesized to perform worse on the second handgrip trial as they had less resources to draw upon following the emotion regulation manipulation. Consistent with their hypotheses, participants who regulated their emotions squeezed the handgrip for less time on the second handgrip trial when compared to the first, whereas control participants' performance remained relatively stable across trials.

Findings from Baumeister and colleagues' early set of experiments seemed to support the idea that self-regulation relies on a limited resource (Baumeister et al., 1998; Muraven et al., 1998). That is, participants who initially exerted a high degree of self-regulation to control their thoughts, emotions, or behaviors tended to perform worse on a subsequent test of self-regulation (across an array of tasks) when compared to control participants who were able to freely self-regulate themselves initially (Hagger et al., 2010b). While this early work sparked significant interest (over 600 studies) across many disciplines investigating an array of behaviors associated with failures at self-regulation (e.g. aggression, impulsive spending, alcohol and drug use), it was not until roughly a decade after the first handgrip study by Muraven et al. (1998) that studies drawing from theorizing within the strength model began examining potential negative carryover effects of prolonged self-regulation exertion on sport and exercise-related outcomes.

While Baumeister and colleagues were not necessarily interested in physical task performance outcomes as they relate to sport and exercise behavior, they recognized certain aspects of these behaviors such as enduring physical discomfort or muscle fatigue also require self-regulation and, in turn, task performance may be sensitive to ego depletion effects. In the first controlled lab-based study to examine this idea, Bray et al. (2008) used a similar design to Muraven et al. (1998) that involved two isometric endurance handgrip squeezes – but this time using a calibrated handgrip dynamometer – separated by a cognitive self-regulation manipulation (i.e. Stroop task; Stroop, 1935). Participants in the experimental condition performed a modified incongruent version of the Stroop task, whereas control participants performed the congruent version of the Stroop task. In both versions, participants were presented with lists of color words. In the congruent version, the text and the ink color of the words were matched (e.g. the word "*yellow*" was printed in yellow ink) and participants were asked to read aloud the word presented (i.e. yellow). In the incongruent version, the text and ink color of the words were mismatched (e.g. the word "*yellow*" was printed in green ink) and participants were asked to say aloud the color of the printed ink (i.e. green) while ignoring the text for each word presented. In addition, experimental participants were asked to override these general rules and read aloud the printed text of each word presented in red ink (e.g. the word "*yellow*" was printed in red ink, and so participants had to say "yellow" instead of "red"). Findings from Bray et al. (2008) replicated initial work by Muraven et al. (1998) showing participants who exerted a high degree of self-regulation to perform an incongruent version of the Stroop task (experimental condition) persisted for less time on the second handgrip endurance trial (when compared to their first endurance trial). In comparison, participants who completed the easier congruent version of the Stroop task (control condition) did not show any decrements in performance on the second endurance trial. Subsequent work has shown ego depletion effects across a range of aerobic, resistance, and isometric tasks requiring physical endurance (see Table 9.1b), including cycling (Martin Ginis & Bray, 2010), push-ups and sit-ups (Dorris, Power, & Kenefick, 2012), bench press and leg extension (Graham, Martin Ginis, & Bray, 2017), and wall-sits (Boat & Taylor, 2017).

Based on the notion that self-regulation resources are limited in nature, it is relatively easy to understand how a prior act of self-regulation can negatively affect subsequent physical endurance performance. That is, when in a state of ego depletion, people's ability to endure pain and fatigue is compromised and so they give up sooner. Furthermore, research also suggests that ego depletion negatively affects people's ability to selectively regulate their attention (Schmeichel & Baumeister, 2010). These findings led to work investigating ego depletion effects across various motor-based sport and exercise-related tasks where attentional control is crucial for successful performance (see Table 9.1b). For instance, ego depletion negatively affects dart throwing accuracy (McEwan, Martin Ginis, & Bray, 2013), sprint start reaction time (Englert & Bertrams, 2014), and basketball free throw shooting accuracy (Englert, Bertrams, et al., 2015). In addition, even controlling one's exercise-related thoughts using a popular sport and exercise psychology technique (i.e. mental imagery) can also induce ego depletion and negatively affect aspects of physical performance (Graham et al., 2014). Although most of the research examining ego depletion effects has been conducted with young adults, ego depletion has also been shown to negatively affect physical performance among older adults (Bray, Martin Ginis, & Woodgate, 2011) and children (Graham, Li, Bray, & Cairney, 2018).

Taken together, ample research shows that prior exertion of self-regulation negatively affects physical performance across a diverse range of sport and exercise-related tasks and age groups. Based on the strength model, researchers have generally assumed that these performance decrements are primarily due to self-regulation resources being depleted on the first task leaving less resources available to draw upon on the second task. However, this is still an assumption as researchers have struggled to identify where these resources manifest in the human body and how to properly measure them. In turn, much debate and concern has evolved over the application of the strength model when examining the aftereffects of self-regulation exertion on physical performance.

Considerations and Pitfalls

Support for the strength model comes from over 300 independent studies among the broader psychology literature showing initial self-regulatory exertion impairs self-regulation on a subsequent task (Dang, 2018). Of particular relevance to the present chapter is that these effects have been observed across a variety of physical tasks in over 50 studies involving participants of different ages and expertise levels (see Tables 9.1b and 9.1c). However, evidence in the broader ego depletion literature has since emerged that is incompatible with a resource-based account of self-regulation, bringing the strength model into question (Beedie & Lane, 2012; Molden et al., 2012).

While the strength model provides an intuitive explanation often likened to muscle fatigue for why ego depletion occurs, research has identified three primary concerns that challenge this model. Perhaps the most concerning issue that has been raised surrounds the proposed underlying depletable mechanism. Despite an abundance of research attempting to uncover a biologically based "resource" (Gailliot & Baumeister, 2007), the origin as well as methods to measure or operationalize the state of the resource outlined within the strength model of self-regulation remains unknown (Friese, Loschelder, Gieseler, Frankenbach, & Inzlicht, 2019). Given that a central resource is identified as the mechanism driving these effects, without having a mechanism to test, the strength model is virtually unfalsifiable – a characteristic of a poor theory (see Gieseler, Loschelder, & Friese, 2019). The second challenge to the strength model comes from work showing that manipulating motivation can attenuate ego depletion effects (Brown & Bray, 2017b; Luethi et al., 2016; Muraven & Slessareva, 2003). For instance, Brown and Bray (2017b) showed that offering a performance contingent incentive to depleted participants can restore handgrip endurance performance to levels achieved in a non-depleted state. To accommodate these findings within the strength model, Baumeister and Vohs (2016) have argued that people do not exhaust their resources completely on the initial self-regulatory task and simply dig deeper into their resource stores when adequately motivated. But this still assumes that a central resource exists. The final challenge to the strength model involves studies that have manipulated people's beliefs and perceptions. That is, when people believe willpower is unlimited (Job, Dweck, & Walton, 2010; Job, Walton, Bernecker, & Dweck, 2013, 2015; Martijn, Tenbült, Merckelbach, Dreezens, & de Vries, 2002) or feel invigorated following self-regulatory exertion (Clarkson, Hirt, Jia, & Alexander, 2010), typical ego depletion effects are not observed.

Collectively, these findings have fueled considerable criticism of the strength model and whether a resource-based account is the appropriate explanation for why we often experience self-regulatory lapses after performing an initial task requiring self-regulation. This has prompted alternative theorizing that self-regulation is not dependent upon a resource, but on motivation and a reasoned assessment of benefits and costs of one's response alternatives (Inzlicht & Schmeichel, 2012; Kotabe & Hofmann, 2015; Kurzban, Duckworth, Kable, & Myers, 2013). Although motivational accounts of self-regulation have received limited attention in the sport and exercise domain to date, prominent theories such as the shifting priorities model of self-control failure[2] provide mechanistic approaches that can and should be tested in this domain (Inzlicht et al., 2014; Inzlicht & Schmeichel, 2012; Milyavskaya & Inzlicht, 2017).

Whether an ego depletion effect actually exists has also been significantly debated with some suggesting ego depletion does not exist, and if it does, the effect is small (for recent examples, see Baumeister, 2019; Baumeister & Vohs, 2016; Carter, Kofler, Forster, & McCullough, 2015; Cunningham & Baumeister, 2016; Dang, 2018; Dang et al., 2021; Friese et al., 2019; Hagger et al., 2016; Inzlicht & Friese, 2019). Despite the controversy of whether an ego depletion effect exists based on previous meta-analyses (Carter et al., 2015; Carter & McCullough, 2014; Dang, 2018) and multi-site replication attempts (Dang et al., 2021; Hagger et al., 2016), it is critical to note several limitations with regard to the conclusions drawn from these studies as they pertain to sport and exercise performance. For instance, although some of the meta-analyses included studies examining physical outcomes, none conducted a sub analysis that quantified the magnitude of the ego depletion effect on sport and exercise performance, which discounts the possibility that ego depletion may vary across domains (e.g. cognitive versus physical outcomes). In addition, while the results are mixed from multi-lab replication studies (Dang et al., 2021; Hagger et al., 2016), these attempts did not involve a physical task as the outcome measure. Therefore, the findings and conclusions drawn from recent meta-analyses, multi-site replication attempts, and commentaries need to be interpreted with caution when inferring about sport and exercise performance. In fact, meta-analyses of studies that have examined ego depletion (or mental fatigue) strictly in a sport and exercise context have found evidence of small ($g = -0.38$; Brown et al., 2020) and moderate (ES = −0.51; Giboin & Wolff, 2019) sized deleterious effects.

Psychobiological Model

While there has been much debate over whether resource or motivation-based models best explain self-regulatory behavior more broadly, these theories lack specificity with regard to factors inherently unique to sport and exercise performance. Consider going for a run. Most people would agree that one of the most salient factors while running is their perception of physical exertion and that these sensations largely influence our decisions regarding whether to speed up, slow down, give up, or keep going (Staiano, Bosio, Morree, Rampinini, & Marcora, 2018). Physical exertion and the sensations that accompany the effort required to move are unique characteristics of sport and exercise performance that influence self-regulation of this behavior. Roughly a decade after the first self-regulation studies were published, including some that involved physical endurance tasks (e.g. isometric handgrip squeeze; Muraven et al., 1998), the psychobiological model emerged as an effort-based decision-making theory to explain exercise tolerance (Marcora, 2008; Marcora, Bosio, & de Morree, 2008; Marcora et al., 2009; Marcora & Staiano, 2010). Although the psychobiological model was originally designed to explain how both physiological and psychological factors influence self-regulation of exercise performance, this model has received significant attention for its ability to explain the effects of prior cognitive exertion on self-regulation of sport and exercise performance.

Rooted in motivational intensity theory (Brehm & Self, 1989), the psychobiological model posits that exercise-induced fatigue (e.g. task disengagement or reduced intensity) is not simply due to physiological exhaustion, but rather a conscious decision driven by the interplay between two factors: (1) Perception of effort, and (2) potential motivation. Perception of effort refers to the conscious sensations of how hard, heavy, or strenuous an individual perceives a physical task to be (Marcora, 2010). However, potential motivation refers to the maximum effort an individual is willing to exert to attain their goal (Wright, 2008). Considered together, the psychobiological model predicts that individuals decide to quit exercising or reduce their current level of effort because the effort required to continue at the current intensity exceeds their potential motivation or perceived ability to sustain such a level of effort. Support for this model stems from studies that have shown manipulating perception of effort (de Morree, Klein & Marcora, 2012) and potential motivation (Cabanac, 1986) can influence exercise performance independently from physiological mechanisms (i.e. cardiovascular, respiratory, metabolic, neuromuscular) assumed to underly exercise tolerance (Allen, Lamb, & Westerblad, 2008; Amann & Calbet, 2008; Burnley & Jones, 2007; McKenna & Hargreaves, 2008; Noakes & Gibson, 2004; Secher et al., 2008; Walsh, 2000). Despite exercise performance being proposed to be driven by the interplay between perception of effort and potential motivation, research has consistently shown a strong association between maximal perceptions of exertion and exercise termination, which supports the notion that perception of effort is the primary determinant of endurance/exercise performance (Crewe, Tucker, & Noakes, 2008; Eston, Faulkner, St Clair Gibson, Noakes, & Parfitt, 2007; Horstman, Morgan, Cymerman, & Stokes, 1979; Nakamura et al., 2008; Noakes, 2008). This has led to perception of effort being termed the "cardinal exercise stopper" (Staiano et al., 2018).

The psychobiological model also recognizes that various factors can affect exercise performance through influencing perception of effort and/or potential motivation. Of relevance to the focus of the present chapter, mental fatigue has been found to influence self-regulation of exercise performance through its impact on perceived exertion (see Van Cutsem et al., 2017 for a review). Mental fatigue refers to a complex psychophysiological phenomenon that results in feelings of tiredness or lack of energy following exposure to tasks that require prolonged cognitive exertion (Boksem & Tops, 2008). It is through this indirect pathway that the psychobiological model has been applied to understand the effects of prior cognitive exertion on exercise performance. Evidence in support of this line of theorizing began to materialize shortly after the psychobiological model was proposed. The seminal study investigating the effects of mental fatigue on aerobic endurance performance was a within-subject crossover trial that involved 16 participants cycling to exhaustion at 80% of their peak power output after performing a demanding cognitive task (i.e. continuous performance task – AX version; AX-CPT) or watching a documentary for 90 minutes (Marcora et al., 2009). In the AX-CPT, cue-probe sequences consisting of four letters are continuously presented on a screen. Each cue-probe sequence involves presentation of a red cue letter first, followed by two white distractor letters, and finishing with a red probe letter. Participants are instructed to respond whether a target (A appears as cue; X appears as probe) or non-target (any other cue-probe combination) trial appears. This task involves higher order cognitive control and sustained attention. Significant declines in vigor were observed following both experimental manipulations; however, participants only reported significant increases in fatigue after performing the demanding cognitive task. With regard to exercise performance, the results showed that participants quit exercising significantly earlier after completing the demanding cognitive task. Closer inspection of the data revealed high levels of motivation prior to exercising that were relatively equivalent between the conditions, thus ruling out motivation as an influential factor. However, during exercise, participants reached their maximal level of perceived exertion earlier following the demanding cognitive task (i.e. in a mentally fatigued state) despite no observed differences in the peripheral physiological responses (e.g. heart rate, oxygen consumption) that were assessed. At the time of this publication, several more studies have shown similar effects at different intensities across a variety of exercise modalities, including self-paced aerobic exercise (Brown & Bray, 2019b; Brownsberger, Edwards, Crowther, & Cottrell, 2013; MacMahon, Schücker, Hagemann, & Strauss, 2014) and resistance exercise (Head et al., 2016; Pageaux, Marcora, & Lepers, 2013) (see Table 9.1a). Taken together, these findings further support Marcora et al.'s (2009) conclusions that perceived effort is the key intermediary variable driving the effects of mental fatigue on exercise performance and highlight the ability of the psychobiological model to explain the mental fatigue–exercise performance relationship.

Although the psychobiological model accounts for the indirect effects of mental fatigue on exercise performance through increases in perception of effort, initial theorizing was broad and as a result, failed to identify mechanisms by which psychological factors such as mental fatigue would exacerbate perception of effort. Drawing on their results, Marcora et al. (2009) suggested mental fatigue disrupts central processing of the corollary discharge associated with the central motor command. This means that, when in a state of mental fatigue, a greater central motor command is necessary to produce the same force output as when not in a state of mental fatigue and, as a result, an increase in perception of exertion is experienced. The authors proposed that the anterior cingulate cortex (ACC) likely plays a significant role in this process due to its involvement in motor control, perception of effort, and higher order cognitive functions involved in effort-related decision making. However, research to date has yet to test this theory in its totality.

After Marcora et al. (2009) demonstrated convincing evidence that exposure to a cognitively demanding task can impair subsequent self-regulation of exercise performance, several academics turned their attention to this area, given the implications for sport. Naturally, this involved conducting studies to test boundary conditions of the mental fatigue–exercise performance relationship, but this also spurred further theorizing around the mechanisms by which mental fatigue may affect perception of effort and/or potential motivation. As emerging evidence continues to indicate physiological variables traditionally believed to limit endurance performance are unaffected by mental fatigue, extensions of the psychobiological model have focused on brain-based mechanisms. The first extension of the psychobiological model provided a neurobiological explanation focused on how mental fatigue influences perception of effort (Pageaux, Lepers, Dietz, & Marcora, 2014). Specifically, Pageaux et al. (2014) proposed that performing a demanding cognitive task leads to an accumulation of extracellular adenosine within the ACC, and, in turn, exacerbates perceptions of effort. These predictions were based on research showing the ACC is activated while performing cognitive tasks (Bush, Luu, & Posner, 2000; Swick & Jovanovic, 2002), including those commonly used to induce a state of mental fatigue (e.g. AX-CPT, Stroop task), and involved in perception of effort during exercise (Williamson et al., 2001, 2002). While this extension of the psychobiological model provides an interesting and plausible physiological explanation of how mental fatigue elicits a deleterious effect on exercise performance through increased perception of effort, there is one major shortcoming that needs to be acknowledged. That is, the psychobiological model posits that the interplay between perception of effort and potential motivation drives exercise performance; thus, the neurobiological explanation put forth by Pageaux et al. (2014) fails to consider the totality of the model in that it ignores the role of potential motivation.

Martin, Meeusen, Thompson, Keegan, and Rattray (2018) have since extended upon the initial physiological explanation proposed by Pageaux et al. (2014). Importantly, this updated physiological explanation encompasses both central tenets of the psychobiological model: Accounting for how mental fatigue affects exercise performance through not only affecting perception of exertion, but also potential motivation. Adenosine was again identified as the key mechanism driving this cascade of events. In addition to adenosine accumulation causing increased perception of effort, Martin et al. (2018) proposed a second pathway by which the buildup of adenosine due to effortful cognitive engagement inhibits the release of dopamine within the ACC, and, in turn, reduces one's motivation to exert further effort. This intuitive proposition is centered around neuroanatomical research and experimental work involving reward sensitivity and decision making among animal models (Fredholm & Svenningsson, 2003; Salamone et al., 2018; Schweimer & Hauber, 2006; Stanwood, Washington, Shumsky, & Levitt, 2001). Although Martin et al.'s (2018) physiological explanation is all encompassing with regard to the central constructs identified within the psychobiological model, it has not been tested within humans and would be challenging to do so.

The revised physiological explanation proposed by Martin et al. (2018) also includes a notable conceptual overlap with the strength model of self-regulation. According to their model, Martin et al. (2018) suggest that effortful cognitive exertion depletes localized cerebral fuel stores and, in turn, produces a bi-product: Cerebral adenosine. This line of theorizing was informed by a study comparing exercise performance following exposure to a mentally fatiguing cognitive task between recreational and professional cyclists (Martin et al., 2016). The results showed that professional cyclists made less errors on a response inhibition task (i.e. Stroop task) than recreational cyclists and were resilient to the effects of prior cognitive exertion on a subsequent cycling task, whereas recreational cyclists demonstrated a significant decline in performance. Martin et al. (2018) have interpreted these findings as potential genetic or training-induced adaptations that provide superior inhibitory control due to increased neuronal efficiency. That is, those with greater neuronal efficiency would use less "cerebral fuel" during tasks involving mental exertion, and, as a result, have less adenosine accumulation. This would have a twofold effect where perception of effort and potential motivation are both affected to a lesser extent, ultimately contributing to superior exercise performance. Overall, Martin et al.'s (2018) extended physiological explanation of the psychobiological model provides a more thorough account of how mental fatigue impairs subsequent self-regulation of exercise performance through an intuitive multi-process pathway.

Considerations and Pitfalls

Evidence to date in support of the psychobiological model overwhelmingly indicates perception of effort is the primary driver of exercise performance following exposure to mental exertion (Van Cutsem et al., 2017). Since Marcora et al.'s (2009) seminal findings were published, studies have shown the characteristics of the exercise task (e.g. fixed versus variable demand) shape behavioral responses to mental fatigue through perception of effort. For tasks involving fixed demands such as cycling to exhaustion, perception of effort is the "cardinal exercise stopper" whereby individuals tend to give up once they have reached the peak perception of effort they are willing to tolerate (Staiano et al., 2018). This peak is reached sooner in a mentally fatigued state. In contrast, for variable demand exercise tasks in which individuals can adjust their pace (e.g. running a 5 km race), perception of effort may be considered the "cardinal effort regulator". In this case, when perception of effort is exacerbated due to mental fatigue, individuals simply down-regulate their pace to bring their perception of effort in line with what they would typically experience in an optimal state. Taken together, findings support theorizing of the psychobiological model in which perception of effort plays a central role in performance of exercise tasks involving prolonged effortful exertion.

However, and similar to findings discussed in the previous section, research to date has shown limited support for the motivational component of the psychobiological model. Studies have assessed various forms of motivation (e.g. task, success, intrinsic) but for the most part have failed to detect any motivational shifts that can be attributed to mental fatigue. As noted previously (Brown & Bray, 2019b; Martin et al., 2018), measures of motivation may be too broad or abstract to objectively quantify shifts in motivation that occur when people are mentally fatigued. Measures of motivation are also confounded by the voluntary nature of participation in research: Participants often come into the lab highly motivated to perform the task at hand, often leading to ceiling effects when reporting motivation. This issue has been brought to attention by Martin et al. (2018). Moving forward, we need to gain a better understanding of how motivation affects self-regulation of exercise performance if we are to unanimously adopt the psychobiological model to understand the effects of prior cognitive exertion on exercise performance.

Finally, recent extensions of the psychobiological model have provided an intuitive physiological explanation for why mental fatigue has a deleterious effect on sport and exercise performance through influencing perception of effort and potential motivation (Martin et al., 2018; Pageaux, 2014). These propositions have focused primarily on neurobiological processes involving adenosine accumulation and, more recently, inhibition of dopamine release. However, the pathways outlined in these physiological explanations are based on research investigating animal models and have yet to be tested in humans. While we can infer about this relationship from findings using animal models, the neurobiological pathways by which this phenomenon occurs in humans is currently unknown. It is apparent that we will need methodological advances in neurobiological measurement before we can comprehensively test this model in humans.

Where Do We Currently Stand?

As noted earlier in this chapter, research investigating self-regulation of sport and exercise performance following an initial task involving cognitive exertion has been conceptualized as due to either ego depletion or mental fatigue. Within these emerging bodies of literature, there have been several recent efforts to synthesize current evidence through conducting systematic reviews (Englert, 2016; Pageaux & Lepers, 2018; Silva-Júnior et al., 2016; Van Cutsem et al., 2017) and meta-analyses (Brown et al., 2020; Giboin & Wolff, 2019; McMorris, Barwood, Hale, Dicks, & Corbett, 2018). Studies from both areas have generally concluded that performing an initial demanding cognitive task leads to subsequent performance impairments across a broad range of aerobic and resistance-based tasks that require prolonged effort regulation, in addition to sport-specific motor tasks. In the first attempt to quantify the magnitude and direction of the effects of prior cognitive exertion on subsequent physical performance, McMorris et al. (2018) demonstrated a small negative effect ($g = -0\ 26$), although statistical tests suggested that this effect may be due to random error. However, these results were only drawn from studies that examined mental (or cognitive) fatigue, which resulted in only eight studies being included. Significant concerns have since been expressed regarding the comprehensiveness and replicability of their search, as well as the rationale for their exclusion criteria (Magariño & Madhivanan, 2019). Therefore, considering the substantial methodological similarities between ego depletion and mental fatigue studies, the meta-analysis of McMorris et al. (2018) failed to consider what is a much larger body of literature.

The major difference that has been argued to stand between the unification of the mental fatigue and ego depletion literatures has been the duration of the cognitive manipulations (Englert, 2016; Pageaux et al., 2013; Van Cutsem et al., 2017). Most mental fatigue studies have used cognitive manipulations lasting 30 minutes or more (e.g., Marcora et al., 2009), whereas ego depletion studies typically use manipulations of shorter duration, with some as brief as 3.5 minutes (e.g., Bray et al., 2008). Researchers examining mental fatigue have argued the cognitive manipulations employed to cause ego depletion are too brief to induce a state of mental fatigue (Pageaux et al., 2013). Simply stated, only after prolonged mental exertion can mental fatigue be experienced. In their recent review, Van Cutsem et al. (2017) argued the minimum task duration necessary to induce mental fatigue is 30 minutes. This claim was based on studies showing decrements in vigilance (Nuechterlein, Parasuraman, & Jiang, 1983) and increments in mental fatigue occurring around the 30-minute time point (Smith, Coutts, et al., 2016). Van Cutsem et al. (2017) also argued against including research from the ego depletion area due to a replication crisis. Unfortunately, the evidence upon which this 30-minute point is based on is both weak and suspect for two reasons. First, only a small proportion of studies in the ego depletion literature have investigated effects of cognitive exertion on physical performance and none of the failed replication efforts undertaken thus far have involved effects of cognitive tasks on physical tasks. Second, it fails to recognize multiple ego depletion studies that have documented significant increases in self-reported mental fatigue following cognitive manipulations lasting much less than 30 minutes (Bray et al., 2011; Brown & Bray, 2017a, 2019a; Graham & Bray, 2012; Muraven et al., 1998). These findings have led theorists to posit ego depletion is a form of mental fatigue (Hagger et al., 2010a; Inzlicht & Berkman, 2015). In addition to task duration, there is compelling evidence that the difficulty of a cognitive task also contributes to perceptions of mental fatigue. That is, difficult cognitive tasks can result in high levels of fatigue in a fraction of the time required by less difficult cognitive tasks (Boksem & Tops, 2008; Mackworth, 1964; Warm, Parasuraman, & Matthews, 2008). For example, performing a highly demanding Stroop task for 10 minutes (Brown & Bray, 2017a) has been shown to produce similar levels of mental fatigue to engaging in a moderately demanding continuous performance task (i.e. AX-CPT) for 50 minutes (Brown & Bray, 2019b). In light of this evidence and the substantial overlap in methodologies, it makes sense to examine these bodies of literature together in totality.

To fully describe and interpret the greater body of literature examining the effects of prior cognitive exertion on self-regulation of sport and exercise performance, we undertook a comprehensive synthesis and meta-analysis that integrated the mental fatigue and ego depletion literatures (Brown et al., 2020). Our rigorous search of the literature found a total of 79 studies (which included 98 comparisons) that involved performance of a physical task following completion of an initial task requiring effortful cognitive exertion. Of the 79 studies, we were able to obtain sufficient statistical information to include 73 studies (which included 91 comparisons) in the meta-analysis.

The results of our meta-analysis of the effects of prior cognitive exertion on self-regulation of a subsequent physical performance task revealed a significant, small-to-medium-sized negative overall effect ($g = -0.38$). Of the 91 independent comparisons included in the meta-analysis, 81 suggested evidence of a deleterious effect, of which 46 indicated a significant performance impairment (all p's < 0.05). Further statistical tests demonstrated significant heterogeneity in the data which led us to conclude that the observed effect is likely not due to chance. Another comprehensive meta-analysis of the ego depletion and mental fatigue literature reached a similar conclusion. Looking strictly at endurance performance, Giboin and Wolff (2019) found evidence of a significant medium-sized negative effect (ES $= -0.51$) across 42 independent comparisons. Therefore, by unifying ego depletion and mental fatigue studies to investigate this greater body of literature in its totality (Brown et al., 2020; Giboin & Wolff, 2019), these meta-analyses were able to reduce potential selection bias which may have influenced conclusions drawn by previous reviews and meta-analyses in the area.

Beyond providing a comprehensive investigation of the overall effect of prior cognitive exertion on subsequent physical performance, our meta-analysis included a closer look at several potential moderators of this relationship. One of the most important subgroup analyses pertained to the aforementioned differences in cognitive manipulation durations used in studies aiming to induce a state of ego depletion or mental fatigue. Given that 30 minutes has been suggested to be the minimum duration needed to induce a state of mental fatigue and, in turn, impair physical performance (Van Cutsem et al., 2017), we stratified studies into two groups based on the duration of the cognitive manipulation utilized: Those < 30 minutes, and those ≥ 30 minutes. The results of our subgroup analysis failed to reveal a difference between the two groups. Simply stated, cognitive manipulations lasting less than 30 minutes ($g = -0.45$) and those lasting 30 minutes or longer ($g = -0.30$) had similar small-to-medium-sized negative carryover effects on physical performance. However, using this arbitrary cut-point failed to consider the possibility of a potential dose-response relationship. To explore this issue, we conducted a post-hoc meta-regression of the relationship between cognitive task duration and physical performance. The results did not support a linear dose-response relationship. Taken together, evidence suggests time on task may not be the driving factor underlying subsequent self-regulatory impairments.

Another major advance provided by our meta-analysis was the quantification of the effects of prior cognitive exertion on different types of sport and exercise tasks. Our study built upon previous findings of a qualitative synthesis of the effects of prior cognitive exertion on a variety of sport and exercise performance outcomes (Pageaux & Lepers, 2018). In their review, Pageaux and Lepers (2018) concluded that tasks requiring precision (i.e. motor skills) or sustained regulation of effort (i.e. aerobic, dynamic resistance, isometric resistance performance) are most sensitive to prior cognitive exertion, whereas performance of tasks requiring maximal anaerobic performance such as a sprint appears unaffected. The results from our meta-analysis provide statistical support for these findings. Specifically, we found prior cognitive exertion to have significant negative effects on motor performance ($g = -0.57$) and tasks requiring prolonged effort regulation (i.e. aerobic [$g = -0.26$], isometric resistance [$g = -0.57$], dynamic resistance performance [$g = -0.51$]). Tasks requiring maximal anaerobic performance showed trivial effects that were not significant. Similar effects have also been reported for endurance tasks grouped based on whether they involved an isolated group of muscles (e.g. handgrip squeeze; ES = −0.72) or the whole body (e.g. cycling; coefficient = 0.34) (Giboin & Wolff, 2019).

The physiological model proposed by Martin et al. (2018) provides an explanation for why prior cognitive exertion negatively affects tasks involving the sustained regulation of effort (i.e. aerobic, dynamic resistance, isometric resistance performance) to a greater extent than tasks involving maximal anaerobic performance. That is, "all out" tasks requiring brief maximal anaerobic performance do not require pacing strategies; thus, individuals are able to endure higher perceptions of effort for short durations that would otherwise derail performance of longer tasks. Theorizing pertaining to the negative carryover effects of cognitive exertion on tasks requiring sustained attention and motor skills, however, has received much less attention to date. Building on Martin et al.'s (2018) model, it is plausible that shared neural pathways governing cognition (e.g. attention) and motor behavior become compromised due to extracellular increases in adenosine and the subsequent dysregulation of dopaminergic neurons governing motor skills, leading to a cascade of psychophysiological processes that affect physical task performance (Brown et al., 2020, p. 524; Graham et al., 2018, p. 11). Nevertheless, additional research is needed to investigate the effect of prior cognitive exertion on maximal anaerobic performance while also testing the aforementioned propositions for reductions in various types of physical task performance.

Potential Mediators and Moderators of Performance

Despite the consistent effects of prior cognitive exertion on self-regulation of sport and exercise performance, very few studies have examined potential mediators and moderators of performance. By identifying mediators and moderators, we can build on theory to understand underlying mechanisms. For example, the shifting priorities (or process) model proposes that self-regulation is the product of multiple psychological inputs – motivation, emotion, and attention – that increase or decrease the value of exerting further effort (Inzlicht et al., 2014; Milyavskaya & Inzlicht, 2017). Understanding the role of these processes could provide insight for recreational exercisers and professional athletes regarding the structure or timing of their workouts and competitions as well as recommendations for coaches and trainers when instructing individuals performing effortful tasks in succession. But only one study to date has comprehensively tested the assumptions of the shifting priorities model within a sport or exercise context and evidence of mediation was not observed (Stocker, Seiler, Schmid, & Englert, 2020). On its own, motivation has received much more attention. Evidence indicates manipulating motivation through providing performance contingent incentives (Brown & Bray, 2017a) and autonomy supportive instructions (Graham, Bray, et al., 2014) can attenuate the negative effects of prior cognitive exertion on physical performance. Therefore, in the right circumstances, individuals are able to overcome the negative aftereffects of cognitive exertion when they are sufficiently motivated to do so.

Studies have shown that perceptions of fatigue (Marcora et al., 2009), affective valence (Brown & Bray, 2017a), and task self-efficacy (Brown & Bray, 2017a; Graham & Bray, 2015) are altered following cognitive exertion and likely contribute to alterations in one's ability to self-regulate their physical performance. Indeed, based on theorizing within self-efficacy theory (Bandura, 1997), Graham et al. (2017) tested single and sequential mediation pathways, including perceptions of fatigue and self-efficacy. They found that cognitive exertion led to higher perceptions of fatigue which, in turn, led to lower perceptions of self-efficacy (i.e. less confident to perform the upcoming physical task), and ultimately reduced physical task performance. Other research has shown that following cognitive exertion people plan to exert less effort on a subsequent test of physical performance which resulted in less work performed during the self-paced exercise session (Brown & Bray, 2019a, 2019b). Taken together, subjective and likely instinctive responses to cognitive exertion, such as increased perceptions of fatigue and reduced affect, seem to trigger a cascade of psychological and decisional processes (e.g. "I feel tired and less confident in my ability to perform so I don't think I can work as hard on this upcoming physical test") that ultimately contribute to reduced physical task performance. Researchers, coaches, and trainers are encouraged to monitor these subjective experiences following cognitive exertion to not only understand why performance decrements occur but to also develop ways to intervene. In fact, recent work has shown that using a heart rate monitor to provide biofeedback to self-monitor performance can successfully attenuate the effects of prior cognitive exertion (Brown & Bray, 2019a). Commonly used self-monitoring tools that track distance, pace, and heart rate may be able to create a motivational structure in which feedback can be leveraged to drive goal-directed behavior in alignment with previously held standards or intentions through enhanced self-efficacy.

As previously discussed, ratings of perceived exertion are a prominent construct within the psychobiological model and are a consistent predictor of physical task cessation and performance. However, it would be interesting to investigate whether certain alterations in psychological processes experienced prior to task performance lead to (i.e. mediate) or enhance (i.e. moderate) changes in perceived exertion during task performance. We encourage researchers to use freely accessible software such as PROCESS (Hayes, 2017) and MEMORE (Montoya & Hayes, 2017) to test for mediation and moderation in between-subject and within-subject study designs. By doing so, we will begin to form a deeper understanding of the prior cognitive exertion – physical performance relationship.

Recent research has also begun to investigate various individual level factors that moderate the prior cognitive exertion – physical performance relationship. For example, while many of the studies investigating the negative aftereffects of cognitive exertion on physical performance have primarily involved inactive or recreationally active individuals, the findings with regard to highly trained individuals have been mixed. That is, recent research suggests that highly trained athletes or expert performers may not be as susceptible to physical performance decrements following cognitive exertion (Kosack, Staiano, Folino, Hansen, & Lønbro 2020; Martin et al., 2016). Other work in children suggests children with low levels of motor coordination experience even greater negative effects of cognitive exertion on physical performance, whereas high levels of motor coordination seem to buffer against the negative effects typically observed (Graham et al., 2018).

Future Directions

There are several promising avenues for future research investigating the effects of prior cognitive exertion on physical exertion. First and foremost, more research is needed investigating cognitive exertion and the self-regulation of physical activity behavior in everyday life outside of contrived lab environments. Of the handful of naturalistic studies that have been conducted using daily diaries and ecological momentary assessment thus far, it seems that self-control dwindles across the course of one's day and negatively impacts physical activity intentions and behavior (Englert & Rummel, 2016; Finne, Englert, & Jekauc, 2019; Pfeffer & Strobach, 2017; Rebar, Dimmock, Rhodes, & Jackson, 2018; Schöndube, Bertrams, Sudeck, & Fuchs, 2017). However, additional research is needed using device-based physical activity measures alongside self-reported measures.

With regard to lab environments, there are several opportunities for refinement and future research. For instance, one of the major limitations idenfitied across studies within Brown et al.'s (2020) risk-of-bias assessment was the lack of blinding procedures. Future research should employ double-blinding procedures whereby one experimenter delivers the cognitive manipulation and another administers the physical task. Crossover and/or multi-task (i.e. physical task-cognitive task-physical task) experimental designs are also encouraged so that change in performance on the physical task can be compared within individuals and between conditions. Similarily, standardizing the physical task to participants' strength (i.e. percent of maximum voluntary contraction) or ability levels should be utlized whenever possible. A familiaration session with the physical task is also encouraged. While there is a strong rationale for selecting the cognitive manipulations previously employed within this body of literature, future work should also consider using cognitive manipulations with greater external validity such as playing video games or scrolling through social media platforms (Fortes et al., 2020).

Finally, undertaking studies involving additional neurophysiological measures alongside self-report measures is strongly encouraged. Theorizing and limited findings based on the strength model and the psychobiological model suggest that various psychological, neurophysiological, and physiological processes are altered during cognitive exertion as well as during subsequent task performance (Lopez, Vohs, Wagner, & Heatherton, 2015; Martin et al., 2018). That is, alterations in muscle activity patterns (Bray et al., 2008; Brown & Bray, 2017b; Graham, Sonne, et al., 2014; Pageaux et al., 2014) and brain activation patterns (Brownsberger et al., 2013; Pires et al., 2018) have been observed following cognitive exertion and during physical task performance. In addition, as previously mentioned in the potential mediators and moderators of performance section, various alterations in psychological processes have also been observed following cognitive exertion and during task performance. It would be very interesting to examine psychological, neurophysiological, and physiological processes either concurrently or sequentially in an experiment to understand how changes in one process may lead to changes in another.

Conclusion

In this chapter, we provided an in-depth overview of the current state of the literature examining the influence of prior cognitive exertion on self-regulation of subsequent sport and exercise performance. We outlined the two most common theoretical perspectives that have been adopted to interpret this body of research, while also highlighting why effects from ego depletion and mental fatigue studies should be considered collectively. At present, research indicates that prior cognitive exertion has a small-to-moderate-sized negative effect on subsequent physical performance; however, this effect is not dependent on time, and is most pronounced for motor-based tasks and tasks requiring prolonged effort regulation (e.g. aerobic or resistance exercise). Research has shown that the negative effects of prior cognitive exertion manifest before an individual even begins to exercise, and once they do get started, they can expect to experience exacerbated perceptions of effort. Intervention strategies aiming to overcome these effects may be most effective when targeting motivational processes. Moving forward, researchers need to design better studies that reduce bias, step outside the lab to tackle this question in the real world, and take a multidisciplinary approach to better understand the mechanisms underlying these effects.

Notes

1 Studies appearing in Tables 9.1a–c and Figures 9.1 and 9.2 adhered to the eligibility criteria and search terms used by Brown et al. (2020) which reviewed studies that investigated the carryover effects of cognitive exertion on physical performance without including any other manipulations

(e.g., motivational incentives, performance at high altitude). True control and experimental conditions (i.e. the no manipulation conditions) were pulled from studies that included auxiliary manipulations, although in some cases this was not possible and these studies were not included in these tables and figures. Some examples are included in the "Potential Mediators and Moderators of Performance" and "Future Directions" subsections near the end of this chapter.

2 The shifting priorities model was originally known as the process model of ego depletion (Inzlicht & Schmeichel, 2012; Inzlicht, Schmeichel, & Macrae, 2014).

10

THE EFFECTS OF MENTAL FATIGUE ON SPORT PERFORMANCE

An Update

Jeroen Van Cutsem and Samuele Marcora

Introduction

Sport training and competitions pose very high demands on the brain and not just the cardiorespiratory, metabolic, and neuromuscular systems (Walsh, 2014). Therefore, sport training and competitions can be mentally as well as physically fatiguing. Furthermore, media engagements, study and work commitments, repetitive tasks, over-analysis, thinking about the sport in question, and environmental instability are thought to cause mental fatigue in athletes (Russell, Jenkins, Rynne et al., 2019). Given all of the above, it is not surprising that athletes and coaches often complain about mental fatigue and believe it negatively affects sport performance (Russell, Jenkins, Rynne et al., 2019).

From a scientific point of view, mental fatigue (also known as cognitive fatigue) can be defined as a psychobiological state induced by prolonged and demanding cognitive tasks and it is experienced as feelings of tiredness and lack of energy, as a reduction in cognitive performance, or as an increase in the effort required to maintain performance (Ackerman, 2011). Mental fatigue can be differentiated from sleepiness because the subjective feelings of mental fatigue can often be counteracted by having a break or shifting the focus onto another task (Van Cutsem et al., 2017), whereas sleepiness needs sleep to be relieved (Borragán, Slama, Bartolomei, & Peigneux, 2017). Albeit different in many respects, mental fatigue and sleep deprivation interact with each other with the mental fatigue-induced reduction in cognitive performance being exacerbated by sleep deprivation (Balkin & Wesensten, 2011). Furthermore, both mental fatigue and sleepiness can be counteracted by stimulants like caffeine, thus suggesting some shared biological mechanisms like the accumulation of adenosine in the brain (Plumb, Sterlace, Cavanaugh, & Minor, 2013). It is also useful to differentiate acute mental fatigue and chronic mental fatigue. The negative effects of the former can be quickly reversed with rest (Smith, Chai, Nguyen, Marcora, & Coutts, 2019), while the symptoms of chronic mental fatigue are often associated with the overtraining syndrome and can take several months to resolve despite a reduction in training load or total rest (Meeusen et al., 2013).

This chapter focuses on experimental studies investigating the effects of acute mental fatigue induced by prolonged and demanding cognitive tasks on the physical and psychomotor components of sport performance. Physical performance measures include measures of muscle strength and power, anaerobic performance (maximal effort lasting less than 75 seconds), and endurance (aerobic) performance (maximal effort lasting more than 75 seconds) (McCormick, Meijen, & Marcora, 2016). Endurance performance can be further subdivided in muscular endurance (i.e. mostly involving a single muscle or muscle group, e.g. sit-ups, weight holding, handgrip tasks, and leg-raise tasks) and whole-body endurance (i.e. involving multiple large muscle groups, e.g. running, cycling, and rowing) (McCormick et al., 2016; Wilmore, Costill, & Kenney, 2008). Psychomotor performance can be defined as highly complex motor behavior that results from the cognitive processing of sensory and perceptual information in a sport-specific context and typically encompasses reaction time and accuracy as main outcome measures (Hindmarch, 2014).

Methodological Approaches to Experimentally Induce Mental Fatigue

In order to adequately understand the experimental studies reviewed in this chapter, it is necessary to have a good understanding of the methodology used to manipulate mental fatigue. The standard method to induce mental fatigue in a laboratory setting is a prolonged cognitive task at a personal computer (Boksem & Tops, 2008; Van Cutsem et al., 2017; Pageaux & Lepers, 2018). For example, specifically within sport science-research, the AX Continuous Performance Test (AX-CPT) and the Stroop task are two of the most-often employed tasks to induce mental fatigue (McMorris, Barwood, Hale, Dicks, & Corbett, 2018; Van Cutsem et al., 2017). In the AX-CPT, sequences of letters are visually presented one at a time in a continuous fashion on a computer screen. By pushing a button, participants have to indicate when target trials appear in the sequences of letters. Target trials are defined as a cue-probe sequence in which the letter A appears as the cue and the letter X appears as the probe. The remaining letters of the alphabet serve as invalid cues and non-target probes. In the Stroop task, colored words (red, blue, green, and yellow) are presented one at a time on a computer screen, and participants are required to indicate the color of the word, ignoring the meaning of the word itself. Often, this Stroop task is also modified in mental fatigue research, e.g. when the ink color of the word is red, the button to be pressed by the participant is not the button that corresponds to the color of the word (i.e. red) but the button that is linked to the real meaning of the word (Van Cutsem et al., 2019). Performance on both these tasks relies on the ability to sustain attention, inhibit responses, working memory, and cognitive flexibility (Carter et al., 1998; MacLeod & MacDonald, 2000). These important executive functions (i.e. "higher-level" cognitive processes that exert top-down regulation of "lower-level" cognitive processes to support flexible and adaptive goal-directed behavior) are also engaged during sport activities, both during training and competitions (Hyland-Monks, Cronin, McNaughton, & Marchant, 2018).

For example, a tennis player has to focus attention on informative cues of the opponent's movements and tune out any noises of the crowd, movements of the linesman, or destructive thoughts (inhibition); among other things, a player has to keep in mind and continuously update previous strokes, knowledge about the opponent's characteristic play, and his tactical approaches (working memory); and a player has to flexibly adjust to the opponent's strokes and the continuously changing situations within a rally (cognitive flexibility) (Krenn, Finkenzeller, Würth, & Amesberger, 2018). Therefore, the AX-CPT and the Stroop task are believed to be appropriate laboratory-controlled tasks that require the same executive functions used during, for example, a tennis or a soccer match (Pageaux & Lepers,

2018). Crucially from an experimental perspective, prolonged engagement with these tasks (Pageaux & Lepers, 2018; Van Cutsem et al., 2019; Marcora, Staiano, & Manning, 2009) can induce mental fatigue without causing, at the same time, the significant neuromuscular, metabolic, and cardiorespiratory fatigue associated with intense and/or prolonged exercise (Joyner, 2016). Furthermore, both the AX-CPT (Carter et al., 1998) and the Stroop task (MacLeod & MacDonald, 2000) are associated with significant activation of the anterior cingulate cortex (ACC). This area of the prefrontal cortex is involved in mental fatigue (Cook, O'Connor, Lange, & Steffener, 2007; Lorist, Boksem, & Ridderinkhof, 2005) and is related to the perception of effort during exercise (Williamson et al., 2001, 2002). Based on the assumption that perception of effort is an important determinant of endurance performance (Wright, 2008; Marcora et al., 2009), such a connection between mental fatigue and perception of effort via the ACC provides a neurobiological rationale for the negative effects of mental fatigue on endurance performance. Although most researchers investigating mental fatigue use cognitive tasks lasting more than 30 minutes up to several hours (Boksem & Tops, 2008), it is worth noting that some authors have investigated the effects of cognitive tasks lasting as little as three to five minutes on performance during subsequent physical or psychomotor tasks (Bray, Martin Ginis, Hicks, & Woodgate, 2008; Boat, Taylor, & Hulston, 2017; Englert & Bertrams, 2014; Englert, Persaud et al., 2015; Hagger et al., 2016). This kind of research usually describes the intervention-effect as an ego depletion, or a self-regulatory depletion instead of mental fatigue, and is based on the "strength" model of self-control (see also Chapters 8 and 9) (Hagger et al., 2016). According to this model, performance on tasks requiring self-control is governed by a generalized, unitary, and finite "internal" resource. It proposes that engaging in tasks requiring self-control will lead to the depletion of this resource and reduced performance on subsequent tasks requiring self-control, including endurance tasks (Hagger et al., 2016). Indeed, a common subsequent task in this literature is a sustained submaximal handgrip task to exhaustion (Hagger et al., 2010b). In our previous systematic review on the effects of mental fatigue on physical performance, we excluded studies from the ego depletion literature where prior cognitive exertion lasted less than 30 minutes. However, two recent meta-analyses have demonstrated significant decrements in subsequent physical performance after performing both shorter (less than 30 minutes) and longer (more than 30 minutes) cognitive tasks (Brown et al., 2020; Giboin & Wolff, 2019). Furthermore, new theoretical models from mainstream psychology argue that ego depletion is a type of mental fatigue rather than a separate phenomenon (Francis & Inzlicht, 2016; Inzlicht & Marcora, 2016). All considered, it seems justifiable to use the umbrella term "mental fatigue" for the negative effects of cognitive exertion (of any duration) on performance and/or the subjective markers of fatigue like feeling tired/drained of energy or that more effort is required to perform a task. In our opinion, the terms "ego depletion" and "self-regulatory depletion" imply that a depletion of a (metaphorical or real) resource underlies the negative effects of cognitive exertion on performance, while mechanistically, an accumulation (e.g. of adenosine; Martin, Meeusen, Thompson, Keegan, & Rattray, 2018) could also lay at the base of the occurrence of mental fatigue and its negative effects. Therefore, the terms "ego depletion" and "self-regulatory depletion" do, in our opinion, not really serve the field of mental fatigue research and the term "mental fatigue" will be used as an umbrella term in this chapter.

The surprising fact that cognitive task duration does not have a large moderating effect on subsequent physical performance may be due to the complex interaction between task duration, task difficulty, and task engagement during cognitive tasks. During physical tasks, where engagement can be easily controlled by fixing the workload on the exercise ergometer, the relationship between task duration and muscle fatigue is clear (Marcora & Staiano, 2010). It is far more complex/almost impossible to accurately control engagement in a cognitive task. For example, because of boredom or the learning of strategies to reduce the difficulty of the task (e.g. squinting to reduce the Stroop interference), engagement can be reduced after, for example, 5 minutes into a 90-minute Stroop task and one can still be able to perform at an acceptable level. Unlike total disengagement with a task, it is very hard to distinguish this kind of disengagement from the performance effects of mental fatigue or individual differences in cognitive performance. Therefore, a 10-minute Stroop task performed with high engagement could be as fatiguing or even more fatiguing than the 90-minute Stroop task described above. In support of this hypothesis, O'Keeffe, Hodder, & Lloyd (2020) recently compared five different tasks (set up control, documentary control, AX-CPT, a dual task test, and an individualized dual task test) in their ability to induce mental fatigue, and achieved mental fatigue to a greater extent in a short (16 minutes), but more difficult, individualized dual task, compared to the longer (90 minutes) AX-CPT. However, when task difficulty is similar, task duration has been shown to be positively correlated with the ability of a task to induce mental fatigue. Fortes et al. (2019) (i.e. smart-phone use) and Gantois et al. (2019) (i.e. a Stroop task) both compared different durations of a mentally fatiguing task and both reported that the 15-minute task failed to induce mental fatigue to the same extent as the 30- and 45-minute tasks. In contrast, a recent high-powered study by Wolff, Sieber et al. (2019) demonstrated that performance on a secondary self-control task did not suffer from a prior self-control task. Moreover, task duration of the primary self-control task did not affect these findings (Wolff, Sieber et al., 2019). Clearly, more research is needed to better understand the main effects and the interaction of cognitive task duration and difficulty on task engagement, mental fatigue, and performance during a subsequent physical or psychomotor task. We also need to develop and use better objective measures of task engagement (and disengagement) at an individual level while performing the cognitive tasks (e.g. heart rate/blood pressure or EEG markers) and employ motivational strategies (e.g. monetary reward) to ensure prolonged engagement with the mentally fatiguing task. Prolonged engagement is important because if people do not engage during the mentally fatiguing task, it is unlikely that the task will cause mental fatigue. Premature partial disengagement during the mentally fatiguing task might, as such, create individual differences in the effects of mental fatigue on physical and psychomotor performance thus reducing the statistical effect sizes. The use of more sport-specific cognitive tasks to induce mental fatigue in athletes has been proposed (Russell et al., 2018). Although there is no convincing neurobiological rationale for the proposal that mental fatigue induced by sport-specific cognitive tasks would be different from mental fatigue induced by non-specific but equally demanding cognitive tasks (Russell, Jeknkins, Smith et al., 2019), a sport-specific cognitive tasks (e.g. a simulated soccer game) may be more engaging to an athlete than, for example, a 90-minute AX-CPT task. However, it has to be considered that enjoyable cognitive tasks are less mentally fatiguing than boring tasks for which the participant has some aversion (Ackerman, 2011). Again, the complexity of the factors involved in mental fatigue (Ackerman, 2011) makes its experimental inducement much more challenging than inducing muscle fatigue, and it should be considered when planning and interpreting experiments on the effects of mental fatigue on sport performance.

The complex interaction between task duration, task difficulty, task enjoyment/aversion, and task engagement may also explain the variability in the observed performance effects of mental fatigue. If a study uses a 30-minute cognitive task to induce mental fatigue, but one participant reduces his/her engagement after 2 minutes, another one after 18 minutes, and another one remains highly engaged for the whole 30 minutes, it should not be surprising that the extent of mental fatigue that was triggered in each of these individuals can be different and subsequently also the effect of mental fatigue on performance in the subsequent physical or psychomotor task (see the importance of prolonged engagement during the mentally fatiguing task; as explained above). This interindividual variability in task engagement may explain the variability of the fatiguing effects of the cognitive tasks used in mental fatigue research and, as a result, reduce the statistical effect size of mental fatigue on physical and psychomotor performances. It is worth noting, however, that the point estimate of the effect of mental fatigue on high-intensity endurance cycling performance is similar to that of pre-fatiguing the leg muscles with 100 drop jumps (Marcora, Bosio, & de Morree, 2008; Marcora et al., 2009); in other words, the average effect of mental fatigue on endurance performance seems to be as large as the average effect of locomotor muscle fatigue.

Even if both, cognitive task duration and engagement, could be controlled, it is likely that interindividual differences exist in the extent of mental fatigue induced by the cognitive tasks used in experimental research, as some individuals may be more resistant than others to the negative effects of prolonged cognitive exertion. Therefore, it is important to use manipulation checks to monitor whether a state of mental fatigue has been induced. However, unlike the presence of muscle fatigue which can be easily quantified by voluntary or stimulated muscle contractions before and after exercise, proving the presence of a complex psychobiological state like mental fatigue is challenging. Multiple subjective (e.g. visual analogue scale, VAS; i.e. a horizontal line of 10 cm that ranges from 0 (= not at all) to 100 (= completely exhausted) on which participants have to indicate how mentally fatigued they feel; Lee, Hicks, & Nino-Murcia, 1991), behavioral (e.g. cognitive performance), and physiological (e.g. brain activity) measures can be employed to check the occurrence of mental fatigue, but there is no consensus on a gold standard (Ackerman, 2011). Therefore, at present, the best approach seems to be the use of several measures in each specific area, i.e. subjective, behavioral, and physiological. The interpretation of the interaction between these different measures is crucial because changes in all three of these areas do not necessarily have to be present for mental fatigue to be proven. For instance, cognitive performance does not necessarily decline when one is mentally fatigued because compensatory effort may alleviate its negative effects on cognitive function (Van Cutsem et al., 2017). Conversely, several studies of operator fatigue show that performance can be objectively impaired even when participants do not report feeling fatigued or impaired (Ackerman, 2011). Future research on the psychophysiological and neural correlates of effort (i.e. task engagement) and mental fatigue is required, so that we can become better at identifying mental fatigue without relying primarily on self-reports and changes in cognitive performance.

Effects of Mental Fatigue on Sport Performance

This section is a qualitative update of our systematic review on the effects of mental fatigue on physical performance (Van Cutsem et al., 2017) subdivided into strength, power, and anaerobic performance, and endurance (aerobic) performance. Because of the importance of

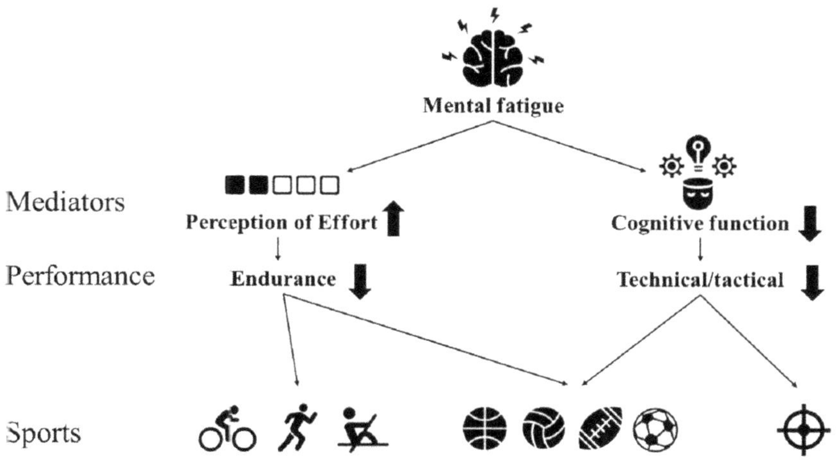

FIGURE 10.1 Overview of the impact of mental fatigue on sport performance and the underlying mechanisms (mediators).

psychomotor skills for sport performance, we have also reviewed experimental studies on the effects of mental fatigue on various measures of psychomotor performance (see Figure 10.1).

Effects of Mental Fatigue on Strength, Power, and Anaerobic Performance

One of the main conclusions of our systematic review was that there is no evidence that muscle strength, power, and anaerobic performance are significantly affected by mental fatigue (Van Cutsem, 2017). Up to date this conclusion has been further substantiated by studies of Fortes, Lima-Júnior, Gantois et al. (2020), Le Mansec et al. (2018), Kosack, Staiano, Folino, Hansen, & Lønbro, (2020), and Campos et al. (2019). Fortes, Lima-Júnior, Gantois et al. (2020) analyzed the performance effects of using smartphone social media apps on the 50-, 100-, and 200-m freestyle high-level swimmers. While smartphone usage was not associated with performance differences on the 50-m race (i.e. the race with the greatest anaerobic character), it did impair performance on the 100- and 200-m race. Le Mansec et al. (2017) confirmed that mental fatigue does not decrease force production capacity of the knee extensors and additionally also demonstrated that the force production capacity of the elbow flexors is not impaired by mental fatigue. Kosack et al. (2020) evaluated the effects of mental fatigue on badminton performance by means of a badminton-specific test that consisted of a sensor in each of the four corners of a badminton court. A computer placed in the middle, front court, showed a visual signal indicating to which corner the subjects were supposed to move. Kosack et al. (2020) found no effect of mental fatigue on this badminton-specific test and in addition reported blood lactate values above 8 mmol/L on average during the test. This indicates that the workload has put great demands on anaerobic metabolism and suggests that mental fatigue may not affect performance on the badminton-specific test due the high anaerobic demands of the test. Campos et al. (2019) used a special judo fitness test, with a high anaerobic demand, to assess the effect of mental fatigue on judo-specific performance. Similarly as Kosack et al. (2020), Campos et al. (2019) also did not observe an effect of mental fatigue on performance. Even though there is considerable evidence to state that mental fatigue does not appear to affect strength, power, and anaerobic performance, we do believe that further research is required to investigate the effects of mental fatigue on strength and power sports like Olympic weightlifting, jumping, and throwing. These sports require high levels of psychomotor skills and the supporting evidence that mental fatigue has a negative influence on psychomotor performance suggests that it may negatively influence performance in these sports normally classified as "strength and power sports". Moreover, the competition format in these skilled "strength and power sports" also requires the athlete to sustain focus and control emotions over a prolonged period of time. A study of Silva, Dias, Corte-Real, and Fonseca (2017) provides a good example in a judo-specific context that can be translated to multiple other strength and power sports. A sub-elite coach and former Olympic athlete that was interviewed in this study (2017) mentions:

> Even the progression throughout the competition requires psychological preparation, because you are advancing [in the competition] and you reach a certain point: Well, now I will enter the stage of winning or not a medal or winning the competition or not. And that's a different fight from the ones in the preliminaries. And these are situations that are more psychologically demanding.

This cognitive exertion may induce substantial mental fatigue during competitions, and further research is required to investigate its influence on performance in Olympic weightlifting, jumping, throwing, and similar sports.

Effects of Mental Fatigue on Endurance (Aerobic) Performance

Our systematic review suggested that endurance performance can be significantly impaired by mental fatigue (Van Cutsem et al., 2017). Since then, several studies have investigated the effects of mental fatigue on endurance performance (Azevedo, Silva-Cavalcante, Gualano, Lima-Silva, & Bertuzzi, 2016; Otani, Kaya, Tamaki, & Watson, 2017; Veness, Patterson, Jeffries, & Waldron, 2017), and the majority found that mental fatigue significantly reduces endurance performance. Salam, Marcora, and Hopker (2018) found that time-to-exhaustion (TTE) was reduced by an average of ~15% across exercise intensities equivalent to Δ40, Δ60, Δ80, and 100% $VO_{2peak.}$ Penna, Filho, Wanner et al. (2018) observed a ~1.2% increase in time to complete a 1500-m swim time trial (TT). Pires et al. (2018) reported that the time to complete a 20-km TT was ~2.7% slower when mentally fatigued and Slimani, Znazen, Bragazzi, Zguira, and Tod (2018) observed a decreased performance (i.e. a lower attained maximal running speed; ~8.2%) on the 20-m multistage fitness test (i.e. an incremental shuttle run test) due to mental fatigue. In contrast, Silva-Cavalcante et al. (2018) found no effect of mental fatigue on time to complete a 4-km cycling TT. Vrijkotte et al. (2018) did not observe any significant differences in the maximal wattage reached in two consecutive incremental cycling tests due to mental fatigue. Filipas, Mottola, Tagliabue, and La Torre (2018) reported no effects of prior mentally demanding activities on 1500-m rowing performance in prepubertal athletes and Head et al. (2016) showed that the amount of muscle resistance exercise repetitions was also not altered by mental fatigue. Taking all behavioral findings into account, the effect of mental fatigue on endurance performance is thus mostly replicated, yet not consistently. Possible moderating factors of the effects of mental fatigue on endurance performance could be a high anaerobic component, the cognitive load of the sport performance (e.g. when little/no pacing is required, the cognitive load decreases and the effect of mental fatigue might be less apparent) (Silva-Cavalcante et al., 2018; Vrijkotte et al., 2018) and physical activity prior to sport performance (e.g. preloaded TT in the study of Van Cutsem et al. 2017). Another moderating factor could be heat, as in our own mental fatigue study in the heat (Van Cutsem et al., 2017), heat appeared to prevent the negative effects of mental fatigue on endurance performance. A plausible explanation for this is that the higher perception of effort experienced during endurance exercise in a hot environment or when mentally fatigued may share a common psychobiological mechanism: negative valence (Van Cutsem et al., 2017). Exercising in the heat is associated with thermal discomfort, whereas mental fatigue is known to induce a more negative mood. As such, in conditions of thermal discomfort, the negative effects of mild mental fatigue on mood may not lead to further increase in negative valence and perception of effort. However, others demonstrated that the negative effect of heat might also work synergistically with mental fatigue to further decrease endurance performance (Otani et al., 2017). This is not the first fatigue-related line of research where heat has been found to act as a moderating variable (Roelands, De Pauw, & Meeusen, 2015) and calls for further research to explore the moderating role of heat on the effects of mental fatigue on endurance performance.

Effects of Mental Fatigue on Psychomotor Performance

As already mentioned in the introduction, besides endurance performance, the effect of mental fatigue on psychomotor performance has also been investigated in recent years (Russell et al., 2018). Psychomotor performance can be defined as highly complex motor behavior that results from the cognitive processing of sensory and perceptual information in a sport-specific context and typically encompasses reaction time and accuracy as primary outcome measures. In sports, psychomotor performance can for example be recognized as an immeasurable amount of high-risk and high-pressure decisions within a game of basketball, or in the particular stimulus-response situation (i.e. anticipating the opponent) in one-on-one games (e.g. fencing, badminton). In general, similarly as for endurance performance, a negative impact of mental fatigue on psychomotor performance can be observed. Mental fatigue impairs sport-specific cricket (Veness et al., 2017), badminton (Van Cutsem et al., 2019) and table tennis (Le Mansec et al., 2017) performance, marksmanship decision-making performance (Head et al., 2017), and soccer-specific technical and perceptual-cognitive psychomotor performance (Badin, Smith, Conte, & Coutts, 2016; Coutinho et al., 2017; Smith et al., 2016). This evidence has already been summarized in topic-related narrative reviews (Pageaux & Lepers, 2018; Russell et al., 2018) and a soccer-specific systematic review (Kunrath, Cardoso et al., 2020). To give a few concrete examples, in the study of Coutinho et al. (2018), mental fatigue resulted in a likely ~8% decrease in the time that players spent synchronized in the longitudinal displacements, while in the study of Moreira et al. (2018), mental fatigue was associated with an increased total number of turnovers in basketball (i.e. when a team loses possession of the ball to the opposing team before a player takes a shot at their team's basket) and Le Mansec et al. (2017) found that ball speed decreased and number of faults increased in mentally fatigued participants, resulting in a lower overall table tennis performance. However, there are also some studies that did not find significant effects of mental fatigue on psychomotor performance (Campos et al., 2019; Kosack et al., 2020; Vogt et al., 2018). Vogt and colleagues (2018) reasoned that the absence of an effect of mental fatigue on the Footbonaut test (i.e. an agility and passing accuracy test in a 14 × 14-m play zone that is equipped with walls, light panels, and ball-throwing machines) was due to possible talent influence, motivation-related aspects, and missing evidence regarding the validity of the Footbonaut task. While in the studies of Kosack et al. (2020) and Campos et al. (2019) the big anaerobic component of the employed psychomotor task might explain why no effect of mental fatigue was observed. In general, anaerobic performance has been shown to not be affected by mental fatigue (Brown et al., 2020; Van Cutsem et al., 2017).

Mechanisms Underlying the Negative Effects of Mental Fatigue on Sport Performance

Physiological Mechanisms

Most studies investigating the effects of mental fatigue on endurance performance monitored standard exercise physiology measures like heart rate (HR), heart rate variability (HRV), blood lactate concentration [Bla], oxygen uptake capacity, electromyography, etc. (Van Cutsem et al., 2017). On the whole, these studies suggest that mental fatigue does not substantially alter the cardiorespiratory, metabolic, or neuromuscular responses to aerobic exercise. Some of these studies also suggest that mental fatigue and central fatigue, defined as the exercise-induced reduction in the capacity of the central nervous system (CNS) to recruit the fatigued muscles during maximal voluntary contractions (Taylor & Gandevia, 2008), are not linked (Pageaux, Marcora, & Lepers, 2013; Pageaux, Marcora, Rozand, & Lepers, 2015). Therefore, these two types of fatigue should not be conflated despite both involving the CNS.

More recently, Salam et al. (2018) found no effect of mental fatigue on HR but did find an effect on [Bla], Penna et al. (2018) did not observe any significant changes in HRV due to mental fatigue and Azevedo et al. (2016) showed that mental fatigue does not affect EMG during sport performance. Pires et al. (2018) is one of the only studies that went one step further and directly assessed brain activity during endurance exercise using electroencephalography (EEG). Specifically, they assessed prefrontal brain activity during the 20-km TT and observed that θ-activity (i.e. a low-frequency brain activity-band (3.5–7.5 Hz) that has been proposed to be a valid and reliable indicator of mental fatigue; Wascher et al., 2014) was higher when mentally fatigued. Brain activity in this study (Pires et al., 2018) is however only measured at the FP1 position, which inevitably limits artifact-rejection possibilities and does not provide a window on the entire brains' activity. The interpretation of EEG data, as for any other physiological data, is also not ideal during TTs because of the changes in workload often observed in these studies (Nicolò et al., 2019). Despite these methodological constraints, it is only the second study – after the study of Brownsberger et al. (2013) – to provide further insight into the prefrontal cortex activation during endurance performance in a mentally fatigued state. Pires et al. (2018) correctly point out that the increased θ-activity in mentally fatigued cyclists could reflect their lower ability to maintain adequate inhibitory control and attentional focus during exercise.

Clearly, more research is needed to further investigate how mental fatigue affects brain activity during exercise and which neurophysiological alterations underlie these brain activity changes. This is very challenging because of the artifacts (e.g. movement, facial muscle contractions, sweating) associated with the vigorous aerobic exercise normally used to measure endurance performance in the laboratory (Perrey & Besson, 2018). However, measurements of brain activity during exercise and psychopharmacological studies interfering with relevant neurotransmitters/neuromodulators like dopamine and adenosine (Salamone et al., 2018) are the only way to gather insight into the brain mechanisms underlying the negative effects of mental fatigue on endurance performance in humans. Using a psychobiological approach, it is also important to investigate whether changes at the brain level are associated with changes in the perception of effort, potential motivation, and other variables at the psychological level (see the next section). As an example of this psychobiological approach from a different field, Roelands, Hasegawa et al. (2008) showed that reboxetine (a noradrenaline reuptake inhibitor) decreased whole-body endurance performance in normal and high ambient temperatures. Interestingly, despite a decreased power output during the TT in this study, there was no change in absolute RPE values, consequently increasing the level of perceived exertion to power output ratio (meaning less power output is generated for the same RPE value). The intake of methylphenidate [a dopamine (DA) reuptake inhibitor], in contrast, allowed subjects to maintain a higher power output and improve TT performance in the heat, again without influencing absolute RPE values (Roelands, Goekint et al., 2008). This finding demonstrates that altered brain neurotransmission is able to affect whole-body endurance performance and that this effect is associated with an altered level of perceived exertion to power output ratio (in the case of DA, a decreased ratio).

Concerning the studies on the effects of mental fatigue on psychomotor performance (see also Pageaux & Lepers, 2018), they mostly point out that mental fatigue negatively affects this type of performance as well. Consequently, these studies provide excellent insights at the behavioral level. In contrast, still a lot has to be elucidated mechanistically. Only the studies of Badin et al. (2016) and Moreira et al. (2018) attempted to provide some further insight into the possible physiological markers and/or mediators of the effects of mental fatigue on psychomotor performance. Badin et al. (2016) measured HR but did not find any conclusive evidence on a possible effect of mental fatigue. Moreira et al. (2018) measured HR and salivary parameters in response to basketball performance, but subsequently employed a magnitude-based inferential statistical approach resulting in a difficult interpretation of the gathered data. One possible explanation for the current scarcity of studies assessing physiological mechanisms of the effects of mental fatigue on psychomotor performance is the complexity of objectively measuring sport-specific psychomotor performance and its mechanisms. The challenge of measuring performance is relatively straightforward in situations where there is a clear and measurable performance outcome (e.g. cycling, swimming). However, effectively capturing performance in sport-specific psychomotor tasks is far more complex, since it is based on several interrelated component skills (e.g. perceptual, cognitive, and motor). These skills may be harder to isolate under controlled and reproducible settings, and performance decrements in these skills may even be harder to link to neurophysiological alterations. Nonetheless, in order to advance this field of research, future studies should consider monitoring possible neurophysiological mediators in addition to psychomotor variables (see Figure 10.1).

Psychological Mechanisms

Based on the psychobiological model of endurance performance (Marcora, 2008), motivation and perception of effort are two of the most frequently monitored psychological constructs in this line of research. The conclusion of our systematic review was that the most important factor responsible for the negative impact of mental fatigue on endurance performance is a higher perception of effort with little evidence supporting a negative effect of mental fatigue on motivation related to the physical performance task (Van Cutsem et al., 2017). With the exception of Otani et al. (2017) (who, however, compared RPE only at minute zero of the TTE test they used to measure endurance performance) and Silva-Cavalcante et al. (2018), studies published since our systematic review have provided further evidence that mental fatigue significantly increases perception of effort during aerobic exercise (see Figure 10.1) (Salam et al., 2018; Penna, Filho, Wanner et al., 2018; Pires et al., 2018).

With regard to motivation, Pires et al. (2018) reported that motivation rated on a very simple 5-point scale ranging from "very unmotivated" to "highly motivated" was lower at 2 km in the 20-km TT. However, motivation appeared to be higher in the later stages of the TT in the mental fatigue condition compared to the control condition. Overall, it seems that studies using self-reports of motivation do not provide strong evidence that mental fatigue reduces endurance performance by reducing motivation related to the physical endurance task. However, measuring motivation by self-reports has several limitations, and studies experimentally manipulating motivation are needed to provide a more complete answer. The first of such studies using endurance performance as the main dependent variable is the study by Brown and Bray (2017). The results of this study (main effect of monetary incentive) support the psychobiological model's prediction that, when participants are not already highly motivated, a monetary incentive that increases potential motivation can increase endurance performance (Marcora, 2019). This study also shows that a monetary incentive can counteract the negative effect of mental fatigue on endurance performance. However, the lack of a significant interaction between monetary incentive and mental fatigue on endurance performance does not fully support the hypothesis that a reduction in motivation is an important mediator of the negative effect of mental fatigue on endurance performance. Indeed, if this was the case, we would expect a larger effect of monetary incentive in mentally fatigued individuals compared to non-mentally fatigued individuals. Furthermore, the generalizability of the findings of Brown and Bray (2017) to sport performance is limited by the use of a handgrip rather than a whole-body (e.g. running or cycling) task to measure endurance. Clearly, more experimental studies on the effects of motivational manipulations and mediation analysis of studies employing self-reports of motivation are required to test the hypothesis that reduced motivation is an important mediator of reduced endurance performance in mentally fatigued individuals.

In terms of psychomotor performance, the first three studies on the effects of mental fatigue (Badin et al., 2016; Smith, Couts et al., 2016; Smith, Zeuwts et al., 2016) all indicated the mental fatigue-induced performance impairment was not moderated by an altered level of motivation. In addition to motivation, Badin et al. (2016) also assessed RPE and suggested mental fatigue might increase RPE related to a soccer-specific small-sided game. Both the studies of Van Cutsem et al. (2019) and Veness et al. (2017) assessed motivation toward the upcoming physical task. In both studies, it was found that motivation was unaffected by mental fatigue. In addition, in the studies of Le Mansec et al. (2017) and Moreira et al. (2018), perceived exertion was assessed. Le Mansec et al. (2017) reported that RPE tended to be higher when mentally fatigued. Although perception of effort may play a role, theoretically it is linked more to endurance rather than psychomotor performance. Therefore, future studies looking into the psychological mechanisms of reduced psychomotor performance in mentally fatigued athletes should investigate more relevant variables like arousal, self-efficacy, and attentional focus in addition to RPE and motivation (Martin & Gill, 1991).

Strategies to Reduce Mental Fatigue and Its Negative Impact on Sport Performance

The bulk of evidence briefly reviewed here and in our previous systematic review (Van Cutsem et al., 2017) as well as the results of three published meta-analyses (McMorris et al., 2018; Brown et al., 2020; Giboin & Wolff, 2019) suggest that mental fatigue has a significant effect on both endurance performance and psychomotor performance. The performance of athletes competing in sports that require both components, for example, soccer and other team sports, is very likely to be affected by mental fatigue (Smith, Thompson et al., 2018). From a practical point of view, it seems therefore prudent to recommend athletes to avoid/limit mentally demanding tasks before and during games/competitions. Because cognitive exertion cannot be totally avoided during competitions, it is also important to develop strategies to counteract mental fatigue. Such strategies include the use of ergogenic aids and psychological interventions during games/competitions, and develop resistance to mental fatigue during training.

Avoid/Limit Mentally Demanding Tasks before and during Games/Competitions

The most important guideline that currently has been suggested to prevent mental fatigue and its negative effects on sport performance is that mentally demanding tasks should be avoided before games/competitions (Russell et al., 2018; Smith et al., 2018). Tasks and their associated demands that regularly proceed a game/competition and could possibly trigger states of mental fatigue are, for example, interviews and the emotion control that goes with it, or tactical meetings. More qualitative and quantitative research is required to understand which pre-competition tasks athletes find mentally fatiguing and that could be avoided/reduced.

In addition to preventing acute mental fatigue, athletes should avoid the development of chronic fatigue syndromes like non-functional overreaching and overtraining that clearly have a strong mental as well as physical component (Purvis, Gonsalves, & Deuster, 2010). Although, for obvious ethical and logistical reasons, there are no experimental studies on the effects of chronic mental fatigue on sport performance, we feel it is safe to assume that its effects on sport performance are larger than those of acute mental fatigue. An indication of the possible deleterious effects of chronic mental fatigue in athletes can be found in the study of Mann et al. (2016), who found that in examination periods, the odds for a college football player to have an injury restriction were nearly twice as high as during non-examination periods. Therefore, preventing non-functional overreaching and overtraining in their athletes should be a primary goal for coaches and other support staff. Prevention strategies should include not only the monitoring of training load and recovery, but also the monitoring and, if necessary, reduction of the psychological load that athletes experience in all dimensions of their lives (Kellmann et al., 2018).

As discussed in the Introduction, sport itself can be a mentally demanding task. However, athletes and coaches may be able to use certain strategies to reduce the mental demands of competing and, thus, reduce mental fatigue. Brick, Campbell et al. (2016) demonstrated that external control over pacing (also called "cognitive drafting"; currently new technologies are emerging in this field, e.g. Wavelight) may facilitate endurance performance, possibly mediated through reducing the cognitive load and promoting appropriate attentional strategies that optimize performance. Neuroimaging studies also show that cognitive and motor skills training reduces the activity of brain areas associated with mental fatigue such as the ACC (Patel, Spreng, & Turner, 2013). The practical implication is that using well-rehearsed skills and offensive/defensive plays should reduce the development of mental fatigue during team sports, tennis, and other sports that require complex skills, tactical thinking, as well as endurance. Conversely, the decision to introduce novel skills and offensive/defensive plays during a game (albeit possibly beneficial in other respects) may increase mental fatigue and negatively affect the player's performance. More research is definitively warranted to further test these strategies and develop new ones that may reduce the mental demands of sport competitions at high levels of performance.

Before ending this section, it is important to reinforce the notion that poor sleep exacerbates mental fatigue. Therefore, strategies to improve sleep in athletes (Bonnar, Bartel, Kakoschke, & Lang, 2018; Halson & Juliff, 2017) are likely to reduce the development of mental fatigue before and during sport competitions.

Ergogenic Aids and Psychological Strategies to Counteract Mental Fatigue

Nutritionally, caffeine has been put forward as a promising intervention to counteract mental fatigue and its effects on sport performance (Pageaux, Lepers, Dietz, & Marcora, 2014; Franco-Alvarenga et al., 2019). The mental fatigue-counteracting properties of caffeine are attributed to its ability to easily cross the blood-brain barrier and bind to cell membrane receptors for adenosine, thus blocking the inhibitory effects of adenosine on neuronal-excitability, neurotransmitter release, and arousal (Martin et al., 2018). Staiano et al. (2012) were the first to confirm the mental fatigue-counteracting properties of caffeine in terms of endurance performance. Subsequently, Azevedo et al. (2016) conducted an experiment, demonstrating that caffeine ingestion successfully reversed the mental fatigue-induced impairment in cycling TTE at 80% of the maximal power output. This positive effect of caffeine ingestion was accompanied by a tendency to an improvement in mood state (i.e. vigor). Franco-Alvarenga et al. (2019) further confirmed the ability of caffeine ingestion to counteract the mental fatigue-induced impairment in endurance performance. They observed that endurance performance on a 20-km cycling TT was restored back to normal after caffeine ingestion. This restoration of endurance performance was associated with a reversal of the mental fatigue-induced increase in EEG theta wave post the mentally fatiguing task, a lower RPE/power output ratio and higher affect, motivation, and emotional arousal throughout the 20-km cycling TT. In addition, McLellan, Bell, and Kamimori (2004) concluded that caffeine is an effective strategy to maintain sport performance during an overnight period of sleep loss at levels comparable to the rested state.

Another possible countermeasure of mental fatigue that has already been evaluated is serially mouth rinsing a solution containing caffeine and maltodextrin (Van Cutsem, De Pauw et al., 2017). Serially rinsing a caffeine and maltodextrin solution offers a suitable "nutritional" countermeasure for those that want to restrict caloric intake or participate in Ramadan. Perhaps more importantly, this specific study also resulted in further insights in the mediating mechanisms of mental fatigue. Multiple possible mechanisms for the effectiveness of serial caffeine-maltodextrin mouth rinsing are proposed in our mouth rinse-study (Van Cutsem, De Pauw et al., 2017). The mechanism that seems the most important is the brain activating properties of mouth rinsing. Mouth rinsing is known to activate multiple brain areas (Chambers, Bridge, & Jones, 2009), e.g. the activation of specific brain regions (i.e. the ACC and the right caudate that forms part of the striatum) known to produce DA (Turner, Byblow, Stinear, & Gant, 2014), and has also been shown to do so in our mouth rinse-study (Van Cutsem, De Pauw et al., 2017). Mental fatigue has already been associated with alterations in the ACC (Boksem, Meijman, & Lorist, 2005; Boksem & Tops, 2008; Mostofsky & Simmonds, 2008). This way, a mouth rinse containing caffeine and maltodextrin might be able to (partly) restore dopaminergic transmission in the striatum and ACC and postpone mental fatigue by activating sensory neurons in the mouth and initiating a signal transduction cascade toward the brain. The sensory neurons that triggered this transduction cascade could be the neurons that caused the participants to score the caffeine-maltodextrin mouth rinse less pleasant (i.e. more bitter) than the placebo mouth rinse (Van Cutsem, De Pauw et al., 2017). At the end of each trial, participants had to rate the pleasantness of the sweet/bitterness taste of the mouth rinse, and participants scored the caffeine-maltodextrin mouth rinse as significantly less pleasant/more bitter (−0,9 on a 5-point scale) than the placebo mouth rinse. This clearly indicates that a taste-difference was present between both mouth rinses and could explain why a specific transduction cascade was triggered in the caffeine-maltodextrin mouth rinse trial and not in the placebo mouth rinse trial. Kishi, Sadachi, Nakamura, and Tonoike (2017) reported that tasting bitter is associated with activation of the ACC and as such substantiates that the caffeine-maltodextrin mouth rinse might have triggered a specific transduction cascade.

In addition to ergogenic aids, psychological interventions may also be able to improve performance in mentally fatigued athletes. Hopstaken, Van Der Linden, Bakker, and Kompier (2015) demonstrated that increasing motivation, by providing a monetary incentive near the end of a prolonged cognitively demanding task, reversed cognitive performance declines despite previous signs of mental fatigue. A study by Brown and Bray (2017) further substantiated this ability of motivational strategies to counteract mental fatigue in a sport performance-setting. Increased motivation by a monetary incentive reversed the mental fatigue-induced decrease in performance in an endurance handgrip task. Caution is however warranted as Gergelyfi, Jacob, Olivier, and Zénon (2015) also altered the motivational state through monetary incentives during a 120-minute Sudoku task and failed to compensate for the effects of mental fatigue. Although motivation seems to possess the ability to somewhat counteract mental fatigue, more research is required as the effect may be more limited in athletes with high and qualitatively more intrinsic motivation. It is also important to investigate the effects of other psychological interventions known to improve sport performance (e.g. motivational self-talk and focus of attention) specifically in mentally fatigued athletes.

Training Resistance to Mental Fatigue

A final possibility to counteract mental fatigue and the subsequent impairment in sport performance is by training the resistance to mental fatigue. A first insight on this matter was given in a study of Martin et al. (2016), who designed a study to specifically assess whether the level of training in endurance sport had any influence on the effects of mental fatigue on perception of effort and endurance performance. Interestingly, these authors found that professional cyclists exhibited superior performance during a 30-minute Stroop task compared to recreational cyclists, which is indicative of stronger inhibitory control. Moreover, professional cyclists displayed a greater resistance to the negative effects of mental fatigue on a 20-minute cycling TT than recreational cyclists (Martin et al., 2016). However, these findings were not replicated in a study with badminton-athletes (Van Cutsem et al., 2019). Multiple reasons could account for failing to replicate the results of Martin et al. (2016), the two most prominent being: (1) More severe mental fatigue was induced in the study of Van Cutsem et al. (2019) (if one assumes that longer task duration leads to higher mental fatigue) and (2) badminton-athletes were not on the same elite-level as the cyclists in the study of Martin et al. (2016). To explain the superior resistance to mental fatigue of elite athletes, Martin et al. (2016) pointed to genetic and environmental factors (i.e. aerobic training required by professional road cycling may induce morphological and functional adaptations in the ACC and other brain areas that increase resistance to mental fatigue). In a follow-up study of Filipas et al. (2020), the usefulness of four weeks of endurance training to increase resistance to mental fatigue in untrained individuals was demonstrated. This finding indicates that the tolerance to mental fatigue is at least trainable in some aspects. Further research is however necessary to determine what might explain the possible superior resistance to mental fatigue present in elite athletes.

Experimental investigations are also being conducted on the effects of combining cognitive tasks and endurance performance, the so-called Brain Endurance Training (BET), to improve endurance performance and increase the resistance to mental fatigue (Marcora, Staiano, & Merlini, 2015). BET seeks to increase the load on the brain during endurance performance, to induce adaptations in the ACC and other relevant cortical areas and as such increase resistance to mental fatigue and its negative effects on endurance performance. The BET that was developed in this study (Marcora et al., 2015) consisted of cycling on a cycle ergometer for 60 minutes at 65% VO_2max. While cycling, participants performed a mentally fatiguing task on a computer. This training was performed three times a week for 12 weeks and was compared to a control training in which participants did not have to perform a mentally fatiguing task during cycling. TTE-performance throughout the 12 weeks increased significantly more in the BET-group compared to the control group. If confirmed, the beneficial effects of BET may give athletes and coaches a training method to specifically enhance resistance to mental fatigue.

Conclusion

The research reviewed in the present chapter forms an excellent basis for future studies exploring the impact of mental fatigue on sport performance. Continuation of this research is of significant importance as mental fatigue – and other neurophysiological and psychobiological moderators of sport performance – have only recently gained attention in sports science despite being often mentioned by coaches as an important factor affecting sport performance. A better understanding of the impact and mechanisms of mental fatigue in athletes should lead to novel interventions to counteract mental fatigue. Such novel interventions have the potential to improve sport performance beyond the improvements already obtained using the traditional training and nutritional interventions aimed at reducing physical fatigue. Besides being an important topic in sports science, mental fatigue is an issue that is encountered in a multitude of other settings such as military operations, driving a car, and cancer and its treatment. Therefore, research on mental fatigue in athletes may translate to other populations like soldiers, pilots, car and lorry drivers, and patients suffering from fatigue.

11

NEUROSCIENTIFIC APPROACHES TO SELF-REGULATORY CONTROL IN SPORTS

Wanja Wolff, Anna Hirsch, Maik Bieleke, and Amitai Shenhav

Introduction

Sports performance critically depends on physical fitness and skill level. However, success also hinges on how well athletes deal with psychological obstacles that threaten optimal performance (Wolff, Bieleke, & Schüler, 2019). For example, in order to make a critical free-throw, basketball players have to ward off challenges to effective movement execution, triggered both externally (e.g. distraction by hostile chants) and internally (e.g. fear of failure). In the same vein, cyclists whose muscles are aching need to overcome their automatic inclination to ease up and slow down. These exemplary challenges are well within the scope of current definitions of self-regulatory control[1] as the "efforts people exert to stimulate desirable responses and inhibit undesirable responses" (de Ridder, Lensvelt-Mulders, Finkenauer, Stok, & Baumeister, 2012, p. 77) or "the set of mechanisms required to pursue a goal, especially when distraction and/or strong (e.g., habitual) competing responses must be overcome" (Shenhav, Botvinick, & Cohen, 2013, p. 217). Thus, it seems plausible that, in addition to fitness and skill, sports performance hinges on the successful exertion of mental effort in the service of self-regulatory control.

Indeed, a large body of research has found support for the importance of self-regulatory control in sports (Englert, 2016), both at the trait level (i.e. stable self-regulatory tendencies within an individual) and at the state level (i.e. situationally defined influences on one's tendency to self-regulate). For instance, on the trait level, one study has shown that elite cyclists outperform non-elite peers in a reaction-time-based measure of trait self-control (Martin et al., 2016). In another study, youth athletes in an elite talent development program scored higher on a self-report measure of self-regulatory control than their non-selected peers (Wolff, Bertrams, & Schüler, 2019). In the recreational context, high self-regulatory control has been linked with better adherence to exercise regimens (Stork, Graham, Bray, & Martin Ginis, 2016). This makes intuitive sense, as self-regulatory control has been shown to help people deal with the difficulties of adhering to valued behaviors (Wolff, Martarelli, Schüler, & Bieleke, 2020). At the state level, the application of self-regulatory control detrimentally affects subsequent sports performance (for a meta-analysis, please see Giboin & Wolff, 2019, but see also Holgado, Troya, Perales, Vadillo, & Sanabria, 2019). For example, impaired performance after prior self-regulatory control has been found in such diverse sport settings as sprint-running (Englert, Persaud, Oudejans, & Bertrams, 2015) and dart throwing (Yang, Park, & Shin, 2019). Finally, it has been shown that physical effort causes feelings of mental exertion, impairs self-regulatory control, and leads to hypoactivations in control-relevant areas of the brain (Blain et al., 2019; Wolff, Schüler et al., 2019). This is consistent with the claim that physical performance requires self-regulatory control.

A multitude of theoretical accounts have been proposed that specify *why* and *when* self-regulatory control is applied and why it sometimes appears to *fail* (Beedie & Lane, 2012; Inzlicht, Schmeichel, & Macrae, 2014; Kotabe & Hofmann, 2015; Kurzban, Duckworth, Kable, & Myers, 2013; Shenhav et al., 2013). In particular, recent years have seen substantial advancements in our understanding of the guiding principles of self-regulatory control, as well as the neuronal structures that orchestrate its allocation (Munakata et al., 2011; Holroyd & Yeung, 2012; Cavanagh & Frank, 2014; Shenhav et al., 2017). In the present chapter, we will demonstrate how these developments can inform and advance neuroscientific research on self-regulatory control in sports. In part one of this chapter, we will follow recent mechanistic approaches and conceptualize self-regulatory control as a reward-based decision. Specifically, we introduce the expected value of control (EVC) theory (Shenhav et al., 2013) as a mathematically explicit framework that provides a value-based computational expression for the allocation of self-regulatory control and that specifies the mechanistic foundation of self-regulatory control.

In part two of the chapter, we will discuss recent technological advancements that have enabled neuroscientific research even during full body movements, an important prerequisite for investigating neural processes during sports performance (Ekkekakis, 2009a; Perrey & Besson, 2018). This has enabled researchers to satisfy recent calls to investigate the "sporting brain" (Walsh, 2014, R859) and to examine whether findings from basic cognitive neuroscience can be applied to the field of sports and exercise. We will summarize neuroscientific research in sports through the lens of self-regulatory control, with a specific focus on functional near-infrared spectroscopy (fNIRS) as a neuroscientific method that appears to be particularly suited for research in sports.

Computational and Mechanistic Operating Principles of Self-Regulatory Control

In this section, we will elaborate on the concept of mental effort and why it is central to the definition of self-regulatory control. We will then introduce a mechanistic account of the processes that guide the allocation of mental effort in the service of self-regulatory control, based on the EVC theory.

Self-Regulatory Control Is Effortful and Costly

In keeping with this chapter's focus on physical performance, we will use an analogy from physical effort to aid the definition of mental effort. Assume, for instance, that a marathon runner is able to run a marathon in 02:08:00h (i.e. capacity). To qualify for the Olympics, he needs to run it in < 02:11:30h (i.e. task characteristics). Physical effort is what mediates between his running capacity and the time that is required for qualification, on the one hand, and the ultimately achieved finishing time, on the other hand. Likewise, mental effort can be conceptualized as that which "mediates between (a) the characteristics of a target task and the subject's available information-processing capacity and (b) the fidelity of the information-processing operations actually performed, as reflected in task performance" (Shenhav et al., 2017, p. 100). Self-regulatory control is believed to be the force through which mental effort is exerted (Shenhav et al., 2017). Tasks vary in the degree to which they can rely on controlled vs. more automatic processes (Posner & Snyder 1975; Schneider & Shiffrin, 1977). One of the major factors that can determine the control requirements of a task is the extent to which pursuing the task goal requires the individal to overcome more automatic (e.g. default) responses (Cohen, Dunbar, & Mcclelland, 1990; Shenhav et al., 2013). To illustrate, when the runner is hurting, the automatic response tendency would be to stop. However, to qualify for the Olympics, this response needs to be controlled. Thus, although in this case the behavioral output relies on physical effort (e.g. engagement of locomotor muscles), self-regulatory control (and therefore mental effort) is needed to override the automatic response tendency of stopping or slowing down.

Although it is often crucial for success, people tend to avoid engaging in self-regulatory control because the mental effort required (and associated experiences of fatigue and frustration; Wolff, Sieber, Bieleke, & Englert, 2019) is experienced as aversive (Kool & Botvinick, 2018; Westbrook & Braver, 2015; see also Box 1). Thus, applying self-regulatory control appears to carry an intrinsic disutility (Kool & Botvinick, 2018). Accordingly, people tend to mobilize effort only if the goal is subjectively worth it (Gendolla & Richter, 2010) and not to a greater degree than is warranted by the difficulty of a given task (Wright, Mlynski, & Carbajal, 2019). This indicates an aversion against mobilizing more effort than necessary (Richter, Gendolla, & Wright, 2016). Returning to the example of the marathon runner: If the *only* goal is to qualify for the Olympics (i.e. no other incentives like winning the race or beating a rival are present), he should only run as fast as needed to qualify. This reasoning is in accordance with a large body of research showing that people try to conserve their resources when it comes to the mobilization of effort (Richter et al., 2016). Taken together, research suggests that self-regulatory control is treated as if it is costly and limited.

Box 1: When Effort Adds Value

Mental effort plays a key role in our understanding of self-regulatory control. An overwhelming body of research shows that mental effort produces costs that people generally try to avoid (Kurzban, 2016). Sports seems to be at odds with this *law of least effort* (Hull, 1943). For most sports, especially endurance sports like running or cycling, physical and mental efforts are not only instrumental to reaching one's goal; they often constitute the goal itself – that is, effort is often *central* to the sporting experience. To use the words of multiple Tour de France champion Greg LeMond: "it never gets easier, you just go faster" (Missel, 2017, para. 7). Yet, every year, millions of people pay considerable amounts of money to participate in running competitions with neither the chance nor the expectation of winning (Andersen, 2020). For most of them, the cost of participating in such events – ranging from entry fees and costs for equipment and travel to the opportunity costs of training and the risk of suffering an injury (Maxcy, Wicker, & Prinz, 2019) – seems disproportionate compared to what they receive in return. This makes it difficult to explain why so many people freely choose to participate in sporting competitions. Interestingly, one experience recreational athletes appear to seek out in a marathon, or an ultra-marathon might simply be the experience of pushing through perceived boundaries and still keep going (Finn, 2018).

As this example illustrates, some people engage in sports *because* it requires mental and/or physical effort and not despite of it (Loewenstein, 1999). This implies that effort (mental or physical) may in a certain case add value to an activity. From the perspective of the EVC framework, effort can add value in two different ways (Inzlicht, Shenhav, & Olivola, 2018): First, it might amplify the value of the expected outcome. Thus, success is more rewarding when it is achieved with high effort and failure feels worse when one had invested a lot of effort. In the words of Brazilian soccer legend Pelé: "The more difficult the victory, the greater the happiness in winning" (Keville, 2015, para. 3). Second, effort itself might be intrinsically rewarding irrespective of the outcome. One possible explanation for this might be a phenomenon referred to as learned industriousness (Eisenberger, 1992): If athletes learn to directly associate effort with reward, the effort assumes the role of a secondary reinforcer. Indeed, athletes and their coaches often emphasize the need to make an effort, irrespective of the direct outcome. For example, golfer Arnold Palmer stressed that one should "always make a total effort, even when the odds are against you" (Park, 2013, para. 38). And the value of effort is very clearly expressed by Eddy Merckx – considered by many to be the greatest cyclist of all time – who stated that "when it's hurting you, that's when you can make a difference" (Alé La Merckx, 2018, para. 5). The paradoxical nature of effort as both costly and rewarding is not limited to experiences in the sports setting, and has recently started to receive research interest (for a review, please see Inzlicht et al., 2018), although comparatively little research has yet been conducted to investigate the ways in which effort adds value. Sports seems to be a domain where effort is held in very high regard and treated as an incentive in its own right. The field of sports and exercise thus serves as a prime target for the investigation of this effort paradox.

Various explanations have been proposed for *why* the capacity for self-regulatory control might be limited. For example, resource-based accounts suggest that self-regulatory control depletes a metabolic resource (see Chapter 8, this volume; Baumeister, Bratslavsky, Muraven, & Tice, 1998). In contrast to such structural limitations in the capacity for self-regulatory control, other accounts focus on the computational properties of the neuronal systems that govern control. From this perspective, exertion of self-regulatory control is perceived as effortful not because a resource has been depleted but to index the costs that arise in tasks that compete for the same neural representations (Feng et al., 2014; Musslick et al., 2016). This explanation can be transferred to the context of sports and exercise: If an athlete is applying self-regulatory control to perform at her best in a cycling time trial, performance in concurrent tasks that rely on control will likely be impaired (if performance is not impaired, then the task should at least be perceived as more effortful). For example, while the athlete has to control the impulse to go slower, a concurrent task that also relies on impulse control (e.g. to control one's emotional expression) would require self-regulatory control to manage both tasks concurrently, thereby leading to impaired performance and/or increased sensation of mental effort. Tentative support for this interpretation in the context of physical performance comes from the occurrence of cognitive motor interference that already occurs in simple motor tasks like walking (for a meta-analysis, please see Al-Yahya et al., 2011). Likewise, impaired cognitive performance in dual-task situations has been found in diverse sport settings such as table tennis (Schaefer & Scornaienchi, 2020), swimming (Stets, Smith, & Helton, 2019), or climbing (Darling & Helton, 2014). For example, when participants were asked to perform an n-back task while returning table tennis balls from a ball machine, this led to impaired n-back performance (Schaefer & Scornaienchi, 2020). Interestingly, this dual-task cost was signifcantly more pronounced in novices than in experts, which might point toward more automated processing of demands in experts (Schneider & Shiffrin, 1977).

While the exact reasons that limit the brain's capacity for self-regulatory control are still debated (Kurzban et al., 2013; Shenhav et al., 2017), it appears to be clear that people invest mental effort sparingly and treat its mobilization as if the capacity for control is limited. Consequently, researchers have tried to understand the factors that determine how people choose to allocate self-regulatory control.

The Expected Value of Control Theory

Research on self-regulatory control in sports has long been dominated by resource-based conceptualizations of self-regulatory control (for an overview, please see Englert, 2016). Recently, these resource-based accounts have been challenged empirically (Carter & McCullough, 2014; Hagger, Chatzisarantis et al., 2016; Wolff, Baumann, & Englert, 2018) as well as conceptually (Inzlicht et al., 2014; Kurzban et al., 2013), and recent theoretical accounts now converge toward conceptualizing self-regulatory control as some form of reward-based choice (Berkman, Hutcherson, Livingston, Kahn, & Inzlicht, 2017; Inzlicht et al., 2014; Kool & Botvinick, 2014; Kurzban et al., 2013; Wolff & Martarelli, 2020). However, these theoretical accounts have so far rarely been adopted in research on self-regulatory control in sports and exercise. This is puzzling because reward-based accounts play an important role in research on motor control (Körding, Fukunaga, Howard, Ingram, & Wolpert, 2004; Manohar et al., 2015; Morel, Ulbrich, & Gail, 2017; Shadmehr, Huang, & Ahmed, 2016), which is fundamental to any sporting activity. Here, we present the EVC theory as one such reward-based model of self-regulatory control (Shenhav et al., 2013, Shenhav, Cohen, & Botvinick, 2016). The EVC theory synthesizes core concepts of various control theories into an integrative framework that specifies the computational properties as well as the mechanistic underpinnings of self-regulatory control (for an illustration, please see Figure 11.1a).

Computation of the EVC

According to the EVC theory, people allocate self-regulatory control in a way that maximizes the expected payoff while minimizing the mental effort that is required. These collectively determine the expected value of a given control allocation (EVC). The outcome of this cost-benefit analysis (the EVCs of candidate control configurations) determines which task(s) are most worth allocating self-regulatory control to, and how much control should be allocated (Figure 1b). Equation 11.1 formalizes how the EVC is calculated (Shenhav et al., 2013):

$$\text{EVC}(\text{signal, state}) = \left[\sum_i \Pr(\text{outcome}_i \mid \text{signal, state}) \cdot \text{Value}(\text{outcome}_i)\right] - \text{Cost}(\text{signal}) \quad (11.1)$$

The situation (denoted as *state*) a person applies control to is shaped by internal and external states the person finds itself in. For example, a marathon runner might face a strong headwind (external) and also have some lingering doubts regarding her stamina over the full distance (internal). In any given state, different potential control signals of varying vigor can be specified (Figure 1a). The marathon runner's overall goal might be to qualify for the Olympic Games. To do so, she has to complete the distance faster than a set target time and this is likely to be very hard. Thus, while running, she has to control the automatic impulse to ease up and instead stick with her target running pace. Over the course of the competition, the effort required for sticking to the race pace will rise due to fatigue that is setting in.[2] The athlete might reason that she can only consistently resist the impulse to ease up as long as perceived physical exertion does not go beyond 80% of her maximum in the first half of the race, to avoid what runners refer to as "hitting the wall". Further, this might allow her to increase the intensity late in the race and produce a final spurt if needed. Control signals therefore vary in *identity* (e.g. "run" and "inhibit inclination to ease up") and in *intensity* (e.g. for running this might vary from 0% to 100% of maximum effort).

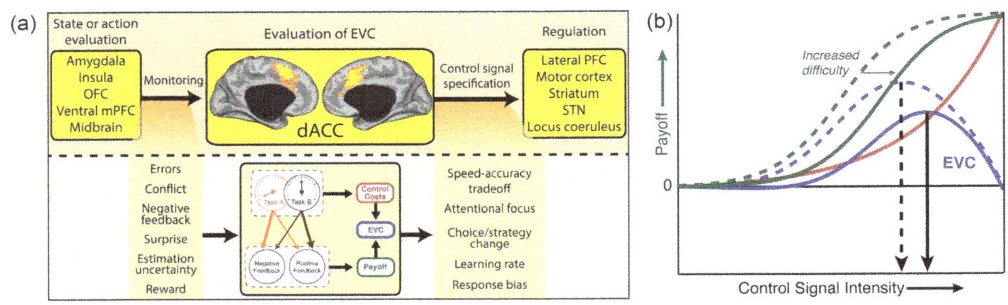

FIGURE 11.1 The Expected Value of Control (EVC) theory. (a) The EVC theory predicts that dACC integrates information about relevant incentives and task demand to determine the overall EVC of potential control configurations. On the basis of this EVC calculation, the dACC specified the optimal (EVC-maximizing) set of control signals, and signals these to relevant downstream regions which guide the execution of these control signals. Adapted from Shenhav et al. (2016). (b) Within the EVC framework, increases in the expected difficulty of a task (bold vs. dashed lines) will often lead to the prediction that additional control is needed to achieve a given level of payoff (green curves). This expected payoff is discounted by the expected cost (red curves) of exerting the necessary mental effort (control intensity), determining the overall EVC of that control intensity (blue curves). The maximum of this EVC curve determines the optimal control setting (black arrows). Adapted from Shenhav et al. (2013).

EVC can be calculated for any available configuration of control signal identities and intensities. As can be seen in the right part of Equation 11.1, the EVC of any given control signal configuration comprises two main components: An expected payoff and a cost. The expected payoff is determined by considering potential future outcomes that are relevant to one's task – including potential praise and pride that come with success, and potential admonishment and embarrasment that come with failure – and weighing these potential outcomes by the likelihood that they would occur under a particular control setting. For instance, as someone increases their physical exertion, they increase the likelihood of success (and attendant positive incentives) and decrease the likelihood of failure (and attendant negative incentives). However, increasing physical exertion is also costly: All things being equal, exercise at very high intensities (e.g. 95% of maximum) generally elicits a more negative affective response than exercise at lower intensity (e.g. 80% of maximum) (Ekkekakis, Parfitt, & Petruzzello, 2011; Roloff et al., 2020). This cost is accounted for by the final term in the equation, which trades off against the expected payoffs, discounting the potential positive outcomes that accrue from increasing intensities of physical exertion. As can be inferred from Equation 11.2,

$$\text{Value}(\text{outcome}) = \text{ImmediateReward}(\text{outcome}) + \gamma \max_i \lfloor \text{EVC}(\text{signal}_i, \text{outcome}) \rfloor \quad (11.2)$$

the outcome value reflects the value of the immediate change that occurs due to applying self-regulatory control (denoted as *ImmediateReward*), as well as accounting for the EVC of future control signals that are feasible based on the chosen signal (expressed as a maximization of EVC taking into account feasible control signals). This recursive definition of outcome value is important, because it highlights that the chosen EVC is not only maximized based on the immediate reward but also on the value of more distal states. For example, the *ImmediateReward* of running only at 80% of maximum exertion might in fact be negative, because the athlete will run slower than at 95% of maximum exertion and this might lead to the athlete being dropped from the lead group. However, specifying a control signal of such (comparably) little intensity might allow this athlete to maintain the target pace over the full distance, better positioning her to achieve her goal of qualifying for the Olympics. Thus, the value of an outcome is the sum of proximal and distal changes that are brought about by the specified control signal. However, as humans prefer immediate rewards over future rewards (Critchfield & Kollins, 2001; Frederick, Loewenstein, & O'Donoghue 2002), a discounting factor γ is introduced to discount the impact of future EVCs in determining the overall value of the outcome that is achieved by the current control signal. This discounting factor is a variable ranging from zero to one to account for intra- and inter-individual differences in discounting. Interestingly, a large-scale analysis of 1.7 million recreational runners' pacing strategies showed that relatively fast starts and fast finishes were both predictors of poor overall performance (Smyth, 2018). From an EVC perspective, this might be attributed to a suboptimal discounting factor (i.e. by over- or underweighting future EVCs).

EVC theory proposes that the human control system performs these calculations, compares the EVCs for different control signals, and then selects the one where EVC is maximized. Recent work has validated these predictions by showing that simulated agents that are designed to maximize their EVC adjust their task performance based on the incentives and task demands in similar ways as has been observed in empirical studies of motivation and self-regulatory control (Musslick, Shenhav, Botvinick, & Cohen, 2015; Lieder, Shenhav, Musslick, & Griffiths, 2018; Bustamante, Lieder, Musslick, Shenhav, & Cohen, 2020).

Mechanistic Underpinnings of Self-Regulatory Control

In addition to specifying the computational properties that underlie self-regulatory control, EVC theory also specifies candidate neural structures that mediate different processes involved in allocating and adjusting self-regulatory control (Shenhav et al., 2013). EVC theory delineates three core functions: *Specification*, *Regulation*, and *Monitoring*. Self-regulated control consists of a continuous loop in which control signals are specified, applied, and the outcome is monitored to assess whether the control signal needs to be adjusted. EVC theory proposes that the dorsal anterior cingulate cortex (dACC) sits at the interface of monitoring and specification, whereas regulation is primarily mediated by regions downstream of dACC that execute specific types of self-regulatory control, such as the lateral prefrontal cortex (lPFC). The functions EVC theory ascribes to dACC and lPFC are well supported by a large body of research (for reviews, please see Badre, 2008; Heatherton, 2011; Miller & Cohen, 2001; Shenhav et al., 2013).

Adaptive control thus requires an individual to monitor their current state and the value of potential future outcomes that might be attained with available control. Such monitoring is intuitively important in sports and exercise: For athletic success, it is crucial to perform at (or close to) one's physiological limit without overextending oneself. Thus, athletes need to closely monitor their current state (e.g. pace) and flexibly adjust their behavior if this state is at odds (e.g. too slow) with the goal they aim to achieve (e.g. qualifying for the Olympics). As we have outlined above, these adjustments are made in order to invest self-regulatory control efficiently. In regard to control signal intensity, this means that the EVC is maximized when the intensity is as low as possible while still enabling goal attainment. For a marathon runner trying to qualify for the Olympic games, this implies that she will only invest the amount of mental effort needed to *just* achieve the qualifying time.[3] However, the emphasis on not wasting resources might sometimes lead to the specification of a control signal intensity that is too low. The marathon runner might, for example, follow a conservative pacing strategy (e.g. negative split times) but if she is unable to make up for lost time later in the race, she might eventually miss the qualification time. Thus, selecting an optimal pacing strategy[4] is crucial to athletic success (Abbiss & Laursen, 2008).

Research shows that the dACC monitors various indicators of state information (e.g. information that is relevant for control signal identity and intensity specification) in a fashion that is likely to subserve the computation of the EVC (Shenhav et al., 2013, 2016). The plethora of different bits of information that might be monitored during exercise is provided by various brain areas (Figure 11.1a): Research indicates that interoceptive information (e.g. heavy breathing, locomotor fatigue) is processed by the insula (e.g. Gehrlach et al., 2019; Livneh et al., 2020), rewards (e.g. joy of running fast, achieving the qualification) are encoded by the ventromedial PFC (Gläscher, Hampton, & O'Doherty, 2009; Strait, Blanchard, & Hayden, 2014), and the amygdala may signal negative affective states such as fear of failure and exercise-induced pain (Neugebauer, Li, Bird, & Han, 2004). The dACC monitors signals from these and other structures as information for computing the EVC. The monitored information then needs to be integrated to specify a control signal that maximizes EVC. Research indicates that the specification and, if required, adjustment of the control signal is performed by the dACC (Cavanagh & Frank, 2014; Phillips, Johnston, & Everling, 2011; Shackman et al., 2011; Ullsperger, Danielmeier, & Jocham, 2014).

The EVC-maximizing control signal is then relayed to relevant downstream regions for execution. For many forms of self-regulatory control (e.g. controlling the impulse to get into a shoving match with an opponent after a foul; pulling oneself together to go out to train in the pouring rain), the region that appears to be most critical for this execution is lPFC (Miller & Cohen, 2001). The dACC and lPFC share strong reciprocal connections (Heilbronner & Hayden, 2016), and tend to co-activate in most control-demanding tasks (Duncan, 2010; Niendam et al., 2012). The strength of this dACC-lPFC co-activation has been shown to be predictive of good self-regulatory control, for instance improved performance on a rotation-letter task (Kondo, Osaka, & Osaka, 2004). Of particular relevance to our central proposition in this chapter, namely that self-regulatory control is important for controlling sports performance, lPFC is also well-connected to structures in the motor system, including the premotor cortex, which is, in turn, extensively connected to areas of relevance for direct motor output, like the primary motor cortex and the basal ganglia (Miller & Cohen, 2001). The connections between PFC and the basal ganglia are of interest in the domain of sports because the basal ganglia are believed to play a key role in generating central fatigue. Physical performance depends strongly on the capacity to tolerate fatigue, which may depend on top-down regulation of striatum by prefrontal cortical structures (Chaudhuri & Behan, 2000).

Cortical Activity during Self-Regulated Sports Performance

The bulk of the neuroscientific evidence that we have presented above stems from animal studies or human imaging studies that were performed under conditions that do not mirror real-world situations. Although it has been proposed that sports might be the "brain's biggest challenge" (Walsh, 2014, p. 859), research on the brain *while* a person is doing sport is still comparably scarce (Perrey & Besson, 2018). However, this is rapidly changing. Over the last 25 years, researchers have become increasingly capable of and interested in the investigation of the sporting brain (Figure 11.2a). Of particular interest for the present chapter is the drastic uptick in research on the brain *during* sports. To illustrate this, we conducted a web of science search that combined the topics "sports" and "brain" and that also required the word "during" in the title of published articles (Figure 11.2b). This search returned only eight hits during the 20-year time span from 1995 and 2004. In the following 15 years, another 171 papers have been published and in 2019 alone, 26 papers fulfilled these search criteria. Thus, while this literature search is by no means comprehensive, it seems safe to say that research on the sporting brain is garnering momentum.

One likely reason for this momentum is the introduction of more portable and more robust technologies for measuring cortical processes during sports. Particularly, fNIRS and, to a lesser extent, electroencephalography (EEG) have been increasingly used in the sports context in recent years (Perrey & Besson, 2018). While most readers are likely familiar with the basic operating principles of EEG, fNIRS is a comparatively recent neuroimaging technology whose specific advantages and disadvantages are less well known. Thus, prior to summarizing the literature on self-regulated sports performance, we will briefly describe the operating principles of fNIRS.

Measuring the Sporting Brain: fNIRS

Neuronal activity consumes energy and local changes in neuronal activity cause local increases in oxygenated blood. In the blood, oxygen is transported by the chromophore hemoglobin, which occurs in an oxygenated (HbO) and a deoxygenated (HbR) variant. Like functional magnetic resonance imaging, fNIRS tracks the resultant change of balance between HbO and HbR as a marker for neuronal activity. fNIRS uses NIR light to measure

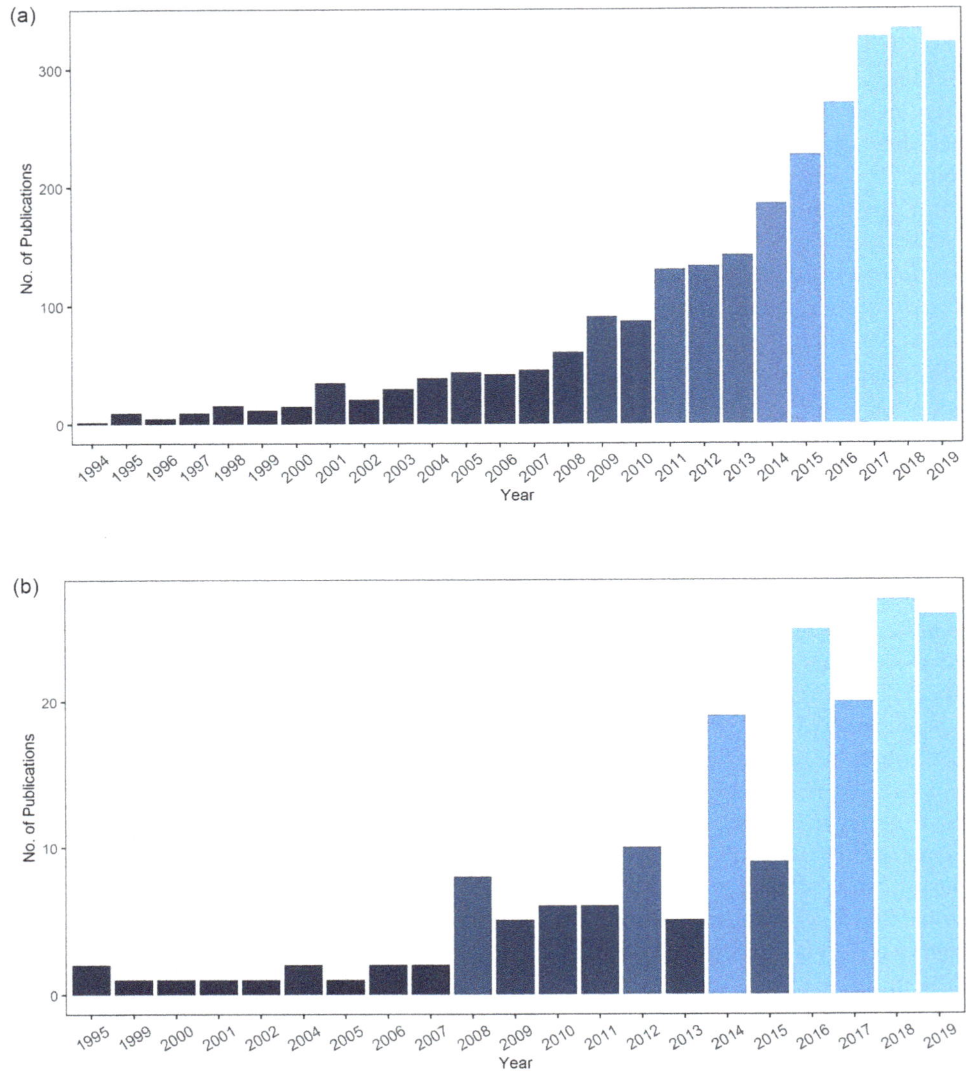

FIGURE 11.2 Web of Science Search (per January 2020) on the publication trends for neuroscientific research in regard to sports. Panel (a) illustrates the broad increase in research into the sporting brain (search terms: Sports AND brain). Panel (b) only includes papers that additionally have the term "during" in their title, to illustrate the relative scarcity and the increase in research on brain activity while people do sports.

changes in HbO and HbR non-invasively in the cerebral cortex (Scholkmann et al., 2014). To do so, NIR light emitting senders and NIR light sensitive detectors are placed on the participants' scalp (see Figure 11.3a), according to a predefined setup (see Figure 11.3b) that is designed to capture regions of interest (see Figure 11.3c). The NIR light spectrum ranges from 700nm to 1400nm and within this spectrum, Hb0 absorbs substantially more light at ranges above 830nm and HbR absorbs more light at 760nm (Ekkekakis, 2009). Capitalizing on this differentiation in absorption spectra, fNIRS senders emit light in two wavelengths

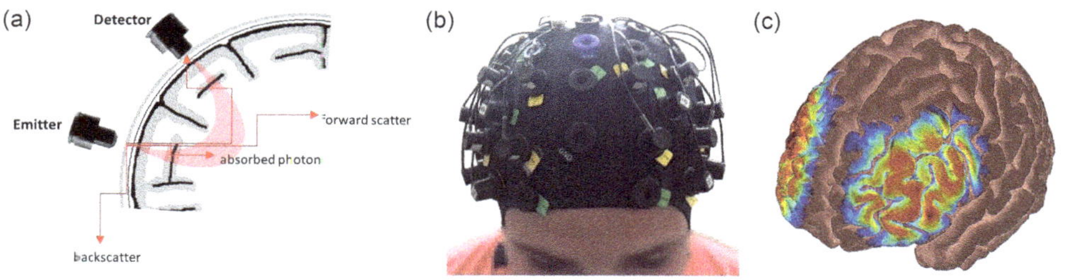

FIGURE 11.3 fNIRS Setup: (a) Schematic illustration of NIR light pathway between emitter and detector, (b) illustration of fNIRS montage designed to capture oxygenation changes in the dorsolateral prefrontal cortex, and (c) illustration of the sensitivity profile for capturing specific regions based on the montage designed to capture changes in the dorsolateral prefrontal cortex.

(e.g. 760nm and 850nm) and detectors nearby[5] track how much of the emitted NIR light leaves the scalp. Relative changes in the detected light are then analyzed as indicators for Hb0/HbR fluctuations, which serve as a proxy for change in cortical activity (Ferrari, Mottola, & Quaresima, 2004). For assessing cortical activity during sports, fNIRS has been regarded as the best suited technology that is currently available (Ekkekakis, 2009; Herold, Wiegel, Scholkmann, & Müller, 2018). Most important for sports settings, fNIRS is comparatively robust to motion artifacts, has acceptable temporal resolution and – due to its portability – can be used in settings with high external validity (Ekkekakis, 2009; Strangman, Culver, Thompson, & Boas, 2002). fNIRS has even been used to measure activity in the motor cortex in freely moving participants (Piper et al., 2014). Specifically, these authors were interested in whether hemodynamic changes that originate from hand movement could be captured while participants were sitting on a bike in decreasingly less-controlled conditions: Participants either sat on a stationary bike without pedalling, were pedalling on a stationary bike, or were freely riding their bike outside. Although an increase in external validity was acompanied by an increase in motion artifacts, the hemodynamic response that was triggered by the hand movement in the contralateral motor cortex could still be recovered (Piper et al., 2014). In addition, compared to technologies like fMRI, fNIRS is cheap to acquire and produces little running costs (Wolff, 2017). Finally, compared to fMRI and EEG, fNIRS measurements tend to be perceived as less invasive and aversive by participants (Cutini & Brigadoi, 2014). Constraining its applicability, fNIRS can only be used to reliably measure oxygenation changes in superficial cortical areas, whereas limited depth penetration prevents the measurement of deep brain areas (Ferrari & Quaresima, 2012). With respect to the key cortical structures involved in self-regulatory control, fNIRS is therefore well-suited for monitoring activity in the lPFC but not in the dACC. Thus, most of the literature we review below has focused on lPFC, whereas research on dACC is scarce. Further, although the spatial resolution of current fNIRS devices is ≤1 cm (Ferrari & Quaresima, 2012), fNIRS is less accurate than the spatial resolution that can be achieved with fMRI. Thus, for research that requires very precise localization or is concerned with subcortical areas, fNIRS is less well-suited. However, to assess group-level effects (e.g. comparing groups of trained and non-trained participants), fNIRS has proven to be a reliable neuroimaging technique (Scholkmann et al., 2014) and has accordingly gained in popularity in the domain of sports in recent years (for a more comprehensive introduction of fNIRS to research in sports, please see Ekkekakis, 2009; Perrey & Besson, 2018).

Brain Activity during Self-Regulated Sports Performance

Only recently have researchers started to explicitly conceptualize sports performance as a self-regulatory challenge (Marcora, 2008; McCormick, Meijen, Anstiss, & Jones, 2018; Pageaux, 2014; Wolff, Bieleke et al., 2018). Consequently, many early studies on the brain's role in exercising have focused on explaining exercise-induced activation changes in the brain from a physiological point of view (Rooks, Thom, McCully, & Dishman, 2010; Secher, Seifert, & Van Lieshout, 2008). For example, a systematic review of 25 fNIRS studies that were published between 1999 and 2009 concluded that with increasing exercise intensity, activation in the lPFC increased until it dropped at very high intensities (Rooks et al., 2010). One interpretation of this pattern suggested that this reflects an automatic physiological response that is initiated to prevent harmful threats to bodily homeostasis when exercise intensity is dangerously high[6] (Noakes, Peltonen, & Rusko, 2001; Rooks et al., 2010). However, rather than reflecting an obligatory response to a physiological limitation, these same findings could reflect the endpoint of a decision process, which weighs the value of applying further effort against the cost of this effort. Specifically, these changes in lPFC activity could be conceptualized in terms of variability in self-regulatory control: During an incremental exercise protocol (for example, riding on a cycling ergometer until exhaustion), the self-regulatory demands rise steadily because the task becomes increasingly more challenging and participants have to fight the impulse to quit. From an EVC perspective, to apply the self-regulatory control that is required to continue in spite of these aversive sensations, the control signal intensity needs to be constantly upregulated by the dACC and more regulative control needs to be applied by the lPFC (Figure 1b). Thus, if one understands an incremental exercise task as a self-regulatory challenge (Wolff, Bieleke et al., 2018), an increase in lPFC oxygenation is expected over time. This assumption is supported by findings of recent fNIRS studies. For example, in one study, lPFC oxygenation during a 30-minute cycling task increased as a function of duration and intensity in a sample of regularly exercising athletes (Giles et al., 2014), probably accompanying increasing levels of self-regulatory control. Similarly, when participants had to produce 50% of their maximum voluntary handgrip force, this self-control-demanding performance was associated with higher lPFC oxygenation, compared to a condition when only 30% of maximum force was required (Guo, Ma, & Chen, 2019). However, at a certain exercise intensity, the cost of exerting the level of self-regulatory control that would be required to continue with the task (e.g. controlling the impulse to stop) will exceed the expected payoff from the task (e.g. from receiving course credit for participating in an experiment). From an EVC perspective, this shift in EVC should motivate the person to reduce the intensity of self-regulatory control they are applying (Frömer, Lin, Dean Wolf, Inzlicht, & Shenhav, 2020), leading to a drop in PFC oxygenation and subsequent task termination. Indeed, an EEG study where cyclists completed an incremental cycling test showed that after an initial rise in PFC activation, a significant drop was observed after the respiratory compensation point (Robertson & Marino, 2015). A similar result could be observed in an fNIRS study with trained cyclists: In a progressive maximal cycling exercise to exhaustion, lPFC oxygenation increased in the first part of the cycling task but decreased significantly prior to task termination (Rupp & Perrey, 2008). Interestingly, a drop in lPFC activation does not lead to immediate task termination but participants continue for some more time[7] (Wolff, Bieleke et al., 2018). One possible explanation for this finding is that exercisers specify control signal intensities that have a built-in anticipatory buffer to be prepared in case exercise gets more demanding. The quick drop in lPFC oxygenation that has been observed prior to task termination might then reflect the dropping of EVC until the specified control intensity does not suffice to continue with the task. This is in line with research showing that a certain activity level in lPFC is required to engage in an effortful task (Hosking, Cocker, & Winstanley, 2016). In addition, this pattern might also reflect some form of task inertia: Changing a self-regulatory control signal produces costs in itself and these reconfiguration costs can deter people from switching to another activity (Monsell, 2003; Musslick, et al., 2018).

Trained Athletes Process Exercise-Induced Demands More Efficiently

Some studies have compared exercise-induced cortical activation changes in trained athletes and untrained participants (Ludyga, Gronwald, & Hottenrott, 2016; Rooks et al., 2010; Seidel, Carius, Roediger, Rumpf, & Ragert, 2019). Interestingly, in the systematic review by Rooks et al. (2010), the drop in PFC oxygenation prior to task termination has been observed in untrained participants but not in trained athletes. Trained athletes have extensive experience in adjusting their mental and physical efforts as a function of the challenge at hand, by interpreting sensations from their body. It is therefore conceivable that trained athletes are better able to anticipate expected control costs and the likelihood of potential future rewards, resulting in better-calibrated estimates of EVC. Behavioral data in support of this hypothesis comes from an analysis of the pacing profiles of 190,228 finishers of the New York Marathon. Here, the variability in 5km split times was substantially lower for top runners compared to less successful runners (Santos-Lozano, Collado, Foster, Lucia, & Garatachea, 2014).

Further, the *neural efficiency hypothesis* suggests that experts are more efficient in using their cortical resources for performing mental operations (Dunst et al., 2014). For example, more intelligent individuals perform cognitive tasks with lower brain activation, indicating the investment of less mental effort (Dunst et al., 2014). Applying this finding to the sports setting, trained athletes exhibit a less pronounced increase in PFC oxygenation during incremental exercise than untrained participants (Rooks et al., 2010). This is also in line with research showing that participants who score highly on a self-report measure of trait self-regulatory control display a less steep increase in lPFC oxygenation over the course of a fatiguing static muscular endurance task (Wolff, Schüler et al., 2019). This might point toward a more efficient use of processing resources. Interestingly, when task demands were standardized with respect to participants' individual capability (e.g. 60% of one's maximum power output on a cycling task), these expert-novice differences in brain oxygenation have not been observed (Dunst et al., 2014; Seidel et al., 2019). Adding to evidence from fNIRS studies, a recent study used EEG to measure the α-wave/β-wave ratio as a marker for neural efficiency,[8] and compared well-trained to less well-trained cyclists (Ludyga et al., 2016). Higher α/β ratios were observed over frontal sites in well-trained cyclists, supporting the neural efficiency hypotheses. Although they do not explicitly refer to self-regulatory control, the authors suggest that superior athletes might be better at inhibiting task-irrelevant cognitive processes. Going back to the proposition that the control demands of a task vary as a function of its automaticity and of its reliance on shared local processing pathways, these findings fit well into the theorizing on self-regulatory control we present here. Compared to non-athletes, trained athletes have been repeatedly exposed to the multitude of self-regulatory challenges one faces during exercise (McCormick, Meijen, & Marcora, 2016) and this experience likely leads to a greater automatization in the processing of these regulatory demands.[9] Thus, it is conceivable that trained athletes process self-regulatory demands during sports more efficiently and specify more realistic EVCs that are more accurately matched to the current task demands.

Psychological Manipulations Affect Cortical Changes during Sports

Recently, researchers have started to investigate the effect psychological manipulations have on effort-related sensations and on cortical activity while participants perform sports. For example, one way to reduce the self-regulatory costs of an action is to make that action more automatic (Bayer, Achtziger, Gollwitzer, & Moskowitz, 2009; Gollwitzer, 1999; see also Chapter 12 for an in-depth discussion of the topic). Accordingly, researchers have investigated the effects of self-regulatory strategies that aim to automatize behavior (Bieleke & Wolff, 2017; Wolff, Bieleke et al., 2018). Interestingly, while such a self-regulatory intervention did not lead to improved performance in a static muscular endurance task, participants were able to perform the task with a less pronounced increase in lPFC activation, indicating that the task had been performed in a neuronally more efficient way (Wolff, Bieleke et al., 2018). Another study used the multi-action plan (MAP) model (Robazza, Bertollo, Filho, Hanin, & Bortoli, 2016) to derive functional and dysfunctional pacing strategies and assess their effect on cycling performance and on EEG coherence (as a measure of functional connectivity; Di Fronso et al., 2018). When applying the dysfunctional strategy, participants were asked to focus their attention internally on feelings of muscle exertion. According to the MAP model, this internal focus on aversive sensations is detrimental to performance because it enhances perceived fatigue. Indeed, applying a dysfunctional strategy was associated with higher EEG coherence at high intensities, potentially indicating excessive attentional focus on muscle exertion (Di Fronso et al., 2018). Interpreting this finding from the perspective of self-regulatory control, adopting a dysfunctional pacing strategy might have resulted in inefficient or excessive allocation of self-regulatory control. In line with this argument, low coherence was observed when participants adopted a functional pacing strategy. Other researchers induced heat stress to alter the costs of exercise. Here, changes in frontal areas of the brain were observed, again likely reflecting changes in the "capacity to sustain mental readiness and arousal" (Périard, Pauw, Zanow, & Racinais, 2018, p. 1).

We are aware of only one study that has investigated the influence of experimentally manipulating the value of self-regulatory control on lPFC oxygenation and physical performance: In this fNIRS study, participants performed an isometric knee extension task until voluntary task termination on two occasions (Giboin, Gruber, Schüler, & Wolff, 2019). In the control group, participants received the same reward per minute in both sessions. Participants in the experimental group received 50% less reward per minute in Session 2 compared to Session 1, but were also compensated with an upfront payment that was calibrated so they would earn exactly the same total reward in the second session if they performed the task for the same duration as in the first session. Previous research has shown that this form of *income-compensated wage decrease* (ICWD) reduces the willingness to invest self-regulatory control during that second session (Kool & Botvinick, 2014). Consistent with this finding, lPFC oxygenation was lower in the ICWD group in the second session. However, counter to expectations, this decrease was not associated with poorer performance, as would be expected if this group was exerting less mental effort. Instead, the ICWD group in fact persisted *longer* in the knee extension task. One potential explanation for this is that the unexpected performance improvement we observed was achieved by a more efficient execution of the task. Indeed, post-hoc analyses revealed that participants in the ICWD group deviated less from the target force that had to be produced, thereby executing the task with less force than the control group. There were no group differences in perceived effort and in a host of objective markers of physiological exertion (maximal voluntary contraction, voluntary activation, potentiated twitch at rest, and electromyographic activity). Collectively, these findings suggest that, under certain conditions, increasing the value of self-regulatory control might lead to an overexertion of physiological resources and thereby produce more costs and hamper performance. Interestingly, this aligns well with recent work showing that predictions people make from previous reward learning can cause them to overexert self-regulatory control (Bustamante et al., 2020).

Another branch of research has investigated the effects of providing inaccurate information regarding the duration of an endurance task on lPFC oxygenation and performance. For example, in one study, participants either knew or did not know how long a cycling task was going to last (Wingfield, Marino, & Skein, 2018). Withholding information on task duration can be understood as a manipulation that complicates the initial computation of the EVC and, subsequently, the adequate updating of EVC based on ones' current state. In line with this reasoning, participants who knew the distance invested more effort at the end of the task which was accompanied by an increase in lPFC oxygenation. In contrast, participants without this information adopted a more conservative pacing strategy and performed worse (Wingfield et al., 2018). A similar pattern was observed in a cycling study where one group of cyclists was told to cycle for ten minutes, while a second group was told to cycle for sixty minutes (Radel, Brisswalter, & Perrey, 2017). However, in the second group, the task was terminated after ten minutes as well. Participants who expected to expend their effort over a longer period of time displayed lower lPFC activation than participants who expected to cycle for only ten minutes.

Beyond Endurance Performance

The bulk of the neuroscientific literature we reviewed here concerned endurance performance. This has at least two reasons: First, the self-regulatory challenges of endurance performance are ideal to study self-regulatory control, given that the regulation of effort is at the heart of endurance sports and that perceived exertion is a fundamental sensation that characterizes the application of self-regulatory control (Wolff & Martarelli, 2020). Second, endurance performance – especially time trial cycling or static muscular endurance – allows for a comparatively controlled and stable measurement of cortical processes because the upper body is relatively stable and athletes usually do not make abrupt movements.

However, researchers have also investigated other types of sports, and their findings are compatible with those obtained in the domain of endurance performance. For example, a recent study found that a more complex juggling task (e.g. 5-ball cascade vs. 2-ball cascade) was accompanied by more oxygenation over motor areas, whereas a higher level of juggling expertise tended to be associated with less oxygenation (Carius et al., 2016). However, as activity was only monitored over motor areas it remains unclear whether the juggling task also elicited an increase in lPFC oxygenation. Considering the projections from the lPFC to premotor areas (Miller & Cohen, 2001) and the self-regulatory demands imposed by the task (i.e. attentional control for tracking ball trajectories), this would be likely. Another recent study investigated changes in oxygenation in the lPFC during a series of sprint start sequences (Wolff, Thürmer, Stadler, & Schüler, 2019). Participants were instructed to either produce a fast sprint start on the Go-signal or *not* to start on the Go-signal (no-start condition). Thus, in the condition where participants actually had to start, they had to balance the impulse to start too fast with the requirement of starting as fast as possible on the Go-signal. In the no-start condition, by contrast, participants only had to restrain the impulse of accidentally starting upon the Go-signal. From an EVC perspective, both tasks required a control signal to be specified to prevent a false start (i.e. response inhibition). However, when actual starts were required, an additional control signal needed to be specified to initiate a fast start as soon as the Go-signal occurred (i.e. action initiation). In line with this reasoning, an increase in PFC oxygenation in the period between the Set-signal and the Go-signal was observed in both conditions. However, this increase was even more pronounced in the condition where participants actually had to produce a start.

Conclusion

Taken together, the literature reviewed in this chapter demonstrates that research on the neuroscience of self-regulatory control in sports is still in its infancy but has started to gather considerable momentum (see Figure 11.2). Performance in sports is increasingly understood as a task with inherent self-regulatory demands that athletes must cope with effectively. This perspective opens the field for innovative insights from research addressing the "whys" and "whens" of successful self-regulatory control. In particular, theories that conceive of self-regulatory control as the output of a reward-based decision offer a comprehensive computational framework that allows specific predictions regarding behavior and its neurophysiological mechanisms. As we have shown, components of one such framework, the EVC theory, can be plausibly related to various aspects of performance in sports, ranging from the initial willingness to invest effort to the decision to terminate a task. Fortunately, state-of-the-art brain imaging technology nowadays permits several intriguing ways of capturing and manipulating neurophysiological processes during exercise, providing glimpses into what has been referred to as the "sporting brain" (Walsh, 2014, R859). That said, we feel it is important to call for more neuroscientific research on self-regulated sports performance because key questions have not yet been addressed comprehensively. It will be important to test the dACC's proposed role during sports performance, to analyze the effect of directly manipulating the value of self-regulatory control, to investigate the potential neurocomputational overlap between physical and mental efforts (Ritz, Frömer, & Shenhav, 2020), and to get a better understanding of the differences between elite and recreational athletes in the neuronal processing of the self-regulatory demands in sports. We believe these are exciting questions and with this chapter we hope to encourage further research on self-regulatory control in sports.

Notes

1 Sometimes also referred to as *self-control* or *cognitive control.*
2 Indeed, research indicates that perceived exertion, rather than physiological resource depletion (e.g. locomotor muscle fatigue), might be the signal that ultimately leads to the termination of an

exercise (e.g. Chapter 10, this volume; Marcora, Staiano, & Manning, 2009; Staiano, Bosio, de Morree, Rampinini, & Marcora, 2018).

3 Clearly, this example only applies to a scenario where the runners' only goal is to qualify and not to achieve a personal best or win the race.

4 Interestingly, research on pacing implies a process with a striking similarity to EVC theory, when it comes to how athletes pace themselves during competition: "intensity is regulated within the brain based on a complex algorithm involving peripheral sensory feedback and the anticipated workload remaining" (Abbiss & Laursen, 2008, p. 239).

5 Research suggests that sender-detector separations of ca. 3 cm optimize signal-to-noise ratio (Boas, Elwell, Ferrari, & Taga, 2014; Ekkekakis, 2009).

6 Indeed, research shows that task termination occurs well before physiological resources are fully depleted or bodily homeostasis is threatened (Marcora & Staiano, 2010; Morales-Alamo et al., 2015).

7 Systematic research on how long participants continue after this drop is currently lacking and represents an exciting future research question.

8 α-waves are associated with mental inactivity and β-waves have been linked with cognitive information processing. Thus, if a demanding task is performed with a high α-wave/β-wave ratio, this can be interpreted as an indicator for energy-efficient cortical functioning (Ludyga et al., 2016).

9 It has to be noted that, while some research supports the notion that specific physical or cognitive trainings generalize beyond the specific functions they presumably address (Jaeggi, Buschkuehl, Jonides, & Perrig, 2008; Sherrington, Tiedemann, Fairhall, Close, & Lord, 2011), there is also an accumulating body of research that indicates that such effects are task-specific and do not generalize (Giboin, Gruber, & Kramer, 2015; Giboin et al., 2019, Melby-Lervag & Hulme, 2013).

12

PLANNING AND IMPLEMENTATION INTENTION INTERVENTIONS IN PHYSICAL ACTIVITY

Susette A. Moyers and Martin S. Hagger

Introduction

Physical inactivity is one of the leading causes of morbidity, premature mortality, and disability worldwide (Guthold, Stevens, Riley, & Bull, 2018; Lee et al., 2012; WHO, 2010). Conversely, regular participation in physical activity engagement has multiple health benefits, including reduced risk for chronic illness and health conditions (Warburton & Bredin, 2017; Warburton, Nicol, & Bredin, 2006; Pedersen & Saltin, 2015) and better mental health (Biddle, Ciaccioni, Thomas, & Vergeer, 2019; Dunn, Trivedi, & O'Neal, 2001). However, 23% of adult men and 32% of adult women worldwide do not participate in sufficient physical activity to meet public health recommendations of 150 min/week of moderate-vigorous intensity physical activity (WHO, 2016). Many interventions have been developed to promote population-level physical activity participation (Heath et al., 2012; Reis et al., 2016; Sallis et al., 2016). However, existing interventions have had limited success in promoting long-term maintenance of physical activity participation, especially in sedentary individuals (Artinian et al., 2010; Kahn et al, 2002). This highlights the need for effective interventions to promote population-level participation in regular physical activity through evidence-based strategies that have been shown to be effective in promoting uptake and maintenance.

Behavioral science is playing an increasingly important role in informing organizations and stakeholders on means to develop optimally effective campaigns and initiatives to promote physical activity (Hagger, Moyers, McAnally, & McKinley, 2020a; Hagger & Weed, 2019; Hennessy, Johnson, Acabchuk, McCloskey, & Stewart-James, 2019). (Bartholomew, Parcel, Kok, Gottlieb, & Fernández, 2011). Behavioral scientists have sought to apply theories derived from social science, particularly psychology, that identify behaviors that are potentially modifiable through interventions (Glanz & Bishop, 2010; Johnson & Acabchuk, 2018). One approach has been to apply social psychological theories to identify the determinants of health behavior participation. If these determinants can be reliably linked to health behavior participation, they can then form the basis for intervention development (Hagger, Cameron, Hamilton, Hankonen, & Lintunen, 2020b, 2020c; Rothman, Klein, & Sheeran,

2020; Suls et al., 2020). In particular, identifying techniques or strategies that are effective in changing the determinants of physical activity can form the content of interventions (Kok et al., 2016; Michie et al., 2013). Theories applied to identify the determinants of physical activity have typically been from the social cognition tradition, that is, theories that aim to predict behavior based on beliefs, attitudes, and interpretation of social information (Conner & Norman, 2015b). While such theories have been successfully adopted to identify the determinants of physical activity, and the processes involved, they have tended to leave substantive variance in physical activity participation unexplained (Ekkekakis & Brand, this volume; Hagger & Chatzisarantis, 2014; Rhodes, McEwan et al., 2019). Importantly, social cognition theories have tended to be more effective in explaining intentions and motivation to participate in physical activity, rather than the behavior itself. This has led to the observation that individuals do not always follow through and enact their good intentions to participate in a physical activity, a so-called 'intention-behavior gap' (Orbell & Sheeran, 1998; Rhodes & de Brujin, 2013a; Rhodes et al., this volume; Sheeran & Webb, 2016).

Theorists and researchers have, therefore, aimed to describe the processes by which individuals are successful in enacting their intentions, and propose strategies that may bolster efforts to support long-term changes in physical activity behavior (Conner & Norman, 2015b; Hagger, Cameron, Hamilton, Hankonen, & Lintunen, 2020d; Heckhausen & Gollwitzer, 1987; Rhodes, McEwan et al., 2019; Schwarzer, 2008). This chapter aims to review research focusing on the role of planning in promoting intention enactment and how planning can be leveraged to improve participation in physical activity. Planning is a deliberate, cognitive process that requires the individual to make decisions about behavior in advance to achieve a future outcome or goal (Owen, 1997). In the context of the present chapter, planning requires individuals to make explicit links between their intended goal-directed action and an external or internal cue or prompt (Gollwitzer, 1999, 2014). The chapter will first outline the importance and prevalence of the 'intention-behavior gap' in physical activity contexts (Orbell & Sheeran, 1998; Rhodes & de Brujin, 2013a; Sheeran & Webb, 2016). It will then describe theoretical approaches to intention enactment, and the role that volitional processes, and the associated behavior change technique of planning, play in promoting individuals acting on their intentions. Research applying these theoretical approaches to promote better intention enactment is then outlined, together with suggestions for future research needed to further understand the role of planning interventions in changing and maintaining physical activity behavior (Gollwitzer, 1996; Keller, Gollwitzer, & Sheeran, 2020).

Application of Social Cognition Theories in Physical Activity

A key assumption of the social cognition theories that have been applied to identify the determinants of health behaviors like physical activity (Armitage & Conner, 2000; Conner & Norman, 2015b; Hardeman et al., 2002; Plotnikoff, Costigan, Karunamuni, & Lubans, 2013) is that the determinants are modifiable through intervention (Michie, Webb, & Sniehotta, 2010; Sheeran, Klein, & Rothman, 2017). Social cognition theories feature prominently among these theoretical approaches. These theories focus on how individuals' processing of social information reflected in beliefs, attitudes, and expectancies impact their future decision-making, reflected in constructs like intention, and actual behavior. The social cognition approach encompasses many well-cited theories and models applied to predict health behaviors, including the theories of reasoned action and planned behavior (Ajzen, 1991; Ajzen & Fishbein, 1980; Fishbein & Ajzen, 1975), protection motivation theory (Rogers, 1983), and social cognitive theory (Bandura, 1991).

A central premise of social cognition theories is that individuals' beliefs and expectations affect future decisions and actions (Ajzen, 1985; Ajzen & Fishbein, 1980; Armitage & Conner, 2000; Conner & Norman, 2015b). For example, many social cognition theories encompass beliefs about expected outcomes of the behavior, such that if a behavior is perceived to have beneficial or utilitarian outcomes, an individual is more likely to be motivated to perform that behavior in future. Intention is a central construct to many social cognition theories. Intention reflects individuals' stated motivation to enact a future target behavior and is considered as the most proximal antecedent of action (Ajzen & Fishbein, 1980; Fishbein et al., 2001). Strong, stable intentions are more likely to lead to action in the future (Cooke & Sheeran, 2004; Sheeran & Abraham, 2003; Sheeran, Orbell, & Trafimow, 1999). Intentions are usually considered the immediate determinant of behavior and mediate effects of other belief-based determinants on behavior. For example, in the theory of planned behavior, a highly prominent social cognition theory, intentions are proposed to mediate the effects of attitudes (positive and negative beliefs regarding performing the target behavior in future), subjective norms (beliefs that significant others support performing the target behavior in future), and perceived behavioral control (beliefs in personal capacity in performing the target behavior in future) (Ajzen, 1985, 1991) on behavioral enactment.

Social cognition theories have demonstrated efficacy in predicting behavior across multiple health behaviors, including physical activity (Armitage & Conner, 2000; Conner & Norman, 2015b; Hardeman et al., 2002; Plotnikoff et al., 2013). For example, a meta-analyses of the theories of reasoned action and planned behavior applied to physical activity demonstrate that physical activity behavior is associated with intention and perceived behavioral control, whereas intentions to be physically active were predicted by attitudes and perceived behavioral control (Downs & Hausenblas, 2005; Hagger, Chatzisarantis, & Biddle, 2002). A more recent meta-analysis on the theory of planned behavior applied to health behaviors suggested that the theory accounted for 23.9% of the variance in physical activity behavior (McEachan, Conner, Taylor, & Lawton, 2011). Similarly, research applying protection motivation theory to predict physical activity has demonstrated that coping appraisals including self-efficacy (belief in one's capability to execute the recommended course of action successfully) and response efficacy (the individual's expectancy that carrying out recommendations can remove the threat) predict physical activity behavior (Fruin, Pratt, & Owen, 1992; Plotnikoff & Trinh, 2010; Rhodes, Plotnikoff, & Courneya, 2008). Taken together, these results suggest that social cognition theories have value in explaining variance in future physical activity participation. Moreover, this research suggests that interventions aimed at promoting behavior change should consider targeting change in the immediate belief-based determinants of intentions (Hagger et al., 2020b; Hardcastle et al., 2015).

The 'Intention-Behavior Gap'

The effectiveness of social cognition theories like the theory of planned behavior in predicting physical activity intentions notwithstanding, research has indicated that the intention-behavior relationship is modest in size. For example, meta-analyses have placed the averaged correlation between intention and behavior between $r = 0.43$ and $r = 0.51$ (Armitage & Conner, 2001; Downs & Hausenblas, 2005; Hagger et al., 2002; McEachan et al., 2011). These reflect small-to-medium-sized effects (Cohen, 1992), suggesting that intentions only translate to behavior about half of the time. These associations suggest considerable 'shortfall' in the prediction of physical activity behavior by intention. Similarly, research has demonstrated that a substantive number of individuals in research applying theories like the theory of planned behavior express intentions but fail to enact them. For example, Orbell and Sheeran (1998) identified a number of 'inclined abstainers' in their research indicating those who reported intentions but did not subsequently participate in health behaviors (Orbell & Sheeran, 1998). Similarly, Rhodes and de Bruijn's (2013a) meta-analysis of physical activity studies revealed that 43% of individuals expressing physical activity intentions did not subsequently participate in the intended physical activity (Rhodes & de Bruijn, 2013a). These individuals were labeled 'unsuccessful intenders'; they possess a strong intention and motivation to be physically active but are unsuccessful at carrying out the planned physical activity behavior (Rhodes & de Brujin, 2013a). This discrepancy between intention and behavior has become known as the 'intention-behavior gap' (Orbell & Sheeran, 1998; Rhodes & de Bruijn, 2013a, 2013b; Sheeran, 2002; Sheeran & Webb, 2016; Sniehotta, Scholz, & Schwarzer, 2005). These findings raise concerns over the likely effectiveness of interventions targeting change in the antecedents of intentions because a majority of individuals are already likely to have formed strong intentions to be physically active but fail to follow through on them on a regular basis (Orbell & Sheeran, 2000; Rhodes & de Brujin, 2013a; Webb & Sheeran, 2006). As such, recent literature has been focused on the processes by which physical activity intentions are enacted and maintained over time.

Dual-Phase Theories

One class of theories that have been applied to address issues around intention enactment, and applied to explain and resolve the 'intention-behavior gap' is known as 'dual-phase' theories. These theories, also known as 'action-control' approaches, propose that intention formation and enactment of intentions are carried out in different phases or stages, and the processes in these stages determine the extent to which intentions predict behavior (Hagger & Chatzisarantis, 2014; Heckhausen & Gollwitzer, 1987; Rhodes & de Bruijn, 2013b; Rhodes, Fiala et al., 2012; Rhodes et al., this volume; Schwarzer, 2008). A prototypical action-control approach is the model of action phases (Gollwitzer, 1990; Heckhausen & Gollwitzer, 1987). Others have utilized the dual-phase approach include the health action process approach (HAPA; Schwarzer, 2008), the I-Change model (de Vries et al., 2005), and the Integrated Behavior Change model (Hagger & Chatzisarantis, 2014). According to the model of action phases, fulfillment of a goal-directed action is the result of processes in two broad phases: Motivational and volitional. In the motivational phase, individuals develop intentions based on the motivation to participate in the target behavior. In the volitional phase, individuals enact their intentions by supplementing their goal intentions with volitional components such as plans (Gollwitzer, 1993). Similarly, the HAPA proposes two explicit phases: The pre-intentional or motivational phase which outlines formation of behavioral intentions, and a post-intentional or volitional phase that leads to enactment of the behavior (Lippke, Ziegelmann, & Schwarzer, 2004; Luszczynska & Schwarzer, 2003; Schüz, Sniehotta, Wiedemann, & Seemann, 2006; Sniehotta et al., 2005; Schwarzer &

Hamilton, 2020; Ziegelmann, Lippke, & Schwarzer, 2006; Zhang, Zhang, Schwarzer, & Hagger, 2019). Such approaches allow for more accurate prediction of behavior and provide insight into the potential mechanisms by which individuals enact behaviors (Lippke, Ziegelmann, & Schwarzer, 2005).

Pre-Intentional Motivation Phase

According to dual-phase theories, individuals make decisions to perform a given target behavior in the pre-intentional or motivational phase. This entails a deliberative process in which the costs and benefits of the target behavior are considered, and a committed decision on whether to perform the behavior is made (Gollwitzer, 1990; Keller et al., 2020). Influences on intention formation in the pre-intentional phase are outlined in the numerous social cognition theories that focus on intention as the immediate determinant of behavior and include constructs such as attitudes, risk perceptions, perceived norms, and self-efficacy. In this section, we review the evidence on specific determinants of physical activity intentions based on these social cognition theories.

Theory and research have consistently identified attitudes, or personal beliefs about the perceived outcome of participating in a behavior in the future, as a key determinant of physical activity intentions. Such beliefs reflect individuals' perceptions that participating in physical activity will have utility (e.g. help make one fitter, assist in losing weight, improve mood, give one more energy in daily life) or have emotional benefits (e.g. improve mood, be enjoyable). Attitude is a central construct to many social cognition theories, such as the theory of planned behavior (Ajzen, 1991). Applications of the theory of planned behavior have linked attitudes with intentions to perform a physical activity (Bentler & Speckart, 1979; Hagger, Chatzisarantis, & Biddle, 2001). Another determinant of physical activity intention is risk perception, which reflects individuals' beliefs of the probable risk for particular health problems or conditions (Renner, Spivak, Kwon, & Schwarzer, 2007). If individuals perceive that they are at risk of a particular health problem but also believe that physical activity can attenuate their risk, they may be more likely to form intentions to participate in physical activity. Many social cognition theories such as the health belief model (Rosenstock, 1974a), protection motivation theory (Rogers, 1975), and the extended parallel process model (Witte, 1992) consider risk perceptions as a key determinant of health behaviors. Evidence for the contribution of risk perception to the prediction of physical activity intentions has been reported in previous research (Renner et al., 2007). Further, risk perceptions may also impact intentions to continue participating in physical activity behavior after initiation (Amireault, Godin, & Vézina-Im, 2012). This evidence supports the idea that risk perception may contribute to forming intentions and maintaining physical activity behavior over time. Normative beliefs have also been shown to influence physical activity intentions. Normative beliefs reflect the perceived influence, positive or negative, of significant others with respect to performing the behavior in the future. It is a key determinant of intentions in social cognition theories, such as the theory of planned behavior. Meta-analyses of studies on the theory of planned behavior have demonstrated that normative beliefs significantly predict physical activity intentions (Hagger et al., 2002; McEachan et al., 2011). Finally, perceived self-efficacy to perform physical activity behavior is a key determinant of intention. Self-efficacy reflects individuals' beliefs in their personal capacity to perform the behavior and overcome potential barriers and obstacles to perform that behavior. Some barriers to initiating and maintaining physical activity participation include certain situational and social contexts that may create a conflict with intended physical activity participation. These include distractions (e.g. needing to look after children), competing goals and sedentary habits (e.g. watching TV), multiple goal pursuits (e.g. working from home), unwanted social influence (e.g. demands to socialize with others), and conflicting self-states such as physical discomfort, fatigue, bad mood, and disruptive thoughts and feelings about physical activity. A number of studies have shown that self-efficacy significantly predicts physical activity intentions (Dzewaltowski, 1989; Dzewaltowski, Noble, & Shaw, 1990; Hagger et al., 2001; Yordy & Lent, 1993). Overall, there is considerable evidence that these determinants predict intentions to be physically active, and intentions mediate the effect of the determinants on physical activity behavior (Hagger et al., 2002). However, consistent with research on the intention-behavior gap, indirect effects of these determinants on physical activity behavior are modest in size, and are dependent on the strength of the intention-behavior relationship. This means that determinants of intentions are important insofar as they likely contribute to intention formation and strength to perform physical activity in the future, and yet they are not implicated in the process by which intentions are converted into behavior. According to dual-phase theories, these determinants operate in a phase that precedes a volitional phase in which intentions are implemented. This latter phase is outlined next.

Volitional or Implemental Phase

As research highlighting the intention-behavior 'gap' has demonstrated, intentions alone do not always lead to behavioral enactment (Orbell & Sheeran, 1998; Rhodes & de Bruijn, 2013a, Sheeran & Webb, 2016). According to dual-phase models, execution of intentions to act is implemented in a subsequent volitional or implemental phase of action. In this phase, volitional processes such as making plans to carry out the intended behavior help bridge the 'gap' between intention and behavior. For example, in the model of action phases, individuals who supplement their intentions with specific plans, known as implementation intentions, in which individuals pinpoint specific conditions on which the intended behavior will be enacted, such as identifying when and where the behavior will be performed (Heckhausen & Gollwitzer, 1987). Similarly, in the HAPA, two types of plans, action and coping plans, are important parts of the process that enable individuals to carry out the intended behavior (Schwarzer, 2008). Action planning is akin to implementation intentions, as outlined in the model of action phases, while coping planning refers to the anticipation of barriers that may interfere with an intended behavior and well thought out alternative behaviors that could be enacted to overcome them (Scholz, Sniehotta, Burkert, & Schwarzer, 2007; Sniehotta et al., 2005; Zhang et al., 2019). For example, action planning consists of planning when, where, and how to engage in physical activity; such as planning to go for a run during lunch hour at work. Coping planning consists of planning alternative actions to pursue in case barriers arise, such as planning to go to the gym to run on the treadmill at lunch time if the weather does not permit an outdoor run, as initially planned. The model of action phases and HAPA differ in the processes by which plans relate to intentions and behavior. In the model of action phases, implementation intentions are proposed to moderate the relationship between intention and behavior. As such, individuals who form plans are more likely to carry out intentions to be physically active. In the HAPA, action and coping planning are proposed to mediate the effects of intentions on behavior and, as such, help address why intentions are converted into behavior. However, there are theorists who suggest that action and coping planning should moderate the intention-behavior relationship within the HAPA (Sutton, 2008), and this has been corroborated empirically (Hamilton & Schwarzer, 2018; Norman & Conner, 2005; Schwarzer, Lippke, & Luszczynska, 2011).

Implementation Intentions

Implementation intentions are one of the most prominent forms of planning within dual-phase approaches to behavior and have received considerable attention in the literature (Adriaanse, Vinkers, De Ridder, Hox, & De Wit, 2011b; Bélanger-Gravel, Godin, & Amireault, 2013a; Gollwitzer, 1999; Gollwitzer & Sheeran, 2006). Implementation intentions are 'if-then' framed plans that provide individuals with an effective strategy to enact their intentions (Gollwitzer, 1993). Implementation intentions are relevant to the volitional phase in the model of action phases and are hypothesized to bind performance of the intended behavior to conditions in the environment, or cues, that will lead to the enactment of the behavior (Gollwitzer, 1999; Keller et al., 2020). Implementation intentions, therefore, involve specifying an event, internal or external, and associating that event with the intended behavior to help enact intentions. Gollwitzer proposed that these plans should make the link between the contingent event and the behavior clear, suggesting that the 'if-then' format may be most appropriate means to do so (Gollwitzer, 1993, 2014). This might involve specifying when or where the target behavior might be enacted. For example, in a physical activity context, an 'if-then' plan would involve an individual explicitly stating the proposed link between the contingency and the behavior (e.g. 'if my alarm goes off at lunch break, then I will collect my gym bag and go to the gym'). Implementation intentions are effective in resolving some of the issues individuals face when attempting to initiate and maintain their goal intentions, and meta-analysis of research on implementation intentions has revealed a medium-to-large effect of forming an implementation intention on behavioral enactment ($d = 0.65$; Gollwitzer & Sheeran, 2006).

Implementation intentions are proposed to operate by tapping into automatic cognitive processes to aid behavior enactment. Implementation intentions are proposed to reduce the need for conscious and effortful control of goal-directed behaviors (Gollwitzer, 1993). Planning how to implement intended behaviors in a given situation in advance may therefore make the behavior easier to enact. Deciding in advance on what course of action to take to carry out an intended behavior reduces the need to make effortful deliberations in 'in-the-moment' situations where the behavior should be carried out. Therefore, behavior initiation should be more efficient and demand fewer cognitive resources (Gollwitzer, 1993, 1996). This automatization of goal implementation through pre-determining the appropriate behavioral response to situations makes it easier to recall intentions to perform the behavior in the appropriate situation and may also protect performance of the intended behavior from distractions, bad habits, or competing goal-directed behaviors. Research has demonstrated that implementation intentions lead to behavioral enactment by facilitating low-effort, automatic enactment of the intended behavior. For example, implementation intentions have been shown to improve perceptual readiness for specified cues (Gollwitzer, 2014; Orbell, Hodgkins, & Sheeran, 1997; Webb & Sheeran, 2004; Wiedemann, Lippke, & Schwarzer, 2012), making the specified cue more salient, and as a result, leads to more efficient enactment of the behavior paired with the cue. Implementation intentions have also been shown to increase the automaticity with which the intended behavior is enacted (Sheeran, Webb, & Gollwitzer, 2005; Webb & Sheeran, 2008; Webb, Sheeran, & Luszczynska, 2009). These automatic cognitive mechanisms also underlie habit and may support the development of habitual behavior (Aarts & Dijksterhuis, 2000; Adriaanse, Gollwitzer, De Ridder, De Wit, & Kroese, 2011a; Hagger, 2019). Therefore, utilizing implementation intentions may help the enactment of the intended behavior to become more automated, which may be important in supporting long-term changes in physical activity behavior.

Research suggests that the formation of implementation intentions is effective in changing physical activity behavior in a variety of populations and contexts. Prompting individuals to form an implementation intention increases the likelihood that individuals will initiate physical activity behavior (Milne, Orbell, & Sheeran, 2002). Interventions utilizing implementation intentions to change physical activity behavior have demonstrated success in promoting greater participation in physical activity. A meta-analysis examining the effects of implementation intentions interventions aiming to increase physical activity behavior demonstrated a small-to-medium-sized effect (standardized mean difference, SMD = 0.31) on physical activity at post-intervention, and also provided evidence of successfully increasing physical activity after no-contact follow-up periods (SMD = 0.24; Bélanger-Gravel et al., 2013a). This suggests that forming implementation intentions has promise in attenuating the intention-behavior gap in physical activity behavior, and influences behavior maintenance after the intervention. Therefore, public health interventions aiming to initiate physical activity behavior with the goal of long-term behavior change may be more successful if the target population is prompted to form an implementation intention. While implementation intentions offer promise in physical activity behavior change interventions, intention strength has been shown to moderate the effectiveness of implementation intentions on physical activity behavior (Pfeffer & Strobach, 2019), and should be considered a necessary antecedent before implementing planning interventions. It is also important to consider other factors that may moderate the effectiveness of implementation of these interventions, as such, these potential moderators will be discussed in the next section.

Moderators of Implementation Intention Effects

A number of factors have been implicated to impact the effectiveness of implementation intentions on physical activity behavior. Variables that have been shown to moderate effects of implementation intention interventions in physical activity include population/sample type, format of the plan ('if-then' versus unstructured; the inclusion of a barrier management component versus without), the complexity of implementation intentions (multiple implementation intentions versus fewer/a single implementation intention/s), format of the intervention (researcher-imposed versus self-generated), delivery mode of the intervention (researcher-present, self-administered, or technology-based; dyadic or group delivery; reinforcement techniques utilized). These factors should be considered when designing implementation intention interventions to change physical activity behavior.

Population Type

There is evidence suggesting that implementation intentions are effective in promoting intended behaviors in many populations. Implementation intention interventions have been successful in increasing physical activity participation in older obese adults (Bélanger-Gravel, Godin, Bilodeau, Poirier, & Dagenais, 2012), older adult women (Hall, Zehr, Paulitzki, & Rhodes, 2014), student populations (Bélanger-Gravel et al., 2013a), clinical populations (Latimer, Ginis, & Arbour, 2006; Rodgers et al., 2014), children with low socioeconomic status (SES; Armitage & Sprigg, 2010), and sedentary women (Arbour & Martin Ginis, 2009). Evidence from Bélanger-Gravel et al.'s (2013a) meta-analysis suggests that population type significantly moderates the effect of implementation intentions on physical activity behavior. Implementation intentions were more effective in student and clinical populations, and less effective in general population samples (Bélanger-Gravel et al., 2013a). This implies that there may be individuals or subgroups in the general population that may benefit less than others from implementation intention interventions for physical activity.

As such, individual traits may also contribute to the observed heterogeneity in effects. For example, implementation intention interventions seem to be less effective among impulsive individuals (Burkard, Rochat, & Van der Linden, 2013; Churchill & Jessop, 2010, 2011), as it is thought that impulsivity may impair in-the-moment reasoning, and override well-conceived plans (Schweizer, 2002). In contrast, these interventions seem to be more efficacious in individuals high in conscientiousness (Webb, Christian, & Armitage, 2007) and those who have high self-efficacy (French, Olander, Chisholm, & McSharry, 2014; Kompf, 2020; Luszczynska & Haynes, 2009; Olander et al., 2013), as these individuals may feel like they are able to carry out the behavior and successfully override other competing behavioral impulses. Therefore, certain traits may impact how an individual responds to this type of implementation intention intervention and how successful it is in changing the targeted behavior. While these examples of individual traits are not all specifically related to physical activity behavior change, they provide evidence in support of moderator effects that may be worthwhile testing in a physical activity context to provide a better understanding of the factors that may determine the efficacy of these interventions in a physical activity context. These factors could help identify groups that may benefit from implementation intention interventions tailored to meet their specific needs (Hagger, Luszczynska et al., 2016). Research exploring effects of implementation intention interventions in groups of individuals characterized by these individual difference factors may help explain the observed variance in intervention effects. While there is promise in the effectiveness of implementation intentions to increase physical activity in many populations, these findings suggest that more research is needed to identify which individuals or subgroups of the general population may benefit more or less from the application of implementation intentions in interventions to increase physical activity participation. It also points to the need for interventionists to pilot test implementation intention interventions in a sample drawn from the populations of interest in order to provide formative data that verifies the effectiveness of the intervention prior to rolling it out as part of a larger population-based intervention.

Format of the Plan

Another potential moderator of the effectiveness of implementation intention interventions in physical activity is the format in which it is specified. Gollwitzer suggested that implementation intentions should be specified in the form of an 'if-then' statement, linking a cue with the intended behavior (Gollwitzer, 2014; Gollwitzer & Sheeran, 2006; Hagger & Luszczynska, 2014). There is evidence that interventions employing the 'if-then' format are more effective in promoting physical activity behavior change than those that prompt participants to determine when, where, and how physical activity behavior will be carried out (Bélanger-Gravel et al., 2013a). There is also a suggestion that incorporating elements related to coping plans (barrier management) may increase the effectiveness of implementation intention interventions (Carraro & Gaudreau, 2013). Including elements from coping planning techniques that specify potential barriers and obstacles that might arise when implementing intended behaviors alongside the specification of implementation intentions in 'if-then' statements (e.g. 'if it is raining at the time I plan to go for a run outdoors, then I will go to the gym and run on the treadmill instead') have been shown to be more effective in changing physical activity behavior than implementation intentions alone (Armitage & Arden, 2010). In Bélanger-Gravel et al.'s (2013a) meta-analysis, results also showed that implementation intention interventions that included an additional barrier management component (a coping planning technique) were more successful (SMD = 0.33) than those that did not (SMD = 0.23; Bélanger-Gravel et al., 2013a). However, while initial evidence from two reviews suggests that adding coping plans increases the efficacy of implementation intention interventions in changing physical activity behavior (Bélanger-Gravel et al., 2013a; Olander et al., 2013), other reviews have found that such additions do not tend to increase their efficacy (Conn, Hafdahl, & Mehr, 2011; French et al., 2014). Therefore, additional research is warranted to understand circumstances in which it may be advantageous to include coping plans alongside implementation intention interventions to increase physical activity participation, and should adopt high quality factorial designs to provide definitive data on whether including coping plans alongside implementation intentions improves intervention effects in physical activity.

Multiple Plans

The number of plans may also moderate the effectiveness of implementation intentions on physical activity behavior. Physical activity behavior is a complex behavior (Gardner, Rebar, & Lally, 2019; Hagger, 2020), and persistent change is likely to require multiple plans that may assist individuals to not only enact the behavior but also overcome any barriers or obstacles that may arise. However, research on health behavior change has shown that forming a single plan instead of multiple plans makes health behavior more salient and more likely to be carried out (Dalton & Spiller, 2012; Verhoeven, Adriaanse, De Ridder, De Vet, & Fennis, 2013). It may be that forming multiple 'if-then' plans may place too many demands on the individual, may be distracting, or the plans may interfere with each other. While the complexity of physical activity behavior may require multiple plans, this may limit the effectiveness of such interventions. In contrast, there is evidence that the number of plans may not be as important as some other moderators in the effects of implementation intentions on physical activity behavior. For example, one study found that the number of implementation intentions does not predict physical activity behavior (de Vet, Oenema, & Brug, 2011), suggesting that having multiple plans may be just as effective as forming fewer plans or having a single plan. As such, future research should seek to replicate these findings to understand the impact that the number of plans has on the efficacy of implementation intention interventions.

It may also be advantageous to investigate how 'if-then' plans can be worded in such a way that they take a more 'generalized' form, necessitating fewer plans, and decreasing cognitive load. Therefore, it has been recommended that specifying abstract and inclusive 'if-then' plans that cover many different critical situations and instrumental responses may be more advantageous than forming multiple, specific 'if-then' plans that may be difficult to remember and put into practice (Hagger, Luszczynska et al., 2016). Future research should investigate how the number of plans impact physical activity behavior, and whether implementation intentions that are specified in a more generalized, flexible way are more effective at changing physical activity behavior. Such practice may reduce the burden on the planner and minimize problems of recall. Therefore, forming implementation intentions that are more inclusive, covering multiple critical situations and many potentially instrumental responses, may be more advantageous than forming multiple, specific 'if-then' plans that may be hard to remember and put into practice. However, this needs to be tested empirically.

Implementation Intention Intervention Format

The format of implementation intention interventions may also be an important moderator of the effect of implementation intentions on physical activity behavior. Implementation intention interventions have been applied in both open-ended formats and experimenter-provided formats (Bélanger-Gravel, Godin, Bilodeau, & Poirier, 2013b; Armitage & Arden, 2010; Chapman, Fletcher, Flight, & Wilson, 2018). Open-ended formats allow participants to select any critical situation and link it to any critical cue, and experimenter-provided formats provide a list of situations and behavioral responses to participants, limiting them to selecting cues and behaviors from the list provided (Achtziger, Gollwitzer, & Sheeran, 2008; Gollwitzer & Sheeran, 2006). Open-ended formats allow participants to tailor plans to meet specific goals which may make them more personally relevant to the participant.

However, open-ended formats have some important limitations. While they have been shown to be successful in changing physical activity participation, the variance in open-ended plans makes coding responses challenging and limits which components of the implementation intention intervention are responsible for the change (Elliott & Armitage, 2006). Another limitation is that individuals may vary in their level of planning skill. Open-ended formats require individuals to reflect on future behavior and insightfully select salient situations or cues that apply to their enactment of the intended behavior in their everyday routine, and plan ways to overcome predetermined barriers. Some individuals may find it difficult to have sufficient insight to identify relevant situational cues and barriers that may arise, possibly limiting the effectiveness of the intervention.

Evidence also supports that those with lower levels of executive functioning benefit less from implementation intention interventions than those with higher executive functioning, suggesting a critical role for planning capacity in implementation intention effectiveness (Hall et al., 2014). Executive functioning refers to the ability to coordinate thought and action and direct it toward obtaining goals. The extent of these abilities will influence individuals' capacity to plan and orchestrate complex sequences of behavior and prioritize goals and sub-goals (Miller & Wallace, 2009). As such, executive functioning may be crucial for planning, and carrying out planned physical activity behavior. Furthermore, planning to select appropriate cues and behavioral responses may be challenging if the individual has never participated in the behavior before, such as those who have not previously participated in regular physical activity (Hagger, 2010). As such, an individual's planning skills may moderate the effect of implementation interventions. Implementation intention interventions applied to individuals with low planning skills may be less effective (Allan, Sniehotta, & Johnston, 2013).

Employing an implementation intervention in the experimenter-provided format may help overcome these issues by providing a list of critical cues and appropriate behavioral responses for the individual. In addition, this structured format enables researchers to better identify the components of the implementation intention that are more efficacious in producing behavior change. Furthermore, the experimenter-provided format may be more effective for participants with low planning skills or low executive function. One example of an experimenter-provided format for implementation intentions is the volitional help sheet (see Table 12.1). The volitional help sheet prompts participants to form implementation intentions by linking critical situations and appropriate behavioral responses from a provided list that was constructed based on empirically supported concepts of temptation and processes of change in the transtheoretical model (Armitage, 2008; DiClemente & Graydon, 2020; Gollwitzer, 1993; Hausenblas et al., 2001; Marcus, Selby, Niaura, & Rossi, 1992a; Marcus, Rakowski, & Rossi, 1992b; Prochaska & DiClemente, 1983). Volitional help sheets have been applied to a number of interventions to change health behavior (Armitage, 2008; Armitage, Norman, Noor, Alganem, & Arden, 2014; Armitage, 2015; Armitage, Alganem, & Norman, 2017). Initial experimental tests have shown that interventions using volitional help sheets have been successful at increasing physical activity participation (Armitage & Arden, 2010; Chapman et al., 2018). However, limiting the selection of cues and responses that participants are able to choose from may de-personalize the meaning behind the cue; however, it is possible that the participant selects cues that are close to, but do not properly capture the intricacies of their situation from the list. Along this line, research testing the effects of experimenter-provided lists has shown that providing participants with one versus ten critical cues to choose from were both equally effective at increasing physical activity participation (Epton & Armitage, 2017). Participants assigned to the condition with multiple cues were more likely to select cues that were more personally relevant, while those assigned to the single cue and no choice conditions received cues that were less personally relevant. This suggests that personal relevance of cues may be less relevant to planning and provides evidence of the utility of experimenter-provided cues in planning interventions. Therefore, it may be advantageous to utilize volitional help sheets to assist individuals with planning, especially those with low executive functioning, limited planning ability, and limited physical activity experience to develop plans to participate in physical activity. Future research should provide more systematic experimental and randomized controlled tests of these formats on intervention effectiveness in physical activity contexts, and also explore ways to make implementation intentions that are derived from volitional help sheets personally relevant to the individual to enhance personal meaning and effectiveness.

Method of Delivery

Method of delivery also plays a role in the efficacy of implementation intention interventions in physical activity contexts. Implementation intention interventions can be delivered in a number of ways, including self-administered, self-administered with experimenter feedback, technologically based, administered in groups, dyads, or to a single participant, and administered with various repetitions or forms of reinforcement (Bélanger-Gravel et al., 2013a). Self-administered implementation intention interventions provide no form of

TABLE 12.1 Volitional Help Sheet: Physical Activity Behavior Change

Situations	*Solutions*
If I'm tempted not to be physically active when I'm under a lot of stress	Then I will think about information from articles and advertisements on how to make physical activity a part of my life
If I'm tempted not to be physically active when I am depressed	Then I will remember how warnings about health hazards of physical inactivity move me emotionally
If I'm tempted not to be physically active when I am anxious	Then I think how I would be a better role model for others if I were more physically active
If I'm tempted not to be physically active because I feel I don't have the time	Then I will think about how my inactivity affects those people who are close to me
If I'm tempted not to be physically active because I don't feel like it	Then I will tell myself that being more physically active would make me a healthier, happier person to be around
If I'm tempted not to be physically active because I am busy	Then I will tell myself that I will feel more confident in myself if I were more physically active
If I'm tempted not to be physically active because I am alone	Then I will use physical activity to relieve my worries
If I'm tempted not to be physically active because I have to exercise alone	Then I will think about all the people encouraging me to be more physically active these days
If I'm tempted not to be physically active because my exercise partner does not exercise that day	Then I will make myself do some physical activity anyway because I know I will feel better afterward
If I'm tempted not to be physically active because I don't have access to exercise equipment	Then I will tell myself that society is changing in ways that make it easier for people who want to be more physically active
If I'm tempted not to be physically active because I am traveling	Then I will seek out someone whom I can depend when I am having problems with keeping physically active
If I'm tempted not to be physically active because my gym is closed	Then I will seek out someone who encourages me to be physically active when I don't feel up to it
If I'm tempted not to be physically active because my friends don't want me to exercise	Then I will try to set realistic goals for myself rather than setting myself up for failure by expecting too much
If I'm tempted not to be physically active because my significant other does not want me to exercise	Then I will tell myself that I am being good to myself by taking care of my body in this way
If I'm tempted not to be physically active because I am spending time with friends or family who do not exercise	Then I will tell myself that I am the only one who is responsible for my health and well-being, and that only I can decide whether or not I am physically active
If I'm tempted not to be physically active because it's raining or snowing	Then I will tell myself that if I try hard enough I can keep being physically active
If I'm tempted not to be physically active because it's cold outside	Then I will put things around my home that remind me to be physically active
If I'm tempted not to be physically active because the roads or pavements are icy/snowy	Then I will keep things around my place of work that remind me to be physically active
If I'm tempted not to be physically active because I don't feel I have the time	Then I will think how I would be a better role model for others if I were more physically active
	Then I will tell myself that I am being good to myself by taking care of my body in this way

Note: Adapted from Armitage and Arden (2010). Copyright 2010 by Taylor & Francis.

assistance to the individual forming their plan. In self-administered interventions with experimenter feedback, the experimenter ensures that the implementation intention manipulation was properly executed, and participants usually meet individually and/or in group sessions once, or on several occasions over the course of the intervention to receive feedback on goal progress. Evidence suggests that interventions that offer intermittent feedback from the researcher were slightly more effective in increasing physical activity than those that were purely self-administered (Bélanger-Gravel et al., 2013a), and this seems to be especially true in older samples (Ziegelmann, Lippke, & Schwarzer, 2006). While this difference was not statistically significant, this preliminary evidence suggests that the different delivery modes should be compared formally in future research. In particular, studies should aim to provide a more systematic evaluation of the effects of augmenting implementation intention interventions with intermittent feedback and the groups in which such modifications are most effective. Also, it is important to explore how often feedback should be given, and what type of feedback is most effective.

Research has also used different technological tools to deliver implementation intention interventions. Results from meta-analytic reviews suggest that the effects of implementation intention interventions delivered by mobile technology (e.g. smartphones, tablets) are effective but with overall small effect sizes (Direito, Carraça, Rawstorn, Whittaker, & Maddison, 2016; Fanning, Mullen, & McAuley, 2012). Technology-based implementation intention interventions have the potential to examine effects of in-the-moment and contextual factors that may influence the efficacy of implementation intention interventions on physical activity participation. Technology-based interventions can be utilized to test the impact that implementation intentions may have on 'in-the-moment' decision-making in a variety of contexts, and also support intervention efforts (e.g. sending text message reminders with relevant implementation intention included). Initial evidence supports the notion that implementation intentions can be successfully delivered via various technologies and are effective in changing physical activity behavior (Hurling et al., 2007; Prestwich, Perugini, & Hurling, 2010; Prestwich et al., 2012). While this line of research is still developing, technology-based delivery of implementation intention interventions may allow for greater integration of other potentially effective planning components alongside the implementation intention interventions such as coping planning (Sullivan & Lachman, 2017). Furthermore, implementation intention interventions to promote physical activity that are delivered in-person may benefit from using technology to support participants in carrying out their plans through text message reminders (Prestwich, Perugini, & Hurling, 2009). Devices can be programmed to assist or employ implementation intentions in a number of ways, and research on the utility of innovative ways to deliver implementation intention interventions is warranted. For example, research has demonstrated how smartphones can be programmed to present, or remind the user of, the situational cue (e.g. triggered by a certain time of day or a certain geographic location it detects the user in) paired with a reminder of the target behavior (Pinder, Vermeulen, Wicaksono, Beale, & Hendley, 2016). Therefore, future research should explore the aspects of technology-based interventions that make them most successful, who may benefit more or less from these forms of delivery, and when it may be most appropriate to consider using technology as a means or supplement to the intervention delivery. Furthermore, researchers should test innovative ways that technology can be used to enhance the effectiveness of implementation intention interventions in physical activity behavior.

Implementation intention interventions may be delivered to one participant at a time, in dyads, or in larger groups. Dyadic and group implementation intention interventions employ collaborative planning techniques. Collaborative planning involves the support of both members of a dyad or members of the group to plan to carry out a behavior together, facilitating social exchange and support. Incorporating significant others in the decision-making process and encouraging direct coaction on the behavior with the individual forming the plan may increase the probability of enactment of the intended behavior. Increasing evidence suggests that dyadic planning techniques may reinforce implementation intention interventions effects (Prestwich & Kellar, 2014; Prestwich et al., 2005; Scholz, Berli, Lüscher, & Knoll, 2020), including in physical activity (Burkert, Knoll, Luszczynska, & Gralla, 2012; Burkert, Scholz, Gralla, Roigas, & Knoll, 2011; Keller et al., 2017; Knoll et al., 2017; Prestwich et al., 2012; Radtke, Luszczynska, Schenkel, Biddle, & Scholz, 2018). There is also evidence that collaborative implementation intention interventions are more efficacious in increasing physical activity than those focused on one member of the dyad (Prestwich et al., 2012). Furthermore, employing group-oriented implementation intentions may also increase social support and make goal realization more likely (Wieber, Thürmer, & Gollwitzer, 2013). Preliminary evidence of interventions utilizing dyadic and group-based implementation intentions has demonstrated promise in changing physical activity behavior. Future research should explore the utility of implementation intention interventions that involve others in the process of forming implementation intentions (Hagger, Luszczynska et al., 2016). This is a relatively new area of research and systematic research comparing the effectiveness of interventions that incorporate dyadic and collaborative planning techniques against individual techniques is needed. Future research should also look at potential moderators of dyadic and group-based intervention, outlining the conditions under which involving others in the intervention may be advantageous.

Another important aspect of the method of delivery that may impact the efficacy of implementation intention interventions is whether the implementation intention is reinforced after initial development. Implementation intention interventions may be reinforced in a number of ways. One method that has been tested is repetition of the implementation intention. In this method, experimenters prescribe a certain frequency for the implementation intention to be repeated by the participant. Repetition may ensure that the link between the critical condition and the behavioral response is reinforced and may lead to greater efficacy in evoking a behavioral response. Repetition may be incorporated into the protocol of implementation intention interventions (e.g. repeated writing of plans in which participants 'press harder' on a pen when writing out their plan; Verhoeven, Adriaanse, de Vet, Fennis, & de Ridder, 2014), and there is preliminary evidence that physical activity participation increased in proportion to the number of repetitions of the implementation intention (Bélanger-Gravel et al., 2013a). Although this effect was not statistically significant, this initial evidence should provide impetus for further research examining the role of repetition in promoting physical activity behavioral enactment (Hagger, Luszczynska et al., 2016).

An alternate technique that may reinforce implementation intentions is providing reminders to participants at certain time intervals during the intervention. In this method, reminders of implementation intentions are previously set on the participant's smartphone or sent to the participant during the intervention to facilitate reinforcement. A recent meta-analysis found that adult participants who received reinforcement of their implementation intention during the intervention were more likely to carry out the intention to be physically active than interventions that did not include this aspect (da Silva et al., 2018). As such, implementation intention interventions aiming to increase physical activity participation should consider including aspects of reinforcement such as prescribed repetition and experimenter-provided reminders to determine who may or may not respond well to these types of reinforcement strategies, and who they may be most effective for. Also, the optimal temporal frequency of repetitions and plan reminders should be examined in future studies. Future research should also consider how reminders should be framed, and the scheduling protocol (i.e. the time interval between presentations – such as a presentation 3 days consecutively versus once a week for a month). Further, exploring factors related to repetition should include alternative ways to reinforce plans, such as writing down the plan a number of times to increase the saliency of the mental link between the situational cue and behavioral response (Verhoeven et al., 2014).

Additional Directions for Future Research

Research has supported the efficacy of planning interventions in promoting physical activity behavior initiation and maintenance (Bélanger-Gravel et al., 2013a; Hagger et al., 2002; Lippke et al., 2004; Sniehotta et al., 2005; Ziegelmann et al., 2006). However, there remains substantial variability in the efficacy of planning interventions in physical activity contexts. Future research should, therefore, aim to identify potential moderators of the effects of these interventions on physical activity behavior that reduce variability and produce consistent changes in physical activity behavior. While the previous section outlined the rationale behind some potential variables that have been shown to impact the efficacy of implementation intention interventions in physical activity, we note additional aspects related to the study that may impact the efficacy of implementation intention interventions to change physical activity behavior in this section for further consideration.

First, study design may be an important focus of future research on implementation intention interventions in physical activity. While there is an increasing number of studies adopting experimental and randomized controlled designs to test implementation intention effects (Arbour & Martin Ginis, 2009; Armitage, 2008; Armitage et al., 2017; Bélanger-Gravel et al., 2013b; Chapman et al., 2018; Prestwich et al., 2012), studies that optimally implement these designs and related features that ensure their quality are rare. Experiments and randomized controlled trials examining the efficacy of implementation intentions in physical activity should report the intervention protocol, include fidelity checks, make clear the content and features of the control and/or comparison groups, include long-term follow-up measures of behavioral outcomes, and include the necessary measures and apply the appropriate analytic methods to allow for tests of mediators (Hagger, Luszczynska et al., 2016). Researchers should also include open access data to permit secondary analyses of effects and sub-group analyses.

Another potential factor that may impact the efficacy of implementation intention interventions is the simultaneous inclusion of other intervention components alongside the implementation intention component, such as health education, diet, or motivational components to enhance physical activity intervention efficacy on the targeted outcome. Research has suggested that including other intervention components improves the efficacy of implementation intention interventions when compared to implementation intention interventions alone (Hagger et al., 2012; McEwan et al., 2016; Milne et al., 2002; Prestwich,

Lawton, & Conner, 2003). However, while such multicomponent interventions may have efficacy, including multiple intervention components together with implementation intentions in single group designs may hinder scientific progress in identifying the mechanisms of action unless such interventions employ factorial designs (Hagger et al., 2020a; Suls et al., 2020). Multicomponent interventions prevent the meaningful tests of the independent effectiveness of each component, and their mechanisms of effect, because the independent and synergistic effects of the other intervention components alongside with implementation intention component cannot be separated unless executed within a factorial design. This also limits tests of independent effects and mediators using meta-analysis. Moving forward, best practice for testing effects of multiple components within implementation intention interventions should employ appropriate factorial designs that permit tests of the independent and interactive effects of individual components (Peters, De Bruin, & Crutzen, 2015; Suls et al., 2020; Wilson et al., 2020).

Summary and Conclusion

Regular participation in physical activity has numerous health benefits, including reduced risk of chronic disease and better psychological well-being and mental health (Dunn et al., 2001; Pedersen & Saltin, 2015; Warburton et al., 2006; Warburton & Bredin 2017). However, 23% of adult men and 32% of adult women worldwide do not participate in sufficient physical activity to meet public health recommendations of 150 min/week of moderate-vigorous intensity physical activity (WHO, 2016). Many public health organizations have focused on developing interventions that are efficacious in promoting physical activity behavior in the general population (Artinian et al., 2010; Kahn et al., 2002). Effective physical activity interventions should be based on psychological theory, which provide a means to identify the determinants of physical activity participation and the processes involved. If these theories are effective in identifying the factors reliably related to physical activity participation, they may have utility in informing interventions designed to change physical activity behavior. Social cognition theories have played a prominent role in identifying the determinants of physical activity behavior, and have identified factors such as attitudes, risk perceptions, normative beliefs, self-efficacy, and behavioral intentions as salient determinants of physical activity behavior.

However, research has suggested that although many people intend to change their behavior, those intentions are not always acted upon, and forming an intention may be necessary but not sufficient to enact a behavior (Orbell & Sheeran, 1998; Rhodes & de Bruijn, 2013a). This has led researchers to become interested in dual-phase models to identify how intentions translate into subsequent behavior. Dual-phase models suggest that beyond intentions, planning is a key process that leads to effective behavioral engagement by increasing the probability that individuals will act on their intentions. Planning interventions, such as action plans, coping plans, and implementation intentions have been developed to assist individuals acting on their intentions and increasing their physical activity participation. Implementation intention interventions, in particular, have shown considerable promise in bridging the intention-behavior gap and contributing to long-term maintenance of physical activity behavior (Bélanger-Gravel et al., 2013a).

Research employing implementation intention interventions has demonstrated their promise promoting physical activity behavior. In addition, research has suggested that implementation intentions that are aimed to increase physical activity participation have been effective in specific subpopulations (clinical and student populations); however, overall, they seem to be less effective in samples that reflect the general population (Bélanger-Gravel et al., 2013a). Further, the format of the implementation intention should be constructed as an 'if-then' statement, possibly including aspects of barrier management (coping planning techniques) (Bélanger-Gravel et al., 2013a), and careful consideration should be given to the number of plans that participants formulate (Dalton & Spiller, 2012; de Vet et al., 2011; Verhoeven et al., 2013). Researchers should also provide guidance to participants, especially those with limited planning ability or limited experience with physical activity participation to formulate their implementation intentions and provide feedback in the implementation intention development process (Armitage & Arden, 2010; Bélanger-Gravel et al., 2013a; Chapman et al., 2018). However, there are many areas where more research is needed to establish the moderators of the effects of implementation intention interventions and the conditions that exacerbate or attenuate their effects. Potential moderators that should be explored include incorporating aspects of technology or utilizing technology to deliver the intervention. Initial evidence suggests that implementation intention interventions may benefit from having a technological component or to be completely delivered via technology (Hurling et al., 2007; Preswich et al., 2012; Sullivan & Lachman, 2017), although specific populations may respond differently to technological incorporation, and this should be tested in the future. Dyadic or group-based implementation intention interventions should be explored further and build on initial evidence supporting the efficacy in incorporating partners or groups in the intervention (Knoll et al., 2017; Thürmer, Wieber, & Gollwitzer, 2017). Finally, means of reinforcement should be explored; the participant may repeat the implementation intention to reinforce the mental link between the action and cue, or the experimenter may remind the participant of their implementation intention during the course of the intervention. Both of these methods have been successful at increasing the efficacy of the intervention in promoting physical activity behavior (Bélanger-Gravel et al., 2013a; da Silva et al., 2018; Verhoeven et al., 2014). Alternative methods to reinforce the implementation intention should also be explored, as well as the optimal temporal application of reinforcement cues. Overall, research adopting planning interventions, and implementation intentions specifically, has shown utility in promoting physical activity participation and may be useful in developing efficacious interventions at the population level.

13

SUMMARY, COMMON THEMES, AND FUTURE DIRECTIONS

Ian M. Taylor and Chris Englert

The chapters presented in this book have provided detailed overviews and insights into the latest theory and research concerning motivation and self-regulation in sport and exercise contexts. It is clear that a sophisticated understanding of motivation and self-regulation is essential if many important issues in sport and exercise are to be addressed, from helping to tackle global physical inactivity and reduce non-communicable disease, to ensuring a lifetime of enjoyable and psychologically healthy exercise, to optimizing performance at the highest levels of elite sport (Hagger, 2010; Taylor, Boat & Murphy, 2018). Each chapter is written by leading experts in their respective fields; hence, all chapters are at the cutting edge of motivation and self-regulation science. At this point, we would like to thank the contributing authors for their efforts in producing outstanding scientific contributions to the field. The aim of this final section is to summarize the content of the chapters and adopt a broad perspective to draw out some common themes which could provide the basis for future scientific endeavors.

It is apparent from reading the chapters that our understanding of motivation and self-regulation in sport and exercise is evolving rapidly. The first common theme that can be observed in many of the book chapters is a shift away from cognitive, rationale models of motivation for physical activity and exercise behavior. As Ekkekakis and Brand point out in Chapter 3, sport and exercise psychology has been firmly camped in cognitivist traditions for several decades (see also Ekkekakis & Zenko, 2016). Within this paradigm, social-cognitive frameworks, such as self-determination theory (Ryan & Deci, 2000), achievement goal theory (Duda & Nicholls, 1992), and the theory of planned behavior (Ajzen & Manstead, 2007), dominated the sport and exercise motivation literature. These theories and others that focus on rationale, deliberative motivation remain significant in helping us understand motivation today, but they have been joined by other theories and models that adopt different perspectives to answer motivational questions. Several book chapters make the case that theory development and practical interventions will be ineffective if they do not consider motivation in all its guises, including cognition and affect, as well as conscious and more automatic motivational tendencies that currently are not easily measured (Ekkekakis,

Zenko, Ladwig, & Hartman, 2018). The role of affect, in particular, is a burgeoning area of research. In competitive sport contexts especially, affect and emotion have been typically viewed as states to reduce, minimize, or control. In physical activity contexts, affect has been studied often as an outcome of physical activity but as a motivating antecedent to a lesser extent. This is different from research outside of sport and exercise, which views affect and emotion as a core motivator of any human behavior (Inzlicht, Bartholow, & Hirsh, 2015). It is important for sport and exercise psychology researchers not to ignore the large history of this work. Although in Chapter 3 the importance of an exercise-specific theory was advocated, there are also generalizable principles of affect as a motivator that could be used to inform exercise-specific nuances (Carver, & Scheier, 2011).

Many of the chapter authors in this book argue that a move away from cognitivist principles is essential because existing attempts to increase intentional physical activity and exercise have failed to sufficiently reduce the "intention-behavior gap" and this reflects a second theme across many book chapters. To recap, this gap refers to intentions to be active failing to transform into behavior (Rhodes & de Bruijn, 2013), a phenomenon that many people will be familiar with. It is becoming abundantly clear, therefore, that reflective, logical processes that help build an intention are often insufficient to energize and sustain activity. Potential motivational and self-regulatory solutions to the intention-behavior gap are extremely important to communicate to lay people and fellow scientists not specializing in motivation and self-regulation. Often, there is a downplaying of the role of motivation and self-regulation in public health because it is often misperceived that motivational and self-regulatory processes are only relevant to the formation of intention. The phrase "I am motivated but..." is all too commonly used to imply that motivation and self-regulation skills are deemed sufficient, but some other barrier prevents action (e.g. environmental or social barriers). Motivation and self-regulation concern much more than the forming of intentions. Individuals can often downplay motivational solutions to public health problems because of this misunderstanding. The underappreciation of motivation and self-regulatory processes that lead to successful behavior change and an overemphasis on behavior is like trying to build a roof on the house before the walls. It is paramount that we do not revisit behaviorism from the early 20th century; otherwise, we might still be repeating a phrase cited in Chapter 3: "if scientific psychology were to succeed, mentalistic concepts would have to integrate and explain the behavioral data" (Miller, 2003, p. 142).

Several chapters in this book attempt to tackle this intention-behavior gap from new perspectives. In Chapter 2, Rhodes and his colleagues presented the Multi-Process Action Control (M-PAC) framework to explain how motivational and self-regulatory processes can explain intentional physical activity engagement. The model is built on a systematic program of research conducted over many years, which is combined with useful insights from other research agendas. The authors detail different mechanisms through which intentional physical activity can be intended, initiated, and sustained. The comprehensiveness of this model is impressive, and this strength is balanced with very specific hypothesized paths that are empirically testable. Thus, the M-PAC is a very useful model to understand the overall motivational and self-regulatory picture underpinning intentional physical activity.

Chapter 3 by Ekkekakis and Brand expands on the problems transforming intentions into behavior in a detailed historical analysis of exercise psychology. In doing so, they present an emerging theory of exercise and physical activity engagement: Affective-reflective theory of inactivity and exercise. The theory draws on several fields of psychology and neuroscience to develop specific testable postulates, many of which focus on the importance of affect in physical activity-based decision making. However, as the title of the theory implies, it is necessary to consider the dual processes of affect and reflective cognition and how they work in tandem to influence motivational decision making toward exercise. If one wished to understand why exercise psychology needs a paradigm shift, this is the chapter to read.

Stemming from the same dual-process or dual-system traditions as Chapter 3, Chapter 4 by Zenko and colleagues also emphasizes affect's role in motivation and self-regulation. The authors build on the affect heuristic and lead the way in integrating behavioral economics with the sport and exercise psychology field. Behavioral economics has become extremely fashionable, potentially due to the increased focus on the work of Daniel Kahneman and Amos Tversky (Kahneman & Tversky, 1979) and subsequent books on their lives and works aimed at non-scientists (e.g. The Undoing Project; Lewis, 2017). This movement has also spawned governmental Nudge Units and Behavioral Insights Teams and a plethora of suggested "life hacks" aimed at living more effectively. The chapter provides many empirically supported examples in which humans do not always behave in a rational reflective manner and take advantage of this information to propose a variety of motivational and self-regulatory strategies that can be used to initiate and maintain physical activity and exercise behavior. Many of the ideas contained in this chapter are not based on existing exercise motivation theory; hence, they are novel and represent a different way of thinking about physical activity promotion. The strategies in this chapter may help individuals sustain physical activity and exercise because they commonly minimize effort. Simultaneously, this will allow the reflexive processes that sustain exercise engagement in the long term to develop, such as those outlined by Rhodes and colleagues in Chapter 2.

A third common thread across several chapters is one we highlighted in our introductory chapter (i.e. Chapter 1) and, indeed, is reflected in the title of this book. Over the last decade or so, motivation research has become increasingly integrated with the science of self-regulation. Many previous textbooks on motivation have focused on theories from the cognitive tradition of reflective motivation, while chapters on self-regulation have been less prevalent. The term self-regulation is not new in sport and exercise psychology; however, it has been used very broadly, often in applied sport psychology to refer to the optimal use of psychological skills such as imagery and pre-performance routines. In motivation psychology, self-regulation refers to processes that are initiated to persistently pursue specific goals and monitor goal progress (Fishbach, Zhang, & Koo, 2009). In a similar fashion, De Ridder and De Witt (2006) postulate that "self-regulation broadly refers to the processes of goal setting and goal striving, and includes dealing with a range of challenges that individuals may face when trying to achieve something that is important but, almost by definition, difficult to attain" (p. 1). These definitions support the assumption that motivation and self-regulation are now being considered as complementary systems that assist in forming an intention, initiating a behavior, and sustaining an activity. Some models operationalize motivation as the reflective processes that help form an intention, and self-regulatory processes refer to processes that help transform the intention into behavior (e.g. The Rubicon model; Gollwitzer, 1990; Heckhausen & Gollwitzer, 1987). The M-PAC model in Chapter 2 expands on this idea, albeit with different terminology. Rhodes and colleagues outline reflective processes, which are predominately factors determining intention formation; regulatory processes, which refer to behavioral, affective, and cognitive strategies to increase the value of the intended act and reduce the value of other possible options; and reflexive processes, which determine more sustained action and typically refer to habit and identity formation.

The link between motivation and self-regulation can be witnessed in the context of endurance performance in Chapter 7. Taylor explains that a motivational basis in which performance goals are consistent with one's identity will provide the necessary foundation for effective self-regulation during endurance tasks. These self-regulatory strategies take the shape of less cognitive resources employed toward the desire to reduce effort, more cognitive resources dedicated toward goal pursuit, and effective emotional regulation in the face of disturbances in goal pursuit. Although the distinction between motivation and self-regulation is not made explicit in the chapter, there is a clear overlap in conceptualization with the action control perspectives detailed in the introductory chapter. Chapters 2 and 7 also share common ground by highlighting identity as a robust motivational foundation, yet do so in the very different contexts of sustaining physical activity and endurance performance. Clearly, identity represents an important motivational bedrock that should be investigated to a greater degree. It will be useful in future research to continue this trend to integrate motivation and self-regulation to provide a more comprehensive understanding of physical activity and exercise engagement, but also more performance-oriented outcomes, such as endurance. The amalgamation of motivation and self-regulation research endeavors makes this area an exciting place to work.

A final theme in the motivation chapters is the analysis of the potential dark side of motivation. Many people often incorrectly focus on behavior to make inferences about underlying motivation. For example, if an individual attends an exercise class or an athlete is successful in their competition, then it is often assumed that they are sufficiently motivated. In fact, human behavior tells us very little about the underlying motivational processes at work. Self-determination theory (Ryan & Deci, 2000) and achievement goal theory (Duda & Nicholls, 1992) clearly detail that the quality of motivation is as, if not more, important than the quantity of motivation. Chapters 5 and 6 are excellent examples of potentially maladaptive motivational and self-regulatory processes. Chapter 5, written by Sabiston and colleagues, describes and evaluates a series of body-related self-conscious emotions, such as social physique anxiety, pride, embarrassment, and shame. They explain how these emotions play a key motivational role in sport and exercise engagement. On the one hand, body-related emotions can energize exercise and sport participation because one likes to feel positively valenced emotions and possess a healthy body image. Exercise and sport participation can also help to reduce negatively valenced body-related emotions. On the other hand, many of these emotions are central to suboptimal experiences within sport and exercise. For example, the authors highlight many facets of sport and exercise (e.g. mirrors in gyms, mandatory sport uniforms) that can enhance social physique anxiety. In turn, this emotional state can motivate exactly what most of us are trying to avoid: Sport drop out, disordered eating, and depression. Emotions have huge potential to be used to facilitate sport and exercise engagement, and importantly, high-quality experiences within those contexts. Nonetheless, sport and exercise contexts are also the primary context in which body-related self-conscious emotions may manifest and precipitate negative consequences.

Sabiston and colleagues' chapter begins to open the door on a potential dark side to sport and exercise motivation and participation; however, Chapter 6 on perfectionism takes a more direct approach. Hill's chapter on perfectionism is timely and interesting because perfectionism is often misconstrued as a positive facet that athletes should be striving for. Hill dispels several separate myths; perfectionism only resides in some people; perfectionism refers only to personal standards; perfectionism is a personal quality; and perfectionism is necessary in order to be successful and can even be good for your health. Hill's response to these myths can be summed up in one line from the chapter: "*There is no evidence for healthy perfectionism.*"

Chapters 5 and 6 have the potential to form the basis of many different future research directions aimed at focusing on the dark side of sport and exercise engagement and learn how we can promote positive experiences. There is often a simplistic perspective adopted with claims that the sport and exercise context is a panacea that helps young people develop character and provides adults with mood boosting positive social experiences. Sport has the potential to do all these things and more, but whether this is achieved is largely down to individuals' underlying motivational processes, something which Chapters 5 and 6 clearly explain.

There are several other key themes that cross the chapters that primarily focus on self-regulation. One of the main questions in self-regulation research is why self-regulation does not always work efficiently. Several theoretical models have been developed – and heavily criticized – over the years, demonstrating the high dynamics in this field (see also Englert, 2019). As outlined by Englert in Chapter 8, the strength model has been one of the most dominating theories when it comes to explaining why individuals often fail to control themselves in sport and exercise contexts. However, recent replication attempts in general psychology have failed to support the basic assumption that there is a limited self-regulatory resource which can become temporarily depleted (Hagger, Chatzisarantis et al., 2016). In Chapter 9, Brown and Graham add to this discussion but also refer to two sports-related recent meta-analyses which revealed that sports-related performance is more likely to suffer after having previously engaged in another self-regulation task (Brown et al., 2019; Giboin & Wolff, 2019). Given these seemingly contradicting findings, the question arises whether self-regulatory processes act differently in sports-related contexts with sport-specific tasks than in rather artificial laboratory settings.

Furthermore, Englert (Chapter 8) and Brown and Graham (Chapter 9) also discuss the differences and similarities between research on ego depletion and mental fatigue and also offer intriguing recommendations how these two lines of research, which have oftentimes operated independently from each other over the years, can be integrated. One major difference between ego depletion and mental fatigue research seems to be that, traditionally, ego depletion research primarily focused on the psychological determinants of self-regulatory performance, while mental fatigue research from the very beginning tried to integrate findings from psychology and physiology. As discussed by Van Cutsem and Marcora (Chapter 10), as well as Wolff and colleagues (Chapter 11), cognitive processes such as action monitoring or inhibitory control interact with perceptual, motivational, and emotional processes in the brain to determine our goal-directed behaviors in sport and exercise settings. Future research should therefore continue to dig deeper into the interplay between psychological, physiological, and neuronal processes to improve our understanding of how self-regulation works and why it often fails.

Another important key theme which has been tackled in this book is which factors might moderate/mediate the effect of ego depletion/mental fatigue on sport and exercise performance. Englert (Chapter 8) and Brown and Graham (Chapter 9) argue that changes in motivation, emotion, and attention after a straining self-regulatory task might cause performance decrements in subsequent sport-specific self-regulatory tasks (see also Inzlicht & Schmeichel, 2012). Van Cutsem and Marcora (Chapter 10) and also Wolff and colleagues (Chapter 11) postulate that self-regulation leads to changes in several physiological as well as neuronal processes which consequently affect subsequent performance. More research in this area is highly necessary in order to shed more light on the influence of potential moderators and mediators on sports-related performance.

After the previous chapters on self-regulation demonstrated that self-regulation can often fail, one final key theme discussed in this book regards the question how self-regulatory performance can be improved. In Chapter 12, Moyers and Hagger introduce implementation intentions as an effective strategy to support individuals' control over themselves (Gollwitzer, 1999). In a nutshell, implementation intentions link an intended, desired behavior to a specific situation in which the respective behavior should be displayed in order to achieve a desirable (long-term) outcome. The authors provide compelling evidence that implementation intentions are a powerful tool in this regard. However, and in sync with the other key themes previously discussed, it seems highly important to also investigate *how* implementation intentions affect self-regulatory performance. Is it simply the consequence of a repeated stimulus-response-coupling or do implementation intentions also affect other psychological, physiological, or neuronal processes?

To conclude, the common themes identified in this chapter suggest that motivation and regulation in sport and exercise is an exciting and dynamic field of science to study and explore. It is central to the big issues in sport science and health promotion, including getting the population more active, and athletes performing better. Within the field, we may be currently at the beginning of a paradigm shift away from pure cognitivism to a more encompassing description of motivation and self-regulation. We are still far from completely understanding the dynamics between motivation and self-regulation; yet, we are beginning to offer valid solutions for why people do not exercise despite intending to do so. Motivation also offers insight into why exercise and sport may not be the psychological utopia that some claim it to be. The exploration of motivation and self-regulation during endurance performance is now burgeoning, and the link between psychology, neuroscience, and physiology in this area makes it a fascinating line of inquiry. We hope you have enjoyed digesting the thoughts and theories of leading scholars in motivation and self-regulation and use them to develop new questions and new solutions.

REFERENCES

Aarts, H., & Dijksterhuis, A. (2000). Habits as knowledge structures: Automaticity in goal-directed behavior. *Journal of Personality and Social Psychology, 78*(1), 53–63. https://doi.org/10.1037/0022-3514.78.1.53

Abbiss, C. R., & Laursen, P. B. (2008). Describing and understanding pacing strategies during athletic competition. *Sports Medicine, 38*, 239–252. https://doi.org/10.2165/00007256-200838030-00004

Abbott, B. D., & Barber, B. L. (2011). Differences in functional and aesthetic body image between sedentary girls and girls involved in sports and physical activity: Does sport type make a difference? *Psychology of Sport and Exercise, 12*(3), 333–342. https://doi.org/10.1016/j.psychsport.2010.10.005

Ach, N. (1905). *Uber die Willenstatigkeit und das Denken*. Gottingen: Vandenhoeck & Ruprecht.

Ach, N (1935). An analysis of the will. In E. Abderhalden (Ed.), *Handbook of biology research methods* (pp. 1–460). Germany: Urban and Schwarzenber.

Achtziger, A., & Gollwitzer, P. M. (2009). Rubicon model of the action phases. In V. Brandstätter & J. H. Otto (Eds.), *Handbuch der allgemeinen psychologie – Motivation und emotion* (pp. 150–156). Göttingen: Hogrefe.

Achtziger, A., & Gollwitzer, P. M. (2010). Motivation and volition in the course of action. In J. Heckhausen & H. Heckhausen (Eds.), *Motivation and action* (pp. 309–335). Berlin: Springer.

Achtziger, A., Gollwitzer, P. M., & Sheeran, P. (2008). Implementation intentions and shielding goal striving from unwanted thoughts and feelings. *Personality and Social Psychology Bulletin, 34*(3), 381–393. https://doi.org/10.1177/0146167207311201

Ackerman, P. L. (2011). *Cognitive fatigue: Multidisciplinary perspectives on current research and future applications* (pp. xviii–333). Washington, DC: American Psychological Association. https://doi.org/10.1037/12343-000

Adriaanse, M. A., de Ridder, D. T., & de Wit, J. B. (2009). Finding the critical cue: Implementation intentions to change one's diet work best when tailored to personally relevant reasons for unhealthy eating. *Personality and Social Psychology Bulletin, 35*(1), 60–71. https://doi.org/10.1177/0146167208325612

Adriaanse, M. A., Gollwitzer, P. M., De Ridder, D. T., De Wit, J. B., & Kroese, F. M. (2011a). Breaking habits with implementation intentions: A test of underlying processes. *Personality and Social Psychology Bulletin, 37*(4), 502–513. https://doi.org/10.1177/0146167211399102

Adriaanse, M. A., Vinkers, C. D., De Ridder, D. T., Hox, J. J., & De Wit, J. B. (2011b). Do implementation intentions help to eat a healthy diet? A systematic review and meta-analysis of the empirical evidence. *Appetite, 56*(1), 183–193. https://doi.org/10.1016/j.appet.2010.10.012

Ainslie, G. (1975). Specious reward: A behavioral theory of impulsiveness and impulse control. *Psychological Bulletin*, *82*(4), 463–496.

Ajzen, I. (1985). From intentions to actions: A theory of planned behavior. In J. Kuhl & J. Beckmann (Eds.), *Action-control: From cognition to behavior* (pp. 11–39). Germany: Springer. https://doi.org/10.1007/978-3-642-69746-3_2

Ajzen, I. (1991). The theory of planned behavior. *Organizational Behavior and Human Decision Processes*, *50*(2), 179–211. https://doi.org/10.1016/0749-5978(91)90020-T

Ajzen, I. (2011). The theory of planned behaviour: Reactions and reflections. *Psychology and Health*, *26*(9), 1113–1127. https://doi.org/10.1080/08870446.2011.613995

Ajzen, I., & Fishbein, M. (1980). *Understanding attitudes and predicting social behavior.* London: Pearson.

Ajzen, I., & Fishbein, M. (2005). The influence of attitudes on behavior. In D. Albarracín, B. T. Johnson, & M. P. Zanna (Eds.), *The handbook of attitudes* (pp. 173–221). Mahwah, NJ: Lawrence Erlbaum. https://doi.org/10.4324/9781410612823.ch5

Ajzen, I., & Manstead, A. S. R. (2007). Changing health-related behaviours: An approach based on the theory of planned behaviour. In M. Hewstone, H. A. W. Schut, J. B. F. De Wit, K. Van Den Bos, & M. S. Stroebe (Eds.), *The scope of social psychology: Theory and applications* (pp. 43–63). New York: Psychology Press. https://doi.org/10.4324/9780203965245-10

Alberts, H. J. E. M., Martijn, C., & de Vries, N. K. (2011). Fighting self-control failure: Overcoming ego depletion by increasing self-awareness. *Journal of Experimental Social Psychology*, *47*, 58–62. https://doi.org/10.1016/j.jesp.2010.08.004

Alberts, H. J. E. M., Martijn, C., Greb, J., Merckelbach, H., & Vries, N. K. de. (2007). Carrying on or giving in: The role of automatic processes in overcoming ego depletion. *British Journal of Social Psychology*, *46*, 383–399. https://doi.org/10.1348/014466606X130111

Alberts, H. J. E. M., Martijn, C., Nievelstein, F., Jansen, A., & de Vries, N. K. (2008). Distracting the self: Shifting attention prevents ego depletion. *Self and Identity*, *7*, 322–334. https://doi.org/10.1080/15298860801987583

Alé La Merckx (2018, June 7). Eddy Merckx: Mind traits of a legend. Retrieved March 24, 2020, from https://www.alelamerckx.com/en/news/eddy-merckx-i-tratti-psicologici-di-una-leggenda

Allan, J. L., Sniehotta, F. F., & Johnston, M. (2013). The best laid plans: Planning skill determines the effectiveness of action plans and implementation intentions. *Annals of Behavioral Medicine*, *46*(1), 114–120. https://doi.org/10.1007/s12160-013-9483-9

Allen, D. G., Lamb, G. D., & Westerblad, H. (2008). Skeletal muscle fatigue: Cellular mechanisms. *Physiological Reviews*, *88*, 287–332. https://doi.org/10.1152/physrev.00015.2007

Allender, S., Cowburn, G., & Foster, C. (2006). Understanding participation in sport and physical activity among children and adults: A review of qualitative studies. *Health Education Research*, *21*(6), 826–835. https://doi.org/10.1093/her/cyl063

Allom, V., Panetta, G., Mullan, B., & Hagger, M. S. (2016). Self-report and behavioural approaches to the measurement of self-control: Are we assessing the same construct? *Personality and Individual Differences*, *90*, 137–142. https://doi.org/10.1016/j.paid.2015.10.051

Almeida, D. M., Marcusson-Clavertz, D., Conroy, D. E., Kim, J., Zawadzki, M. J., Sliwinski, M., & Smyth, J. M. (2020). Everyday stress components and physical activity: Examining reactivity, recovery and pileup. *Journal of Behavioral Medicine*, *43*, 108–120.

Alós-Ferrer, C., & Strack, F. (2014). From dual processes to multiple selves: Implications for economic behavior. *Journal of Economic Psychology*, *41*, 1–11. https://doi.org/10.1016/j.joep.2013.12.005

Al-Yahya, E., Dawes, H., Smith, L., Dennis, A., Howells, K., & Cockburn, J. (2011). Cognitive motor interference while walking: A systematic review and meta-analysis. *Neuroscience and Biobehavioral Reviews*, *35*, 715–728. https://doi.org/10.1016/j.neubiorev.2010.08.008

Amann, M. (2012). Pulmonary system limitations to endurance exercise performance in humans. *Experimental Physiology*, *97*(3), 311–318. https://doi.org/10.1113/expphysiol.2011.058800

Amann, M., & Calbet, J. A. L. (2008). Convective oxygen transport and fatigue. *Journal of Applied Physiology*, *104*, 861–870. https://doi.org/10.1152/japplphysiol.01008.2007

Amaya, M., & Petosa, R. L. (2012). An evaluation of a worksite exercise intervention using the social cognitive theory: A pilot study. *Health Education Journal*, *71*(2), 133–143.

Amireault, S., Godin, G., & Vézina-Im, L. A. (2012). Determinants of physical activity maintenance: A systematic review and meta-analyses. *Health Psychology Review*, 7(1), 55–91. https://doi.org/10.1123/japa.2017-0234

Andersen, J. (2020, March 30). The state of running 2019. RunRepeat. Retrieved March 24, 2020, from https://runrepeat.com/state-of-running

Anton, S. D., Perri, M. G., & Riley, J. R. (2000). Discrepancy between actual and ideal body images: Impact on eating and exercise behaviors. *Eating Behaviours*, *1*, 153–160.

Antoniewicz, F., & Brand, R. (2014). Automatic evaluations and exercise setting preference in frequent exercisers. *Journal of Sport and Exercise Psychology*, *36*, 631–636.

Antoniewicz, F., & Brand, R. (2016a). Learning to like exercising: Evaluative conditioning changes automatic evaluations of exercising and influences subsequent exercising behavior. *Journal of Sport and Exercise Psychology*, *38*(2), 138–148. https://doi.org/10.1123/jsep.2015-0125

Antoniewicz, F., & Brand, R. (2016b). Dropping out or keeping up? Early-dropouts, late-dropouts, and maintainers differ in their automatic evaluations of exercise already before a 14-week exercise course. *Frontiers in Psychology*, *7*, 00838.

Arbour, K. P., & Martin Ginis, K. A. (2009). A randomised controlled trial of the effects of implementation intentions on women's walking behaviour. *Psychology and Health*, *24*(1), 49–65. https://doi.org/10.1080/08870440801930312

Arem, H., Moore, S. C., Patel, A., Hartge, P., Berrington de Gonzalez, A., Visvanathan, K., & Matthews, C. E. (2015). Leisure time physical activity and mortality: A detailed pooled analysis of the dose-response relationship. *JAMA Internal Medicine*, *175*, 959–967. https://doi.org/10.1001/jamainternmed.2015.0533

Ariely, D., & Carmon, Z. (2000). Gestalt characteristics of experiences: The defining features of summarized events. *Journal of Behavioral Decision Making*, *13*(2), 191–201.

Armitage, C. J. (2008). A volitional help sheet to encourage smoking cessation: A randomized exploratory trial. *Health Psychology*, *27*(5), 557–566. https://doi.org/10.1037/0278-6133.27.5.557

Armitage, C. J. (2015). Evidence that a volitional help sheet reduces alcohol consumption among smokers: A pilot randomized controlled trial. *Behavior Therapy*, *46*(3), 342–349. https://doi.org/10.1016/j.beth.2014.12.003

Armitage, C. J., Alganem, S., & Norman, P. (2017). Randomized controlled trial of a volitional help sheet to encourage weight loss in the Middle East. *Prevention Science*, *18*(8), 976–983. https://doi.org/10.1007/s11121-017-0807-z

Armitage, C. J., & Arden, M. A. (2010). A volitional help sheet to increase physical activity in people with low socioeconomic status: A randomised exploratory trial. *Psychology and Health*, *25*(10), 1129–1145. https://doi.org/10.1080/08870440903121638

Armitage, C. J., & Conner, M. (2000). Social cognition models and health behaviour: A structured review. *Psychology and Health*, *15*(2), 173–189. https://doi.org/10.1080/08870440008400299

Armitage, C. J., & Conner, M. (2001). Efficacy of the theory of planned behavior: A meta-analysis. *British Journal of Social Psychology*, *40*(4), 471–499. https://doi.org/10.1348/014466601164939

Armitage, C. J., Norman, P., Noor, M., Alganem, S., & Arden, M. A. (2014). Evidence that a very brief psychological intervention boosts weight loss in a weight loss program. *Behavior Therapy*, *45*(5), 700–707. https://doi.org/10.1016/j.beth.2014.04.001

Armitage, C. J., & Sprigg, C. A. (2010). The roles of behavioral and implementation intentions in changing physical activity in young children with low socioeconomic status. *Journal of Sport and Exercise Psychology*, *32*(3), 359–376. https://doi.org/10.1123/jsep.32.3.359

Arnold, C. M., Sran, M. M., & Harrison, E. L. (2008). Exercise for fall risk reduction in community-dwelling older adults: A systematic review. *Physiotherapy Canada*, *60*, 358–372.

Artinian, N. T., Fletcher, G. F., Mozaffarian, D., Kris-Etherton, P., Van Horn, L., Lichtenstein, A. H., … & Meininger, J. C. (2010). Interventions to promote physical activity and dietary lifestyle changes for cardiovascular risk factor reduction in adults: A scientific statement from the American Heart Association. *Circulation*, *122*(4), 406–441.

Ashraf, N., Karlan, D., & Yin, W. (2006). Tying Odysseus to the mast: Evidence from a commitment savings product in the Philippines. *The Quarterly Journal of Economics*, *121*(2), 635–672.

Assor, A., Vansteenkiste, M., & Kaplan, A. (2009). Identified versus introjected approach and introjected avoidance motivations in school and in sports: The limited benefits of self-worth strivings. *Journal of Educational Psychology*, *101*(2), 482–497. https://doi.org/10.1037/a0014236

Audiffren, M., & André, N. (2015). The strength model of self-control revisited: Linking acute and chronic effects of exercise on executive functions. *Journal of Sport and Health Science*, *4*, 30–46. https://doi.org/10.1016/j.jshs.2014.09.002

Avalos, L., Tylka, T. L., & Wood-barcalow, N. (2005). The body appreciation scale: Development and psychometric evaluation. *Body Image*, *2*, 285–297. https://doi.org/10.1016/j.bodyim.2005.06.002

Avishai, A., Conner, M., & Sheeran, P. (2019). Setting realistic health goals: Antecedents and consequences. *Annals of Behavioral Medicine*, *53*, 1020–1031.

Azevedo, R., Silva-Cavalcante, M. D., Gualano, B., Lima-Silva, A. E., & Bertuzzi, R. (2016). Effects of caffeine ingestion on endurance performance in mentally fatigued individuals. *European Journal of Applied Physiology*, *116*, 2293–2303. https://doi.org/10.1007/s00421-016-3483-y

Baars, B. J. (1986). *The cognitive revolution in psychology*. New York: Guilford.

Baars, B. J., & Franklin, S. (2003). How conscious experience and working memory interact. *Trends in Cognitive Sciences*, 7(4), 166–172. https://doi.org/10.1016/S1364-6613(03)00056-1

Badin, O. O., Smith, M. R., Conte, D., & Coutts, A. J. (2016). Mental fatigue: Impairment of technical performance in small-sided soccer games. *International Journal of Sports Physiology and Performance*, *11*, 1100–1105. https://doi.org/10.1123/ijspp.2015-0710

Badre, D. (2008). Cognitive control, hierarchy, and the rostro–caudal organization of the frontal lobes. *Trends in Cognitive Sciences*, *12*(5), 193–200. https://doi.org/10.1016/j.tics.2008.02.004

Bagozzi, R. P. (1992). The self-regulation of attitudes, intentions, and behavior. *Social Psychology Quarterly*, *55*, 178–204.

Bailey, R. P., Madigan, D. J., Cope, E., & Nicholls, A. R. (2018). The prevalence of pseudoscientific ideas and neuromyths among sports coaches. *Frontiers in Psychology*, *9*, 641.

Balk, Y. A., & Englert, C. (2020). Recovery self-regulation in sport: Theory, research, and practice. *International Journal of Sports Science and Coaching*, *15*, 273–281. https://doi.org/10.1177/1747954119897528

Balkin, T. J., & Wesensten, N. J. (2011). Differentiation of sleepiness and mental fatigue effects. In P. L. Ackerman (Ed.), *Decade of behavior/science conference. Cognitive fatigue: Multidisciplinary perspectives on current research and future applications* (pp. 47–66). Washington, DC: American Psychological Association. https://doi.org/10.1037/12343-002

Bandura, A. (1977). Self-efficacy: Toward a unifying theory of behavioral change. *Psychological Review*, *84*, 191–215.

Bandura, A. (1986). *Social foundations of thought and action: A social cognitive theory*. Englewood Cliffs, NJ: Prentice-Hall.

Bandura, A. (1989). Human agency in social cognitive theory. *American Psychologist*, *44*(9), 1175–1184. https://doi.org/10.1037/0003066X.44.9.1175

Bandura, A. (1991). Social cognitive theory of self-regulation. *Organizational Behavior and Human Decision Processes*, *50*(2), 248–287. https://doi.org/10.1016/07495978(91)90022L

Bandura, A. (1997). Self-efficacy: The exercise of control. New York: W.H. Freeman and Company.

Bandura, A. (1998). Health promotion from the perspective of social cognitive theory. *Psychology and Health*, *13*, 623–649. doi: https://doi.org/10.1080/08870449808407422

Bandura, A. (2004). Health promotion by social cognitive means. *Health Education and Behavior*, *31*(2), 143–164. https://doi.org/10.1177/1090198104263660

Bane, S., & McAuley, E. (1998). Body image and exercise. In J. L. Duda (Ed.), *Advances in sport and exercise psychology measurement* (pp. 311–324). Morgantown, WV: Fitness Information Technology.

Banting, L. K., Dimmock, J. A., & Lay, B. S. (2009). The role of implicit and explicit components of exerciser self-schema in the prediction of exercise behavior. *Psychology of Sport and Exercise*, *10*, 80–86.

Bargh, J. A. (1994). The four horsemen of automaticity: Awareness, intention, efficiency, and control in social cognition. In R. S. Wyer, Jr. & T. K. Srull (Eds.), *Handbook of social cognition: Basic processes* (pp. 1–40). Hillsdale, NJ: Lawrence Erlbaum.

Bargh, J. A., & Chartrand, T. L. (1999). The unbearable automaticity of being. *American Psychologist, 54*(7), 462–479. https://doi.org/10.1037/0003066X.54.7.462

Bartholomew, L. K., Parcel, G. S., Kok, G., Gottlieb, N. H., & Fernández, M. E. (2011). *Planning health promotion programs: An intervention mapping approach* (3rd edition). San Francisco, CA: Jossey-Bass.

Bartulovic, D., Young, B. W., & Baker, J. (2017). Self-regulated learning predicts skill group differences in developing athletes. *Psychology of Sport and Exercise, 31*, 61–69. https://doi.org/10.1016/j.psychsport.2017.04.006

Bassett-Gunter, R., Tanna, S., Arbour-Nicitopoulos, K., Rhodes, R. E., & Leo, J. (2020). Understanding parent support for physical activity among parents of children and youth with disabilities: A behavior change theory perspective. *European Journal of Adaptive Physical Activity, 13*(2), 11. https://doi.org/10.5507/euj.2020.008

Baumeister, R. F. (1984). Choking under pressure: Self-consciousness and paradoxical effects of incentives on skillful performance. *Journal of Personality and Social Psychology, 46*, 610–620. https://doi.org/10.1037/0022-3514.46.3.610

Baumeister, R. F. (2014). Self-regulation, ego depletion, and inhibition. *Neuropsychologia, 65*, 313–319. https://doi.org/10.1016/j.neuropsychologia.2014.08.012

Baumeister, R. F. (2019). Self-control, ego depletion, and social psychology's replication crisis [Preprint]. PsyArXiv. https://doi.org/10.31234/osf.io/uf3cn

Baumeister, R. F., Bratslavsky, E., Muraven, M., & Tice, D. M. (1998). Ego depletion: Is the active self a limited resource? *Journal of Personality and Social Psychology, 74*, 1252–1265. https://doi.org/10.1037/0022-3514.74.5.1252

Baumeister, R. F., Gailliot, M., DeWall, C. N., & Oaten, M. (2006). Self-regulation and personality: How interventions increase regulatory success, and how depletion moderates the effects of traits on behavior. *Journal of Personality, 74*, 1773–1801. https://doi.org/10.1111/j.1467-6494.2006.00428.x

Baumeister, R. F., & Heatherton, T. F. (1996). Self-regulation failure: An overview. *Psychological Inquiry, 7*, 1–15. https://doi.org/10.1207/s15327965pli0701_1

Baumeister, R. F., Heatherton, T. F., & Tice, D. M. (1994). *Losing control: How and why people fail at self-regulation*. Cambridge, MA: Academic Press.

Baumeister, R. F., & Vohs, K. D. (2016a). Misguided effort with elusive implications. *Perspectives on Psychological Science, 11*, 574–575. https://doi.org/10.1177/1745691616652878

Baumeister, R. F., & Vohs, K. D. (2016b). Strength model of self-regulation as limited resource: Assessment, controversies, update. In J. M. Olson & M. P. Zanna (Eds.), *Advances in experimental social psychology* (Vol. 54, pp. 67–127). Cambridge, MA: Academic Press. https://doi.org/10.1016/bs.aesp.2016.04.001

Baumeister, R. F., Vohs, K. D., DeWall, C. N., & Zhang, L. (2007). How emotion shapes behavior: Feedback, anticipation, and reflection, rather than direct causation. *Personality and Social Psychology Review, 11*, 167–203.

Baumeister, R. F., Vohs, K. D., & Tice, D. M. (2007). The strength model of self-control. *Current Directions in Psychological Science, 16*(6), 351–355. https://doi.org/10.1111/j.1467-8721.2007.00534.x

Bayer, U. C., Achtziger, A., Gollwitzer, P. M., & Moskowitz, G. B. (2009). Responding to subliminal cues: Do if-then plans facilitate action preparation and initiation without conscious intent? *Social Cognition, 27*, 183–201. https://doi.org/10.1521/soco.2009.27.2.183

Bechara, A., & Damasio, A. R. (2005). The somatic marker hypothesis: A neural theory of economic decision. *Games and Economic Behavior, 52*(2), 336–372. https://doi.org/10.1016/j.geb.2004.06.010

Bechara, A., Damasio, H., & Damasio, A. R. (2000). Emotion, decision making and the orbitofrontal cortex. *Cerebral Cortex, 10*(3), 295–307. https://doi.org/10.1093/cercor/10.3.295

Beedie, C. J., & Lane, A. M. (2012). The role of glucose in self-control: Another look at the evidence and an alternative conceptualization. *Personality and Social Psychology Review, 16*, 143–153. https://doi.org/10.1177/1088868311419817

Beer, J. S., & Keltner, D. (2004). What is unique about self-conscious emotions? *Psychological Inquiry, 15*, 126–170.

Beilock, S. L., & Gray, R. (2007). Why do athletes choke under pressure? In G. Tenenbaum & R. C. Ecklund (Eds.), *Handbook of sport psychology* (Vol. 3, pp. 425–444). Hoboken, NJ: Wiley.

Bélanger-Gravel, A., Godin, G., & Amireault, S. (2013). A meta-analytic review of the effect of implementation intentions on physical activity. *Health Psychology Review*, 7(1), 23–54. https://doi.org/10.1080/17437199.2011.560095

Bélanger-Gravel, A., Godin, G., Bilodeau, A., & Poirier, P. (2013). The effect of implementation intentions on physical activity among obese older adults: A randomised control study. *Psychology & Health*, *28*(2), 217–233. https://doi.org/10.1080/08870446.2012.723711

Bélanger-Gravel, A., Godin, G., Bilodeau, A., Poirier, P., & Dagenais, G. R. (2012). Physical activity beliefs among overweight/obese older adults. *International Journal of Sport Psychology*, *44*(2), 145–159. https:/doi.org/10.7352/IJSP 2012.43.000

Bem, D. J. (1972). *Self-perception theory*. New York: Academic Press.

Bennie, J. A., De Cocker, K., Teychenne, M. J., Brown, W. J., & Biddle, S. J. H. (2019). The epidemiology of aerobic physical activity and muscle-strengthening activity guideline adherence among 383,928 U.S. adults. *International Journal of Behavioral Nutrition and Physical Activity*, *16*, 34. https://doi.org/10.1186/s12966-019-0797-2

Bentler, P. M., & Speckart, G. (1979). Models of attitude–behavior relations. *Psychological Review*, *86*(5), 452–464. https://doi.org/10.1037/0033-295X.86.5.452

Berkman, E. T., Hutcherson, C. A., Livingston, J. L., Kahn, L. E., & Inzlicht, M. (2017). Self-control as value-based choice. *Current Directions in Psychological Science*, *26*, 422–428. https://doi.org/10.1177/0963721417704394

Berkman, E. T., Livingston, J. L., & Kahn, L. E. (2017). Finding the "self" in self-regulation: The identity-value model. *Psychological Inquiry*, *28*(2–3), 77–98. https://doi.org/10.1080/1047840X.2017.1323463

Bernard, P., Carayol, M., Gourlan, M., Boiché, J., Romain, A. J., Bortolon, C., Lareyre, O., & Ninot, G. (2017). Moderators of theory-based interventions to promote physical activity in 77 randomized controlled trials. *Health Education and Behavior*, *44*(2), 227–235. https://doi.org/10.1177/1090198116648667

Berridge, K. C., Ho, C.-Y., Richard, J. M., & DiFeliceantonio, A. G. (2010). The tempted brain eats: Pleasure and desire circuits in obesity and eating disorders. *Brain Research*, *1350*, 43–64. https://doi.org/10.1016/j.brainres.2010.04.003

Berridge, K. C., & Robinson, T. E. (2016). Liking, wanting, and the incentive-sensitization theory of addiction. *American Psychologist*, *71*(8), 670–679. https://doi.org/10.1037/amp0000059

Berry, T. R. (2006). Who's even interested in the exercise message? Attentional bias for exercise and sedentary-lifestyle related words. *Journal of Sport and Exercise Psychology*, *28*, 4–17.

Berry, T. R., Rodgers, W. M., Divine, A., & Hall, C. (2018). The relationship of explicit-implicit evaluative discrepancy to exercise dropout in middleaged adults. *Journal of Sport and Exercise Psychology*, *40*(2), 92–100. https://doi.org/10.1123/jsep.20170267

Bertrams, A., & Dickhäuser, O. (2009). Messung dispositioneller Selbstkontroll-Kapazität: Eine deutsche Adaptation der Kurzform der Self-Control Scale (SCS-K-D) [Measuring dispositional self-control capacity. A German adaptation of the short form of the Self-Control Scale (SCS-K-D)]. *Diagnostica*, *55*, 2–10. https://doi.org/10.1026/0012–1924.55.1.2

Bertrams, A., & Englert, C. (2013). Umsetzung subjektiver Sporthäufigkeitsstandards – Zur Rolle dispositionell verfügbarer Selbstkontrollkraft [Implementing subjective standards of exercise frequency – On the role of dispositionally available self-control strength]. *German Journal of Exercise and Sport Research*, *43*, 276–282. https://doi.org/10.1007/s12662-013-0304-x

Bertrams, A., Englert, C., & Dickhäuser, O. (2010). Self-control strength in the relation between trait test anxiety and state anxiety. *Journal of Research in Personality*, *44*, 738–741. https://doi.org/10.1016/j.jrp.2010.09.005

Bertrams, A., Englert, C., Dickhäuser, O., & Baumeister, R. F. (2013). Role of self-control strength in the relation between anxiety and cognitive performance. *Emotion*, *13*, 668–680. https://doi.org/10.1037/a0031921

Bertrams, A., Unger, A., & Dickhäuser, O. (2011). Momentan verfügbare Selbstkontrollkraft: Vorstellung eines Messinstruments und erste Befunde aus pädagogisch-psychologischen Kontexten [Momentarily available self-control strength – Introduction of a measure and first findings from educational-psychological contexts]. *Zeitschrift für Pädagogische Psychologie, 25*, 185–196. https://doi.org/10.1024/1010-0652/a000042

Bessenoff, G. R., & Snow, D. (2006). Absorbing society's influence: Body image self-discrepancy and internalized shame. *Sex Roles, 54*, 727–731. https://doi.org/10.1007/s11199-006-9038-7

Bettman, J. R. (1993). The decision maker who came in from the cold. *Advances in Consumer Research, 20*, 7–11.

Bhattacharya, J., Garber, A. M., & Goldhaber-Fiebert, J. D. (2015). *Nudges in exercise commitment contracts: A randomized controlled trial* (No. W21406). National Bureau of Economic Research. https://doi.org/10.3386/w21406

Biddle, S. J., Ciaccioni, S., Thomas, G., & Vergeer, I. (2019). Physical activity and mental health in children and adolescents: An updated review of reviews and an analysis of causality. *Psychology of Sport and Exercise, 42*, 146–155. https://doi.org/10.1016/j.psychsport.2018.08.011

Bieleke, M., & Wolff, W. (2017). That escalated quickly-Planning to ignore RPE can backfire. *Frontiers in Physiology, 8*, 736. https://doi.org/10.3389/fphys.2017.00736

Blain, B., Schmit, C., Aubry, A., Hausswirth, C., Le Meur, Y., & Pessiglione, M. (2019). Neuro-computational impact of physical training overload on economic decision-making. *Current Biology, 29*, 3289–3297.e4. https://doi.org/10.1016/j.cub.2019.08.054

Blasberg, J. S., Hewitt, P. L., Flett, G. L., Sherry, S. B., & Chen, C. (2016). The importance of item wording: The distinction between measuring high standards versus measuring perfectionism and why it matters. *Journal of Psychoeducational Assessment, 34*, 702–717.

Blázquez, D., Botella, J., & Suero, M. (2017). The debate on the ego-depletion effect: Evidence from meta-analysis with the p-uniform method. *Frontiers in Psychology, 8*, 197. https://doi.org/10.1177/1745691616652878

Bluemke, M., Brand, R., Schweizer, G., & Kahlert, D. (2010). Exercise might be good for me, but I don't feel good about it: Do automatic associations predict exercise behavior? *Journal of Sport and Exercise Psychology, 32*(2), 137–153. https://doi.org/10.1123/jsep.32.2.137

Boas, D. A., Elwell, C. E., Ferrari, M., & Taga, G. (2014). Twenty years of functional near-infrared spectroscopy: Introduction for the special issue. *NeuroImage, 85*(Pt. 1), 1–5. https://doi.org/10.1016/j.neuroimage.2013.11.033

Boat, R., Atkins, T., Davenport, N., & Cooper, S. (2018). Prior self-control exertion and perceptions of pain and motivation during a physically effortful task. In M. Sarkar & S. Marcora (Eds.), *Sport and the brain: The science of preparing, enduring and winning, part C* (Vol. 240, pp. 19–34). Cambridge, MA: Academic Press. https://doi.org/10.1016/bs.pbr.2018.08.007

Boat, R., & Cooper, S. B. (2019). Self-control and exercise: A review of the bi-directional relationship. *Brain Plasticity, 5*, 97–104. https://doi.org/10.3233/BPL-190082

Boat, R., & Taylor, I. M. (2017). Prior self-control exertion and perceptions of pain during a physically demanding task. *Psychology of Sport and Exercise, 33*, 1–6. https://doi.org/10.1016/j.psychsport.2017.07.005

Boat, R., Taylor, I. M., & Hulston, C. J. (2017). Self-control exertion and glucose supplementation prior to endurance performance. *Psychology of Sport and Exercise, 29*, 103–110. https://doi.org/10.1016/j.psychsport.2016.12.007

Boksem, M. A., Meijman, T. F. & Lorist, M. M. (2005). Effects of mental fatigue on attention: An ERP study. *Cognitive Brain Research, 25*, 107–116. https://doi.org/10.1016/j.cogbrainres.2005.04.011

Boksem, M. A., & Tops, M. (2008). Mental fatigue: Costs and benefits. *Brain Research Reviews, 59*, 125–139. https://doi.org/10.1016/j.brainresrev.2008.07.001

Bonnar, D., Bartel, K., Kakoschke, N., & Lang, C. (2018). Sleep interventions designed to improve athletic performance and recovery: A systematic review of current approaches. *Sports Medicine, 48*, 683–703. https://doi.org/10.1007/s40279-017-0832-x

Borragán, G., Slama, H., Bartolomei, M., & Peigneux, P. (2017). Cognitive fatigue: A time-based resource-sharing account. *Cortex, 89*, 71–84. https://doi.org/10.1016/j.cortex.2017.01.023

Bottos, S., & Dewey, D. (2004). Perfectionists' appraisal of daily hassles and chronic headache. *Headache: The Journal of Head and Face Pain, 44*, 772–779.

Botvinick, M., & Braver, T. (2015). Motivation and cognitive control: From behavior to neural mechanism. *Annual Review of Psychology, 66*, 83–113.

Brand, R., & Antoniewicz, F. (2016). Affective evaluations of exercising: The role of automatic-reflective evaluation discrepancy. *Journal of Sport and Exercise Psychology, 38*(6), 631–638. https://doi.org/10.1123/jsep.2016-0171

Brand, R., & Cheval, B. (2019). Theories to explain exercise motivation and physical inactivity: Ways of expanding our current theoretical perspective. *Frontiers in Psychology, 10*, 1147. https://doi.org/10.3389/fpsyg.2019.01147

Brand, R., & Ekkekakis, P. (2018). Affective-reflective theory of physical inactivity and exercise: Foundations and preliminary evidence. *German Journal of Exercise and Sport Research, 48*(1), 48–58. https://doi.org/10.1007/s12662-017-0477-9

Brand, R., & Ekkekakis, P. (2018). Affective–reflective theory of physical inactivity and exercise. *German Journal of Exercise and Sport Research, 48*, 48–58. https://doi.org/10.1007/s12662-017-0477-9

Brand, R., & Schweizer, G. (2015). Going to the gym or to the movies? Situated decisions as a functional link connecting automatic and reflective evaluations of exercise with exercising behavior. *Journal of Sport and Exercise Psychology, 37*(1), 63–73. https://doi.org/10.1123/jsep.20140018

Brand, R., & Ulrich, L. (2019). I can see it in your face: Affective valuation of exercise in more or less physically active individuals. *Frontiers in Psychology, 10*, 2901. https://doi.org/10.3389/fpsyg.2019.02901

Brandstätter, V., & Schüler, J. (2013). Action crisis and cost–benefit thinking: A cognitive analysis of a goal-disengagement phase. *Journal of Experimental Social Psychology, 49*(3), 543–553. https://doi.org/10.1016/j.jesp.2012.10.004

Bratland-Sanda, S., & Sundgot-Borgen, J. (2013). Eating disorders in athletes: Overview of prevalence, risk factors and recommendations for prevention and treatment. *European Journal of Sport Science, 13*, 499–508. https://doi.org/10.1080/17461391.2012.740504

Braver, T. S. (2012). The variable nature of cognitive control: A dual mechanisms framework. *Trends in Cognitive Sciences, 16*, 106–113. http://dx.doi.org/10.1016/j.tics.2011.12.010

Bray, S. R., Graham, J. D., & Saville, P. D. (2015). Self-control training leads to enhanced cardiovascular exercise performance. *Journal of Sports Sciences, 33*, 534–543. http://dx.doi.org/10.1080/02640414.2014.949830

Bray, S. R., Martin Ginis, K. A., Hicks, A. L., & Woodgate, J. (2008). Effects of self-regulatory strength depletion on muscular performance and EMG activation. *Psychophysiology, 45*, 337–343. http://dx.doi.org/10.1111/j.1469-8986.2007.00625.x

Bray, S. R., Martin Ginis, K. A., & Woodgate, J. (2011). Self-regulatory strength depletion and muscle-endurance performance: A test of the limited-strength model in older adults. *Journal of Aging and Physical Activity, 19*, 177–188. http://dx.doi.org/10.1123/japa.19.3.177

Bray, S. R., Oliver, J. P., Graham, J. D., & Ginis, K. A. M. (2013). Music, emotion, and self-control: Does listening to uplifting music replenish self-control strength for exercise? *Journal of Applied Biobehavioral Research, 18*, 156–173. https://doi.org/10.1111/jabr.12008

Brehm, J. W., & Self, A. (1989). The intensity of motivation. *Annual Reviews in Psychology, 40*, 109–131. https://doi.org/10.1146/annurev.ps.40.020189.000545

Brick, N. E., Campbell, M. J., Metcalfe, R. S., Mair, J. L., & MacIntyre, T. E. (2016). Altering pace control and pace regulation: Attentional focus effects during running. *Medicine and Science in Sports and Exercise, 48*(5), 879–886. https://doi.org/10.1249/MSS.0000000000000843

Brick, N. E., MacIntyre, T. E., & Campbell, M. J. (2015). Metacognitive processes in the self-regulation of performance in elite endurance runners. *Psychology of Sport and Exercise, 19*, 1–9. https://doi.org/10.1016/j.psychsport.2015.02.003

Brick, N. E., MacIntyre, T. E., & Campbell, M. J. (2016). Thinking and action: A cognitive perspective on self-regulation during endurance performance. *Frontiers in Physiology, 7*, 159. https://doi.org/10.3389/fphys.2016.00159

Broman-Fulks, J. J., Hill, R. W., & Green, B. A. (2008). Is perfectionism categorical or dimensional? A taxometric analysis. *Journal of Personality Assessment, 90*, 481–490.

Brown, D. M., & Bray, S. R. (2017a). Effects of mental fatigue on physical endurance performance and muscle activation are attenuated by monetary incentives. *Journal of Sport and Exercise Psychology, 39*, 385–396. https://doi.org/10.1123/jsep.2017–0187

Brown, D. M., & Bray, S. R. (2017b). Graded increases in cognitive control exertion reveal a threshold effect on subsequent physical performance. *Sport, Exercise, and Performance Psychology, 6*, 355–369. https://doi.org/10.1037/spy0000091

Brown, D. M. Y., & Bray, S. R. (2019a). Heart rate biofeedback attenuates effects of mental fatigue on exercise performance. *Psychology of Sport and Exercise, 41*, 70–79. https://doi.org/10.1016/j.psychsport.2018.12.001

Brown, D. M. Y., & Bray, S. R. (2019b). Effects of mental fatigue on exercise intentions and behavior. *Annals of Behavioral Medicine, 53*, 405–414. https://doi.org/10.1093/abm/kay052

Brown, D. M. Y., Graham, J. D., Innes, K. I., Harris, S., Flemington, A., & Bray, S. R. (2020). Effects of prior cognitive exertion on physical performance: A systematic review and meta-analysis. *Sports Medicine, 50*, 497–529. https://doi.org/10.1007/s40279-019-01204-8

Brownsberger, J., Edwards, A., Crowther, R., & Cottrell, D. (2013). Impact of mental fatigue on self-paced exercise. *International Journal of Sports Medicine, 34*, 1029–1036. https://doi.org/10.1055/s-0033–1343402

Brunet, J., Pila, E., Solomon-Krakus, S., Sabiston, C. M., & O'Loughlin, J. (2019). Self-esteem moderates the associations between body-related self-conscious emotions and depressive symptoms. *Journal of Health Psychology, 24*(6), 833–843. https://doi.org/10.1177/1359105316683786

Brunet, J., & Sabiston, C. M. (2011). In the company we keep: Social physique anxiety levels differ around parents and peers. *Journal of Health Psychology, 16*(1), 42–49. https://doi.org/10.1177/1359105310367530

Brunet, J., Sabiston, C., Castonguay, A., Ferguson, L., & Bessette, N. (2012). The association between physical self-discrepancies and women's physical activity: The mediating role of motivation. *Journal of Sport and Exercise Psychology, 34*(1), 102–123. https://doi.org/10.1123/jsep.34.1.102

Brunet, J., Sabiston, C. M., Dorsch, K. D., & McCreary, D. R. (2010). Exploring a model linking social physique anxiety, drive for muscularity, drive for thinness and self-esteem among adolescent boys and girls. *Body Image, 7*(2), 137–142. https://doi.org/10.1016/j.bodyim.2009.11.004

Bryan, A. D., & Rocheleau, C. A. (2002). Predicting aerobic versus resistance exercise using the theory of planned behavior. *American Journal of Health Behavior, 26*(2), 83–94.

Buck, R. (1999). The biological affects: A typology. *Psychological Review, 106*(2), 301–336. https://doi.org/10.1037/0033295X.106.2.301

Buckley, J., Cohen, J. D., Kramer, A. F., McAuley, E., & Mullen, S. P. (2014). Cognitive control in the self-regulation of physical activity and sedentary behavior. *Frontiers in Human Neuroscience, 8*. https://doi.org/10.3389/fnhum.2014.00747

Buehler, R., & Pucher, J. (2012). Cycling to work in 90 large American cities: New evidence on the role of bike paths and lanes. *Transportation, 39*, 409–432.

Burcher, P. (2013). The Ulysses contract in obstetrics: A woman's choices before and during labour. *Journal of Medical Ethics, 39*(1), 27–30.

Burger, J. M., & Shelton, M. (2011). Changing everyday health behaviors through descriptive norm manipulations. *Social Influence, 6*(2), 69–77.

Burkard, C., Rochat, L., & Van der Linden, M. (2013). Enhancing inhibition: How impulsivity and emotional activation interact with different implementation intentions. *Acta Psychologica, 144*(2), 291–297. https://doi.org/10.1016/j.actpsy.2013.07.008

Burke, P. J. (2006). Identity change. *Social Psychology Quarterly, 69*, 81–96. https://psycnet.apa.org/doi/10.1177/019027250606900106

Burke, P. J., & Stets, J. E. (2009). *Identity theory*. New York: Oxford University Press.

Burkert, S., Knoll, N., Luszczynska, A., & Gralla, O. (2012). The interplay of dyadic and individual planning of pelvic-floor exercise in prostate-cancer patients following radical prostatectomy. *Journal of Behavioral Medicine, 35*(3), 305–317. https://doi.org/10.1007/s10865-012-9416-2

Burkert, S., Scholz, U., Gralla, O., Roigas, J., & Knoll, N. (2011). Dyadic planning of health-behavior change after prostatectomy: A randomized-controlled planning intervention. *Social Science & Medicine, 73*(5), 783–792. https://doi.org/10.1016/j.socscimed.2011.06.016

Burnley, M., & Jones, A. M. (2007). Oxygen uptake kinetics as a determinant of sports performance. *European Journal of Sport Science*, 7, 63–79. https://doi.org/10.1080/17461390701456148

Burnley, M., & Jones, A. M. (2018). Power-duration relationship: Physiology, fatigue, and the limits of human performance. *European Journal of Sport Science*, *18*(1), 1–12. https://doi.org/10.1080/17461391.2016.1249524

Burnley, M., Vanhatalo, A., & Jones, A. M. (2012). Distinct profiles of neuromuscular fatigue during muscle contractions below and above the critical torque in humans. *Journal of Applied Physiology*, *113*(2), 215–223. https://doi.org/10.1152/japplphysiol.00022.2012

Burns, D. D. (1980). *Feeling good: The new mood therapy*. New York: The New American Library Inc.

Bush, G., Luu, P., & Posner, M. I. (2000). Cognitive and emotional influences in anterior cingulate cortex. *Trends in Cognitive Sciences*, *4*, 215–222. https://doi.org/10.1016/S1364-6613(00)01483-2

Bustamante, L. A., Lieder, F., Musslick, S., Shenhav, A., & Cohen, J. D. (2020). Learning to overexert cognitive control in a Stroop task. https://doi.org/10.31234/osf.io/3rynj

Cabanac, M. (1986). Money versus pain: Experimental study of a conflict in humans. *Journal of the Experimental Analysis of Behavior*, *46*, 37–44. https://doi.org/10.1901/jeab.1986.46-37

Cabanac, M. (1992). Pleasure: The common currency. *Journal of Theoretical Biology*, *155*, 173–200.

Calitri, R., Lowe, R., Eves, F. F., & Bennett, P. (2009). Associations between visual attention, implicit and explicit attitude and behavior for physical activity. *Psychology & Health*, *24*, 1105–1123.

Calogero, R. M., & Pina, A. (2011). Body guilt : Preliminary evidence for a further subjective experience of self-objectification. https://doi.org/10.1177/0361684311408564

Campbell, D. T. (1958). Common fate, similarity, and other indices of the status of aggregates of persons as social entities. *Systems Research and Behavioral Science*, *3*(1), 14–25.

Campbell, J. D., & Di Paula, A. (2002). Perfectionistic self-beliefs: Their relation to personality and goal pursuit. In G. L. Flett, & P. L. Hewitt (Eds.), *Perfectionism: Theory, research, and treatment* (pp. 181–198). Washington, DC: American Psychological Association.

Campo, M., Champely, S., Louvet, B., Rosnet, E., Ferrand, C., Pauketat, J. V. T., & Mackie, D. M. (2019). Group-based emotions: Evidence for emotion- performance relationships in team sports. *Research Quarterly for Exercise and Sport*, *90*(1), 54–63. https://doi.org/10.1080/02701367.2018.1563274

Campos, B. T., Penna, E. M., Rodrigues, J. G., Mendes, T. T., Maia-Lima, A., Nakamura, F. Y., ... & Prado, L. S. (2019). Influence of mental fatigue on physical performance, and physiological and perceptual responses of judokas submitted to the special judo fitness test. *Journal of Strength and Conditioning Research*. https://doi.org/10.1519/jsc.0000000000003453

Carius, D., Andrä, C., Clauß, M., Ragert, P., Bunk, M., & Mehnert, J. (2016). Hemodynamic response alteration as a function of task complexity and expertise-An fNIRS study in jugglers. *Frontiers in Human Neuroscience*, *10*, 126. https://doi.org/10.3389/fnhum.2016.00126

Carmack, M. A., & Martens, R. (1979). Measuring commitment to running: A survey of runner's attitudes and mental states. *Journal of Sport Psychology*, *1*(1), 25–42.

Carraro, N., & Gaudreau, P. (2013). Spontaneous and experimentally induced action planning and coping planning for physical activity: A meta-analysis. *Psychology of Sport and Exercise*, *14*(2), 228–248. https://doi.org/10.1016/j.psychsport.2012.10.004

Carter, C. S., Braver, T. S., Barch, D. M., Botvinick, M. M., Noll, D., & Cohen, J. D. (1998). Anterior cingulate cortex, error detection, and the online monitoring of performance. *Science*, *280*(5364), 747–749. https://doi.org/10.1126/science.280.5364.747

Carter, E. C., Kofler, L. M., Forster, D. E., & McCullough, M. E. (2015). A series of meta-analytic tests of the depletion effect: Self-control does not seem to rely on a limited resource. *Journal of Experimental Psychology: General*, *144*, 796–815. https://doi.org/10.1037/xge0000083

Carter, E. C., & McCullough, M. E. (2014). Publication bias and the limited strength model of self-control: Has the evidence for ego depletion been overestimated? *Frontiers in Psychology*, 5. https://doi.org/10.3389/fpsyg.2014.00823

Carver, C. S. (2006). Approach, avoidance, and the self-regulation of affect and action. *Motivation and Emotion*, *30*(2), 105–110. https://doi.org/10.1007/s11031-006-9044-7

Carver, C. S., & Scheier, M. F. (1982). Control theory: A useful conceptual framework for personality-social, clinical, and health psychology. *Psychological Bulletin, 92*(1), 111–135. https://doi.org/10.1037/0033-2909.92.1.111

Carver, C. S., & Scheier, M. F. (1998). *On the self-regulation of behavior*. Cambridge: Cambridge University Press. https://doi.org/10.1017/CBO9781139174794

Carver, C. S., & Scheier, M. F. (2000). On the structure of behavioral self-regulation. In M. Boekaerts, P. R. Pintrich, & M. Zeidner (Eds.), *Handbook of self-regulation* (pp. 41–84). Cambridge, MA: Academic Press. https://doi.org/10.1016/B978-012109890-2/50032-9

Carver, C. S., & Scheier, M. F. (2001). *On the self-regulation of behavior*. Cambridge: Cambridge University Press.

Carver, C. S., & Scheier, M. F. (2011). Self-regulation of action and affect. In K. D. Vohs & R. F. Baumeister (Eds.), *Handbook of self-regulation: Research, theory, and applications* (pp. 3–21). New York: Guilford Press.

Casey, B. J., & Jones, R. M. (2010). Neurobiology of the adolescent brain and behavior: Implications for substance use disorders. *Journal of the American Academy of Child and Adolescent Psychiatry, 49*(12), 1189–1201. https://doi.org/10.1016/j.jaac.2010.08.017

Cash, T. F., Santos, M. T., & Williams, E. F. (2005). Coping with body-image threats and challenges: Validation of the body image coping strategies inventory. *Journal of Psychosomatic Research, 58*(2), 190–199. https://doi.org/10.1016/j.jpsychores.2004.07.008

Castonguay, A. L., Brunet, J., Ferguson, L., & Sabiston, C. M. (2012). Weight-related actual and ideal self-states, discrepancies, and shame, guilt, and pride: Examining associations within the process model of self-conscious emotions. *Body Image, 9*(4), 488–494. https://doi.org/10.1016/j.bodyim.2012.07.003

Castonguay, A. L., Gilchrist, J. D., Mack, D. E., & Sabiston, C. M. (2013). Body-related pride in young adults : An exploration of the triggers, contexts, outcomes and attributions. *Body Image, 10*, 335–343. https://doi.org/10.1016/j.bodyim.2013.03.001

Castonguay, A. L., Pila, E., Wrosch, C., & Sabiston, C. M. (2015). Body-related self-conscious emotions relate to physical activity motivation and behavior in men. *American Journal of Men's Health, 9*(3), 209–221. https://doi.org/10.1177/1557988314537517

Castonguay, A. L., Sabiston, C. M., Crocker, P. R. E., & Mack, D. E. (2014). Development and validation of the body and appearance self-conscious emotions scale (BASES). *Body Image, 11*(2), 126–136. https://doi.org/10.1016/j.bodyim.2013.12.006

Castonguay, A. L., Sabiston, C. M., Kowalski, K. C., & Wilson, P. M. (2015). Introducing an instrument to measure body and fitness-related self-conscious emotions: The BSE-FIT. *Psychology of Sport and Exercise*, In Press.

Cavanagh, J. F., & Frank, M. J. (2014). Frontal theta as a mechanism for cognitive control. *Trends in Cognitive Sciences, 18*, 414–421. https://doi.org/10.1016/j.tics.2014.04.012

Cavanagh, J. F., & Shackman, A. J. (2015). Frontal midline theta reflects anxiety and cognitive control: Meta-analytic evidence. *Journal of Physiology, Paris, 109*, 3–15. https://doi.org/10.1016/j.jphysparis.2014.04.003

Chambers, E. S., Bridge, M. W., & Jones, D. A. (2009). Carbohydrate sensing in the human mouth: Effects on exercise performance and brain activity. *The Journal of Physiology, 587*, 1779–1794. https://doi.org/10.1113/jphysiol.2008.164285

Chapman, J., Fletcher, C., Flight, I., & Wilson, C. (2018). Pilot randomized trial of a volitional help sheet-based tool to increase leisure time physical activity in breast cancer survivors. *British Journal of Health Psychology, 23*(3), 723–740. https://doi.org/10.1111/bjhp.12313

Chase, M. A., & DiSanti, J. S. (2017). Talent development recommendations for coaches to consider. *Journal of Sport Psychology in Action, 8*, 1–11.

Chaudhuri, A., & Behan, P. C. (2000). Fatigue and basal ganglia. *Journal of the Neurological Sciences, 179*, 34–42. https://doi.org/10.1016/S0022-510X(00)00411-1

Cheval, B., Miller, M. M., Orsholits, D., Berry, T., Sander, D., & Boisgontier, M. P. (2020). Physically active individuals look for more: An eye-tracking study of attentional bias. *Psychophysiology, 57*(6), e13582. https://doi.org/10.1111/psyp.13582

Cheval, B., Radel, R., Neva, J. L., Boyd, L. A., Swinnen, S. P., Sander, D., & Boisgontier, M. P. (2018). Behavioral and neural evidence of the rewarding value of exercise behaviors: A systematic review. *Sports Medicine, 48*(6), 1389–1404. https://doi.org/10.1007/s4027901808980

Cheval, B., Sarrazin, P., Isoard-Gautheur, S., Radel, R., & Friese, M. (2015). Reflective and impulsive processes explain (in)effectiveness of messages promoting physical activity: A randomized controlled trial. *Health Psychology, 34*, 10–19.

Cheval, B., Sarrazin, P., Isoard-Gautheur, S., Radel, R., & Friese, M. (2016). How impulsivity shapes the interplay of impulsive and reflective processes involved in objective physical activity. *Personality and Individual Differences, 96*, 132–137.

Cheval, B., Sarrazin, P., & Pelletier, L. (2014). Impulsive approach tendencies towards physical activity and sedentary behaviors, but not reflective intentions, prospectively predict non-exercise activity thermogenesis. *PLoS One, 9*, e115238.

Cheval, B., Sarrazin, P., Pelletier, L., & Friese, M. (2016). Effect of retraining approach-avoidance tendencies on an exercise task: A randomized controlled trial. *Journal of Physical Activity and Health, 13*, 1396–1403.

Cheval, B., Tipura, E., Burra, N., Frossard, J., Chanal, J., Orsholits, D., Radel, R., & Boisgontier, M. P. (2018). Avoiding sedentary behaviors requires more cortical resources than avoiding physical activity: An EEG study. *Neuropsychologia, 119*, 68–80. https://doi.org/10.1016/j.neuropsychologia.2018.07.029

Chevance, G., Bernard, P., Chamberland, P. E., & Rebar, A. (2019). The association between implicit attitudes toward physical activity and physical activity behaviour: A systematic review and correlational meta-analysis. *Health Psychology Review, 13*(3), 248–276. https://doi.org/10.1080/17437199.2019.1618726

Chevance, G., Berry, T., Boiché, J., & Heraud, N. (2019). Changing implicit attitudes for physical activity with associative learning. *German Journal of Exercise and Sport Research, 49*(2), 156–167. https://doi.org/10.1007/s12662-018-0559-3

Chevance, G., Caudroit, J., Henry, T., Guerin, P., Boiché, J., & Héraud, N. (2018). Do implicit attitudes toward physical activity and sedentary behavior prospectively predict objective physical activity among persons with obesity? *Journal of Behavioral Medicine, 41*, 31–42.

Chevance, G., Caudroit, J., Romain, A. J., & Boiché, J. (2017). The adoption of physical activity and eating behaviors among persons with obesity and in the general population. The role of implicit attitudes within the theory of planned behavior. *Psychology, Health, & Medicine, 22*, 319–324.

Chidnok, W., Fulford, J., Bailey, S. J., Dimenna, F. J., Skiba, P. F., Vanhatalo, A., & Jones, A. M. (2013). Muscle metabolic determinants of exercise tolerance following exhaustion: Relationship to the "critical power". *Journal of Applied Physiology (Bethesda, Md.: 1985), 115*(2), 243–250. https://doi.org/10.1152/japplphysiol.00334.2013

Christian, M. S., & Ellis, A. P. (2011). Examining the effects of sleep deprivation on workplace deviance: A self-regulatory perspective. *Academy of Management Journal, 54*, 913–934. https://doi.org/10.5465/amj.2010.0179

Churchill, S., & Jessop, D. (2010). Spontaneous implementation intentions and impulsivity: Can impulsivity moderate the effectiveness of planning strategies? *British Journal of Health Psychology, 15*(3), 529–541. https://doi.org/10.1348/135910709X475423

Churchill, S., & Jessop, D. C. (2011). Too impulsive for implementation intentions? Evidence that impulsivity moderates the effectiveness of an implementation intention intervention. *Psychology and Health, 26*(5), 517–530. https://doi.org/10.1080/08870441003611536

Ciarocco, N. J., Sommer, K. L., & Baumeister, R. F. (2001). Ostracism and ego depletion: The strains of silence. *Personality and Social Psychology Bulletin, 27*, 1156–1163. https://doi.org/10.1177/0146167201279008

Ciarocco, N. J., Twenge, J. M., Muraven, M., & Tice, D. M. (2007). *Measuring state self-control: Reliability, validity, and correlations with physical and psychological stress.* West Long Branch, NJ: Monmouth University. Unpublished manuscript.

Clark, I. E., Goulding, R. P., DiMenna, F. J., Bailey, S. J., Jones, M. I., Fulford, J., McDonagh, S. T. J., Jones, A. M., & Vanhatalo, A. (2019). Time-trial performance is not impaired in either competitive athletes or untrained individuals following a prolonged cognitive task. *European Journal of Applied Physiology, 119*, 149–161. https://doi.org/10.1007/s00421-018-4009-6

Clarkson, J. J., Hirt, E. R., Jia, L., & Alexander, M. B. (2010). When perception is more than reality: The effects of perceived versus actual resource depletion on self-regulatory behavior. *Journal of Personality and Social Psychology, 98*, 29–46. https://doi.org/10.1037/a0017539

Cohen, J. (1992). A power primer. *Psychological Bulletin, 112*, 155–159. https://doi.org/10.1037/0033–2909.112.1.155

Cohen, J., Dunbar, K., & Mcclelland, J. (1990). On the control of automatic processes: A parallel distributed processing account of the Stroop effect. *Psychological Review, 97*, 332–361. https://doi.org/10.1037/0033-295X.97.3.332

Conn, V. S., Hafdahl, A. R., & Mehr, D. R. (2011). Interventions to increase physical activity among healthy adults: Meta-analysis of outcomes. *American Journal of Public Health, 101*(4), 751–758. https://doi.org/10.2105/AJPH.2010.194381

Conner, M., Abraham, C., Prestwich, A., Hutter, R., Hallam, J., Sykes-Muskett, B., … Hurling, R. (2016). Impact of goal priority and goal conflict on the intention–health-behavior relationship: Tests on physical activity and other health behaviors. *Health Psychology, 35*, 1017–1026.

Conner, M., Godin, G., Sheeran, P., & Germain, M. (2013). Some feelings are more important: Cognitive attitudes, affective attitudes, anticipated affect, and blood donation. *Health Psychology, 32*(3), 264–272. https://doi.org/10.1037/a0028500

Conner, M., & Norman, P. (2015a). *Predicting health behaviour: Research and practice with social cognition models*. Berkshire: Open University Press.

Conner, M. T., & Norman, P. (2015b). Predicting and changing health behaviour: A social cognition approach. In M. T. Conner & P. Norman (Eds.), *Predicting and changing health behaviour: Research and practice with social cognition models* (3rd ed., pp. 1–29). Maidenhead: Open University Press.

Conradt, M., Dierk, J.-M., Schlumberger, P., Rauh, E., Hevebrand, J., & Rief, W. (2007). Development of the weight- and body-related shame and guilt scale (WEB-SG) in a non-clinical sample of obese subjects. *Journal of Personality Assessment, 88*, 317–327.

Conroy, D. E., & Berry, T. R. (2017). Automatic affective evaluations of physical activity. *Exercise and Sport Sciences Reviews, 45*(4), 230–237. https://doi.org/10.1249/JES.0000000000000120

Conroy, D. E., Hyde, A. L., Doerksen, S. E., & Ribeiro, N. F. (2010). Implicit attitudes and explicit motivation prospectively predict physical activity. *Annals of Behavioral Medicine, 39*, 112–118.

Cook, D. B., O'Connor, P. J., Lange, G., & Steffener, J. (2007). Functional neuroimaging correlates of mental fatigue induced by cognition among chronic fatigue syndrome patients and controls. *Neuroimage, 36*, 108–122. https://doi.org/10.1016/j.neuroimage.2007.02.033

Cooke, R., & Sheeran, P. (2004). Moderation of cognition-intention and cognition-behaviour relations: A meta-analysis of properties of variables from the theory of planned behaviour. *British Journal of Social Psychology, 43*(2), 159–186. https://doi.org/10.1348/0144666041501688

Cordova, D. I., & Lepper, M. R. (1996). Intrinsic motivation and the process of learning: Beneficial effects of contextualization, personalization, and choice. *Journal of Educational Psychology, 88*(4), 715–730. https://doi.org/10.1037/0022-0663.88.4.715

Corrigan, P. W., Powell, K. J., & Michaels, P. J. (2015). Beyond the rational patient: Implications for health decisions and behaviors. In P. W. Corrigan (Ed.), *Person-centered care for mental illness: The evolution of adherence and selfdetermination* (pp. 29–51). Washington, DC: American Psychological Association. https://doi.org/10.1037/14644-003

Corrigan, P. W., Rüsch, N., BenZeev, D., & Sher, T. (2014). The rational patient and beyond: Implications for treatment adherence in people with psychiatric disabilities. *Rehabilitation Psychology, 59*(1), 85–98. http://dx.doi.org/10.1037/a0034935

Courneya, K. S., & Friedenreich, C. M. (1999). Utility of the theory of planned behavior for understanding exercising during breast cancer treatment. *Psycho-Oncology, 8*(2), 112–122.

Coutinho, D., Gonçalves, B., Travassos, B., Wong, D. P., Coutts, A. J., & Sampaio, J. E. (2017). Mental fatigue and spatial references impair soccer players' physical and tactical performances. *Frontiers in Psychology, 8*, 1645. https://doi.org/10.3389/fpsyg.2017.01645

Coutinho, D., Gonçalves, B., Wong, D. P., Travassos, B., Coutts, A. J., & Sampaio, J. (2018). Exploring the effects of mental and muscular fatigue in soccer players' performance. *Human Movement Science, 58*, 287–296. https://doi.org/10.1016/j.humov.2018.03.004

Cox, A. E., Sabiston, C. M., Karlinsky, A., Manzone, J., Neyedli, H., & Welsh, T. N. (2020). The impact of athletic clothing style and body awareness on motor performance in women. *Psychonomic Bulletin & Review, 27*(5), 1025–1035. https://doi.org/10.3758/s13423-020-01755-2.

Cox, A. E., Ullrich-French, S., & Sabiston, C. M. (2013). Using motivation regulations in a person-centered approach to examine the link between social physique anxiety in physical education and physical activity-related outcomes in adolescents. *Psychology of Sport and Exercise, 14*(4), 461–467. https://doi.org/10.1016/j.psychsport.2013.01.005

Craft, L. L., Magyar, T. M., Becker, B. J., & Feltz, D. L. (2003). The relationship between the Competitive State Anxiety Inventory-2 and sport performance: A meta-analysis. *Journal of Sport and Exercise Psychology, 25*, 44–65. https://doi.org/10.1123/jsep.25.1.44

Craft, L. L., & Perna, F. M. (2004). The benefits of exercise for the clinically depressed. *Primary Care Companion to the Journal of Clinical Psychiatry, 6*, 104–111.

Craig, A. D. (2003). Interoception: The sense of the physiological condition of the body. *Current Opinion in Neurobiology, 13*(4), 500–505. https://doi.org/10.1016/s0959-4388(03)00090-4

Crane, J., & Temple, V. (2015). A systematic review of dropout from organized sport among children and youth. *European Physical Education Review, 21*(1), 114–131. https://doi.org/10.1177/1356336X14555294

Crescioni, A. W., Ehrlinger, J., Alquist, J. L., Conlon, K. E., Baumeister, R. F., Schatschneider, C., & Dutton, G. R. (2011). High trait self-control predicts positive health behaviors and success in weight loss. *Journal of Health Psychology, 16*, 750–759. https://doi.org/10.1177/1359105310390247

Crewe, H., Tucker, R., & Noakes, T. D. (2008). The rate of increase in rating of perceived exertion predicts the duration of exercise to fatigue at a fixed power output in different environmental conditions. *European Journal of Applied Physiology, 103*, 569–577. https://doi.org/10.1007/s00421-008-0741-7

Critchfield, T. S., & Kollins, S. H. (2001). Temporal discounting: Basic research and the analysis of socially important behavior. *Journal of Applied Behavior Analysis, 34*, 101–122. https://doi.org/10.1901/jaba.2001.34-101

Critchley, H., Daly, E., Phillips, M., Brammer, M., Bullmore, E., Williams, S., Van Amelsvoort, T., Robertson, D., David, A., & Murphy, D. (2000). Explicit and implicit neural mechanisms for processing of social information from facial expressions: A functional magnetic resonance imaging study. *Human Brain Mapping, 9*(2), 93–105. https://doi.org/10.1002/(SICI)1097-0193(200002)9:2<93::AIDHBM4>3.0.CO;2-Z

Critchley, H. D., & Garfinkel, S. N. (2017). Interoception and emotion. *Current Opinion in Psychology, 17*, 7–14. https://doi.org/10.1016/j.copsyc.2017.04.020

Critchley, H. D., & Harrison, N. A. (2013). Visceral influences on brain and behavior. *Neuron*, 77(4), 624–638. https://doi.org/10.1016/j.neuron.2013.02.008

Crocker, J., & Wolfe, C. T. (2001). Contingencies of self-worth. *Psychological Review, 108*(3), 593–623. https://doi.org/10.1037/0033-295X.108.3.593

Crocker, P. R. E., Brune, S. M., Kowalski, K. C., Mack, D. E., Wilson, P. M., & Sabiston, C. M. (2014). Body-related state shame and guilt in women: Do causal attributions mediate the influence of physical self-concept and shame and guilt proneness. *Body Image, 11*, 19–26. https://doi.org/10.1016/j.bodyim.2013.08.002

Crombie, P.-A., Brunet, J., & Sabiston, C. M. (2011). Stop staring! Proposed strategies to reduce students' body-related concerns in physical education. *Journal of Physical Education, Recreation & Dance (JOPERD), 82*(2), 39–43.

Cunningham, M. R., & Baumeister, R. F. (2016). How to make nothing out of something: Analyses of the impact of study sampling and statistical interpretation in misleading meta-analytic conclusions. *Frontiers in Psychology*, 7, 1639. https://doi.org/10.3389/fpsyg.2016.01639

Curran, T., & Hill, A. P. (2019). Perfectionism is increasing over time: A meta-analysis of birth cohort differences from 1989 to 2016. *Psychological Bulletin*, *145*(4), 410.

Cutini, S., & Brigadoi, S. (2014). Unleashing the future potential of functional near-infrared spectroscopy in brain sciences. *Journal of Neuroscience Methods*, *232*, 152–156. https://doi.org/10.1016/j.jneumeth.2014.05.024

da Silva, M. A. V., Sao-Joao, T. M., Brizon, V. C., Franco, D. H., & Mialhe, F. L. (2018). Impact of implementation intentions on physical activity practice in adults: A systematic review and meta-analysis of randomized clinical trials. *PLoS ONE*, *13*(11), e0206294. https://doi.org/10.1371/journal.pone.0206294

Dai, H., Milkman, K. L., & Riis, J. (2014). The fresh start effect: Temporal landmarks motivate aspirational behavior. *Management Science*, *60*(10), 2563–2582.

Dai, H., Milkman, K. L., & Riis, J. (2015). Put your imperfections behind you: Temporal landmarks spur goal initiation when they signal new beginnings. *Psychological Science*, *26*(12), 1927–1936.

Dalgetty, R., Miller, C. B., & Dombrowski, S. U. (2019). Examining the theory-effectiveness hypothesis: A systematic review of systematic reviews. *British Journal of Health Psychology*, *24*, 334–356.

Dalton, A. N., & Spiller, S. A. (2012). Too much of a good thing: The benefits of implementation intentions depend on the number of goals. *Journal of Consumer Research*, *39*(3), 600–614. https://doi.org/10.1086/664500

Damasio, A. R. (1994). *Descartes' error: Emotion, reason, and the human brain*. New York: G. P. Putnam's Sons.

Damasio, A. R. (1996). The somatic marker hypothesis and the possible functions of the prefrontal cortex. *Philosophical Transactions of the Royal Society of London. Series B, Biological Sciences*, *351*(1346), 1413–1420. http://doi.org/10.1098/rstb.1996.0125

Damasio, A. R. (2000). A neurobiology for consciousness. In T. Metzinger (Ed.), *Neural correlates of consciousness: Empirical and conceptual questions* (pp. 111–120). Cambridge, MA: MIT Press.

Dang, J. (2018). An updated meta-analysis of the ego depletion effect. *Psychological Research*, *82*, 645–651. https://doi.org/10.1007/s00426-017-0862-x

Dang, J., Barker, P., Baumert, A., Bentvelzen, M., Berkman, E., Buchholz, N., … & Zinkernagel, A. (2021). A multilab replication of the ego depletion effect. *Social Psychological and Personality Science*, *12*, 14–24. https://doi.org/10.1177/1948550619887702

Darling, K. A., & Helton, W. S. (2014). Dual-task interference between climbing and a simulated communication task. *Experimental Brain Research*, *232*, 1367–1377. https://doi.org/10.1007/s00221-014-3855-7

Davies, C. T., & Sargeant, A. J. (1979). The effects of atropine and practolol on the perception of exertion during treadmill exercise. *Ergonomics*, *22*(10), 1141–1146. https://doi.org/10.1080/00140137908924688

Davis, C., Patte, K., Curtis, C., & Reid, C. (2010). Immediate pleasures and future consequences. A neuropsychological study of binge eating and obesity. *Appetite*, *54*, 208–213. https://doi.org/10.1016/j.appet.2009.11.002

de Azevedo, M. H. P., Soares, M. J., Carvalho Bos, S., Allen Gomes, A., Maia, B., Marques, M., … & Macedo, A. (2009). Perfectionism and sleep disturbance. *The World Journal of Biological Psychiatry*, *10*(3), 225–233.

de Bruin, M., Sheeran, P., Kok, G., Hiemstra, A., Prins, J. M., Hospers, H. J., & van Breukelen, G. J. (2012). Self-regulatory processes mediate the intention-behavior relation for adherence and exercise behaviors. *Health Psychology*, *31*, 695–703. https://doi.org/10.1037/a0027425

De Ridder, D. T., & De Wit, J. B. (2006). Self-regulation in health behavior: Concepts, theories, and central issues. In D. T. De Ridder, & J. B. De Wit (Eds.), *Self-regulation in health behavior*. Hoboken, NJ: Wiley.

De Ridder, D. T., Lensvelt-Mulders, G., Finkenauer, C., Stok, F. M., & Baumeister, R. F. (2012). Taking stock of self-control: A meta-analysis of how trait self-control relates to a wide range of behaviors. *Personality and Social Psychology Review, 16*, 76–99. https://doi.org/10.1177/1088868311418749

De Souto Barreto, P. (2013). Why are we failing to promote physical activity globally? *Bulletin of the World Health Organization, 91*(6), 390–390A. https://doi.org/10.2471/BLT.13.120790

De Souto Barreto, P. (2015). Global health agenda on non-communicable diseases: Has WHO set a smart goal for physical activity? *British Medical Journal, 350*, h23. https://doi.org/10.1136/bmj.h23

de Vet, E., Oenema, A., & Brug, J. (2011). More or better: Do the number and specificity of implementation intentions matter in increasing physical activity? *Psychology of Sport and Exercise, 12*, 471–477. https://doi.org/10.1016/j.psychsport.2011.02.008

de Vries, H., Mesters, I., Van de Steeg, H., & Honing, C. (2005). The general public's information needs and perceptions regarding hereditary cancer: An application of the Integrated Change Model. *Patient Education and Counseling, 56*(2), 154–165. https://doi.org/10.1016/j.pec.2004.01.002

Deci, E. L., Eghrari, H., Patrick, B. C., & Leone, D. R. (1994). Facilitating internalization: The self-determination theory perspective. *Journal of Personality, 62*(1), 119–142. https://doi.org/10.1111/j.1467-6494.1994.tb00797.x

Deci, E. L., & Ryan, R. M. (1980). Self-determination theory: When mind mediates behavior. *Journal of Mind and Behavior, 1*(1), 33–43.

Deci, E. L., & Ryan, R. M. (1985). *Intrinsic motivation and self-determination in human behavior.* New York: Plenum.

Deci, E. L., & Ryan, R. M. (2002). *Handbook of self-determination.* Rochester, NY: University of Rochester.

Dehaene, S., Posner, M. I., & Tucker, D. M. (1994). Localization of a neural system for error detection and compensation. *Psychological Science, 5*(5), 303–305. https://doi.org/10.1111/j.1467-9280.1994.tb00630.x

Deutsch, R. (2017). Associative and propositional processes from the perspective of the reflective-impulsive model. In R. Deutsch, B. Gawronski, & W. Hofmann (Eds.), *Reflective and impulsive determinants of human behavior* (pp. 51–68). New York: Routledge. https://doi.org/10.4324/9781315523095-11

Deutsch, R., & Strack, F. (2010). Building blocks of social behavior: Reflective and impulsive processes. In B. Gawronski & B. K. Payne (Eds.), *Handbook of implicit social cognition: Measurement, theory, and applications* (pp. 62–79). New York: Guilford.

Dhar, R., & Gorlin, M. (2013). A dual-system framework to understand preference construction processes in choice. *Journal of Consumer Psychology, 23*(4), 528–542. https://doi.org/10.1016/j.jcps.2013.02.002

Di Domenico, S. I., Le, A., Liu, Y., Ayaz, H., & Fournier, M. A. (2016). Basic psychological needs and neurophysiological responsiveness to decisional conflict: An event-related potential study of integrative self processes. *Cognitive, Affective & Behavioral Neuroscience, 16*(5), 848–865. https://doi.org/10.3758/s13415-016-0436-1

Di Fronso, S., Tamburro, G., Robazza, C., Bortoli, L., Comani, S., & Bertollo, M. (2018). Focusing attention on muscle exertion increases EEG coherence in an endurance cycling task. *Frontiers in Psychology, 9*, 1249. https://doi.org/10.3389/fpsyg.2018.01249

Dickinson, A. (2012). Associative learning and animal cognition. *Philosophical Transactions of the Royal Society of London. Series B, Biological Sciences, 367*(1603), 2733–2742. https://doi.org/10.1098/rstb.2012.0220

DiClemente, C. C., & Graydon, M. M. (2020). Changing behavior using the transtheoretical model. In M. S. Hagger, L. D. Cameron, K. Hamilton, N. Hankonen, & T. Lintunen (Eds.), *The handbook of behavior change* (pp. 136–149). New York: Cambridge University Press. https://doi.org/10.1017/97811086773180.010

Direito, A., Carraça, E., Rawstorn, J., Whittaker, R., & Maddison, R. (2016). mHealth technologies to influence physical activity and sedentary behaviors: Behavior change techniques, systematic review and meta-analysis of randomized controlled trials. *Annals of Behavioral Medicine, 51*(2), 226–239. https://doi.org/10.1007/s12160-016-9846-0

Dishman R. K. (2003). The impact of behavior on quality of life. *Quality of Life Research, 12*(Suppl. 1), 43–49. https://doi.org/10.1023/a:1023517303411

Dishman, R. K., Sallis, J. F., & Orenstein, D. R. (1985). The determinants of physical activity and exercise. *Public Health Reports, 100*(2), 158–171.

Dodge, T., Clarke, P., & Dwan, R. (2017). The relationship between physical activity and alcohol use among adults in the United States: A systematic review of the literature. *American Journal of Health Promotion, 31*(2), 97–108. https://doi.org/10.1177/0890117116664710

Doré, I., Pila, E., Gilchrist, J., & Sabiston, C. M. (In Press). Investigating the association between social identity and group-based emotions with sport commitment among adolescent female athletes. *International Journal of Sport Psychology.*

Dorris, D. C., Power, D. A., & Kenefick, E. (2012). Investigating the effects of ego depletion on physical exercise routines of athletes. *Psychology of Sport and Exercise, 13*, 118–125. https://doi.org/10.1016/j.psychsport.2011.10.004

Downs, D. S., & Hausenblas, H. A. (2005). The theories of reasoned action and planned behavior applied to exercise: A meta-analytic update. *Journal of Physical Activity and Health, 2*(1), 76–97. https://doi.org/10.1123/jpah.2.1.76

Du, Y., Liu, B., Sun, Y., Snetselaar, L. G., Wallace, R. B., & Bao, W. (2019). Trends in adherence to the Physical Activity Guidelines for Americans for aerobic activity and time spent on sedentary behavior among US adults, 2007 to 2016. *JAMA Network Open, 2*(7), e197597. https://doi.org/10.1001/jamanetworkopen.2019.7597

Duckworth, A. L., Gendler, T. S., & Gross, J. J. (2016). Situational strategies for self-control. *Perspectives on Psychological Science, 11*(1), 35–55.

Duckworth, A. L., & Kern, M. L. (2011). A meta-analysis of the convergent validity of self-control measures. *Journal of Research in Personality, 45*, 259–268. https://doi.org/10.1016/j.jrp.2011.02.004

Duckworth, A. L., Milkman, K. L., & Laibson, D. (2018). Beyond willpower: Strategies for reducing failures of self-control. *Psychological Science in the Public Interest, 19*(3), 102–129.

Duckworth, A. L., & Seligman, M. E. (2017). The science and practice of self-control. *Perspectives on Psychological Science, 12*, 715–718. https://doi.org/10.1177/1745691617690880

Duckworth, A. L., Tsukayama, E., & Kirby, T. A. (2013). Is it really self-control? Examining the predictive power of the delay of gratification task. *Personality and Social Psychology Bulletin, 39*, 843–855. https://doi.org/10.1177/0146167213482589

Duda, J. L. (1992). Motivation in sport settings: A goal perspective approach. In G. C. Roberts (Ed.), *Motivation in sport and exercise* (pp. 57–91). Champaign, IL: Human Kinetics.

Duda, J. L., & Nicholls, J. G. (1992). Dimensions of achievement motivation in schoolwork and sport. *Journal of Educational Psychology, 84*(3), 290–299. https://doi.org/10.1037/0022-0663.84.3.290

Duncan, J. (2010). The multiple-demand (MD) system of the primate brain: Mental programs for intelligent behaviour. *Trends in Cognitive Sciences, 14*, 172–179. https://doi.org/10.1016/j.tics.2010.01.004

Duncan, M. J., Fowler, N., George, O., Joyce, S., & Hankey, J. (2015). Mental fatigue negatively influences manual dexterity and anticipation timing but not repeated high-intensity exercise performance in trained adults. *Research in Sports Medicine, 23*, 1–13. https://doi.org/10.1080/15438627.2014.975811

Dunkley, D. M., Schwartzman, D., Looper, K. J., Sigal, J. J., Pierre, A., & Kotowycz, M. A. (2012). Perfectionism dimensions and dependency in relation to personality vulnerability and psychosocial adjustment in patients with coronary artery disease. *Journal of Clinical Psychology in Medical Settings, 19*, 211–223.

Dunkley, D. M., Zuroff, D. C., & Blankstein, K. R. (2006). Specific perfectionism components versus self-criticism in predicting maladjustment. *Personality and Individuals Differences, 40*, 665–676.

Dunn, A. L., Trivedi, M. H., & O'Neal, H. A. (2001). Physical activity dose-response effects on outcomes of depression and anxiety. *Medicine & Science in Sports & Exercise, 33*(6), S587–S597. https://doi.org/10.1097/00005768-200106001-00027

Dunning, D. (2011). The DunningKruger effect: On being ignorant of one's own ignorance. *Advances in Experimental Social Psychology, 44*, 247–296. https://doi.org/10.1016/B978-0-12-385522-0.00005-6

Dunst, B., Benedek, M., Jauk, E., Bergner, S., Koschutnig, K., Sommer, M., ... Neubauer, A. C. (2014). Neural efficiency as a function of task demands. *Intelligence, 42*, 22–30. https://doi.org/10.1016/j.intell.2013.09.005

Dunton, G. F. (2017). Ecological momentary assessment in physical activity research. *Exercise and Sport Sciences Reviews, 45*, 48–54.

Dweck, C. S. (2017). From needs to goals and representations: Foundations for a unified theory of motivation, personality, and development. *Psychological Review, 124*(6), 689–719. https://doi.org/10.1037/rev0000082

Dzewaltowski, D. A. (1989). Toward a model of exercise motivation. *Journal of Sport and Exercise Psychology, 11*(3), 251–269. https://doi.org/10.1123/jsep.11.3.251

Dzewaltowski, D. A., Noble, J. M., & Shaw, J. M. (1990). Physical activity participation: Social cognitive theory versus the theories of reasoned action and planned behavior. *Journal of Sport and Exercise Psychology, 12*(4), 388–405. https://doi.org/10.1123/jsep.12.4.388

Edelman, G. M. (2003). Naturalizing consciousness: A theoretical framework. *Proceedings of the National Academy of Sciences of the United States of America, 100*, 5520–5524. https://doi.org/10.1073/pnas.0931349100

Edmunds, J., Ntoumanis, N., & Duda, J. L. (2006). A test of self-determination theory in the exercise domain. *Journal of Applied Social Psychology, 36*(9), 2240–2265.

Edmunds, J., Ntoumanis, N., & Duda, J. L. (2008). Testing a self-determination theory-based teaching style intervention in the exercise domain. *European Journal of Social Psychology, 38*(2), 375–388. https://doi.org/10.1002/ejsp.463

Edwards, M. K., Addoh, O., Herod, S. M., Rhodes, R. E., & Loprinzi, P. D. (2017). A conceptual neurocognitive affect-related model for the promotion of exercise among obese adults. *Current Obesity Reports, 6*(1), 86–92. https://doi.org/10.1007/s13679-017-0244-0

Eerland, A., Guadalupe, T. M., Franken, I. H. A., & Zwaan, R. A. (2012). Posture as index for approach-avoidance behavior. *PLoS ONE, 7*(2), e31291. https://doi.org/10.1371/journal.pone.0031291

Eisenberger, R. (1992). Learned industriousness. *Psychological Review, 99*, 248. https://doi.org/10.1037/0033-295X.99.2.248

Ekkekakis, P. (2009a). Illuminating the black box: Investigating prefrontal cortical hemodynamics during exercise with near-infrared spectroscopy. *Journal of Sport and Exercise Psychology, 31*, 505–553. https://doi.org/10.1123/jsep.31.4.505

Ekkekakis, P. (2009b). Let them roam free? Physiological and psychological evidence for the potential of self-selected exercise intensity in public health. *Sports Medicine, 39*(10), 857–888.

Ekkekakis, P. (2017). People have feelings! Exercise psychology in paradigmatic transition. *Current Opinion in Psychology, 16*, 84–88. https://doi.org/10.1016/j.copsyc.2017.03.018

Ekkekakis, P., & Brand, R. (2019). Affective responses to and automatic affective valuations of physical activity: Fifty years of progress on the seminal question in exercise psychology. *Psychology of Sport and Exercise, 42*, 130–137. https://doi.org/10.1016/j.psychsport.2018.12.018

Ekkekakis, P., & Dafermos, M. (2012). Exercise is a many-splendored thing but for some it does not feel so splendid: Staging a resurgence of hedonistic ideas in the quest to understand exercise behavior. In E. O. Acevedo (Ed.), *The Oxford handbook of exercise psychology* (pp. 295–333). New York: Oxford University Press. https://doi.org/10.1093/oxfordhb/9780195394313.013.0016

Ekkekakis, P., Hartman, M. E., & Ladwig, M. A. (2020). Affective responses to exercise. In G. Tenenbaum & R. C. Eklund (Eds.), *Handbook of sport psychology* (4th ed., pp. 233–253). New York: Wiley.

Ekkekakis, P., Parfitt, G., & Petruzzello, S. J. (2011). The pleasure and displeasure people feel when they exercise at different intensities: Decennial update and progress towards a tripartite rationale for exercise intensity prescription. *Sports Medicine, 41*(8), 641–671. https://doi.org/10.2165/11590680-000000000-00000

Ekkekakis, P., Vazou, S., Bixby, W. R., & Georgiadis, E. (2016). The mysterious case of the public health guideline that is (almost) entirely ignored: Call for a research agenda on the causes of the extreme avoidance of physical activity in obesity. *Obesity Reviews, 17*(4), 313–329. https://doi.org/10.1111/obr.12369

Ekkekakis, P., & Zenko, Z. (2016). Escape from cognitivism: Exercise as hedonic experience. In M. Raab, P. Wylleman, R. Seiler, A.-M. Elbe, & A. Hatzigeorgiadis (Eds.), *Sport and exercise psychology research: From theory to practice* (pp. 389–414). London: Academic Press. https://doi.org/10.1016/B978-0-12-803634-1.00018-2

Ekkekakis, P., Zenko, Z., Ladwig, M. A., & Hartman, M. E. (2018). Affect as a potential determinant of physical activity and exercise: Critical appraisal of an emerging research field. In D. M. Williams, R. E. Rhodes, & M. Conner (Eds.), *Affective determinants of health behavior* (pp. 237–261). New York: Oxford University Press. https://doi.org/10.1093/oso/9780190499037.003.0011

Ekkekakis, P., Zenko, Z., & Werstein, K. M. (2018). Exercise in obesity from the perspective of hedonic theory: A call for sweeping change in professional practice norms. In S. Razon & M. L. Sachs (Eds.), *Applied exercise psychology: The challenging journey from motivation to adherence* (pp. 289–315). New York: Routledge. https://doi.org/10.4324/9780203795422223

Ekman, P., & Cordaro, D. (2011). What is meant by calling emotions basic. *Emotion Review, 3*(4), 364–370. https://doi.org/10.1177/1754073911410740

Elliot, A. J. (1997). Integrating the "classic" and "contemporary" approaches to achievement motivation: A hierarchical model of approach and avoidance achievement motivation. In M. L. Maehr & P. R. Pintrich (Eds.), *Advances in motivation and achievement* (Vol. 10, pp. 143–179). Greenwich, CT: JAI Press.

Elliot, A. J., & McGregor, H. A. (2001). A 2 X 2 achievement goal framework. *Journal of Personality and Social Psychology, 80*(3), 501–519. https://doi.org/10.1037/0022-3514.80.3.501

Elliot, A. J., Murayama, K., & Pekrun, R. (2011). A 3 × 2 achievement goal model. *Journal of Educational Psychology, 103*(3), 632–648. https://doi.org/10.1037/a0023952

Elliott, M. A., & Armitage, C. J. (2006). Effects of implementation intentions on the self-reported frequency of drivers' compliance with speed limits. *Journal of Experimental Psychology: Applied, 12*(2), 108–117. https://doi.org/10.1037/1076-898X.12.2.108

Ellis, A. (1958). Rational psychotherapy. *The Journal of General Psychology, 59*(1), 35–49.

Enders, H., Cortese, F., Maurer, C., Baltich, J., Protzner, A. B., & Nigg, B. M. (2016). Changes in cortical activity measured with EEG during a high-intensity cycling exercise. *Journal of Neurophysiology, 115*(1), 379–388. https://doi.org/10.1152/jn.00497.2015

Englert, C. (2015). Choking under Pressure und Ego Depletion: Eine Erweiterung der Attentional Control Theory und mögliche Interventionsmaßnahmen [Choking under pressure and ego depletion: An extension of Attentional Control Theory and possible interventions]. *Zeitschrift für Sportpsychologie, 22*, 137–145. https://doi.org/10.1026/1612–5010/a000151.

Englert, C. (2016). The strength model of self-control in sport and exercise psychology. *Frontiers in Psychology, 7*, 314. https://doi.org/10.3389/fpsyg.2016.00314

Englert, C. (2017). Ego depletion in sports: Highlighting the importance of self-control strength for high-level sport performance. *Current Opinion in Psychology, 16*, 1–5. https://doi.org/10.1016/j.copsyc.2017.02.028

Englert, C. (2019). The self-regulation of human performance: A critical discussion and future directions for self-control research. *Performance Enhancement and Health, 6*(3–4), 156–157.

Englert, C., & Bertrams, A. (2012). Anxiety, ego depletion, and sport performance. *Journal of Sport and Exercise Psychology, 34*, 580–599. https://doi.org/10.1123/jsep.34.5.580

Englert, C., & Bertrams, A. (2013). Too exhausted for operation? Anxiety, depleted self-control strength, and perceptual-motor performance. *Self and Identity, 12*, 650–662. https://doi.org/10.1080/15298868.2012.718865

Englert, C., & Bertrams, A. (2014a). The effect of ego depletion on sprint start reaction time. *Journal of Sport and Exercise Psychology, 36*, 506–515. https://doi.org/10.1123/jsep.2014-0029

Englert, C., & Bertrams, A. (2014b). What is self-control depleting in sports? Effects of vicarious experiences on performance. *International Journal of Sport Psychology, 45*, 1–10.

Englert, C., & Bertrams, A. (2015). Integrating attentional control theory and the strength model of self-control. *Frontiers in Psychology – Personality and Social Psychology, 6*, 824. https://doi.org/10.3389/fpsyg.2015.00824

Englert, C., Bertrams, A., Furley, P., & Oudejans, R. R. D. (2015). Is ego depletion associated with increased distractibility? Results from a basketball free throw task. *Psychology of Sport and Exercise, 18*, 26–31. https://doi.org/10.1016/j.psychsport.2014.12.001

Englert, C., Havik, L., Qian, Z., & Oudejans, R. R. D. (2018). Can you go the extra mile? The effect of ego depletion on endurance performance. *International Journal of Sport Psychology, 49*, 505–520.

Englert, C., Persaud, B., Oudejans, R., & Bertrams, A. (2015). The influence of ego depletion on sprint start performance in athletes without track and field experience. *Frontiers in Psychology, 6*, 1207. https://doi.org/10.3389/fpsyg.2015.01207

Englert, C., & Rummel, J. (2016). I want to keep on exercising but I don't: The negative impact of momentary lacks of self-control on exercise adherence. *Psychology of Sport and Exercise, 26*, 24–31. https://doi.org/10.1016/j.psychsport.2016.06.001

Englert, C., & Wolff, W. (2015). Ego depletion and persistent performance in a cycling task. *International Journal of Sport Psychology, 46*, 137–151.

Englert, C., Zwemmer, K., Bertrams, A., & Oudejans, R. R. D. (2015). Ego depletion and attention regulation under pressure: Is a temporary loss of self-control strength indeed related to impaired attention regulation? *Journal of Sport and Exercise Psychology, 37*, 127–137. https://doi.org/10.1123/jsep.2014-0219

Enns, M. W., Cox, B. J., & Clara, I. (2002). Adaptive and maladaptive perfectionism: Developmental origins and association with depression proneness. *Personality and Individual Differences, 33*, 921–935.

Epstein, L. H., & Saelens, B. E. (2000). Behavioral economics of obesity: Food intake and energy expenditure. In W. K. Bickel & R. E. Vuchinich (Eds.), *Reframing health behavior change with behavioral economics* (pp. 293–311). Mahwah, NJ: Lawrence Erlbaum Associates.

Epstein, S. (1991). Cognitive-experiential self-theory: An integrative theory of personality. In R. C. Curtis (Ed.), *The relational self: Theoretical convergences in psychoanalysis and social psychology* (pp. 111–137). New York: Guilford.

Epstein, S. (1994). Integration of the cognitive and the psychodynamic unconscious. *American Psychologist, 49*(8), 709–724. https://doi.org/10.1037/0003066X.49.8.709

Epstein, S. (2013). Cognitive-experiential self-theory: An integrative theory of personality. In H. Tennen, J. Suls, & I. B. Weiner (Eds.), *Handbook of psychology: Personality and social psychology* (pp. 93–118). New York: Wiley. https://doi.org/10.1002/9781118133880.hop205005

Epstein, S., & Pacini, R. (1999). Some basic issues regarding dual-process theories from the perspective of cognitive–experiential self-theory. In S. Chaiken & Y. Trope (Eds.), *Dual-process theories in social psychology* (pp. 462–482). New York: Guilford.

Epton, T., & Armitage, C. J. (2017). Does situation-specificity affect the operation of implementation intentions? *Behavior Therapy, 48*(6), 860–869. https://doi.org/10.1016/j.beth.2017.08.003

Eston, R., Faulkner, J., St Clair Gibson, A., Noakes, T., & Parfitt, G. (2007). The effect of antecedent fatiguing activity on the relationship between perceived exertion and physiological activity during a constant load exercise task. *Psychophysiology, 44*, 779–786. https://doi.org/10.1111/j.1469-8986.2007.00558.x

Evans, G. W., & Rosenbaum, J. (2008). Self-regulation and the income-achievement gap. *Early Childhood Research Quarterly, 23*, 504–514. https://doi.org/10.1016/j.ecresq.2008.07.002

Evans, J. S. B. T. (2008). Dual-processing accounts of reasoning, judgment, and social cognition. *Annual Review of Psychology, 59*, 255–278. https://doi.org/10.1146/annurev.psych.59.103006.093629

Evans, J. S. B. T., & Stanovich, K. E. (2013). Dual-process theories of higher cognition: Advancing the debate. *Perspectives on Psychological Science, 8*(3), 223–241. https://doi.org/10.1177/1745691612460685

Evans, M. B., Eys, M. A., & Bruner, M. W. (2012). Seeing the "we" in "me" sports: The need to consider individual sport team environments. *Canadian Psychology/Psychologie Canadienne, 53*, 301–308. https://doi.org/10.1037/a0030202

Eves, F. F., Scott, E. J., Hoppé, R., & French, D. P. (2007). Using the affective priming paradigm to explore the attitudes underlying walking behavior. *British Journal of Health Psychology, 12,* 571–585.

Eysenck, M. W., Derakshan, N., Santos, R., & Calvo, M. G. (2007). Anxiety and cognitive performance: Attentional control theory. *Emotion, 7,* 336–353. https://doi.org/10.1037/1528–3542.7.2.336

Fanning, J., Mullen, S. P., & McAuley, E. (2012). Increasing physical activity with mobile devices: A meta-analysis. *Journal of Medical Internet Research, 14*(6), e161. https://doi.org/10.2196/jmir.2171

Faries, M. (2016). Why we don't "just do it": Understanding the intention-behavior gap in lifestyle medicine. *American Journal of Lifestyle Medicine, 10*(5), 322–329.

Fazio, R. H. (1995). Attitudes as object-evaluation associations: Determinants, consequences, and correlates of attitude accessibility. In R. E. Petty & J. A. Krosnick (Eds.), *Attitude strength: Antecedents and consequences* (pp. 247–282). Hillsdale, NJ: Lawrence Erlbaum.

Fazio, R. H. (2001). On the automatic activation of associated evaluations: An overview. *Cognition and Emotion, 15*(2), 115–141. https://doi.org/10.1080/02699930042000024

Feldman Barrett, L. (2006). Valence is a basic building block of emotional life. *Journal of Research in Personality, 40*(1), 35–55. https://doi.org/10.1016/j.jrp.2005.08.006

Feldman Barrett, L., & Bliss-Moreau, E. (2009). Affect as a psychological primitive. *Advances in Experimental Social Psychology, 41,* 167–218. https://doi.org/10.1016/S00652601(08)00404-8

Feldman Barrett, L., Mesquita, B., Ochsner, K. N., & Gross, J. J. (2007). The experience of emotion. *Annual Review of Psychology, 58,* 373–403. https://doi.org/10.1146/annurev.psych.58.110405.085709

Feng, S. (2005). Rationality and self-control: The implications for smoking cessation. The *Journal of Socio-Economics, 34*(2), 211–222.

Feng, S. F., Schwemmer, M., Gershman, S. J., & Cohen, J. D. (2014). Multitasking versus multiplexing: Toward a normative account of limitations in the simultaneous execution of control-demanding behaviors. *Cognitive, Affective, & Behavioral Neuroscience, 14,* 129–146. https://doi.org/10.3758/s13415-013-0236-9

Fenton, S. A., Duda, J. L., & Barrett, T. (2016). Optimising physical activity engagement during youth sport: A self-determination theory approach. *Journal of Sports Sciences, 34*(19), 1874–1884. https://doi.org/10.1080/02640414.2016.1142104

Ferrari, M., Mottola, L., & Quaresima, V. (2004). Principles, techniques, and limitations of near infrared spectroscopy. *Canadian Journal of Applied Physiology, 29,* 463–487. https://doi.org/10.1139/h04-031

Ferrari, M., & Quaresima, V. (2012). A brief review on the history of human functional near-infrared spectroscopy (fNIRS) development and fields of application. *NeuroImage, 63,* 921–935. https://doi.org/10.1016/j.neuroimage.2012.03.049

Festinger, L. (1957). *Cognitive dissonance.* Stanford, CA: Stanford University Press.

Filipas, L., Gallo, G., Pollastri, L., & Torre, A. L. (2019). Mental fatigue impairs time trial performance in sub-elite under 23 cyclists. *PLOS ONE, 14,* e0218405. https://doi.org/10.1371/journal.pone.0218405

Filipas, L., Martin, K., Northey, J. M., La Torre, A., Keegan, R., & Rattray, B. (2020). A 4-week endurance training program improves tolerance to mental exertion in untrained individuals. *Journal of Science and Medicine in Sport.* https://doi.org/10.1016/j.jsams.2020.04.020

Filipas, L., Mottola, F., Tagliabue, G., & La Torre, A. (2018). The effect of mentally demanding cognitive tasks on rowing performance in young athletes. *Psychology of Sport and Exercise, 39,* 52–62. https://doi.org/10.1016/j.psychsport.2018.08.002

Finkel, E. J., Campbell, W. K., Brunell, A. B., Dalton, A. N., Scarbeck, S. J., & Chartrand, T. L. (2006). High-maintenance interaction: Inefficient social coordination impairs self-regulation. *Journal of Personality and Social Psychology, 91,* 456–475. https://doi.org/10.1037/0022-3514.91.3.456

Finkenauer, C., Engels, R. C. M. E., & Baumeister, R. F. (2005). Parenting and adolescent eternalizing and internalizing problems: The role of self-control. *International Journal of Behavioral Development, 29,* 58–69. doi:10.1080/01650250444000333

Finn, A. (2018, April 2). When 26.2 miles just isn't enough – The phenomenal rise of the ultramarathon. The Guardian. Retrieved March 24, 2020, from https://www.theguardian.com/lifeandstyle/2018/apr/02/ultrarunner-ultramarathon-racing-100-miles

Finne, E., Englert, C., & Jekauc, D. (2019). On the importance of self-control strength for regular physical activity. *Psychology of Sport and Exercise, 43*, 165–171. https://doi.org/10.1016/j.psychsport.2019.02.007

Finucane, M. L., Alhakami, A., Slovic, P., & Johnson, S. M. (2000). The affect heuristic in judgments of risks and benefits. *Journal of Behavioral Decision Making, 13*(1), 1–17. https://doi.org/10.1002/(SICI)1099-0771(200001/03)13:1<1::AID-BDM333>3.0.CO;2-S

Finucane, M. L., Peters, E., & Slovic, P. (2003). Judgment and decision making: The dance of affect and reason. In S. L. Schneider & J. Shanteau (Eds.), *Emerging perspectives on judgment and decision research* (pp. 327–364). New York: Cambridge University Press. https://doi.org/10.1017/CBO9780511609978.012

Fishbach, A., & Shah, J. Y. (2006). Self-control in action: Implicit dispositions toward goals and away from temptations. *Journal of Personality and Social Psychology, 90*(5), 820–832. https://doi.org/10.1037/0022-3514.90.5.820

Fishbach, A., Shah, J. Y., & Kruglanski, A. W. (2004). Emotional transfer in goal systems. *Journal of Experimental Social Psychology, 40*(6), 723–738. https://doi.org/10.1016/j.jesp.2004.04.001

Fishbach, A., Zhang, Y., & Koo, M. (2009). The dynamics of self-regulation. *European Review of Social Psychology, 20*(1), 315–344. https://doi.org/10.1080/10463280903275375

Fishbein, M., & Ajzen, I. (1975). *Belief, attitude, intention and behavior: An introduction to theory and research*. Reading, MA: Addison-Wesley.

Fishbein, M., & Ajzen, I. (2010). *Predicting and changing behavior: The reasoned action approach*. New York: Psychology Press.

Fishbein, M., Triandis, H. C., Kanfer, F. H., Becker, M., Middlestadt, S. E., & Eichler, A. (2001). Factors influencing behavior and behavior change. In A. Baum & T. A. Revenson (Eds.), *Handbook of health psychology* (pp. 3–17). Mahwah, NJ: Lawrence Erlbaum Associates.

Fisher, R. J., & Katz, J. E. (2000). Social-desirability bias and the validity of self-reported values. *Psychology and Marketing, 17*, 105–120. https://doi.org/10.1002/(SICI)1520-6793(200002)17:2<105::AID-MAR3>3.0.CO;2-9

Fiuza-Luces, C., Garatachea, N., Berger, N. A., & Lucia, A. (2013). Exercise is the real polypill. *Physiology, 28*, 330–358.

Fletcher, D., & Arnold, R. (2017). Stress in sport: The role of the organizational environment. In C. R. D. Wagstaff (Ed.), *An organizational psychology of sport: Key issues and practical applications* (pp. 83–100). Abingdon: Routledge.

Flett, G. L., Baricza, C., Gupta, A., Hewitt, P. L., & Endler, N. S. (2011). Perfectionism, psychosocial impact and coping with irritable bowel disease: A study of patients with Crohn's disease and ulcerative colitis. *Journal of Health Psychology, 16*, 561–571.

Flett, G. L., & Hewitt, P. L. (2006). Positive versus negative perfectionism in psychopathology. *Behaviour Modification, 30*, 472–495.

Flett, G. L., & Hewitt, P. L. (2007). When does conscientiousness become perfectionism. *Current Psychiatry, 6*(7), 49–60.

Forberger, S., Reisch, L., Kampfmann, T., & Zeeb, H. (2019). Nudging to move: A scoping review of the use of choice architecture interventions to promote physical activity in the general population. *International Journal of Behavioral Nutrition and Physical Activity, 16*, 77. https://doi.org/10.1186/s12966-019-0844-z

Forestier, C., Sarrazin, P., Allenet, B., Gauchet, A., Heuzé, J. P., & Chalabaev, A. (2018). 'Are you in full possession of your capacity?' A mechanistic self-control approach at trait and state levels to predict different health behaviors. *Personality and Individual Differences, 134*, 214–221. https://doi.org/10.1016/j.paid.2018.05.044

Forscher, P. S., Lai, C. K., Axt, J. R., Ebersole, C. R., Herman, M., Devine, P. G., & Nosek, B. A. (2019). A meta-analysis of procedures to change implicit measures. *Journal of Personality and Social Psychology, 117*(3), 522–559. http://dx.doi.org/10.1037/pspa0000160

Fortes, L. S., Lima-Junior, D. D., Fiorese, L., Nascimento-Júnior, J. R. A., Mortatti, A. L., & Ferreira, M. E. C. (2020). The effect of smartphones and playing video games on decision-making in soccer players: A crossover and randomised study. *Journal of Sports Sciences, 38*, 552–558. https://doi.org/10.1080/02640414.2020.1715181

Fortes, L. S., Lima-Junior, D., Nascimento-Júnior, J. R., Costa, E. C., Matta, M. O., & Ferreira, M. E. (2019). Effect of exposure time to smartphone apps on passing decision-making in male soccer athletes. *Psychology of Sport and Exercise, 44*, 35–41. https://doi.org/10.1016/j.psychsport.2019.05.001

Fortes, L. S., Lima-Júnior, D D., Gantois, P., Nasicmento-Júnior, J. R., & Fonseca, F. S. (2020). Smartphone use among high level swimmers is associated with mental fatigue and slower 100-and 200-but not 50-meter freestyle racing. *Perceptual and Motor Skills*, 0031512520952915. https://doi.org/10.1177/0031512520952915

Francis, Z. L., & Inzlicht, M. (2016). Proximate and ultimate causes of ego depletion. In E. R. Hirt, J. J. Clarkson, & L. Jia (Eds.), *Self-regulation and ego control* (pp. 373–398). Cambridge, MA: Academic Press. https://doi.org/10.1016/B978-0-12-801850-7.00018-4

Franco-Alvarenga, P. E., Brietzke, C., Canestri, R., Goethel, M. F., Hettinga, F., Santos, T. M., & Pires, F. O. (2019). Caffeine improved cycling trial performance in mentally fatigued cyclists, regardless of alterations in prefrontal cortex activation. *Physiology & Behavior, 204*, 41–48. https://doi.org/10.1016/j.physbeh.2019.02.009

Frederick, S. (2005). Cognitive reflection and decision making. *Journal of Economic Perspectives, 19*(4), 25–42.

Frederick, S., Loewenstein, G., & O'donoghue, T. (2002). Time discounting and time preference: A critical review. *Journal of Economic Literature, XL*, 351–401. https://doi.org/10.1257/002205102320161311

Fredholm, B. B., & Svenningsson, P. (2003). Adenosine–dopamine interactions. *Neurology, 61*, S5. https://doi.org/10.1212/01.WNL.0000095204.89871.FF

Fredrickson, B. L. (2004). The broaden-and-build theory of positive emotions. *Philosophical Transactions of the Royal Society B: Biological Sciences*. https://doi.org/10.1098/rstb.2004.1512

Fredrickson, B. L., & Harrison, K. (2005). Throwing like a girl: Self-objectification predicts adolescent girls' motor performance. *Journal of Sport & Social Issues, 29*(1), 79–101. https://doi.org/10.1177/0193723504269878

Fredrickson, B. L., & Kahneman, D. (1993). Duration neglect in retrospective evaluations of affective episodes. *Journal of Personality and Social Psychology, 65*(1), 45–55.

Fredrickson, B. L, & Roberts, T.-A. (1997). Objectification theory. *Psychology of Women Quarterly, 21*(2), 173–206. https://doi.org/10.1111/j.1471-6402.1997.tb00108.x

French, D. P., Olander, E. K., Chisholm, A., & McSharry, J. (2014). Which behaviour change techniques are most effective at increasing older adults' self-efficacy and physical activity behaviour? A systematic review. *Annals of Behavioral Medicine, 48*(2), 225–234. https://doi.org/10.1007/s12160-014-9593-z

Freund, A. M., & Baltes, P. B. (2002). Life-management strategies of selection, optimization, and compensation: Measurement by self-report and construct validity. *Journal of Personality and Social Psychology, 82*, 642–662.

Friese, M., Frankenbach, J., Job, V., & Loschelder, D. D. (2017). Does self-control training improve self-control? A meta-analysis. *Perspectives on Psychological Science, 12*, 1077–1099. doi:10.1177/1745691617697076

Friese, M., Loschelder, D. D., Gieseler, K., Frankenbach, J., & Inzlicht, M. (2019). Is ego depletion real? An analysis of arguments. *Personality and Social Psychology Review, 23*, 107–131. https://doi.org/10.1177/1088868318762183

Frömer, R., Lin, H., Dean Wolf, C. K., Inzlicht, M., & Shenhav, A. (2020, May 20). When effort matters: Expectations of reward and efficacy guide cognitive control allocation. https://doi.org/10.1101/2020.05.14.095935.

Frost, R. O., Marten, P., Lahart, C., & Rosenblate, R. (1990). The dimensions of perfectionism. *Cognitive Therapy and Research, 14*(5), 449–468. https://doi.org/10.1007/BF01172967

Fruin, D. J., Pratt, C., & Owen, N. (1992). Protection motivation theory and adolescents' perceptions of exercise. *Journal of Applied Social Psychology, 22*(1), 55–69. https://doi.org/10.1111/j.1559-1816.1992.tb01521.x

Fullerton, C. L., Lane, A. M., Nevill, A. M., & Devonport, T. J. (2018). Does the brief self-control scale assess relatively stable individual differences in self-control among endurance athletes? *Journal of Sport Behavior, 41*, 27–39.

Gailliot, M. T., & Baumeister, R. F. (2007). The physiology of willpower: Linking blood glucose to self-control. *Personality and Social Psychology Review, 11*, 303–327. https://doi.org/10.1177/1088868307303030

Gainforth, H. L., West, R., & Michie, S. (2015). Assessing connections between behavior change theories using network analysis. *Annals of Behavioral Medicine, 49*(5), 754–761. https://doi.org/10.1007/s12160-015-9710-7

Gammage, K. L., Drouin, B., & Lamarche, L. (2016). Comparing a yoga class with a resistance exercise class: Effects on body satisfaction and social physique anxiety in university women. *Journal of Physical Activity and Health*. https://doi.org/10.1123/jpah.2015-0642

Gantois, P., Ferreira, M. E. C., Lima-Junior, D. de, Nakamura, F. Y., Batista, G. R., Fonseca, F. S., & Fortes, L. de S. (2019). Effects of mental fatigue on passing decision-making performance in professional soccer athletes. *European Journal of Sport Science, 20*, 1–10, 534–543. https://doi.org/10.1080/17461391.2019.1656781

Gardner, B. (2015). A review and analysis of the use of 'habit' in understanding, predicting and influencing health-related behaviour. *Health Psychology Review, 9*, 277–295. https://doi.org/10.1080/17437199.2013.876238

Gardner, B., Phillips, L. A., & Judah, G. (2016). Habitual instigation and habitual execution: Definition, measurement, and effects on behaviour frequency. *British Journal of Health Psychology, 21*, 613–630.

Gardner, B., Rebar, A., & Lally, P. (2019). 'Habitually deciding' or 'habitually doing'? A response to Hagger. *Psychology of Sport and Exercise, 47*, 101539. https://doi.org/10.1016/j.psychsport.2019.05.008

Gasbarri, A., Pompili, A., Packard, M. G., & Tomaz, C. (2014). Habit learning and memory in mammals: Behavioral and neural characteristics. *Neurobiology of Learning and Memory, 114*, 198–208. https://doi.org/10.1016/j.nlm.2014.06.010

Gaudreau, P., & Thompson, A. (2010). Testing a 2× 2 model of dispositional perfectionism. *Personality and Individual Differences, 48*(5), 532–537.

Gawronski, B., & Bodenhausen, G. V. (2006). Associative and propositional processes in evaluation: An integrative review of implicit and explicit attitude change. *Psychological Bulletin, 132*(5), 692–731. https://doi.org/10.1037/00332909.132.5.692

Gawronski, B., & Bodenhausen, G. V. (2014). The associative-propositional evaluation model: Operating principles and operating conditions of evaluation. In J. W. Sherman, B. Gawronski, & Y. Trope (Eds.), *Dual-process theories of the social mind* (pp. 188–203). New York: Guilford.

Gawronski, B., Brannon, S. M., & Bodenhausen, G. V. (2017). The associative-propositional duality in the representation, formation, and expression of attitudes. In R. Deutsch, B. Gawronski, & W. Hofmann (Eds.), *Reflective and impulsive determinants of human behavior* (pp. 103–118). New York: Routledge. https://doi.org/10.4324/978131552309515

GBD 2017 Disease and Injury Incidence and Prevalence Collaborators. (2018). Global, regional, and national incidence, prevalence, and years lived with disability for 354 diseases and injuries for 195 countries and territories, 1990–2017: A systematic analysis for the Global Burden of Disease Study 2017. *Lancet*. https://doi.org/10.1016/S0140-6736(18)32279-7

Gehrlach, D. A., Dolensek, N., Klein, A. S., Chowdhury, R. R., Matthys, A., Junghänel, M., … & Conzelmann, K. K. (2019). Aversive state processing in the posterior insular cortex. *Nature Neuroscience, 22*, 1424–1437. https://doi.org/10.1038/s41593-019-0469-1

Geisser, M. E., Haig, A. J., Wallbom, A. S., & Wiggert, E. A. (2004). Pain-related fear, lumbar flexion, and dynamic EMG among persons with chronic musculoskeletal low back pain. *Clinical Journal of Pain, 20*(2), 61–69. https://doi.org/10.1097/00002508-200403000-00001

Gendolla, G. H. E., & Richter, M. (2010). Effort mobilization when the self is involved: Some lessons from the cardiovascular system. *Review of General Psychology, 14*, 212–226. https://doi.org/10.1037/a0019742

Gerber, M., Lindwall, M., Brand, S., Lang, C., Elliot, C., & Pühse, U. (2015). Longitudinal relationships between perceived stress, exercise self-regulation and exercise involvement among physically active adolescents. *Journal of Sports Sciences, 33*, 369–380. https://doi.org/10.1080/02640414.2014.946072

Gergelyfi, M., Jacob, B., Olivier, E., & Zénon, A. (2015). Dissociation between mental fatigue and motivational state during prolonged mental activity. *Frontiers in Behavioral Neuroscience, 9*, 176. https://doi.org/10.3389/fnbeh.2015.00176

Gibala, M. J., & McGee, S. L. (2008). Metabolic adaptations to short-term high-intensity interval training: A little pain for a lot of gain? *Exercise and Sport Sciences Reviews, 36*(2), 58–63. https://doi.org/10.1097/JES.0b013e318168ec1f

Giboin, L. S., Gruber, M., & Kramer, A. (2015). Task-specificity of balance training. *Human Movement Science, 44*, 22–31. https://doi.org/10.1016/j.humov.2015.08.012

Giboin, L. S., Loewe, K., Hassa, T., Kramer, A., Dettmers, C., Spiteri, S., ... & Schoenfeld, M. A. (2019). Cortical, subcortical and spinal neural correlates of slackline training-induced balance performance improvements. *NeuroImage, 202*, 116061. https://doi.org/10.1016/j.neuroimage.2019.116061

Giboin, L.-S., Gruber, M., Schüler, J., & Wolff, W. (2019). Investigating performance in a strenuous physical task from the perspective of self-control. *Brain Sciences*, 9. https://doi.org/10.3390/brainsci9110317

Giboin, L. S., & Wolff, W. (2019). The effect of ego depletion or mental fatigue on subsequent physical endurance performance: A meta-analysis. *Performance Enhancement and Health*, 7, 100150. https://doi.org/10.1016/j.peh.2019.100150

Gieseler, K., Loschelder, D. D., & Friese, M. (2019). What makes for a good theory? How to evaluate a theory using the strength model of self-control as an example. In K. Sassenberg & M. L. W. Vliek (Eds.), *Social psychology in action: Evidence-based interventions from theory to practice* (pp. 3–21). New York: Springer International Publishing. https://doi.org/10.1007/978-3-030-13788-5_1

Gigerenzer, G., Gaissmaier, W., Kurz-Milcke, E., Schwartz, L. M., & Woloshin, S. (2007). Helping doctors and patients make sense of health statistics. *Psychological Science in the Public Interest, 8*(2), 53–96. https://doi.org/10.1111/j.15396053.2008.00033.x

Gilbert, D. T., & Ebert, J. E. T. (2002). Decisions and revisions: The affective forecasting of changeable outcomes. *Journal of Personality and Social Psychology, 82*, 503–514.

Gilbert, P. (2003). Evolution, social roles, and the differences in shame and guilt. *Social Research, 70*(4), 1205–1230.

Gilbert, P. (2007). The evolution of shame as a marker for relationship security: A biopsychosocial approach. In & J. P. Tangney, J. L. Tracy, & R. W. Robins (Eds.), *The self-conscious emotions: Theory and research* (pp. 283–309). New York: Gilford Press.

Gilbert, P., Durrant, R., & McEwan, K. (2006). Investigating relationships between perfectionism, forms and functions of self-criticism, and sensitivity to put-down. *Personality and Individual Differences, 41*(7), 1299–1308.

Gilchrist, J. D., Conroy, D. E., & Sabiston, C. M. (2018). Experienced and anticipated pride and shame as predictors of goal-directed behavior. *Journal of Sport and Exercise Psychology*. https://doi.org/10.1123/jsep.2017-0011

Gilchrist, J. D., Pila, E., Castonguay, A., Sabiston, C. M., & Mack, D. E. (2018). Body pride and physical activity: Differential associations between fitness- and appearance-related pride in young adult Canadians. *Body Image, 27*, 77–85. https://doi.org/10.1016/j.bodyim.2018.08.010

Gilchrist, J. D., & Sabiston, C. M. (2018). Intentions mediate the association between anticipated pride and physical activity in young adults. *Sport, Exercise, and Performance Psychology*, 7(3), 308–317. https://doi.org/10.1037/spy0000139

Gilchrist, J. D., Sabiston, C. M., & Kowalski, K. C. (2018). Associations between actual and ideal self-perceptions and anticipated pride among young adults. *Journal of Theoretical Social Psychology, 3*(2), 127–134. https://doi.org/10.1002/jts5.39

Gilchrist, J. D., Solomon-Krakus, S., Pila, E., Crocker, P., & Sabiston, C. M. (2020). Associations between physical self-concept and anticipated guilt and shame: The moderating role of gender. *Sex Roles, 83*, 763–772. https://doi.org/10.1007/s11199-020-01137-x

Giles, G. E., Brunyé, T. T., Eddy, M. D., Mahoney, C. R., Gagnon, S. A., Taylor, H. A., & Kanarek, R. B. (2014). Acute exercise increases oxygenated and deoxygenated hemoglobin in the prefrontal cortex. *Neuroreport, 25*, 1320–1325. https://doi.org/10.1097/WNR.0000000000000266

Gill, D. L., Hammond, C. C., Reifsteck, E. J., Jehu, C. M., Williams, R. A., Adams, M. M., Lange, E. H., Becofsky, K., Rodriguez, E., & Shang, Y. T. (2013). Physical activity and quality of life. *Journal of Preventive Medicine and Public Health, 46*(Suppl 1), S28–S34. https://doi.org/10.3961/jpmph.2013.46.S.S28

Gillet, N., Vallerand, R. J., Amoura, S., & Baldes, B. (2010). Influence of coaches' autonomy support on athletes' motivation and sport performance: A test of the hierarchical model of intrinsic and extrinsic motivation. *Psychology of Sport and Exercise, 11*(2), 155–161. https://doi.org/10.1016/j.psychsport.2009.10.004

Gino, F., & Pierce, L. (2009). Dishonesty in the name of equity. *Psychological Science, 20*, 1153–1160.

Glanz, K., & Bishop, D. B. (2010). The role of behavioral science theory in development and implementation of public health interventions. *Annual Review of Public Health, 31*, 399–418. https://doi.org/10.1146/annurev.publhealth.012809.103604

Gläscher, J., Hampton, A. N., & O'Doherty, J. P. (2009). Determining a role for ventromedial prefrontal cortex in encoding action-based value signals during reward-related decision making. Cerebral Cortex, *19*, 483–495. https://doi.org/10.1093/cercor/bhn098

Goldenberg, A., Saguy, T., & Halperin, E. (2014). How group-based emotions are shaped by collective emotions: Evidence for emotional transfer and emotional burden. *Journal of Personality and Social Psychology, 107*, 581. https://doi.org/10.1037/a0037462

Gollwitzer, P. (1996). The volitional benefits of planning. In P. M. Gollwitzer, & J. Bargh (Eds.), *The psychology of action: Linking cognition and motivation to behavior* (pp. 287–312). New York: Guilford Press.

Gollwitzer, P. M. (1990). Action phases and mind-sets. In E. T. Higgins & R. M. Sorrentino (Eds.), *Handbook of motivation and cognition: Foundations of social behavior*, (Vol. 2, pp. 53–92). New York: Guilford Press.

Gollwitzer, P. M. (1993). Goal achievement: The role of intentions. *European Review of Social Psychology, 4*(1), 141–185. https://doi.org/10.1080/14792779343000059

Gollwitzer, P. M. (1999). Implementation intentions: Strong effects of simple plans. *American Psychologist, 54*, 493–503. https://doi.org/10.1037/0003–066X.54.7.493

Gollwitzer, P. M. (2014). Weakness of the will: Is a quick fix possible? *Motivation and Emotion, 38*(3), 305–322. https://doi.org/10.1007/s11031-014-9416-3

Gollwitzer, P. M., & Sheeran, P. (2006). Implementation intentions and goal achievement: A meta-analysis of effects and processes. *Advances in Experimental Social Psychology, 38*, 69–119. https://doi.org/10.1016/S0065-2601(06)38002-1

Google Trends. (2020, March). Google Trends. https://trends.google.com/trends/explore?date=all&q=%22exercise%22

Gotwals, J. K. (2011). Perfectionism and burnout within intercollegiate sport: A person-oriented approach. *The Sport Psychologist, 25*(4), 489–510.

Gotwals, J. K. (2016). The tripartite model of perfectionism: Evidence from research in sport and dance. In A. P. Hill (Ed.), *The psychology of perfectionism in sport, dance and exercise* (pp. 166–189). London: Routledge.

Gotwals, J. K., Dunn, J. G., Dunn, J. C., & Gamache, V. (2010). Establishing validity evidence for the Sport Multidimensional Perfectionism Scale-2 in intercollegiate sport. *Psychology of Sport and Exercise, 11*, 423–432.

Gotwals, J. K., Stoeber, J., Dunn, J. G., & Stoll, O. (2012). Are perfectionistic strivings in sport adaptive? A systematic review of confirmatory, contradictory, and mixed evidence. *Canadian Psychology, 53*, 263.

Gould, D., Moffett, K., & Diefenbach, A. (2002). Psychological characteristics and their development in Olympic champions. *Journal of Applied Sport Psychology, 14*, 172–204. https://doi.org/10.1080/10413200290103482

Gourlan, M., Bernard, P., Bortolon, C., Romain, A. J., Lareyre, O., Carayol, M., Ninot, G., & Boiché, J. (2016). Efficacy of theory-based interventions to promote physical activity: A meta-analysis of randomised controlled trials. *Health Psychology Review, 10*(1), 50–66. https://doi.org/10.1080/17437199.2014.981777

Graham, J. D., & Bray, S. R. (2012). Imagery and endurance: Does imagery impair performance by depleting self-control strength? *Journal of Imagery Research in Sport and Physical Activity*, 7. https://doi.org/10.1515/1932-0191.1074

Graham, J. D., & Bray, S. R. (2015). Self-control strength depletion reduces self-efficacy and impairs exercise performance. *Journal of Sport and Exercise Psychology, 37*, 477–488. https://doi.org/10.1123/jsep.2015–0064

Graham, J. D., Bray, S. R., & Martin Ginis, K. A. (2014). 'Pay the piper': It helps initially, but motivation takes a toll on self-control. *Psychology of Sport and Exercise, 15*, 89–96. https://doi.org/10.1016/j.psychsport.2013.09.007

Graham, J. D., Li, Y. C., Bray, S. R., & Cairney, J. (2018). Effects of cognitive control exertion and motor coordination on task self-efficacy and muscular endurance performance in children. *Frontiers in Human Neuroscience, 12*, 379. https://doi.org/10.3389/fnhum.2018.00379

Graham, J. D., Martin Ginis, K. A., & Bray, S. R. (2017). Exertion of self-control increases fatigue, reduces task self-efficacy, and impairs performance of resistance exercise. *Sport, Exercise, and Performance Psychology, 6*, 70–88. https://doi.org/10.1016/j.peh.2019.100150

Graham, J. D., Sonne, M. W. L., & Bray, S. R. (2014). It wears me out just imagining it! Mental imagery leads to muscle fatigue and diminished performance of isometric exercise. *Biological Psychology, 103*, 1–6. https://doi.org/10.1016/j.biopsycho.2014.07.018

Grant, S., Juba, M., Quinlan, A., & Rhodes, R. E. (2018). *Understanding action control of physical activity among mothers with young children*. Paper presented at the Society of Behavioural Medicine Annual Meeting New Orleans, Louisiana.

Gray, J. A. (1994). Three fundamental emotion systems. In D. Ekman & R. Davidson (Eds.), *The nature of emotion: Fundamental questions* (pp. 243–247). New York: Oxford University Press.

Grayot, J. D. (2020). Dual process theories in behavioral economics and neuroeconomics: A critical review. *Review of Philosophy and Psychology, 11*, 105–136. https://doi.org/10.1007/s13164-019-00446-9

Greaves, C. J., Sheppard, K. E., Abraham, C., Hardeman, W., Roden, M., Evans, P. H., & Schwarz, P. (2011). Systematic review of reviews of intervention components associated with increased effectiveness in dietary and physical activity interventions. *BMC Public Health, 11*, 119.

Greenspon, T. S. (2000). "Healthy perfectionism" is an oxymoron!: Reflections on the psychology of perfectionism and the sociology of science. *Journal of Secondary Gifted Education, 11*, 197–208.

Greenspon, T. S. (2008). Making sense of error: A view of the origins and treatment of perfectionism. *American Journal of Psychotherapy, 62*, 263–282.

Grieser, M., Vu, M. B., Bedimo-Rung, A. L., Neumark-Sztainer, D., Moody, J., Young, D. R., & Moe, S. G. (2006). Physical activity attitudes, preferences, and practices in African American, Hispanic, and Caucasian girls. *Health Education and Behavior, 33*(1), 40–51. https://doi.org/10.1177/1090198105282416

Gross, J. J., & Thompson, R. A. (2007). Emotion regulation: Conceptual foundations. In J. J. Gross (Ed.), *Handbook of emotion regulation* (pp. 3–24). New York: Guilford Press.

Grugan, M. C., Jowett, G. E., Mallinson-Howard, S. H., & Hall, H. K. (2020). The relationships between perfectionism, angry reactions, and antisocial behavior in team sport. *Sport, Exercise, and Performance Psychology, 9*(4), 543–557. https://doi.org/10.1037/spy0000198

Gucciardi, D. F., Longbottom, J. L., Jackson, B., & Dimmock, J. A. (2010). Experienced golfers' perspectives on choking under pressure. *Journal of Sport and Exercise Psychology, 32*, 61–83. https://doi.org/10.1123/jsep.32.1.61

Gunnell, K. E., Crocker, P. R. E., Mack, D. E., Wilson, P. M., & Zumbo, B. D. (2014). Goal contents, motivation, psychological need satisfaction, well-being and physical activity: A test of self-determination theory over 6 months. *Psychology of Sport and Exercise, 15*(1), 19–29. https://doi.org/10.1016/j.psychsport.2013.08.005

Guo, Z., Ma, T., & Chen, F. (2019, March). Effects of grip-load force and muscle fatigue on fNIRS signal during handgrip voluntary contraction task. 9th International IEEE EMBS Conference on Neural Engineering, San Francisco, CA.

Gusella, J., Clark, S., & van Roosmalen, E. (2004). Body image self-evaluation colouring lens: Comparing the ornamental and instrumental views of adolescent girls with eating disorders. *European Eating Disorders Review, 12*(4), 223–229. https://doi.org/10.1002/erv.569

Gustafson, H., Hassmèn, H., Kenttä, G., & Johansson, M. (2008). A qualitative analysis of burnout in elite Swedish athletes. *Psychology of Sport and Exercise, 9*, 800–816. https://doi.org/10.1016/j.psychsport.2007.11.004

Guthold, R., Stevens, G. A., Riley, L. M., & Bull, F. C. (2018). Worldwide trends in insufficient physical activity from 2001 to 2016: A pooled analysis of 358 population-based surveys with 1.9 million participants. *Lancet Global Health, 6*(10), e1077–e1086. https://doi.org/10.1016/S2214-109X(18)30357-7

Hagger, M. S. (2010). Current issues and new directions in psychology and health: Physical activity research showcasing theory into practice. *Psychology & Health, 25*(1), 1–5. https://doi.org/10.1080/08870440903268637

Hagger, M. S. (2010). Self-regulation: An important construct in health psychology research and practice. *Health Psychology Review, 4*, 57–65. https://doi.org/10.1080/17437199.2010.503594

Hagger, M. S. (2014). The multiple pathways by which trait self-control predicts health behavior. *Annals of Behavioral Medicine, 48*, 282–283. https://doi.org/10.1007/s12160-014-9631-x

Hagger, M. S. (2019). Habit and physical activity: Theoretical advances, practical implications, and agenda for future research. *Psychology of Sport and Exercise, 42*, 118–129. https://doi.org/10.1016/j.psychsport.2018.12.007

Hagger, M. S. (2020). Redefining habits and linking habits with other implicit processes. *Psychology of Sport and Exercise, 46*, 101606. https://doi.org/10.1016/j.psychsport.2019.101606

Hagger, M. S., Cameron, L. D., Hamilton, K., Hankonen, N., & Lintunen, T. (2020b). *The handbook of behavior change*. New York: Cambridge University Press. https://doi.org/10.1017/9781108677318

Hagger, M. S., Cameron, L. D., Hamilton, K., Hankonen, N., & Lintunen, T. (2020c). Changing behavior: A theory- and evidence-based approach. In M. S. Hagger, L. D. Cameron, K. Hamilton, N. Hankonen & T. Lintunen (Eds.), *The handbook of behavior change* (pp. 1–14). New York: Cambridge University Press. https://doi.org/10.1017/97811086773180.001

Hagger, M. S., Cameron, L. D., Hamilton, K., Hankonen, N., & Lintunen, T. (2020d). The science of behavior change: The road ahead. In M. S. Hagger, L. D. Cameron, K. Hamilton, N. Hankonen & T. Lintunen (Eds.), *The handbook of behavior change* (pp. 677–699). New York: Cambridge University Press.

Hagger, M. S., Chatzisarantis, N., & Biddle, S. J. (2001). The influence of self-efficacy and past behaviour on the physical activity intentions of young people. *Journal of Sports Sciences, 19*(9), 711–725. https://doi.org/10.1080/02640410152475847

Hagger, M. S., & Chatzisarantis, N. L. (2014). An integrated behavior change model for physical activity. *Exercise and Sport Sciences Reviews, 42*(2), 62–69. https://doi.org/10.1249/JES.0000000000000008

Hagger, M. S., & Chatzisarantis, N. L. D. (Eds.). (2007). *Intrinsic motivation and self-determination in exercise and sport*. Champaign, IL: Human Kinetics.

Hagger, M. S., Chatzisarantis, N. L. D., Alberts, H., Anggono, C. O., Batailler, C., Birt, A. R., … & Zwienenberg, M. (2016). A multilab preregistered replication of the ego-depletion effect. *Perspectives on Psychological Science, 11*, 546–573. https://doi.org/10.1177/1745691616652873

Hagger, M. S., Chatzisarantis, N. L. D., & Biddle, S. J. H. (2002). A meta-analytic review of the theories of reasoned action and planned behavior in physical activity: Predictive validity and the contribution of additional variables. *Journal of Sport & Exercise Psychology, 24*(1), 3–32. https://doi.org/10.1123/jsep.24.1.3

Hagger, M. S., & Hamilton, K. (2020). General causality orientations in self-determination theory: Meta-analysis and test of a process model. https://doi.org/10.31234/osf.io/hbs3k

Hagger, M. S., Leaver, E., Esser, K., Leung, C.-M., Te Pas, N., Keatley, D. A., Chan, D. K.-C., & Chatzisarantis, N. L. D. (2013). Cue-induced smoking urges deplete cigarette smokers' self-control resources. *Annals of Behavioral Medicine, 46*, 394–400. https://doi.org/10.1007/s12160-013-9520-8

Hagger, M. S., Lonsdale, A. J., & Chatzisarantis, N. L. D. (2012). A theory-based intervention to reduce alcohol drinking in excess of guideline limits among undergraduate students. *British Journal of Health Psychology, 17*(1), 18–43. https://doi.org/10.1111/j.2044-8287.2010.02011.x

Hagger, M. S., & Luszczynska, A. (2014). Implementation intention and action planning interventions in health contexts: State of the research and proposals for the way forward. *Applied Psychology: Health and Well-Being, 6*(1), 1–47. https://doi.org/10.1111/aphw.12017

Hagger, M. S., Luszczynska, A., De Wit, J., Benyamini, Y., Burkert, S., Chamberland, P. E., ... & Gauchet, A. (2016). Implementation intention and planning interventions in health psychology: Recommendations from the synergy expert group for research and practice. *Psychology & Health, 31*(7), 814–839. https://doi.org/10.1080/08870446.2016.1146719

Hagger, M. S., Moyers, S., McAnally, K., & McKinley, L. E. (2020a). Known knowns and known unknowns on behavior change interventions and mechanisms of action. *Health Psychology Review, 14*(1), 199–212. https://doi org/10.1080/17437199.2020.1719184

Hagger M. S., & Weed, M. (2019). Debate: Do interventions based on behavioral theory work in the real world? *International Journal of Behavioral Nutrition and Physical Activity, 16*(1), 36. https://doi.org/10.1186/s12966-019-0795-4

Hagger M. S., & Weed, M. E. (2019). DEBATE: Do behavioral interventions work in the real world? *International Journal of Behavioral Nutrition and Physical Activity, 16*(1), 36. https://doi.org/10.1186/s12966-019-0795-4

Hagger, M. S., Wood, C., Stiff, C., & Chatzisarantis, N. L. (2009). The strength model of self-regulation failure and health-related behaviour. *Health Psychology Review, 3*, 208–238. https://doi.org/10.1080/17437190903414387

Hagger, M. S., Wood, C. W., Stiff, C., & Chatzisarantis, N. L. (2010a). Self-regulation and self-control in exercise: The strength-energy model. *International Review of Sport and Exercise Psychology, 3*, 62–86. https://doi.org/10.1080/17509840903322815

Hagger, M. S., Wood, C. W., Stiff, C., & Chatzisarantis, N. L. (2010b). Ego depletion and the strength model of self-control: A meta-analysis. *Psychological Bulletin, 136*, 495–525. https://doi.org/10.1037/a0019486

Hall, H K. (2006). Perfectionism: A hallmark quality of world class performers, or a psychological impediment to athletic development? In D. Hackfort, & G. Tenenbaum (Eds.), *Perspectives in sport and exercise psychology. Essential processes for attaining peak performance* (Vol. 1, pp. 178–211). Oxford: Meyer & Meyer Publishers.

Hall, H K., Hill, A. P., & Appleton, P. R. (2012). Perfectionism: A foundation for sporting excellence or an uneasy pathway toward purgatory? In R. C. Roberts & D. Treasure (Eds.), *Advances in motivation in sport and exercise* (pp. 129–168). Champaign, IL: Human Kinetics Publishers. ISBN-13: 978–0736090810

Hall, P. A., Zehr, C., Paulitzki, J., & Rhodes, R. (2014). Implementation intentions for physical activity behavior in older adult women: An examination of executive function as a moderator of treatment effects. *Annals of Behavioral Medicine, 48*(1), 130–136. https://doi.org/10.1007/s12160-013-9582-7

Hallal, P. C., Andersen, L. B., Bull, F. C., Guthold, R., Haskell, W., & Ekelund, U. (2012). Global physical activity levels: Surveillance progress, pitfalls, and prospects. *Lancet, 380*(9838), 247–257. https //doi.org/10.1016/S0140-6736(12)60646-1

Hallam, J. S., & Petosa, R. (2004). The long-term impact of a four-session work-site intervention on selected social cognitive theory variables linked to adult exercise adherence. *Health Education & Behavior, 31*(1), 88–100.

Halson, S. L., & Juliff, L. E. (2017). Sleep, sport, and the brain. *Progress in Brain Research, 234*, 13–31. https://doi.org/10.1016/bs.pbr.2017.06.006

Hamilton, K., & Schwarzer, R. (2018). Making plans to facilitate young children's physical activity: The role of psycho-social mediators and moderators. *Journal of Child and Family Studies, 27,* 421–430. https://doi.org/10.1007/s10826-017-0893-3

Hamlyn-Williams, C. C., Tempest, G., Coombs, S., & Parfitt, G. (2015). Can previously sedentary females use the feeling scale to regulate exercise intensity in a gym environment? An observational study. *BMC Sports Science, Medicine, & Rehabilitation,* 7, 30.

Hampson, D. B., St Clair Gibson, A., Lambert, M. I., & Noakes, T. D. (2001). The influence of sensory cues on the perception of exertion during exercise and central regulation of exercise performance. *Sports Medicine, 31*(13), 935–952. https://doi.org/10.2165/00007256-200131130-00004

Hardcastle, S. J., Hancox, J., Hattar, A., Maxwell-Smith, C., Thogersen-Ntoumani, C., & Hagger, M. S. (2015). Motivating the unmotivated: How can health behaviour be changed in those unwilling to change? *Frontiers in Psychology, 6,* 835. https://doi.org/10.3389/fpsyg.2015.00835

Hardeman, W., Johnston, M., Johnston, D., Bonetti, D., Wareham, N., & Kinmonth, A. L. (2002). Application of the theory of planned behaviour in behaviour change interventions: A systematic review. *Psychology and Health, 17*(2), 123–158. https://doi.org/10.1080/08870440290013644a

Hargreaves, E. A., & Stych, K. (2013). Exploring the peak and end rule of past affective episodes within the exercise context. *Psychology of Sport and Exercise, 14,* 169–178.

Harmon-Jones, E., & Mills, J. (2019). An introduction to cognitive dissonance theory and an overview of current perspectives on the theory. In E. Harmon-Jones (Ed.), *Cognitive dissonance: Reexamining a pivotal theory in psychology* (pp. 3–24). Washington, DC: American Psychological Association. https://doi.org/10.1037/0000135-001

Harris, C. D., Watson, K. B., Carlson, S. A., Fulton, J. E., Dorn, J. M., & Elam-Evans, L. (2013). Adult participation in aerobic and muscle-strengthening physical activities – United States, 2011. *Morbidity and Mortality Weekly Report, 62*(17), 326.

Harris, S., & Bray, S. R. (2019). Effects of mental fatigue on exercise decision-making. *Psychology of Sport and Exercise, 44,* 1–8. https://doi.org/10.1016/j.psychsport.2019.04.005

Hart, E., Leary, M. R., & Rejeski, J. W. (1989). The measurement of social physique anxiety. *Journal of Sport & Exercise Psychology, 11,* 94–104.

Haslam, N., Holland, E., & Kuppens, P. (2012). Categories versus dimensions in personality and psychopathology: A quantitative review of taxometric research. *Psychological Medicine, 42*(5), 903–920.

Hathaway, E. D., & Fedewa, M. V. (2017). Role of behavioral economics in understanding and working with clients. *ACSM's Health & Fitness Journal, 21*(5), 16–20.

Haugaasen, M., & Jordet, G. (2012). Developing football expertise: A football-specific research review. *International Review of Sport and Exercise Psychology, 5,* 177–201. https://doi.org/10.1080/1750984X.2012.677951

Hausenblas, H. A., Carron, A. V., & Mack, D. E. (1997). Application of the theories of reasoned action and planned behavior to exercise behavior: A meta-analysis. *Journal of Sport & Exercise Psychology, 19(1),* 36–51.

Hausenblas, H. A., Nigg, C. R., Dannecker, E. A., Downs, D. S., Gardner, R. E., Fallon, E. A., ... & Loving, M. G. (2001). A missing piece of the transtheoretical model applied to exercise: Development and validation of the temptation to not exercise scale. *Psychology and Health, 16*(4), 381–390. https://doi.org/10.1080/08870440108405514

Hayes, A. F. (2017). *Introduction to mediation, moderation, and conditional process analysis, second edition: A regression-based approach.* New York: Guilford Publications.

Head, J. R., Tenan, M. S., Tweedell, A. J., LaFiandra, M. E., Morelli, F., Wilson, K. M., Ortega, S. V., & Helton, W. S. (2017). Prior mental fatigue impairs marksmanship decision performance. *Frontiers in Physiology,* 8. https://doi.org/10.3389/fphys.2017.00680

Head, J. R., Tenan, M. S., Tweedell, A. J., Price, T. F., LaFiandra, M. E., & Helton, W. S. (2016). Cognitive fatigue influences time-on-task during bodyweight resistance training exercise. *Frontiers in Physiology,* 7. https://doi.org/10.3389/fphys.2016.00373

Heath, G. W., Parra, D. C., Sarmiento, O. L., Andersen, L. B., Owen, N., Goenka, S., ... & Lancet Physical Activity Series Working Group. (2012). Evidence-based intervention in physical activity: Lessons from around the world. *The Lancet, 380*(9838), 272–281. https://doi.org/10.1016/S0140-6736(12)60816-2

Heatherton, T. F. (2011). Neuroscience of self and self-regulation. *Annual Review of Psychology, 62*, 363–390. https://doi.org/10.1146/annurev.psych.121208.131616

Heckhausen, H., & Gollwitzer, P. M. (1987). Thought contents and cognitive functioning in motivational versus volitional states of mind. *Motivation and Emotion, 11*(2), 101–120. https://doi.org/10.1007/BF00992338

Heckhausen, H., Gollwitzer, P. M., & Weinert, F. E. (1987). *Beyond the Rubicon: The will in the human sciences*. Heidelberg: Springer.

Heckhausen, J. (2007). The motivation-volition divide and its resolution in action-phase models of developmental regulation. *Research in Human Development, 4*, 163–180.

Heilbronner, S. R., & Hayden, B. Y. (2016). Dorsal anterior cingulate cortex: A bottom-up view. *Annual Review of Neuroscience, 39*, 149–170. https://doi.org/10.1146/annurev-neuro-070815-013952

Helfer, S. G., Elhai, J. D., & Geers, A. L. (2015). Affect and exercise: Positive affective expectations can increase post-exercise mood and exercise intentions. *Annals of Behavioral Medicine, 49*(2), 269–279.

Helson, H. (1933). The fundamental propositions of Gestalt psychology. *Psychological Review, 40*(1), 13.

Hennessy, E. A., Johnson, B. T., Acabchuk, R. L., McCloskey, K., & Stewart-James, J. (2019). Self-regulation mechanisms in health behaviour change: A systematic meta-review of meta-analyses, 2006–2017. *Health Psychology Review, 14*(1), 6–42. https://doi.org/10.1080/17437199.2019.1679654

Herold, F., Wiegel, P., Scholkmann, F., & Müller, N. G. (2018). Applications of functional near-infrared spectroscopy (fNIRS) neuroimaging in exercise-cognition science: A systematic, methodology-focused review. *Journal of Clinical Medicine*, 7(12), 466. https://doi.org/10.3390/jcm7120466

Hewitt, P. L., & Flett, G. L. (1991). Perfectionism in the self and social contexts: Conceptualization, assessment, and association with psychopathology. *Journal of Personality and Social Psychology, 60*(3), 456–470.

Higgins, E. T., Horwitz, E. K., Horwitz, M. B., Cope, J., Horwitz, E. K., Horwitz, M. B., & Cope, J. (1987). Self-discrepancy: A theory relating self and affect. *Psychological Review, 94*(3), 319–340. https://doi.org/10.1037/0033-295X.94.3.319

Hill, A. P. (2013). Perfectionism and burnout in junior soccer players: A test of the 2× 2 model of dispositional perfectionism. *Journal of Sport and Exercise Psychology, 35*(1), 18–29.

Hill, A. P. (2014). Perfectionistic strivings and the perils of partialling. *International Journal of Sport and Exercise Psychology, 12*, 302–315.

Hill, A. P. (2016). Conceptualizing perfectionism: An overview and unresolved issues. In A. P. Hill (Ed.), *The psychology of perfectionism in sport, dance and exercise* (pp. 19–46). London: Routledge.

Hill, A. P. (2017). Real and imagined perils: A reply to Stoeber and Gaudreau (2017). *Personality and Individual Differences, 108*, 220–224.

Hill, A. P., & Curran, T. (2016). Multidimensional perfectionism and burnout: A meta-analysis. *Personality and Social Psychology Review, 20*(3), 269–288.

Hill, A. P., & Grugan, M. (2019). Introducing perfectionistic climate. *Perspectives in Early Childhood Psychology and Education, 4*, 263–275.

Hill, A. P., Hall, H. K., & Appleton, P. R. (2010). A comparative examination of the correlates of self-oriented perfectionism and conscientious achievement striving in male cricket academy players. *Psychology of Sport and Exercise, 11*(2), 162–168.

Hill, A. P., Hall, H. K., & Appleton, P. R. (2011). The relationship between multidimensional perfectionism and contingencies of self-worth. *Personality and Individual Differences, 50*(2), 238–242.

Hill, A. P., Hall, H. K., Duda, J. L., & Appleton, P. R. (2011). The cognitive, affective and behavioural responses of self-oriented perfectionists following successive failure on a muscular endurance task. *International Journal of Sport and Exercise Psychology, 9*(2), 189–207. https://doi.org/10.1080/1612197X.2011.567108

Hill, A. P., & Madigan, D. J. (2017). A short review of perfectionism in sport, dance and exercise: Out with the old, in with the 2× 2. *Current Opinion in Psychology, 16*, 72–77.

Hill, A. P., Madigan, D, J., Smith, M. M., Mallinson-Howard, S. H., & Donachie, T. C. Perfectionism in sport. To appear in R. J. Schinke & D. Hackfort (Eds.), *Encyclopaedia of sport psychology.* Accepted November 15, 2019.

Hill, A. P., Mallinson-Howard, S. H., & Jowett, G. E. (2018). Multidimensional perfectionism in sport: A meta-analytical review. *Sport, Exercise, and Performance Psychology*, 7(3), 235.

Hill, A. P., Robson, S. J., & Stamp, G. M. (2015). The predictive ability of perfectionistic traits and self-presentational styles in relation to exercise dependence. *Personality and Individual Differences, 86*, 176–183.

Hill, A. P., Stoeber, J., Brown, A., & Appleton, P. R. (2014). Team perfectionism and team performance: A prospective study. *Journal of Sport and Exercise Psychology, 36*(3), 303–315.

Hill, A. P., Witcher, C. S., Gotwals, J. K., & Leyland, A. F. (2015). A qualitative study of perfectionism among self-identified perfectionists in sport and the performing arts. *Sport, Exercise, and Performance Psychology, 4*(4), 237.

Hill, D. M., Hanton, S., Matthews, N., & Fleming, S. (2010). Choking in sport: A review. *International Review of Sport and Exercise Psychology, 3*, 24–39. https://doi.org/10.1080/17509840903301199.

Hindmarch I. (2014) Psychomotor performance in humans. In I. Stolerman & L. Price (Eds.), *Encyclopedia of psychopharmacology.* Berlin, Heidelberg: Springer. https://doi.org/10.1007/978-3-642-27772-6_181-2

Hodgins, H. S. (2008). Motivation, threshold for threat, and quieting the ego. In H. A. Wayment & J. J. Bauer (Eds.), *Transcending self-interest: Psychological explorations of the quiet ego* (pp. 117–124). Washington, WA: American Psychological Association.

Hodgins, H. S., & Knee, C. R. (2002). The integrating self and conscious experience. In E. L. Deci & R. M. Ryan (Eds.), *Handbook of self-determination research* (pp. 87–100). Rochester, NY: University of Rochester Press.

Hodgins, H. S., & Liebeskind, E. (2003). Apology versus defense: Antecedents and consequences. *Journal of Experimental Social Psychology, 39*(4), 297–316. https://doi.org/10.1016/S0022-1031(03)00024-6

Hofmann, W., Baumeister, R. F., Förster, G., & Vohs, K. D. (2012). Everyday temptations: An experience sampling study of desire, conflict, and self-control. *Journal of Personality and Social Psychology, 102*(6), 1318–1335. https://doi.org/10.1037/a0026545

Hofmann, W., Deutsch, R., Lancaster, K., & Banaji, M. R. (2010). Cooling the heat of temptation: Mental self-control and the automatic evaluation of tempting stimuli. *European Journal of Social Psychology, 40*(1), 17–25.

Hofmann, W., Friese, M., & Wiers, R. W. (2008). Impulsive versus reflective influences on health behavior: A theoretical framework and empirical review. *Health Psychology Review, 2*(2), 111–137. https://doi.org/10.1080/17437190802617668

Hofmann, W., & Van Dillen, L. (2012). Desire: The new hot spot in self-control research. *Current Directions in Psychological Science, 21*(5), 317–322. https://doi.org/10.1177/0963721412453587

Hofmann, W., Vohs, K. D., & Baumeister, R. F. (2012). What people desire, feel conflicted about, and try to resist in everyday life. *Psychological Science, 23*, 582–588. https://doi.org/10.1177/0956797612437426

Hogarth, L., Balleine, B. W., Corbit, L. H., & Killcross, S. (2013). Associative learning mechanisms underpinning the transition from recreational drug use to addiction. *Annals of the New York Academy of Sciences, 1282*, 12–24. https://doi.org/10.1111/j.1749-6632.2012.06768.x

Holbrook, C., Piazza, J. R., & Fessler, D. M. T. (2014). Further challenges to the "Authentic"/"Hubristic" model of pride: Conceptual clarifications and new evidence. *Emotion, 14*(1), 38–42. https://doi.org/10.1037/a0035457

Holgado, D., Troya, E., Perales, J. C., Vadillo, M. A., & Sanabria, D. (2019). Does mental fatigue impair physical performance? A replication study. https://doi.org/10.31236/osf.io/tzn6d

Holgado, D., Zabala, M., & Sanabria, D. (2019). No evidence of the effect of cognitive load on self-paced cycling performance. *PLOS ONE, 14*, e0217825. https://doi.org/10.1371/journal.pone.0217825

Holroyd, C. B., & Coles, M. G. H. (2002). The neural basis of human error processing: Reinforcement learning, dopamine, and the error-related negativity. *Psychological Review, 109*(4), 679–709. https://doi.org/10.1037/0033-295X.109.4.679

Holroyd, C. B., & Yeung, N. (2012). Motivation of extended behaviors by anterior cingulate cortex. *Trends in Cognitive Sciences, 16*, 122–128. https://doi.org/10.1016/j.tics.2011.12.008

Homan, K. J., & Tylka, T. L. (2014). Appearance-based exercise motivation moderates the relationship between exercise frequency and positive body image. *Body Image, 11*, 101–108. https://doi.org/10.1016/j.bodyim.2014.01.003

Hopstaken, J. F., Van Der Linden, D., Bakker, A. B., & Kompier, M. A. (2015). A multifaceted investigation of the link between mental fatigue and task disengagement. *Psychophysiology, 52*, 305–315. https://doi.org/10.1111/psyp.12339

Horstman, D. H., Morgan, W. P., Cymerman, A., & Stokes, J. (1979). Perception of effort during constant work to self-imposed exhaustion. *Perceptual and Motor Skills, 48*, 1111–1126. https://doi.org/10.2466/pms.1979.48.3c.1111

Hosking, J. G., Cocker, P. J., & Winstanley, C. A. (2016). Prefrontal cortical inactivations decrease willingness to expend cognitive effort on a rodent cost/benefit decision-making task. *Cerebral Cortex, 26*, 1529–1538. https://doi.org/10.1093/cercor/bhu321

Howlett, N., Trivedi, D., Troop, N. A., & Chater, A. M. (2019). Are physical activity interventions for healthy inactive adults effective in promoting behavior change and maintenance, and which behavior change techniques are effective? A systematic review and meta-analysis. *Translational Behavioral Medicine, 9*(1), 147–157. https://doi.org/10.1093/tbm/iby010

Hull, C. L. (1943). *Principles of behavior.* New York: Appleton-Century-Crofts.

Hurling, R., Catt, M., De Boni, M., Fairley, B., Hurst, T., Murray, P., … & Sodhi, J. (2007). Using internet and mobile phone technology to deliver an automated physical activity program: Randomized controlled trial. *Journal of Medical Internet Research, 9*(2), e7. https://doi.org/10.2196/jmir 9.2.e7

Husband, C., Wharf Higgins, J., & Rhodes, R. E. (2019). A feasibility randomized trial of an identity-based physical activity intervention among university students. *Journal of Health Psychology and Behavioral Medicine*, 7, 128–146.

Hutchinson, J. C., Jones, L., Vitti, S. N., Moore, A., Dalton, P. C., & O'Neil, B. J. (2018). The influence of self-selected music on affect-regulated exercise intensity and remembered pleasure during treadmill running. *Sport, Exercise, and Performance Psychology*, 7, 80–92.

Hutchinson, J. C., & O'Neil, B. J. (2020). Effects of respite music during recovery between bouts of intense exercise. *Sport, Exercise, and Performance Psychology, 9*, 102–114.

Hutchinson, J. C., & Tenenbaum, G. (2007). Attention focus during physical effort: The mediating role of task intensity. *Psychology of Sport and Exercise, 8*(2), 233–245. https://doi.org/10.1016/j.psychsport.2006.03.006

Hutchinson, J. C., Zenko, Z., Santich, S., & Dalton, P. C. (2020). Increasing the pleasure and enjoyment of exercise: A novel resistance training protocol. *Journal of Sport and Exercise Psychology, 42*(2), 143–152.

Hyde, A. L., Doerksen, S. E., Ribeiro, N. F., & Conroy, D. E. (2010). The independence of implicit and explicit attitudes toward physical activity: Introspective access and attitudinal concordance. *Psychology of Sport and Exercise, 11*, 387–393.

Hyde, A. L., Elavsky, S., Doerksen, S. E., & Conroy, D. E. (2012). The stability of automatic evaluations of physical activity and their relations with physical activity. *Journal of Sport and Exercise Psychology, 34*, 715–736.

Hyland-Monks, R., Cronin, L., McNaughton, L., & Marchant, D. (2018). The role of executive function in the self-regulation of endurance performance: a critical review. *Progress in Brain Research, 240*, 353–370. https://doi.org/10.1016/bs.pbr.2018.09.011

Ingledew, D. K., & Markland, D. (2008). The role of motives in exercise participation. *Psychology and Health, 23*(7), 807–828. https://doi.org/10.1080/08870440701405704

Inzlicht, M., Bartholow, B. D., & Hirsh, J. B. (2015). Emotional foundations of cognitive control. *Trends in Cognitive Sciences, 19*(3), 126–132. https://doi.org/10.1016/j.tics.2015.01.004

Inzlicht, M., & Berkman, E. (2015). Six questions for the resource model of control (and some answers). *Social and Personality Psychology Compass, 9*, 511–524. https://doi.org/10.1111/spc3.12200

Inzlicht, M., & Friese, M. (2019). The past, present, and future of ego depletion. *Social Psychology, 50*, 370–378. https://doi.org/10.1027/1864-9335/a000398

Inzlicht, M., & Gutsell, J. N. (2007). Running on empty: Neural signals for self-control failure. *Psychological Science, 18*, 933–937. https://doi.org/10.1111/j.1467–9280.2007.02004.x

Inzlicht, M., & Legault, L. (2014). No pain, no gain: How distress underlies effective self-control (and unites diverse social psychological phenomena). In J. P. Forgas & E. Harmon-Jones (Eds.), *Sydney symposium of social psychology. Motivation and its regulation: The control within* (pp. 115–132). New York: Psychology Press.

Inzlicht, M., & Marcora, S. M. (2016). The central governor model of exercise regulation teaches us precious little about the nature of mental fatigue and self-control failure. *Frontiers in Psychology, 7*, 656. https://doi.org/10.3389/fpsyg.2016.00656

Inzlicht, M., & Schmeichel, B. J. (2012). What is ego depletion? Toward a mechanistic revision of the resource model of self-control. *Perspectives on Psychological Science, 7*, 450–463. https://doi.org/10.1177/1745691612454134.

Inzlicht, M., Schmeichel, B. J., & Macrae, C. N. (2014). Why self-control seems (but may not be) limited. *Trends in Cognitive Sciences, 18*, 127–133. https://doi.org/10.1016/j.tics.2013.12.009

Inzlicht, M., Shenhav, A., & Olivola, C. Y. (2018). The effort paradox: Effort is both costly and valued. *Trends in Cognitive Sciences, 22*, 337–349. https://doi.org/10.1016/j.tics.2018.01.007

Inzlicht, M., Werner, K. M., Briskin, J. L., & Roberts, B. (2021). Integrating models of self-regulation. *Annual Review of Psychology. Annual Review of Psychology, 72*, 319–345. https://doi.org/10.1146/annurev-psych-061020-105721

Jacoby, L. L., Kelley, C. M., & McElree, B. D. (1999). The role of cognitive control: Early selection versus late correction. In S. Chaiken & Y. Trope (Eds.), *Dual-process theories in social psychology* (pp. 383–400). New York: Guilford Press.

Jaeggi, S. M., Buschkuehl, M., Jonides, J., & Perrig, W. J. (2008). Improving fluid intelligence with training on working memory. *Proceedings of the National Academy of Sciences of the United States of America, 105*, 6829–6833. https://doi.org/10.1073/pnas.0801268105.

James, W. (1892/1963). *Psychology*. Greenwich, CT: Fawcett. (Original work published 1892)

Jaworski, R. L., Jensen, A., Niederberger, B., Congalton, R., & Kelly, K. R. (2015). Changes in combat task performance under increasing loads in active duty marines. *Military Medicine, 180*(3 Suppl), 179–186. https://doi.org/10.7205/MILMED-D-14-00432

Jeukendrup, A. E., Hopkins, S., Aragón-Vargas, L. F., & Hulston, C. (2008). No effect of carbohydrate feeding on 16 km cycling time trial performance. *European Journal of Applied Physiology, 104*(5), 831–837. https://doi.org/10.1007/s00421-008-0838-z

Job, V., Dweck, C. S., & Walton, G. M. (2010). Ego-depletion: Is it all in your head? Implicit theories about willpower affect self-regulation. *Psychological Science, 21*, 1686–1693. https://doi.org/10.1177/0956797610384745

Job, V., Walton, G. M., Bernecker, K., & Dweck, C. S. (2013). Beliefs about willpower determine the impact of glucose on self-control. *Proceedings of the National Academy of Sciences, 110*, 14837–14842. https://doi.org/10.1073/pnas.1313475110

Job, V., Walton, G. M., Bernecker, K., & Dweck, C. S. (2015). Implicit theories about willpower predict self-regulation and grades in everyday life. *Journal of Personality and Social Psychology, 108*(4), 637–647. https://doi.org/10.1037/pspp0000014

Joyner, M. J. (2016). Fatigue: Where did we come from and how did we get here? *Medicine and Science in Sports and Exercise, 48*, 2224–2227. https://doi.org/10.1249/MSS.0000000000000938

Jõesaar, H., Hein, V., & Hagger, M. S. (2011). Peer influence on young athletes' need satisfaction, intrinsic motivation and persistence in sport: A 12-month prospective study. *Psychology of Sport and Exercise, 12*(5), 500–508. https://doi.org/10.1016/j.psychsport.2011.04.005

Johnson, B. T., & Acabchuk, R. L. (2018). What are the keys to a longer, happier life? Answers from five decades of health psychology research. *Social Science & Medicine, 196*, 218–226. https://doi.org/10.1016/j.socscimed.2017.11.001

Johnson, E. J., & Goldstein, D. G. (2013). Decisions by default. In E. Shafir (Ed.), *The behavioral foundations of public policy* (pp. 417–427). Princeton, NJ: Princeton University Press.

Johnson, E. J., & Ratcliff, R. (2014). Computational and process models of decision making in psychology and behavioral economic. In P. W. Glimcher & E. Fehr (Eds.), *Neuroeconomics: Decision making and the brain* (2nd edition, pp. 35–47). Cambridge, MA: Elsevier. https://doi.org/10.1016/B978-0-12-416008-8.00003-6

Jowett, G. E., Hill, A. P., Forsdyke, D., & Gledhill, A. (2018). Perfectionism and coping with injury in marathon runners: A test of the 2× 2 model of perfectionism. *Psychology of Sport and Exercise, 37*, 26–32.

Jowett, G. E., Hill, A. P., Hall, H. K., & Curran, T. (2013). Perfectionism and junior athlete burnout: The mediating role of autonomous and controlled motivation. *Sport, Exercise, and Performance Psychology, 2*(1), 48–61. https://doi.org/10.1037/a0029770

Jung, M. E., Locke, S. R., Bourne, J. E., Beauchamp, M. R., Lee, T., Singer, J., MacPherson, M., Barry, J., Jones, C., & Little, J. P. (2020). Cardiorespiratory fitness and accelerometer-determined physical activity following one year of free-living high-intensity interval training and moderate-intensity continuous training: A randomized trial. *International Journal of Behavioral Nutrition and Physical Activity, 17*(1), 25. https://doi.org/10.1186/s12966-020-00933-8

Kagawa, M., Kuroiwa, C., Uenishi, K., Mori, M., Dhaliwal, S., Hills, A., & Bins, C. W. B. (2007). A comparison of body perceptions in relation to measured body composition in young Japanese males and females. *Body Image, 4*, 372–380. https://doi.org/10.1016/j.bodyim.2007.06.002

Kahn, E. B., Ramsey, L. T., Brownson, R. C., Heath, G. W., Howze, E. H., Powell, K. E., ... & Corso, P. (2002). The effectiveness of interventions to increase physical activity: A systematic review. *American Journal of Preventive Medicine, 22*(4), 73–107. https://doi.org/10.1016/S0749-3797(02)00434-8

Kahneman, D. (2003a). A perspective on judgment and choice: Mapping bounded rationality. *American Psychologist, 58*(9), 697–720. https://doi.org/10.1037/0003066X.58.9.697

Kahneman, D. (2003b). Maps of bounded rationality: Psychology for behavioral economics. *The American Economic Review, 93*(5), 1449–1475.

Kahneman, D. (2011). *Thinking, fast and slow*. New York: Farrar, Straus and Giroux.

Kahneman, D., Fredrickson, B. L., Schreiber, C. A., & Redelmeier, D. A. (1993). When more pain is preferred to less: Adding a better end. *Psychological Science, 4*(6), 401–405.

Kahneman, D., Ritov, I., & Schkade, D. (1999). Economic preferences or attitude expressions? An analysis of dollar responses to public issues. *Journal of Risk and Uncertainty, 19*(1–3), 220–242. https://doi.org/10.1023/A:1007835629236

Kahneman, D., & Tversky, A. (1979). Prospect theory: An analysis of decision under risk. *Econometrica, 47*(2), 263–292.

Kahneman, D., & Tversky, A (1992). Advances in prospect theory: Cumulative representation of uncertainty. *Journal of Risk and Uncertainty, 5*, 297–323.

Kahneman, D., Wakker, P. P., & Sarin, R. (1997). Back to Bentham? Explorations of experienced utility. *The Quarterly Journal of Economics, 112*(2), 375–406.

Kamon, E., Pandolf, K., & Cafarelli, E. (1974). The relationship between perceptual information and physiological responses to exercise in the heat. *Journal of Human Ergology, 3*(1), 45–54.

Karoly, P. (1992). Mechanisms of self-regulation: A systems view. *Annual Review of Psychology, 44*, 23–52.

Kaushal, N., & Rhodes, R. E. (2014). The home physical environment and its relationship with physical activity and sedentary behavior: A systematic review. *Preventive Medicine, 67*, 221–237.

Kaushal, N., & Rhodes, R. E. (2015). Exercise habit in new gym members: A longitudinal study. *Journal of Behavioral Medicine, 38*, 652–663.

Kaushal N., Rhodes, R. E., Meldrum, J., & Spence, J. C. (2017). The role of habit in different phases of exercise. *British Journal of Health Psychology, 22*, 429–448.

Kaushal, N., Rhodes, R. E., Spence, J., & Meldrum, J. (2017). Increasing physical activity through principles of habit formation in new gym members: A randomized-controlled trial. *Annals of Behavioral Medicine, 51*, 578–586.

Kavanagh, D. J., Andrade, J., & May, J. (2005). Imaginary relish and exquisite torture: The elaborated intrusion theory of desire. *Psychological Review, 112*(2), 446–467. https://doi.org/10.1037/0033-295X.112.2.446

Kearns, H., Forbes, A., Gardiner, M., & Marshall, K. (2008). When a high distinction isn't good enough: A review of perfectionism and self-handicapping. *Australian Educational Researcher, 35*(3), 21–36.

Keer, M., Conner, M., Van den Putte, B., & Neijens, P. (2013). The temporal stability and predictive validity of affect-based and cognition-based intentions. *British Journal of Social Psychology*, 1–13.

Kehayes, I. L. L., Smith, M. M., Sherry, S. B., Vidovic, V., & Saklofske, D. H. (2019). Are perfectionism dimensions risk factors for bulimic symptoms? A meta-analysis of longitudinal studies. *Personality and Individual Differences, 138*, 117–125.

Keller, J., Fleig, L., Hohl, D. H., Wiedemann, A. U., Burkert, S., Luszczynska, A., & Knoll, N. (2017). Which characteristics of planning matter? Individual and dyadic physical activity plans and their effects on plan enactment. *Social Science & Medicine, 189*, 53–62. https://doi.org/10.1016/j.socscimed.2017.07.025

Keller, L., Gollwitzer, P., & Sheeran, P. (2020). Changing behavior using the model of action phases. In M. S. Hagger, L. D. Cameron, K. Hamilton, N. Hankonen & T. Lintunen (Eds.), *The handbook of behavior change* (pp. 77–88). New York: Cambridge University Press. https://doi.org/10.1017/97811086773180.006

Kellmann, M., Bertollo, M., Bosquet, L., Brink, M., Coutts, A. J., Duffield, R., … & Kallus, K. W. (2018). Recovery and performance in sport: Consensus statement. *International Journal of Sports Physiology and Performance, 13*, 240–245. https://doi.org/10.1123/ijspp.2017-0759

Keltner, D., & Buswell, B. N. (1997). Embarrassment: Its distinct form and appeasement functions. *Psychological Bulletin, 122*(3), 250–270. https://doi.org/10.1037/0033-2909.122.3.250

Kendzierski, D., Furr, R. M., & Schiavoni, J. (1998). Physical activity self-definitions: Correlates and perceived criteria. *Journal of Sport & Exercise Psychology, 20*, 176–193.

Kendzierski, D., & Morganstein, M. S. (2009). Test, revision, and cross-validation of the physical activity self-definition model. *Journal of Sport & Exercise Psychology, 31*, 484–504. https://doi.org/10.1123/jsep.31.4.484

Keren, G., & Schul, Y. (2009). Two is not always better than one: A critical evaluation of two-system theories. *Perspectives on Psychological Science, 4*(6), 533–550. https://doi.org/10.1111/j.1745-6924.2009.01164.x

Kerns, J. G. (2004). Anterior cingulate conflict monitoring and adjustments in control. *Science, 303*, 1023–1026. https://doi.org/10.1126/science.1089910

Keville, G. (2015, January 7). "The more difficult the victory, the greater the happiness in winning" -25 inspirational sports quotes. Independent. Retrieved March 24, 2020, from https://www.independent.ie/sport/other-sports/the-more-difficult-the-victory-the-greater-the-happiness-in-winning-25-inspirational-sports-quotes-30889900.html

Kim, J., Dunn, E., Rellinger, K., Robertson-Wilson, J., & Eyes, M. (2017). Social norms and physical activity in American and Canadian contexts: A scoping review. *International Review of Sport and Exercise Psychology, 12*(1), 26–48.

Kim, K., & Johnson, M. K. (2015). Activity in ventromedial prefrontal cortex during self-related processing: positive subjective value or personal significance? *Social Cognitive and Affective Neuroscience, 10*(4), 494–500. https://doi.org/10.1093/scan/nsu078

Kimm, S. Y., Glynn, N. W., Kriska, A. M., Fitzgerald, S. L., Aaron, D. J., Similo, S. L., McMahon, R. P., & Barton, B. A. (2000). Longitudinal changes in physical activity in a biracial cohort during adolescence. *Medicine and Science in Sports and Exercise, 32*, 1445–1454.

Kishi, M., Sadachi, H., Nakamura, J., & Tonoike, M. (2017). Functional magnetic resonance imaging investigation of brain regions associated with astringency. *Neuroscience Research, 122*, 9–16. https://doi.org/10.1016/j.neures.2017.03.009

Klein, S. B., & Lax, M. L. (2010). The unanticipated resilience of trait self-knowledge in the face of neural damage. *Memory, 18*(8), 918–948. https://doi.org/10.1080/09658211.2010.524651

Knoll, N., Hohl, D. H., Keller, J., Schuez, N., Luszczynska, A., & Burkert, S. (2017). Effects of dyadic planning on physical activity in couples: A randomized controlled trial. *Health Psychology, 36*(1), 8–20. https://doi.org/10.1037/hea0000423

Kohl, H. W., Craig, C. L., Lambert, E. V., Inoue, S., Alkandari, J. R., Leetongin, G., & Kahlmeier, S. (2012). The pandemic of physical inactivity: Global action for public health. *The Lancet, 380*, 9838, 294–305.

Kok, G., Gottlieb, N. H., Peters, G.-J. Y., Mullen, P. D., Parcel, G. S., Ruiter, R. A. C., … Bartholomew, L. K. (2016). A taxonomy of behavior change methods: An intervention mapping approach. *Health Psychology Review, 10*(3), 297–312. https://doi.org/10.1080/17437199.2015.1077155

Kompf, J. (2020). Implementation intentions for exercise and physical activity: Who do they work for? A systematic review. *Journal of Physical Activity and Health, 17*(3), 349–359. https://doi.org/10.1123/jpah.2018-0720

Kondo, H., Osaka, N., & Osaka, M. (2004). Cooperation of the anterior cingulate cortex and dorsolateral prefrontal cortex for attention shifting. *NeuroImage, 23*, 670–679. https://doi.org/10.1016/j.neuroimage.2004.06.014

Kool, W., & Botvinick, M. (2018). Mental labour. *Nature Human Behaviour, 2*, 899–908. https://doi.org/10.1038/s41562-018-0401-9

Kool, W., & Botvinick, M. M. (2014). A labor/leisure tradeoff in cognitive control. *Journal of Experimental Psychology*. General, *143*, 131–141. https://doi.org/10.1037/a0031048

Körding, K. P., Fukunaga, I., Howard, I. S., Ingram, J. N., & Wolpert, D. M. (2004). A neuroeconomics approach to inferring utility functions in sensorimotor control. *PLoS Biology, 2*, e330. https://doi.org/10.1371/journal.pbio.0020330

Kosack, M. H., Staiano, W., Folino, R., Hansen, M. B., & Lønbro, S. (2020). The acute effect of mental fatigue on badminton performance in elite players. *International Journal of Sports Physiology and Performance*, 1–7. https://doi.org/10.1123/ijspp.2019-0361

Kotabe, H. P., & Hofmann, W. (2015). On integrating the components of self-control. *Perspectives on Psychological Science, 10*(5), 618–638. https://doi.org/10.1177/1745691615593382

Kowalski, K. C., Mack, D. E., Crocker, P. R. E., Niefer, C. B., & Fleming, T. (2006). Coping with social physique anxiety in adolescence. *Journal of Adolescent Health, 39*, 275.e9–275.e16.

Krane, V., Waldron, J., Stiles-Shipley, J., & Michalenok, J. (2001). Relationships among body satisfaction, social physique anxiety, and eating behaviors in female athletes and exercisers. *Journal of Sport Behavior, 24*(3), 247–254.

Krenn, B., Finkenzeller, T., Würth, S., & Amesberger, G. (2018). Sport type determines differences in executive functions in elite athletes. *Psychology of Sport and Exercise, 38*, 72–79. https://doi.org/10.1016/j.psychsport.2018.06.002

Kruglanski, A. W., Fishbach, A., Woolley, K., Bélanger, J. J., Chernikova, M., Molinario, E., & Pierro, A. (2018). A structural model of intrinsic motivation: On the psychology of means-ends fusion. *Psychological Review, 125*(2), 165–182. https://doi.org/10.1037/rev0000095

Kruglanski, A. W., & Gigerenzer, G. (2011). Intuitive and deliberate judgments are based on common principles. *Psychological Review, 118*(1), 97–109. https://doi.org/10.1037/a0020762

Kuhl, J. (1984). Motivational aspects of achievement motivation and learned helplessness: Towards a comprehensive theory of action control. In B. A. Maher & W. B. Maher (Eds.), *Progress in experimental personality research* (Vol. 13, pp. 99–171). New York: Academic Press.

Kuhl, J. (1986). Motivation and information processing: A new look at decision making, dynamic change, and action control. In R. M. Sorrentino & E. T. Higgins (Eds.), *Handbook of motivation and cognition: Foundations of social behavior* (pp. 404–434). New York: Guilford.

Kuhl, J., & Beckmann, J. (1994). *Volition and personality: Action versus state orientation volition and personality*. Germany: Hogrefe.

Kuhn, T. S. (1962/1996). *The structure of scientific revolutions*. Chicago, IL: University of Chicago Press.

Kujala, U. M. (2011). Physical activity, genes, and lifetime predisposition to chronic disease. *European Review of Aging and Physical Activity, 8*, 31–36.

Kunrath, C. A., Cardoso, F., Nakamura, F. Y., & Teoldo, I. (2018). Mental fatigue as a conditioner of the tactical and physical response in soccer players: A pilot study. *Human Movement*, *19*, 16–22. https://doi.org/10.5114/hm.2018.76075

Kunrath, C. A., Cardoso, F. D. S. L., Calvo, T. G., & Costa, I. T. D. (2020). Mental fatigue in soccer: A systematic review. *Revista Brasileira de Medicina do Esporte*, *26*, 172–178. https://doi.org/10.1590/1517-869220202602208206

Kunrath, C. A., Nakamura, F. Y., Roca, A., Tessitore, A., & Teoldo Da Costa, I. (2020). How does mental fatigue affect soccer performance during small-sided games? A cognitive, tactical and physical approach. *Journal of Sports Sciences*, 1–11. https://doi.org/10.1080/02640414.2020.1756681

Kurzban, R. (2016). The sense of effort. *Current Opinion in Psychology*, *7*, 67–70. https://doi.org/10.1016/j.copsyc.2015.08.003

Kurzban, R., Duckworth, A., Kable, J. W., & Myers, J. (2013). An opportunity cost model of subjective effort and task performance. *Behavioral and Brain Sciences*, *36*(6), 661–679. https://doi.org/10.1017/S0140525X12003196

Kushi, L. H., Doyle, C., McCullough, M., Rock, C. L., Demark-Wahnefried, W., Bandera, E. V., Gasptur, S., … & Gansler, T. (2012). American Cancer Society guidelines on nutrition and physical activity for cancer prevention: Reducing the risk of cancer with healthy food choices and physical activity. *CA: A Cancer Journal for Clinicians*, *62*, 30–67.

Kwan, M. Y., Cairney, J., Faulkner, G. E., & Pullenayegum, E. E. (2012). Physical activity and other health-risk behaviors during the transition into early adulthood: A longitudinal cohort study. *American Journal of Preventive Medicine*, *42*, 14–20.

Kwasnicka, D., Dombrowski, S. U., White, M., & Sniehotta, F. F. (2016). Theoretical explanations for maintenance of behaviour change: A systematic review of behaviour theories. *Health Psychology Review*, 277–296. https://psycnet.apa.org/doi/10.1080/17437199.2016.1151372

Ladwig, M. A., Vazou, S., & Ekkekakis, P. (2018). "My best memory is when I was done with it": PE memories are associated with adult sedentary behavior. *Translational Journal of the American College of Sports Medicine*, *3*(16), 119–129. https://doi.org/10.1249/TJX.0000000000000067

Lagestad, P., van den Tillaar, R., & Mamen, A. (2018). Longitudinal changes in physical activity level, body mass index, and oxygen uptake among Norwegian adolescents. *Frontiers in Public Health*, *6*, 97.

Lally, P., van Jaarsveld, C. H. M., Potts, H. W. W., & Wardle, J. (2009). How are habits formed: Modelling habit formation in the real world. *European Journal of Social Psychology*, *40*, 998–1009.

Lamoureux, N. R., Fitzgerald, J. S., Norton, K. I., Sabato, T., Tremblay, M. S., & Tomkinson, G. R. (2019). Temporal trends in the cardiorespiratory fitness of 2,525,827 adults between 1967 and 2016: A systematic review. *Sports Medicine*, *49*(1), 41–55. https://doi.org/10.1007/s40279-018-1017-y

Landais, L. L., Damman, O. C., Schoonmade, L. J., Rimmermans, D. R. M., Verhagen, E. A. L. M., & Jelsma, J. G. M. (2020). Choice architecture interventions to change physical activity and sedentary behavior: A systematic review of effects on intention, behavior and health outcomes during and after intervention. *International Journal of Behavioral Nutrition and Physical Activity*, *17*, 47. https://doi.org/10.1186/s12966-020-00942-7

Landers, R. N., Bauer, K. N., & Callan, R. C. (2017). Gamification of task performance with leaderboards: A goal setting experiment. *Computers in Human Behavior*, *71*, 508–515. https://doi.org/10.1016/j.chb.2015.08.008

Lang, P. J. (1979). A bio-informational theory of emotional imagery. *Psychophysiology*, *16*(6), 495–512. https://doi.org/10.1111/j.1469-8986.1979.tb01511.x

Larson, E. B., Wang, L., Bowen, J. D., McCormick, W. C., Teri, L., Crane, P., & Kukull, W. (2006). Exercise is associated with reduced risk for incident dementia among persons 65 years of age or older. *Annals of Internal Medicine*, *144*, 73–81.

Lascar, N., Kennedy, A., Hancock, B., Jenkins, D., Andrews, R. C., Greenfield, S., & Narendran, P. (2014). Attitudes and barriers to exercise in adults with type 1 diabetes (T1DM) and how best to address them: A qualitative study. *PLoS ONE*, *9*(9), e108019. https://doi.org/10.1371/journal.pone.0108019

Latimer, A. E., Ginis, K. A. M., & Arbour, K. P. (2006). The efficacy of an implementation intention intervention for promoting physical activity among individuals with spinal cord injury: A randomized controlled trial. *Rehabilitation Psychology*, *51*(4), 273–280. https://doi.org/10.1037/0090-5550.51.4.273

Latty, T., & Beekman, M. (2011). Irrational decision-making in an amoeboid organism: Transitivity and context-dependent preferences. *Proceedings of the Royal Society B: Biological Sciences*, *278*, 307–312.

Lawton, R., Conner, M., & McEachan, R. (2009). Desire or reason: Predicting health behaviors from affective and cognitive attitudes. *Health Psychology*, *28*(1), 56–65. https://doi.org/10.1037/a0013424

Lazarus, R. S. (1991). Progress on a cognitive-motivational-relational theory of emotion. *American Psychologist*, *46*, 819–834.

Le Mansec, Y., Dorel, S., Nordez, A., & Jubeau, M. (2019). Is reaction time altered by mental or physical exertion? *European Journal of Applied Physiology*, *119*, 1323–1335. https://doi.org/10.1007/s00421-019-04124-7

Le Mansec, Y., Pageaux, B., Nordez, A., Dorel, S., & Jubeau, M. (2018). Mental fatigue alters the speed and the accuracy of the ball in table tennis. *Journal of Sports Sciences*, *36*, 1–9, 2751–2759. https://doi.org/10.1080/02640414.2017.1418647

Ledger, D., & McCaffrey, D. (2014). Inside wearables, how the science of human behaviour change offers the secret to long-term engagement. *Forbes.Com*.

Lee, C. (1998). *Alternatives to cognition: A new look at explaining human social behavior*. Mahwah, NJ: Lawrence Erlbaum.

Lee, C. (2011). Bounded rationality and the emergency of simplicity amidst complexity. *Journal of Economic Surveys*, *25*(3), 507–526.

Lee, I. M., Shiroma, E. J., Lobelo, F., Puska, P., Blair, S. N., Katzmarzyk, P. T., & Lancet Physical Activity Series Working Group. (2012). Effect of physical inactivity on major non-communicable diseases worldwide: An analysis of burden of disease and life expectancy. *The Lancet*, *380*(9838), 219–229. https://doi.org/10.1016/S0140-6736(12)61031-9

Lee, K. A., Hicks, G., & Nino-Murcia, G. (1991). Validity and reliability of a scale to assess fatigue. *Psychiatry Research*, *36*, 291–298. https://doi.org/10.1016/0165-1781(91)90027-M

Legault, L., & Inzlicht, M. (2013). Self-determination, self-regulation, and the brain: Autonomy improves performance by enhancing neuroaffective responsiveness to self-regulation failure. *Journal of Personality and Social Psychology*, *105*(1), 123–138. https://doi.org/10.1037/a0030426

Lelard, T., Stins, J., & Mouras, H. (2019). Postural responses to emotional visual stimuli. *Clinical Neurophysiology*, *49*(2), 109–114. https://doi.org/10.1016/j.neucli.2019.01.005

Leventhal, H., Singer, R., & Jones, S. (1965). Effects of fear and specificity of recommendation upon attitudes and behavior. *Journal of Personality and Social Psychology*, *2*, 20–29.

Lewin, K. (1935). *A dynamic theory of personality: Selected papers*. New York: McGraw-Hill.

Lewin, K. (1951a). *Field theory in social science: Selected theoretical papers*. New York: Harper and Brothers.

Lewin, K. (1951b). Intention, will and need. In D. Rapaport (Ed.), *Organization and pathology of thought: Selected sources* (pp. 95–153). New York: Columbia University Press.

Lewis, M. (2008). Self-conscious emotions: Embarrassment, pride, shame, and guilt. In M. Lewis, J. M. Haviland-Jones, & L. F. Barrett (Eds.), *Handbook of emotions* (3rd ed., pp. 742–756). New York: Guilford Press.

Lewis, M. (2017). *The undoing project: A friendship that changed our minds*. New York: W W Norton & Co.

Lickel, B., Schmader, T., Curtis, M., Scarnie, M., & Ames, D. R. (2005). Vicarious shame and guilt. *Group Processes & Intergroup Relations*, *8*, 145–157. https://doi.org/10.1177/1368430205051064

Lieberman, D. E. (2015). Is exercise really medicine? An evolutionary perspective. *Current Sports Medicine Reports*, *14*, 313–319.

Lieder, F., Shenhav, A., Musslick, S., & Griffiths, T. (2018). Rational metareasoning and the plasticity of cognitive control. *PLOS Computational Biology*, *14*, e1006043. https://doi.org/10.1371/journal.pcbi.1006043

Lim, C., Wharf Higgins, J., & Rhodes, R. E. (in press). Working out with F.I.D.O. (frequency, intensity, duration, & outcomes): A feasibility randomized controlled trial. *Human-Animal Interaction Bulletin*.

Limburg, K., Watson, H. J., Hagger, M. S., & Egan, S. J. (2017). The relationship between perfectionism and psychopathology: A meta-analysis. *Journal of Clinical Psychology, 73*(10), 1301–1326.

Lines, R. L. J., Ntoumanis, N., Thøgersen-Ntoumani, C., McVeigh, J. A., Ducker, K. J., Fletcher, D., & Gucciardi, D. F. (2020). Cross-sectional and longitudinal comparisons of self-reported and device-assessed physical activity and sedentary behavior. *Journal of Science and Medicine in Sport*. https://doi.org/10.1016/j.jsams.2020.03.004

Lippke, S., Ziegelmann, J. P., & Schwarzer, R. (2004). Behavioral intentions and action plans promote physical exercise: A longitudinal study with orthopedic rehabilitation patients. *Journal of Sport and Exercise Psychology, 26*(3), 470–483. https://doi.org/10.1123/jsep.26.3.470

Lippke, S., Ziegelmann, J. P., & Schwarzer, R. (2005). Stage-specific adoption and maintenance of physical activity: Testing a three-stage model. *Psychology of Sport and Exercise, 6*(5), 585–603. https://doi.org/10.1016/j.psychsport.2004.11.002

Little, B. R. (1983). Personal projects a rationale and method for investigation. *Environment and Behavior, 15*, 273–309.

Livneh, Y., Sugden, A. U., Madara, J. C., Essner, R. A., Flores, V. I., Sugden, L. A., … & Andermann, M. L. (2020). Estimation of current and future physiological states in insular cortex. *Neuron*. https://doi.org/10.1016/j.neuron.2019.12.027

Lizmore, M. R., Dunn, J. G., Dunn, J. C., & Hill, A. P. (2019). Perfectionism and performance following failure in a competitive golf-putting task. *Psychology of Sport and Exercise, 45*, 101582. https://doi.org/10.1016/j.psychsport.2019.101582

Locke, E. A., & Latham, G. P. (1990). *A theory of goal setting performance*. Englewood Cliffs, NJ: Prentice Hall.

Locke, E. A., & Latham, G. P. (2006). New directions in goal setting theory. *Current Directions in Psychological Science, 15*, 265–268.

Loewenstein, G. (1996). Out of control: Visceral influences on behavior. *Organizational Behavior and Human Decision Processes, 65*(3), 272–292. https://doi.org/10.1006/obhd.1996.0028

Loewenstein, G. (1999). Because it is there: The challenge of mountaineering … for utility theory. *Kyklos, 52*, 315–343.

Loewenstein, G. F., Weber, E. U., Hsee, C. K., & Welch, N. (2001). Risk as feelings. *Psychological Bulletin, 127*(2), 267–286. https://doi.org/10.1037/00332909.127.2.267

Lopes, T. R., Oliveira, D. M., Simurro, P. B., Akiba, H. T., Nakamura, F. Y., Okano, A. H., Dias, Á. M., & Silva, B. M. (2020). No sex difference in mental fatigue effect on high-level runners' aerobic performance. *Medicine and Science in Sports and Exercise, 52*(10), 2207–2216. https://doi.org/10.1249/MSS.0000000000002346

Lopez, R. B., Vohs, K. D., Wagner, D. D., & Heatherton, T. F. (2015). Self-regulatory strength: Neural mechanisms and implications for training. In G. H. E. Gendolla, M. Tops, & S. L. Koole (Eds.), *Handbook of biobehavioral approaches to self-regulation* (pp. 43–54). New York: Springer. https://doi.org/10.1007/978-1-4939-1236-0_4

Lorist, M. M., Boksem, M. A., & Ridderinkhof, K. R. (2005). Impaired cognitive control and reduced cingulate activity during mental fatigue. *Cognitive Brain Research, 24*, 199–205. https://doi.org/10.1016/j.cogbrainres.2005.01.018

Love, R., Adams, J., & van Sluijs, E. (2019). Are school-based physical activity interventions effective and equitable? A meta-analysis of cluster randomized controlled trials with accelerometer-assessed activity. *Obesity Reviews, 20*(6), 859–870. https://doi.org/10.1111/obr.12823

Ludyga, S., Gronwald, T., & Hottenrott, K. (2016). The athlete's brain: Cross-sectional evidence for neural efficiency during cycling exercise. *Neural Plasticity*, 2016, 4583674. https://doi.org/10.1155/2016/4583674

Luethi, M. S., Friese, M., Binder, J., Boesiger, P., Luechinger, R., & Rasch, B. (2016). Motivational incentives lead to a strong increase in lateral prefrontal activity after self-control exertion. *Social Cognitive and Affective Neuroscience, 11*, 1618–1626. https://doi.org/10.1093/scan/nsw073

Lund, J. P., Donga, R., Widmer, C. G., & Stohler, C. S. (1991). The pain-adaptation model: A discussion of the relationship between chronic musculoskeletal pain and motor activity. *Canadian Journal of Physiology and Pharmacology, 69*(5), 683–694. https://doi.org/10.1139/y91-102

Luque-Suarez, A., Martinez-Calderon, J., & Falla, D. (2019). Role of kinesiophobia on pain, disability and quality of life in people suffering from chronic musculoskeletal pain: A systematic review. *British Journal of Sports Medicine, 53*(9), 554–559. https://doi.org/10.1136/bjsports-2017-098673

Luszczynska, A., & Haynes, C. (2009). Changing nutrition, physical activity and body weight among student nurses and midwives: Effects of a planning intervention and self-efficacy beliefs. *Journal of Health Psychology, 14*(8), 1075–1084. https://doi.org/10.1177/1359105309342290

Luszczynska, A., & Schwarzer, R. (2003). Planning and self-efficacy in the adoption and maintenance of breast self-examination: A longitudinal study on self-regulatory cognitions. *Psychology and Health, 18*(1), 93–108. https://doi.org/10.1080/0887044021000019358

Macdonald, K., Germine, L., Anderson, A., Christodoulou, J., & McGrath, L. M. (2017). Dispelling the myth: Training in education or neuroscience decreases but does not eliminate beliefs in neuromyths. *Frontiers in Psychology, 8*, 1314.

Mack, D. E., Kouali, D., Gilchrist, J. D., & Sabiston, C. M. (2015). Pride and physical activity: Behavioural regulations as a motivational mechanism? *Psychology and Health, 30*(9), 1049–1062. https://doi.org/10.1080/08870446.2015.1022547

Mackie, D. M., Devos, T., & Smith, E. R. (2000). Intergroup emotions: Explaining offensive action tendencies in an intergroup context. *Journal of Personality and Social Psychology, 79*, 602–616. https://doi.org/10.10371/0022-3514.79.4.602

Mackowiak, R., Lucibello, K. M., Gilchrist, J. D., & Sabiston, C. M. (2019). Examination of actual and ideal body-related characteristics and body-related pride in adult males. *American Journal of Men's Health*. https://doi.org/10.1177/1557988319874642

Mackworth, J. F. (1964). Performance decrement in vigilance, threshold, and high-speed perceptual motor tasks. *Canadian Journal of Psychology, 18*, 209–223. https://doi.org/10.1037/h0083302

MacLean, P. D. (1970). The limbic brain in relation to the psychoses. In P. Black (Ed.), *Physiological correlates of emotion* (pp. 129–146). New York: Academic. https://doi.org/10.1016/B978-0-12-102850-3.50013-X

MacLeod, C. M., & MacDonald, P. A. (2000). Interdimensional interference in the Stroop effect: Uncovering the cognitive and neural anatomy of attention. *Trends in Cognitive Sciences, 4*, 383–391. https://doi.org/10.1016/S1364-6613(00)01530-8

MacMahon, C., Hawkins, Z., & Schücker, L. (2019). Beep test performance is influenced by 30 minutes of cognitive work. *Medicine and Science in Sports and Exercise, 51*, 1928–1934. https://doi.org/10.1249/MSS.0000000000001982

MacMahon, C., Schücker, L., Hagemann, N., & Strauss, B. (2014). Cognitive fatigue effects on physical performance during running. *Journal of Sport and Exercise Psychology, 36*, 375–381. https://doi.org/10.1123/jsep.2013-0249

Maddux, J. E. (1993). Social cognitive models of health and exercise behavior: An introduction and review of conceptual issues. *Journal of Applied Sport Psychology, 5*(2), 116–140. https://doi.org/10.1080/10413209308411310

Madigan, D. J. (2019). A meta-analysis of perfectionism and academic achievement. *Educational Psychology Review, 31*, 967–989.

Madigan, D. J., Stoeber, J., Culley, T., Passfield, L., & Hill, A. P. (2018). Perfectionism and training performance: The mediating role of other-approach goals. *European Journal of Sport Science, 18*(9), 1271–1279.

Magariño, L. S., & Madhivanan, P. (2019). Cognitive fatigue effects on physical performance: A systematic review and meta-analysis – Correspondence. *Physiology & Behavior, 198*, 159–160. https://doi.org/10.1016/j.physbeh.2018.05.025

Magen, E., & Gross, J. J. (2007). Harnessing the need for immediate gratification: Cognitive reconstrual modulates the reward value of temptations. *Emotion, 7*(2), 415–428. https://doi.org/10.1037/1528-3542.7.2.415

Maher, J. P., Dzubur, E., Huh, J., Intille, S., Rhodes, R. E., & Dunton, G. F. (2017). Momentary assessment of physical activity intention-behavior coupling in adults. *Translational Behavioral Medicine*, *7*, 709–718. https://doi.org/10.1007/s13142-017-0472-6

Maiman, L. A., & Becker, M. H. (1974). The health belief model: Origins and correlates in psychological theory. *Health Education Monographs*, *2*(4), 336–353. https://doi.org/10.1177/109019817400200404

Maitland, C., Stratton, G., Foster, S., Braham, R., & Rosenberg, M. (2013). A place for play? The influence of the home physical environment on children's physical activity and sedentary behaviour. *The International Journal of Behavioral Nutrition and Physical Activity*, *10*, 99.

Mallinson-Howard, S. H., Hill, A. P., & Hall, H. K. (2019). The 2× 2 model of perfectionism and negative experiences in youth sport. *Psychology of Sport and Exercise*, *45*, 101581.

Mann, J. B., Bryant, K. R., Johnstone, B., Ivey, P. A., & Sayers, S. P. (2016). Effect of physical and academic stress on illness and injury in division 1 college football players. *Journal of Strength and Conditioning Research*, *30*, 20–25. https://doi.org/10.1519/JSC.0000000000001055

Manohar, S. G., Chong, T. T.-J., Apps, M. A. J., Batla, A., Stamelou, M., Jarman, P. R., … Husain, M. (2015). Reward pays the cost of noise reduction in motor and cognitive control. *Current Biology*, *25*, 1707–1716. https://doi.org/10.1016/j.cub.2015.05.038

Maranges, H. M., & Baumeister, R. F. (2016). Self-control and ego depletion. In K. D. Vohs & R. F. Baumeister (Eds.), *The handbook of self-regulation*. New York: Guilford Press.

Marcora, S. M. (2008). Do we really need a central governor to explain brain regulation of exercise performance? *European Journal of Applied Physiology*, *104*, 929–931. https://doi.org/10.1007/s00421-008-0818-3

Marcora, S. (2009). Perception of effort during exercise is independent of afferent feedback from skeletal muscles, heart, and lungs. *Journal of Applied Physiology*, *106*(6), 2060–2062. https://doi.org/10.1152/japplphysiol.90378.2008

Marcora, S. (2010). Counterpoint: Afferent feedback from fatigued locomotor muscles is not an important determinant of endurance exercise performance. *Journal of Applied Physiology*, *108*(2), 454–457.

Marcora, S. (2019). Psychobiology of fatigue during endurance exercise. In C. Meijen (Ed.), *Endurance performance in sport: Psychological theory and interventions* (pp. 15–34). London: Routledge. https://doi.org/10.4324/9781315167312-2

Marcora, S. M., Bosio, A., & de Morree, H. (2008). Locomotor muscle fatigue increases cardiorespiratory responses and reduces performance during intense cycling exercise independently from metabolic stress. *American Journal of Physiology-Regulatory, Integrative and Comparative Physiology*, *294*, R874–R883. https://doi.org/10.1152/ajpregu.00678.2007

Marcora, S. M., & Staiano, W. (2010). The limit to exercise tolerance in humans: Mind over muscle? *European Journal of Applied Physiology*, *109*, 763–770. https://doi.org/10.1007/s00421-010-1418-6

Marcora, S. M., Staiano, W., & Manning, V. (2009). Mental fatigue impairs physical performance in humans. *Journal of Applied Physiology*, *106*, 857–864. https://doi.org/10.1152/japplphysiol.91324.2008

Marcora, S. M., Staiano, W., & Merlini, M. (2015). A randomized controlled trial of brain endurance training (BET) to reduce fatigue during endurance exercise. *Medicine and Science in Sports and Exercise*, *47*(5S), 198. https://doi.org/10.1249/01.mss.0000476967.03579.44

Marcus, B. H., Rakowski, W., & Rossi, J. S. (1992b). Assessing motivational readiness and decision making for exercise. *Health Psychology*, *11*(4), 257–261. https://doi.org/10.1037/0278-6133.11.4.257

Marcus, B. H., Selby, V. C., Niaura, R. S., & Rossi, J. S. (1992a). Self-efficacy and the stages of exercise behavior change. *Research Quarterly for Exercise and Sport*, *63*(1), 60–66. https://doi.org/10.1080/02701367.1992.10607557

Markland, D., Hall, C. R., Duncan, L. R., & Simatovic, J. (2015). The effects of an imagery intervention on implicit and explicit exercise attitudes. *Psychology of Sport and Exercise*, *17*, 24–31. https://doi.org/10.1016/j.psychsport.2014.11.007

Martijn, C., Tenbült, P., Merckelbach, H., Dreezens, E., & de Vries, N. K. (2002). Getting a grip on ourselves: Challenging expectancies about loss of energy after self-control. *Social Cognition*, *20*, 441–460. https://doi.org/10.1521/soco.20.6.441.22978

Martin Ginis, K. A., & Bray, S. R. (2010). Application of the limited strength model of self-regulation to understanding exercise effort, planning and adherence. *Psychology and Health*, *25*, 1147–1160. doi:10.1080/08870440903111696

Martin Ginis, K. A., Jung, M. E., & Gauvin, L. (2003). Effects of exercising in mirrored environments on sedentary women's feeling states and self-efficacy. *Health Psychology*, *22*, 354–361.

Martin Ginis, K. A., McEwan, D., Josse, A. R., & Phillips, S. M. (2012). Body image change in obese and overweight women enrolled in a weight-loss intervention: The importance of perceived versus actual physical changes. *Body Image*, *9*(3), 311–317.

Martin Ginis, K. A., Prapavessis, H., & Haase, A. M. (2008). The effects of physique-salient and physique non-salient exercise videos on women's body image, self-presentational concerns, and exercise motivation. *Body Image*. https://doi.org/10.1016/j.bodyim.2007.11.005

Martin, J. J., & Gill, D. L. (1991). The relationships among competitive orientation, sport-confidence, self-efficacy, anxiety, and performance. *Journal of Sport and Exercise Psychology*, *13*, 149–159. https://doi.org/10.1123/jsep.13.2.149

Martin, K., Meeusen, R., Thompson, K. G., Keegan, R., & Rattray, B. (2018). Mental fatigue impairs endurance performance: A physiological explanation. *Sports Medicine*, *48*, 2041–2051. https://doi.org/10.1007/s40279-018-0946-9

Martin, K., Staiano, W., Menaspà, P., Hennessey, T., Marcora, S., Keegan, R., Thompson, K. G., Martin, D., Halson, S., & Rattray, B. (2016). Superior inhibitory control and resistance to mental fatigue in professional road cyclists. *PLOS ONE*, *11*, e0159907. https://doi.org/10.1371/journal.pone.0159907

Martin, K., Thompson, K. G., Keegan, R., Ball, N., & Rattray, B. (2015). Mental fatigue does not affect maximal anaerobic exercise performance. *European Journal of Applied Physiology*, *115*, 715–725. https://doi.org/10.1007/s00421-014-3052-1

Martin, K., Thompson, K. G., Keegan, R., & Rattray, B. (2019). Are individuals who engage in more frequent self-regulation less susceptible to mental fatigue? *Journal of Sport and Exercise Psychology*, *41*, 289–297. https://doi.org/10.1123/jsep.2018-0222

Mascie-Taylor, C. G. N., & Karim, E. (2003). The burden of chronic disease. *Science*, *302*, 1921–1922.

Maxcy, J., Wicker, P., & Prinz, J. (2019). Happiness as a reward for torture: Is participation in a long-distance triathlon a rational choice? *Journal of Sports Economics*, *20*, 177–197. https://doi.org/10.1177/1527002518758144

McAdams, D. P. (2013). The psychological self as actor, agent, and author. *Perspectives on Psychological Science*, *8*(3), 272–295. https://doi.org/10.1177/1745691612464657

McCormick, A., Meijen, C., Anstiss, P. A., & Jones, H. S. (2018a). Self-regulation in endurance sports: Theory, research, and practice. *International Review of Sport and Exercise Psychology*, *19*, 1–30. https://doi.org/10.1080/1750984X.2018.1469161

McCormick, A., Meijen, C. Anstiss, P. A., & Massey, H. S. (2018b). Self-regulation in endurance sports: theory, research, and practice. *International Journal of Sport and Exercise Psychology*, *12*, 235–264.

McCormick, A., Meijen, C., & Marcora, S. M. (2016). Psychological demands experienced by recreational endurance athletes. *International Journal of Sport and Exercise Psychology*, *6*, 1–16. https://doi.org/10.1080/1612197X.2016.1256341

McEachan, R., Conner, M., Taylor, N. J., & Lawton, R. J. (2011). Prospective prediction of health-related behaviors with the theory of planned behavior: A meta-analysis. *Health Psychology Review*, *5*, 97–144. https://doi.org/10.1080/17437199.2010.521684

McEachan, R., Taylor, N., Harrison, R., Lawton, R., Gardner, P., & Conner, M. (2016). Meta-analysis of the reasoned action approach (RAA) to understanding health behaviors. *Annals of Behavioral Medicine: A Publication of the Society of Behavioral Medicine*, *50*(4), 592–612. https://doi.org/10.1007/s12160-016-9798-4

McEwan, D., Beauchamp, M. R., Kouvousis, C., Ray, C. M., Wyrough, A., & Rhodes, R. E. (2019). Examining the active ingredients of physical activity interventions underpinned by theory versus no stated theory: A meta-analysis. *Health Psychology Review*, *13*(1), 1–17. https://doi.org/10.1080/17437199.2018.1547120

McEwan, D., Harden, S. M., Zumbo, B. D., Sylvester, B. D., Kaulius, M., Ruissen, G. R., … & Beauchamp, M. R. (2016). The effectiveness of multi-component goal setting interventions for changing physical activity behaviour: A systematic review and meta-analysis. *Health Psychology Review, 10*(1), 67–88. https://doi.org/10.1080/17437199.2015.1104258

McEwan, D., Kouvousis, C., Ray, C., Wyrough, A., Beauchamp, M. R., & Rhodes, R. E. (2019). Examining the active ingredients of physical activity interventions underpinned by theory versus no stated theory: A meta-analysis. *Health Psychology Review, 13*, 1–17. https://doi.org/10.1080/17437199.2018.1547120

McEwan, D., Martin Ginis, K. A., & Bray, S. R. (2013). The effects of depleted self-control strength on skill-based task performance. *Journal of Sport and Exercise Psychology, 35*, 239–249. https://doi.org/10.1123/jsep.35.3.239

McFadyen, J., Mermillod, M., Mattingley, J. B., Halász, V., & Garrido, M. I. (2017). A rapid subcortical amygdala route for faces irrespective of spatial frequency and emotion. *Journal of Neuroscience, 37*(14), 3864–3874. https://doi.org/10.1523/JNEUROSCI.3525-16.2017

McHugh, T. L. F., Kowalski, K. C., MacK, D. E., Crocker, P. R. E., Junkin, S. E., Lejbak, L. K., & Martin, S. (2008). Young women's experiences of social physique anxiety. *Feminism and Psychology, 18*(2), 231–252. https://doi.org/10.1177/0959353507088593

McKenna, M. J., & Hargreaves, M. (2008). Resolving fatigue mechanisms determining exercise performance: Integrative physiology at its finest! *Journal of Applied Physiology, 104*, 286–287. https://doi.org/10.1152/japplphysiol.01139.2007

McLellan, T. M., Bell, D. G., & Kamimori, G. H. (2004). Caffeine improves physical performance during 24 h of active wakefulness. *Aviation, Space, and Environmental -Medicine, 75*, 666–672.

McMorris, T., Barwood, M., Hale, B. J., Dicks, M., & Corbett, J. (2018). Cognitive fatigue effects on physical performance: A systematic review and meta-analysis. *Physiology and Behavior, 188*, 103–107. https://doi.org/10.1016/j.physbeh.2018.01.029

Meeusen, R., Duclos, M., Foster, C., Fry, A., Gleeson, M., Nieman, D., … & Urhausen, A. (2013). Prevention, diagnosis and treatment of the overtraining syndrome: Joint consensus statement of the European College of Sport Science (ECSS) and the American College of Sports Medicine (ACSM). *European Journal of Sport Science, 13*, 1–24. https://doi.org/10.1080/17461391.2012.730061

Melby-Lervag, M., & Hulme, C. (2013). Is working memory training effective? A meta-analytic review. *Developmental Psychology, 49*, 270–291. https://doi.org/10.1037/a0028228.

Melnikoff, D. E., & Bargh, J. A. (2018). The mythical number two. *Trends in Cognitive Sciences, 22*(4), 280–293. https://doi.org/10.1016/j.tics.2018.02.001

Méndez-Bértolo, C., Moratti, S., Toledano, R., Lopez-Sosa, F., Martínez-Alvarez, R., Mah, Y. H., Vuilleumier, P., Gil-Nagel, A., & Strange, B. A. (2016). A fast pathway for fear in human amygdala. *Nature Neuroscience, 19*(8), 1041–1049. https://doi.org/10.1038/nn.4324

Michie, S., Abraham, C., Whittington, C., McAteer, J., & Gupta, S. (2009). Effective techniques in healthy eating and physical activity interventions: A meta-regression. *Health Psychology, 28*, 690–701.

Michie, S., Richardson, M., Johnston, M., Abraham, C., Francis, J., Hardeman, W., … Wood, C. E. (2013). The behavior change technique taxonomy (v1) of 93 hierarchically clustered techniques: Building an international consensus for the reporting of behavior change interventions. *Annals of Behavioral Medicine, 46*, 81–95.

Michie, S., Webb, T. L., & Sniehotta, F. F. (2010). The importance of making explicit links between theoretical constructs and behaviour change techniques. *Addiction, 105*(11), 1897–1898. https://doi.org/10.1111/j.1360-0443.2010.03161.x

Michie, S., West, R., Campbell, R., Brown, J., & Gainforth, H. (2014). *ABC of theories of behaviour change*. Great Britain: Silverback Publishing.

Midgley, C., Kaplan, A., & Middleton, M. (2001). Performance-approach goals: Good for what, for whom, under what circumstances, and at what cost? *Journal of Educational Psychology, 93*(1), 77–86. https://doi.org/10.1037/0022-0663.93.1.77

Miles, L. M., Rodrigues, A. M., Sniehotta, F. F., & French, D. P. (2020). Asking questions changes health-related behavior: An updated systematic review and meta-analysis. *Journal of Clinical Epidemiology, 123*, 59–68. https://doi.org/10.1016/j.jclinepi.2020.03.014

Milkman, K. L., Minson, J. A., & Volpp, K. G. M. (2014). Holding the hunger games hostage at the gym: An evaluation of temptation bundling. *Management Science, 60*(2), 283–299.

Miller, G. A. (2003). The cognitive revolution: A historical perspective. *Trends in Cognitive Sciences*, 7(3), 141–144. https://doi.org/10.1016/s1364-6613(03)00029-9

Miller, E. K., & Cohen, J. D. (2001). An integrative theory of prefrontal cortex function. *Annual Review of Neuroscience, 24*, 167–202. https://doi.org/10.1146/annurev.neuro.24.1.167

Miller, E. K., & Wallis, J. D. (2009). Executive function and higher-order cognition: Definition and neural substrates. In L. R. Squire (Ed.) *Encyclopedia of neuroscience* (Vol. 4, pp. 99–104). Oxford: Academic Press.

Miller, W. C., & Eggert, K. E. (1992). Weight loss perceptions, characteristics, and expectations of an overweight male and female population. *Medicine, Exercise, Nutrition and Health, 1*(1), 42–47.

Millet, G. Y. (2011). Can neuromuscular fatigue explain running strategies and performance in ultra-marathons? *Sports Medicine, 41*, 489–506. https://doi.org/10.2165/11588760-000000000-00000

Milne, S., Orbell, S., & Sheeran, P. (2002). Combining motivational and volitional interventions to promote exercise participation: Protection motivation theory and implementation intentions. *British Journal of Health Psychology*, 7(2), 163–184. https://doi.org/10.1348/135910702169420

Milyavskaya, M., & Inzlicht, M. (2017). Attentional and motivational mechanisms of self-control. In D. T. D. de Ridder, M. Adriaanse, & K. Fujita (Eds.), *The Routledge international handbook of self-control in health and well-being* (1st ed., pp. 11–23). New York: Routledge. https://doi.org/10.4324/9781315648576-2

Milyavskaya, M., Inzlicht, M., Hope, N., & Koestner, R. (2015). Saying "no" to temptation: Want-to motivation improves self-regulation by reducing temptation rather than by increasing self-control. *Journal of Personality and Social Psychology, 109*(4), 677–693. https://doi.org/10.1037/pspp0000045

Mischel, W. (1961). Preference for delayed reinforcement and social responsibility. *Journal of Abnormal and Social Psychology, 62*, 1–7. https://doi.org/10.1037/h0048263

Mischel, W., Ayduk, O., Berman, M. G., Casey, B. J., Gotlib, I. H., Jonides, J., Kross, E., Teslovich, T., Wilson, N. L., Zayas, V., & Shoda, Y. (2011). 'Willpower' over the life span: Decomposing self-regulation. *Social Cognitive and Affective Neuroscience, 6*, 252–256. https://doi.org/10.1093/scan/nsq081

Mischel, W., Shoda, Y., & Rodriguez, M. L. (1989). Delay of gratification in children. *Science, 244*, 933–938. https://doi.org/10.1126/science.2658056

Missel, R. (2017, June 6). Cyclist quotes every rider should know. Bicycling. Retrieved March 24, 2020, from https://www.bicycling.com/news/g20042972/quotes-cyclists-should-know/

Moffitt, T. E., Arseneault, L., Belsky, D., Dickson, N., Hancox, R. J., Harrington, H., Houts, R., Poulton, R., Roberts, B. W., Ross, S., Sears, M. R., Thomson, W. M., & Caspi, A. (2011). A gradient of childhood self-control predicts health, wealth, and public safety. *Proceedings of the National Academy of Sciences, 108*, 2693–2698. https://doi.org/10.1073/pnas.1010076108

Mogler, B. K., Shu, S. B., Fox, C. R., Goldstein, N. J., Victor, R. G., Escarce, J. J., & Shapiro, M. F. (2013). Using insights from behavioral economics and social psychology to help patients manage chronic diseases. *Journal of General Internal Medicine, 28*(5), 711–718. https://doi.org/10.1007/s11606-012-2261-8

Molden, D. C., Hui, C. M., Scholer, A. A., Meier, B. P., Noreen, E. E., D'Agostino, P. R., & Martin, V. (2012). Motivational versus metabolic effects of carbohydrates on self-control. *Psychological Science, 23*, 1137–1144. https://doi.org/10.1177/0956797612439069

Molnar, D. S., Flett, G. L., Sadava, S. W., & Colautti, J. (2012). Perfectionism and health functioning in women with fibromyalgia. *Journal of Psychosomatic Research, 73*, 295–300.

Mond, J. M., & Calogero, R. M. (2009). Excessive exercise in eating disorder patients and in healthy women. *Australian and New Zealand Journal of Psychiatry, 43*, 227–234.

Monsell, S. (2003). Task switching. *Trends in Cognitive Sciences*, *7*, 134–140. https://dx.doi.org/10.1016/s1364-6613(03)00028-7

Montoya, A. K., & Hayes, A. F. (2017). Two-condition within-participant statistical mediation analysis: A path-analytic framework. *Psychological Methods*, *22*, 6–27. https://doi.org/10.1037/met0000086

Morales-Alamo, D., Losa-Reyna, J., Torres-Peralta, R., Martin-Rincon, M., Perez-Valera, M., Curtelin, D., ... & Calbet, J. A. (2015). What limits performance during whole-body incremental exercise to exhaustion in humans?. *The Journal of Physiology*, *593*, 4631–4648. https://doi.org/10.1113/JP270487

More, K. R., Phillips, L. A., & Eisenberg Colman, M. H. (2019). Evaluating the potential roles of body dissatisfaction in exercise avoidance. *Body Image*, *28*, 110–114. https://doi.org/10.1016/j.bodyim.2019.01.003

Moreira, A., Aoki, M. S., Franchini, E., da Silva Machado, D. G., Paludo, A. C., & Okano, A. H. (2018). Mental fatigue impairs technical performance and alters neuroendocrine and autonomic responses in elite young basketball players. *Physiology & Behavior*, *196*, 112–118. https://doi.org/10.1016/j.physbeh.2018.08.015

Morel, P., Ulbrich, P., & Gail, A. (2017). What makes a reach movement effortful? Physical effort discounting supports common minimization principles in decision making and motor control. *PLoS Biology*, *15*, e2001323. https://doi.org/10.1371/journal.pbio.2001323

Morgan, W. P., & O'Connor, P. J. (1988). Exercise and mental health. In R. K. Dishman (Ed.), *Exercise adherence: Its impact on public health* (pp. 91–121). Champaign, IL: Human Kinetics.

Morin, A. J. S., Scalas, L. F., & Marsh, H. W. (2015). Tracking the elusive actual-ideal discrepancy model within latent subpopulations. *Journal of Individual Differences*, *36*, 65–72. https://doi.org/10.1027/1614-0001/a000157

Morris, J. S., Öhman, A., & Dolan, R. J. (1999). A subcortical pathway to the right amygdala mediating "unseen" fear. *Proceedings of the National Academy of Sciences of the United States of America*, *96*(4), 1680–1685. https://doi.org/10.1073/pnas.96.4.1680

Morrow, J. R., Jr., Krzewinski-Malone, J. A., Jackson, A. W., Bungum, T. J., & FitzGerald, S. J. (2004). American adults' knowledge of exercise recommendations. *Research Quarterly for Exercise and Sport*, *75*, 231–237.

Mostofsky, S. H., & Simmonds, D. J. (2008). Response inhibition and response selection: Two sides of the same coin. *Journal of Cognitive Neuroscience*, *20*, 751–761. https://doi.org/10.1162/jocn.2008.20500

Mulle, J. G., & Vaccarino, V. (2013). Cardiovascular disease, psychosocial factors, and genetics: The case of depression. *Progress in Cardiovascular Diseases*, *55*, 557–562.

Munakata, Y., Herd, S., Chatham, C., Depue, B., Banich, M., & O'Reilly, R. (2011). A unified framework for inhibitory control. *Trends in Cognitive Sciences*, *15*, 453–459. https://dx.doi.org/10.1016/j.tics.2011.07.011

Muraven, M. (2010). Building self-control strength: Practicing self-control leads to improved self-control performance. *Journal of Experimental Social Psychology*, *46*, 465–468. https://doi.org/10.1016/j.jesp.2009.12.011

Muraven, M., & Slessareva, E. (2003). Mechanisms of self-control failure: Motivation and limited resources. *Personality and Social Psychology Bulletin*, *29*, 894–906. https://doi.org/10.1177/0146167203029007008

Muraven, M., Tice, D. M., & Baumeister, R. F. (1998). Self-control as a limited resource: Regulatory depletion patterns. *Journal of Personality and Social Psychology*, *74*, 774–789. https://doi.org/10.1037/0022–3514.74.3.774

Murphy, S. L., & Taylor, I. M. (2019). Self-determination in recreational exercise: Associations with lapse and post-lapse emotions. *Psychology of Sport and Exercise*, *45*, 101548. https://doi.org/10.1016/j.psychsport.2019.101548

Murphy, S. T., & Zajonc, R. B. (1993). Affect, cognition, and awareness: Affective priming with optimal and suboptimal stimulus exposures. *Journal of Personality and Social Psychology*, *64*(5), 723–739. http://dx.doi.org/10.1037/00223514.64.5.723

Murray, J. M., Brennan, S. F., French, D. P., Patterson, C. C., Kee, F., & Hunter, R. F. (2017). Effectiveness of physical activity interventions in achieving behaviour change maintenance in young and middle aged adults: A systematic review and meta-analysis. *Social Science & Medicine, 192*, 125–133. https://doi.org/10.1016/j.socscimed.2017.09.021

Murray, J. M., Brennan, S. F., French, D. P., Patterson, C. C., Kee, F., & Hunter, R. F. (2018). Mediators of behavior change maintenance in physical activity interventions for young and middle-aged adults: A systematic review. *Annals of Behavioral Medicine, 52*(6), 513–529. https://doi.org/10.1093/abm/kay012

Murtagh, A. M., & Todd, S. A. (2004). Self-regulation: A challenge to the strength model. *Journal of Articles in Support of the Null Hypothesis, 3*, 19–51.

Musslick, S., Cohen, J. D., & Shenhav A. (2019). Decomposing individual differences in cognitive control: A model-based approach. *Proceedings of the 41st Annual Conference of the Cognitive Science Society*, Montreal, CA

Musslick, S., Dey, B., Ozcimder, K., Patwary, M. M. A., Willke, T. L., & Cohen, J. D. (2016). Controlled vs. automatic processing: a graph-theoretic approach to the analysis of serial vs. parallel processing in neural network architectures. *Proceedings of the 38th Annual Conference of the Cognitive Science Society*, Philadelphia, Pen.

Musslick, S., Jang, S. J., Shvartsman, M., Shenhav, A., & Cohen, J. D. (2018). Constraints associated with cognitive control and the stability-flexibility dilemma. *Proceedings of the 40th Annual Conference of the Cognitive Science Society*, Madison, WI.

Musslick, S., Shenhav, A., Botvinick, M. M., & Cohen, J. D. (2015). A computational model of control allocation based on the expected value of control. *Reinforcement Learning and Decision Making Conference*, Edmonton, Alberta, CA.

Myers. J. (2003). Exercise and cardiovascular health. *Circulation, 107*, e2–e5.

Nakamura, F. Y., Okuno, N. M., Perandini, L. A., S. Caldeira, L. F., Simões, H. G., Cardoso, J. R., & Bishop, D. J. (2008). Critical power can be estimated from nonexhaustive tests based on rating of perceived exertion responses. *Journal of Strength and Conditioning Research, 22*, 937–943. https://doi.org/10.1519/JSC.0b013e31816a41fa

NCD Risk Factor Collaboration. (2016). Trends in adult body-mass index in 200 countries from 1975 to 2014: A pooled analysis of 1698 population-based measurement studies with 19.2 million participants. *Lancet, 387*(10026), 1377–1396. https://doi.org/10.1016/S01406736(16)30054X

Nelson, M. C., Taylor, K., & Vella, C. A. (2019). Comparison of self-reported and objectively measured sedentary behavior and physical activity in undergraduate students. *Measurement in Physical Education and Exercise Science, 23*, 237–248.

Neugebauer, V., Li, W., Bird, G. C., & Han, J. S. (2004). The amygdala and persistent pain. *The Neuroscientist, 10*, 221–234. https://doi.org/10.1177/1073858403261077

Newsom, J. T., Huguet, N., McCarthy, M. J., Ramage-Morin, P., Kaplan, M. S., Bernier, J., McFarland, B. H., & Oderkirk, J. (2012). Health behavior change following chronic illness in middle and later life. *Journals of Gerontology: Series B, Psychological Sciences and Social Sciences, 67*(3), 279–288. https://doi.org/10.1093/geronb/gbr103

Newsom, J. T., McFarland, B. H., Kaplan, M. S., Huguet, N., & Zani, B. (2005). The health consciousness myth: Implications of the near independence of major health behaviors in the North American population. *Social Science and Medicine, 60*(2), 433–437. https://doi.org/10.1016/j.socscimed.2004.05.015

Ng, J. Y., Ntoumanis, N., Thøgersen-Ntoumani, C., Deci, E. L., Ryan, R. M., Duda, J. L., & Williams, G. C. (2012). Self-determination theory applied to health contexts: A meta-analysis. *Perspectives on Psychological Science*, 7(4), 325–340. https://doi.org/10.1177/1745691612447309

Nicholls, J. G. (1989). *The competitive ethos and democratic education*. Cambridge, MA: Harvard University Press.

Nicolò, A., Sacchetti, M., Girardi, M., McCormick, A., Angius, L., Bazzucchi, I., & Marcora, S. M. (2019). A comparison of different methods to analyse data collected during time-to-exhaustion tests. *Sport Sciences for Health, 15*, 667–679. https://doi.org/10.1007/s11332-019-00585-7

Niedenthal, P. M., & Brauer, M. (2012). Social functionality of human emotion. *Annual Review of Psychology, 63*, 259–285. https://doi.org/10.1146/annurev.psych.121208.131605

Niendam, T. A., Laird, A. R., Ray, K. L., Dean, Y. M., Glahn, D. C., & Carter, C. S. (2012). Meta-analytic evidence for a superordinate cognitive control network subserving diverse executive functions. *Cognitive, Affective, & Behavioral Neuroscience, 12*, 241–268. https://doi.org/10.3758/s13415-011-0083-5

Nigg, C. R. (2014). *ACSM's behavioral aspects of physical activity and exercise*. Philadelphia, PA: Lippincott Williams and Wilkins.

Noakes, T. D. (2008). Rating of perceived exertion as a predictor of the duration of exercise that remains until exhaustion. *British Journal of Sports Medicine, 42*, 623. http://dx.doi.org/10.1136/bjsm.2007.043612

Noakes, T. D., & Gibson, A. S. C. (2004). Logical limitations to the "catastrophe" models of fatigue during exercise in humans. *British Journal of Sports Medicine, 38*, 648–649. https://doi.org/10.1136/bjsm.2003.009761

Noakes, T. D., Peltonen, J. E., & Rusko, H. K. (2001). Evidence that a central governor regulates exercise performance during acute hypoxia and hyperoxia. *The Journal of Experimental Biology, 204*, 3225–3234.

Norman, J. (2002). Two visual systems and two theories of perception: An attempt to reconcile the constructivist and ecological approaches. *Behavioral and Brain Sciences, 25*(1), 73–144. https://doi.org/10.1017/S0140525X0200002X

Norman, P., & Conner, M. (2005). The theory of planned behavior and exercise: Evidence for the mediating and moderating roles of planning on intention-behavior relationships. *Journal of Sport and Exercise Psychology, 27*(4), 488–504. https://doi.org/10.1123/jsep.27.4.488

Ntoumanis, N. (2014). The strength model of self-control. In R. C. Eklund & G. Tenenbaum (Eds.), *Encyclopaedia of sport and exercise psychology* (pp. 714–717). London: Sage.

Ntoumanis, N., Healy, L. C., Sedikides, C., Duda, J., Stewart, B., Smith, A., & Bond, J. (2014). When the going gets tough: The "why" of goal striving matters. *Journal of Personality, 82*(3), 225–236. https://doi.org/10.1111/jopy.12047

Ntoumanis, N., Ng, J. Y., Barkoukis, V., & Backhouse, S. (2014). Personal and psychosocial predictors of doping use in physical activity settings: A meta-analysis. *Sports Medicine, 44*(11), 1603–1624. https://doi.org/10.1007/s40279-014-0240-4

Nuechterlein, K. H., Parasuraman, R., & Jiang, Q. (1983). Visual sustained attention: Image degradation produces rapid sensitivity decrement over time. *Science, 220*, 327–329. https://doi.org/10.1126/science.6836276

O'Keeffe, K., Hodder, S., & Lloyd, A. (2020). A comparison of methods used for inducing mental fatigue in performance research: Individualised, dual-task and short duration cognitive tests are most effective. *Ergonomics, 63*, 1–12. https://doi.org/10.1080/00140139.2019.1687940

O'Leary, K., Tanghe, D., Pratt, W., & Ralston, J. (2018). Collaborative health reminders and notifications: Insights from prototypes. *AMIA: Annual Symposium Proceedings. AMIA Symposium, 2018*, San Francisco, 837–846.

O'Loughlin, E. K., Sabiston, C. M., Dugas, E. N., & O'Loughlin, J. L. (2015). The association between exercise behavior regulation and exergaming in adolescents. *Journal of Physical Activity and Health, 12*(3), 328–334. https://doi.org/10.1123/jpah.2012-0455

Ochsner, K. N., Silvers, J. A., & Buhle, J. T. (2012). Functional imaging studies of emotion regulation: A synthetic review and evolving model of the cognitive control of emotion. *Annals of the New York Academy of Sciences, 1251*, E1–E24. https://doi.org/10.1111/j.17496632.2012.06751.x

Okun, M. A., Ruehlman, L., Karoly, P., Lutz, R., Fairholme, C., & Schaub, R. (2003). Social support and social norms: Do both contribute to predicting leisure-time exercise? *American Journal of Health Behavior, 27*(5), 493–507.

Olander, E. K, Fletcher, H., Williams, S., Lou, A., Turner, A., & French, D. P. (2013). What are the most effective techniques in changing obese individuals' physical activity self-efficacy and behaviour: A systematic review and meta-analysis. *The International Journal of Behavioral Nutrition and Physical Activity, 10*(29). https://doi.org/10.1186/1479-5868-10-29

Oliver, A., McCarthy, P. J., & Burns, L. (2020). A grounded-theory study of meta-attention in golfers. *The Sport Psychologist, 34*, 11–22. doi:10.1123/tsp.2019-0014

Olsson, L. F., Hill, A. P., Madigan, D. J., & Woodley, G. (2020). Development of perfectionism in junior athletes: Examination of actual and perceived parental perfectionism. *Journal of Sports Sciences, 38*(6), 669–675. https://doi.org/10.1080/02640414.2020.1723387

Orbell S., Hodgkins, S., & Sheeran, P. (1997). Implementation intentions and the theory of planned behavior. *Personality and Social Psychology Bulletin, 23*(9), 945–954. https://doi.org/10.1177/0146167297239004

Orbell S., & Sheeran, P. (1998). "Inclined abstainers": A problem for predicting health-related behaviour. *British Journal of Social Psychology, 37*(2), 151–165. https://doi.org/10.1111/j.2044-8309.1998.tb01162.x

Orbell S., & Sheeran, P. (2000). Motivational and volitional processes in action initiation: A field study of the role of implementation intentions. *Journal of Applied Social Psychology, 30*(4), 780–797. https://doi.org/10.1111/j.1559-1816.2000.tb02823.x

Orehek, E., & Vazeou-Nieuwenhuis, A. (2013). Sequential and concurrent strategies of multiple goal pursuit. *Review of General Psychology, 17*, 339–349.

Osman, M. (2004). An evaluation of dual-process theories of reasoning. *Psychonomic Bulletin and Review, 11*(6), 988–1010. https://doi.org/10.3758/BF03196730

Otani, H., Kaya, M., Tamaki, A., & Watson, P. (2017). Separate and combined effects of exposure to heat stress and mental fatigue on endurance exercise capacity in the heat. *European Journal of Applied Physiology, 117*, 119–129. https://doi.org/10.1007/s00421-016-3504-x

Oudejans, R. R., Karamat, R. S., & Stolk, M. H. (2012). Effects of actions preceding the jump shot on gaze behavior and shooting performance in elite female basketball players. *International Journal of Sports Science and Coaching, 7*, 255–267. https://doi.org/10.1260/1747–9541.7.2.255

Oudejans, R. R., Kuijpers, W., Kooijman, C. C., & Bakker, F. C. (2011). Thoughts and attention of athletes under pressure: Skill-focus or performance worries? *Anxiety, Stress, and Coping, 24*, 59–73. https://doi.org/10.1080/10615806.2010.481331

Owen, A. M. (1997). Cognitive planning in humans: Neuropsychological, neuroanatomical and neuropharmacological perspectives. *Progress in Neurobiology, 53*(4), 431–450. https://doi.org/10.1016/S0301-0082(97)00042-7

Pacht, A. R. (1984). Reflections on perfection. *American Psychologist, 39*, 386–390.

Packard, M. G., & Goodman, J. (2013). Factors that influence the relative use of multiple memory systems. *Hippocampus, 23*(11), 1044–1052. https://doi.org/10.1002/hipo.22178

Packard, M. G., Goodman, J., & Ressler, R. L. (2018). Emotional modulation of habit memory: Neural mechanisms and implications for psychopathology. *Current Opinion in Behavioral Sciences, 20*, 25–32. https://doi.org/10.1016/j.cobeha.2017.09.004

Pageaux, B. (2014). The psychobiological model of endurance performance: An effort-based decision-making theory to explain self-paced endurance performance. *Sports Medicine, 44*, 1319–1320. https://doi.org/10.1007/s40279-014-0198-2

Pageaux, B., & Lepers, R. (2018). The effects of mental fatigue on sport-related performance. In M. Sarkar & S. Marcora (Eds.), *Sport and the brain: The science of preparing, enduring and winning, part C* (Vol. 240, pp. 291–315). Cambridge, MA: Academic Press. https://doi.org/10.1016/bs.pbr.2018.10.004

Pageaux, B., Lepers, R., Dietz, K. C., & Marcora, S. M. (2014). Response inhibition impairs subsequent self-paced endurance performance. *European Journal of Applied Physiology, 114*, 1095–1105. https://doi.org/10.1007/s00421-014-2838-5

Pageaux, B., Marcora, S. M., & Lepers, R. (2013). Prolonged mental exertion does not alter neuromuscular function of the knee extensors. *Medicine & Science in Sports & Exercise, 45*, 2254–2264. https://doi.org/10.1249/MSS.0b013e31829b504a

Pageaux, B., Marcora, S. M., Rozand, V., & Lepers, R. (2015). Mental fatigue induced by prolonged self-regulation does not exacerbate central fatigue during subsequent whole-body endurance exercise. *Frontiers in Human Neuroscience*, 9. https://doi.org/10.3389/fnhum.2015.00067

Parfitt, G., Alrumh, A., & Rowlands, A. V. (2012). Affect-regulated exercise-intensity: Does training at an intensity that feels 'good' improve physical health? *Journal of Science and Medicine in Sport, 15*(6), 548–553.

Park, R. (2013, June 19). 50 best golf quotes of all time. Colorado Avid Golfer. Retrieved March 24, 2020, from https://coloradoavidgolfer.com/50-best-golf-quotes-of-all-time/

Parker, W. D. (1997). An empirical typology of perfectionism in academically talented children. *American Educational Research Journal, 34*(3), 545–562.

Parrott, M. W., Tennant, L. K., Olejnik, S., & Poudevigne, M. S. (2008). Theory of planned behavior: Implications for an email-based physical activity intervention. *Psychology of Sport and Exercise, 9(*4), 511–526.

Patel, R., Spreng, R. N., & Turner, G. R. (2013). Functional brain changes following cognitive and motor skills training: A quantitative meta-analysis. *Neurorehabilitation and Neural Repair, 27*, 187–199. https://doi.org/10.1177/1545968312461718

Patnode, C. D., Evans, C. V., Senger, C. A., Redmond, N., & Lin, J. S. (2017). Behavioral counseling to promote a healthful diet and physical activity for cardiovascular disease prevention in adults without known cardiovascular disease risk factors: Updated evidence report and systematic review for the US Preventive Services Task Force. *Journal of the American Medical Association, 318*(2), 175–193. https://doi.org/10.1001/jama.2017.3303

Paton, J. F., Li, Y. W., & Kasparov, S. (1999). Reflex response and convergence of pharyngoesophageal and peripheral chemoreceptors in the nucleus of the solitary tract. *Neuroscience, 93*(1), 143–154. https://doi.org/10.1016/s0306-4522(99)00098-6

Pattyn, N., Van Cutsem, J., Dessy, E., & Mairesse, O. (2018). Bridging exercise science, cognitive psychology, and medical practice: Is 'cognitive fatigue' a remake of 'The Emperor's New Clothes?' *Frontiers in Psychology, 9*, 1246. https://doi.org/10.3389/fpsyg.2018.01246

Pearl, R. L., Puhl, R. M., & Dovidio, J. F. (2014). Differential effects of weight bias experiences and internalization on exercise among women with overweight and obesity. *Journal of Health Psychology, 20*, 1626–1632. https://doi.org/10.1177/1359105313520338

Pedersen, B. K., & Saltin, B. (2015). Exercise as medicine–evidence for prescribing exercise as therapy in 26 different chronic diseases. *Scandinavian Journal of Medicine & Science in Sports, 25*(S3), 1–72. https://doi.org/10.1111/sms.12581

Penna, E. M., Filho, E., Campos, B. T., Pires, D. A., Nakamura, F. Y., Mendes, T. T., Lopes, T. R., Smith, M., & Prado, L. S. (2018). Mental fatigue does not affect heart rate recovery but impairs performance in handball players. *Revista Brasileira de Medicina Do Esporte, 24*, 347–351. https://doi.org/10.1590/1517-869220182405180483

Penna, E. M., Filho, E., Wanner, S. P., Campos, B. T., Quinan, G. R., Mendes, T. T., Smith, M. R., & Prado, L. S. (2018). Mental fatigue impairs physical performance in young swimmers. *Pediatric Exercise Science, 30*, 208–215. https://doi.org/10.1123/pes.2017-0128

Pennycook, G., De Neys, W., Evans, J. S. B. T., Stanovich, K. E., & Thompson, V. (2018). The mythical dual-process typology. *Trends in Cognitive Sciences, 22*, 667–668.

Périard, J. D., Pauw, K. de, Zanow, F., & Racinais, S. (2018). Cerebrocortical activity during self-paced exercise in temperate, hot and hypoxic conditions. *Acta Physiologica*, 222. https://doi.org/10.1111/apha.12916

Perrey, S., & Besson, P. (2018). Studying brain activity in sports performance: Contributions and issues. *Progress in Brain Research, 240*, 247–267. https://doi.org/10.1016/bs.pbr.2018.07.004

Pessoa, L. (2008). On the relationship between emotion and cognition. *Nature Reviews Neuroscience, 9*(2), 148–158. https://doi.org/10.1038/nrn2317

Pessoa, L. (2017). A network model of the emotional brain. *Trends in Cognitive Sciences, 21*(5), 357–371. https://doi.org/10.1016/j.tics.2017.03.002

Peters, E., & Slovic, P. (2000). The springs of action: Affective and analytical information processing in choice. *Personality and Social Psychology Bulletin, 26*(12), 1465–1475. https://doi.org/10.1177/01461672002612002

Peters, G. J. Y., De Bruin, M., & Crutzen, R. (2015). Everything should be as simple as possible, but no simpler: Towards a protocol for accumulating evidence regarding the active content of health behaviour change interventions. *Health Psychology Review, 9*(1), 1–14. https://doi.org/10.1080/17437199.2013.848409

Petrie, T. A., & Greenleaf, C. A. (2012). Eating disorders in sport: From theory to research to intervention. In *Handbook of sport psychology: Third edition*. https://doi.org/10.1002/9781118270011.ch16

Petter, S., Straub, D., & Rai, A. (2007). Specifying formative constructs in information systems research. *MIS Quarterly, 31*, 623–656.

Pfeffer, I., Englert, C., & Mueller-Alcazar, A. (2020). Perceived stress and trait self-control interact with the intention–behavior gap in physical activity behavior. *Sport, Exercise, and Performance Psychology, 9*, 244–260. https://doi.org/10.1037/spy0000189

Pfeffer, I., & Strobach, T. (2017). Executive functions, trait self-control, and the intention–behavior gap in physical activity behavior. *Journal of Sport and Exercise Psychology, 39*, 277–292. https://doi.org/10.1123/jsep.2017-0112

Pfeffer, I., & Strobach, T. (2019). Effects of a planning intervention on physical activity behavior in an RCT: Intention strength as moderator and action planning, coping planning, and coping self-efficacy as mediators. *Sport, Exercise, and Performance Psychology, 8*(2), 192–209. https://doi.org/10.1037/spy0000137

Phillips, J. M., Johnston, K., & Everling, S. (2011). Effects of anterior cingulate microstimulation on pro-and antisaccades in nonhuman primates. *Journal of Cognitive Neuroscience, 23*, 481–490. https://doi.org/10.1162/jocn.2010.21482

Phillips, L. A. (2019). Challenging assumptions about habit: A response to Hagger. *Psychology of Sport and Exercise, 47*, 101502.

Phillips, L. A., & Gardner, B. (2016). Habitual exercise instigation (vs. execution) predicts healthy adults' exercise frequency. *Health Psychology, 35*, 69–77.

Physical Activity Guidelines Advisory Committee. (2018). 2018 Physical activity guidelines advisory committee scientific report. Washington, DC: U.S. Department of Health and Human Services.

Pila, E., Brunet, J., Crocker, P. R. E., Kowalski, K. C., & Sabiston, C. M. (2016). Intrapersonal characteristics of body-related guilt, shame, pride, and envy in Canadian adults. *Body Image, 16*, 100–106. https://doi.org/10.1016/j.bodyim.2016.01.001

Pila, E., Sabiston, C. M., Brunet, J., Castonguay, A. L., & O'Loughlin, J. (2015). Do body-related shame and guilt mediate the association between weight status and self-esteem? *Journal of Health Psychology, 20*(5). https://doi.org/10.1177/1359105315573449

Pila, E., Sabiston, C. M., Mack, D. E., Wilson, P. M., Brunet, J., Kowalski, K. C., & Crocker, P. R. E. (2020). Fitness and appearance-related self-conscious emotions and sport experiences: A prospective longitudinal investigation among adolescent girls. *Psychology of Sport & Exercise, 47*, 101641. https://doi.org/10.1016/j.psychsport.2019.101641

Pila, E., Solomon-Krakus, S., Egelton, K., & Sabiston, C. M. (2017). "I am a fat baby, who moved to a fat child, who moved to a fat teenager, who moved to a fat adult": Women's reflections of a lifetime of body and weight concern. *Journal of Women and Aging, 30*(2), 158–177. https://doi.org/10.1080/08952841.2017.1295669

Pila, E., Stamiris, A., Castonguay, A., & Sabiston, C. M. (2014). Body-related envy: A social comparison perspective in sport and exercise. *Journal of Sport and Exercise Psychology, 36*, 93–106. https://doi.org/10.1123/jsep.2013-0100

Pinder, C., Vermeulen, J., Wicaksono, A., Beale, R., & Hendley, R. J. (2016, September). If this, then habit: Exploring context-aware implementation intentions on smartphones. In *Proceedings of the 18th International Conference on Human-Computer Interaction with Mobile Devices and Services Adjunct* (pp. 690–697). https://doi.org/10.1145/2957265.2961837

Piper, S. K., Krueger, A., Koch, S. P., Mehnert, J., Habermehl, C., Steinbrink, J., ... & Schmitz, C. H. (2014). A wearable multi-channel fNIRS system for brain imaging in freely moving subjects. *Neuroimage, 85*, 64–71. https://doi.org/10.1016/j.neuroimage.2013.06.062

Pires, F. O., Silva-Júnior, F. L., Brietzke, C., Franco-Alvarenga, P. E., Pinheiro, F. A., de França, N. M., Teixeira, S., & Meireles Santos, T. (2018). Mental fatigue alters cortical activation and psychological responses, impairing performance in a distance-based cycling trial. *Frontiers in Physiology, 9*, 227. https://doi.org/10.3389/fphys.2018.00227

Plotnikoff, R. C., Costigan, S. A., Karunamuni, N., & Lubans, D. R. (2013). Social cognitive theories used to explain physical activity behavior in adolescents: A systematic review and meta-analysis. *Preventive Medicine, 56*(5), 245–253.https://doi.org/10.1016/j.ypmed.2013.01.013

Plotnikoff, R. C., & Trinh, L. (2010). Protection motivation theory: Is this a worthwhile theory for physical activity promotion? *Exercise and Sport Sciences Reviews, 38*(2), 91–98. https://doi.org/10.1097/JES.0b013e3181d49612

Plumb, T. N., Sterlace, S. R., Cavanaugh, K. A., & Minor, T. R. (2013). Stress, brain adenosine signaling, and fatigue-related behavioral processes. In S. Masino & D. Boison (Eds.), *Adenosine* (pp. 535–558). New York: Springer. https://doi.org/10.1007/978-1-4614-3903-5_25

Poldrack, R. A., & Packard, M. G. (2003). Competition among multiple memory systems: Converging evidence from animal and human brain studies. *Neuropsychologia, 41*(3), 245–251. https://doi.org/10.1016/S0028-3932(02)00157-4

Posner, M. I., & Snyder, C. R. R. (1975). Attention and cognitive control. In R. L. Solso (Ed.), *Information processing and cognition: The Loyola symposium*. Hillsdale, NJ: Erlbaum Assoc.

Powers, T. A., Koestner, R., Zuroff, D. C., Milyavskaya, M., & Gorin, A. A. (2011). The effects of self-criticism and self-oriented perfectionism on goal pursuit. *Personality and Social Psychology Bulletin, 37*(7), 964–975.

Pratt, M., Ramirez Varela, A., Salvo, D., Kohl, H. W. III, & Ding, D. (2020). Attacking the pandemic of physical inactivity: What is holding us back? *British Journal of Sports Medicine, 54*(13), 760–762. https://doi.org/10.1136/bjsports-2019-101392

Prestwich, A., Conner, M., Lawton, R., Bailey, W., Litman, J., & Molyneaux, V. (2005). Individual and collaborative implementation intentions and the promotion of breast self-examination. *Psychology and Health, 20*(6), 743–760. https://doi.org/10.1080/14768320500183335

Prestwich, A., Conner, M. T., Lawton, R. J., Ward, J. K., Ayres, K., & McEachan, R. R. C. (2012). Randomized controlled trial of collaborative implementation intentions targeting working adults' physical activity. *Health Psychology, 31*(4), 486–495. https://doi.org/10.1037/a0027672

Prestwich, A., & Kellar, I. (2014). How can the impact of implementation intentions as a behaviour change intervention be improved? *European Review of Applied Psychology, 64*(1), 35–41. https://doi.org/10.1016/j.erap.2010.03.003

Prestwich, A., Lawton, R., & Conner, M. (2003). The use of implementation intentions and the decision balance sheet in promoting exercise behaviour. *Psychology and Health, 18*(6), 707–721. https://doi.org/10.1080/08870440310001594493

Prestwich, A., Perugini, M., & Hurling, R. (2009). Can the effects of implementation intentions on exercise be enhanced using text messages? *Psychology and Health, 24*(6), 677–687. https://doi.org/10.1080/08870440802040715

Prestwich, A., Perugini, M., & Hurling, R. (2010). Can implementation intentions and text messages promote brisk walking? A randomized trial. *Health Psychology, 29*(1), 40–49. https://doi.org/10.1037/a0016993

Prochaska, J. O., & DiClemente, C. C. (1982). Transtheoretical therapy: Toward a more integrative model of change. *Psychotherapy: Theory, Research & Practice, 19*, 276–288. https://doi.org/10.1037/h0088437

Prochaska, J. O., & DiClemente, C. C. (1983). Stages and processes of self-change of smoking: Toward an integrative model of change. *Journal of Consulting and Clinical Psychology, 51*(3), 390–395. https://doi.org/10.1037/0022-006X.51.3.390

Prochaska, J. O., & Marcus, B. H. (1994). The transtheoretical model: Applications to exercise. In R. K. Dishman (Ed.), *Advances in exercise adherence* (pp. 161–180). Champaign, IL: Human Kinetics.

Purvis, D., Gonsalves, S., & Deuster, P. A. (2010). Physiological and psychological fatigue in extreme conditions: Overtraining and elite athletes. *PM&R, 2*, 442–450. https://doi.org/10.1016/j.pmrj.2010.03.025

Rachlin, H., Kagel, J. H., & Battalio, R. C. (1980). Substitutability in time allocation. *Psychological Review, 87*, 355–374.

Radel, R., Brisswalter, J., & Perrey, S. (2017). Saving mental effort to maintain physical effort: A shift of activity within the prefrontal cortex in anticipation of prolonged exercise. *Cognitive, Affective & Behavioral Neuroscience, 17*, 305–314. https://doi.org/10.3758/s13415-016-0480-x

Radtke, T., Luszczynska, A., Schenkel, K., Biddle, S., & Scholz, U. (2018). A cluster randomized controlled trial comparing the effectiveness of an individual planning intervention with collaborative planning in adolescent friendship dyads to enhance physical activity (TWOgether). *BMC Public Health, 18*(1), 911. https://doi.org/10.1186/s12889-018-5818-6

Ramirez, J. M., & Cabanac, M. (2003). Pleasure, the common currency of emotions. *Annals of the New York Academy of Sciences, 1000*, 293–295. https://doi.org/10.1196/annals.1280.028

Rasquinha, A., Dunn, J. G., & Dunn, J. C. (2014). Relationships between perfectionistic strivings, perfectionistic concerns, and competitive sport level. *Psychology of Sport and Exercise, 15*(6), 659–667. https://doi.org/10.1016/j.psychsport.2014.07.008

Read, D. J., Hill, A. P., Jowett, G. E., & Astill, S. L. (2019). The relationship between perfectionistic self-presentation and reactions to impairment and disability following spinal cord injury. *Journal of Health Psychology, 24*, 362–375.

Reber, A. S. (1993). *Implicit learning and tacit knowledge: An essay on the cognitive unconscious*. New York: Oxford University Press.

Rebar, A., & Rhodes, R. E. (in press). Progression of motivation models in exercise science: Where we have been and where we are heading. In G. Tenenbaum & R. C. Eklund (Eds.), *Handbook of sport psychology* (4th ed.). Hoboken, NJ: Wiley, 911–928.

Rebar, A., Rhodes, R. E., & Gardner, B. (2019). How we are misinterpreting physical activity intention-behavior relations and what to do about it. *The International Journal of Behavioral Nutrition and Physical Activity, 16*, 71–71.

Rebar, A. L., Dimmock, J. A., Rhodes, R. E., & Jackson, B. (2018). A daily diary approach to investigate the effect of ego depletion on intentions and next day behavior. *Psychology of Sport and Exercise, 39*, 38–44. https://doi.org/10.1016/j.psychsport.2018.07.010

Rebar, A. L., Elavsky, S., Maher, J. P., Doerksen, S. E., & Conroy, D. E. (2014). Habits predict physical activity on days when intentions are weak. *Journal of Sport and Exercise Psychology, 36*(2), 157–165.

Rebar A. L., Ram, N., & Conroy, D. E. (2015). Using the EZ-diffusion model to score a single-category implicit association test of physical activity. *Psychology of Sport and Exercise, 16*, 96–105.

Rees, T., Hardy, L., Güllich, A., Abernethy, B., Côté, J., Woodman, T., … & Warr, C. (2016). The great British medalists project: A review of current knowledge on the development of the world's best sporting talent. *Sports Medicine, 46*, 1041–1058.

Reeve, J., Nix, G., & Hamm, D. (2003). Testing models of the experience of self-determination in intrinsic motivation and the conundrum of choice. *Journal of Educational Psychology, 95*(2), 375–392. https://doi.org/10.1037/0022-0663.95.2.375

Reis, R. S., Salvo, D., Ogilvie, D., Lambert, E. V., Goenka, S., Brownson, R. C., & Lancet Physical Activity Series 2 Executive Committee. (2016). Scaling up physical activity interventions worldwide: Stepping up to larger and smarter approaches to get people moving. *The Lancet, 388*(10051), 1337–1348. https://doi.org/10.1016/S0140-6736(16)30728-0

Renner, B., Spivak, Y., Kwon, S., & Schwarzer, R. (2007). Does age make a difference? Predicting physical activity of South Koreans. *Psychology and Aging, 22*(3), 482–493. https://doi.org/10.1037/0882-7974.22.3.482

Reyna, V. F., Nelson, W. L., Han, P. K., & Dieckmann, N. F. (2009). How numeracy influences risk comprehension and medical decision making. *Psychological Bulletin, 135*(6), 943–973. https://doi.org/10.1037/a0017327

Rhéaume, J., Freeston, M. H., Ladouceur, R., Bouchard, C., Gallant, L., Talbot, F., & Vallières, A. (2000). Functional and dysfunctional perfectionists: Are they different on compulsive-like behaviors?. *Behaviour Research and Therapy, 38*, 119–128.

Rhodes, R. E. (2017). The evolving understanding of physical activity behavior: A multi-process action control approach. In A. J. Elliot (Ed.), *Advances in motivation science* (Vol. 4, pp. 171–205). Cambridge, MA: Elsevier Academic Press.

Rhodes, R. E., Berry, T., Faulkner, G., Latimer-Cheung, A. E., O'Reilly, N., Tremblay, M. S., … & Spence, J. C. (2019). Application of the multi-process action control framework to understand parental support of child and youth physical activity, sleep, and screen time behaviors. *Applied Psychology: Health and Well-Being, 11*, 223–239.

Rhodes, R. E., Boudreau, P., Weman Josefsson, K., & Ivarsson, A. (in press). Mediators of physical activity behaviour change interventions among adults: A systematic review and meta-analysis. *Health Psychology Review*. https://doi.org/10.1080/17437199.2019.1706614

Rhodes, R. E., Bredin, S. S. D., Janssen, I., Warburton, D. E. R., & Bauman, A. (2017). Physical activity: Health impact, prevalence, correlates and interventions. *Psychology and Health, 32*, 942–975. doi: https://doi.org/10.1080/08870446.2017.1325486

Rhodes, R. E., & de Bruijn, G. J. (2013a). How big is the physical activity intention-behaviour gap? A meta-analysis using the action control framework. *British Journal of Health Psychology, 18*(2), 296–309. https://doi.org/10.1111/bjhp.12032

Rhodes, R. E., & de Bruijn, G. J. (2013b). What predicts intention-behavior discordance? A review of the action control framework. *Exercise and Sports Sciences Reviews, 41*(4), 201–207. https://doi.org/10.1097/JES.0b013e3182a4e6ed

Rhodes, R. E., & Dickau, L. (2012). Meta-analysis of experimental evidence for the intention-behavior relationship in the physical activity domain. *Health Psychology, 31*(6), 724–727.

Rhodes, R. E., & Dickau, L. (2013). Moderators of the intention-behaviour relationship in the physical activity domain: A systematic review. *British Journal of Sports Medicine, 47*, 215–225. https://doi.org/10.1136/bjsports-2011-090411

Rhodes, R. E., Fiala, B., & Conner, M. (2009). Affective judgments and physical activity: A review and meta-analysis. *Annals of Behavioral Medicine, 38*, 180–204. https://doi.org/10.1007/s12160-009-9147-y

Rhodes, R. E., Fiala, B., & Nasuti, G. (2012). Action control of exercise behavior: Evaluation of social cognition, cross-behavioral regulation, and automaticity. *Behavioral Medicine, 38*(4), 121–128. https://doi.org/10.1080/08964289.2012.695411

Rhodes, R. E., Grant, S., & De Bruijn, G. J. (2020). Planning and implementation intention interventions. In M. S. Hagger, L. D. Cameron, K. Hamilton, N. Hankonen & T. Lintunen (Eds.), *Handbook of behavior change* (pp. 572–585). New York, NY: Cambridge University Press.

Rhodes, R. E., & Gray, S. (2018). Affect in the process of action control of health protective behaviors. In D. W. Williams, R. E. Rhodes & M. T. Conner (Eds.), *Affective determinants of health behavior* (pp. 21–47). New York: Oxford Press.

Rhodes, R. E., & Kates, A. (2015). Can the affective response to exercise predict future motives and physical activity behavior? A systematic review of published evidence. *Annals of Behavioral Medicine, 49*(5), 715–731. https://doi.org/10.1007/s12160-015-9704-5

Rhodes, R. E., Kaushal, N., & Quinlan, A. (2016). Is physical activity a part of who I am? A review and meta-analysis of identity, schema and physical activity. *Health Psychology Review, 10*, 204–225. http://dx.doi.org/10.1080/17437199.2016.1143334

Rhodes, R. E., La, H., Quinlan, A., & Grant, S. (this volume). Enacting physical activity intention: A multi-process action control approach. In C. Englert & I. M. Taylor (Eds.), *Motivation & self-regulation in sport & exercise*. London: Routledge.

Rhodes, R. E., McEwan, D., & Rebar, A. L. (2019). Theories of physical activity behaviour change: A history and synthesis of approaches. *Psychology of Sport and Exercise, 42*, 100–109. https://doi.org/10.1016/j.psychsport.2018.11.010

Rhodes, R. E., & Nasuti, G. (2011). Trends and changes in research on the psychology of physical activity across 20 years: A quantitative analysis of 10 journals. *Preventive Medicine, 53*(1–2), 17–23.

Rhodes, R. E., Nasuti, G., & Fiala, B. (2012). Action control of exercise behaviour: Evaluation of social cognition, cross-behavioural regulation and automaticity. *Behavioral Medicine, 38*, 121–128.

Rhodes, R. E., Naylor, P. J., Blanchard, C., Quinlan, A., & Warburton, D. E. R. (2019). Family physical activity planning and child physical activity outcomes: A randomized trial. *American Journal of Preventive Medicine, 57*, 135–292.

Rhodes, R. E., Naylor, P. J., & McKay, H. A. (2010). Pilot study of a family physical activity planning intervention among parents and their children. *Journal of Behavioral Medicine, 33*, 91–100.

Rhodes, R. E., & Lim, C. (2016). Understanding action control of daily walking behavior among dog owners: A community survey. *BMC Public Health, 16*, 1165–1174.

Rhodes, R. E., & Nigg, C. R. (2011). Advancing physical activity theory: A review and future directions. *Exercise and Sport Sciences Reviews, 39*(3), 113–119. https://doi.org/10.1097/JES.0b013e31821b94c8

Rhodes, R. E., & Plotnikoff, R. C. (2006). Understanding action control: Predicting physical activity intention-behavior profiles across six months in a Canadian sample. *Health Psychology, 25*, 292–299.

Rhodes, R. E., Plotnikoff, R. C., & Courneya, K. S. (2008). Predicting the physical activity intention–behavior profiles of adopters and maintainers using three social cognition models. *Annals of Behavioral Medicine, 36*(3), 244–252. https://doi.org/10.1007/s12160-008-9071-6

Rhodes, R. E., Quinlan, A., & Mistry, C. (2016). Do other goals influence physical activity? A systematic review examining the relationship between other goals and physical activity behaviour. *Preventive Medicine, 91*, 306–317.

Rhodes, R. E., Quinlan, A., Naylor, P. J., Warburton, D. E. R., & Blanchard, C. M. (2020). Predicting personal physical activity of parents during participation in a family intervention targeting their children. *Journal of Behavioral Medicine, 43*, 209–224.

Rhodes, R. E., & Rebar, A. (2017). Conceptualizing and defining the intention construct for future physical activity research. *Exercise and Sports Sciences Reviews, 45*, 209–216.

Rhodes, R. E., & Rebar, A (2018). Physical activity habit: Complexities and controversies. In B. Verplanken (Ed.), *The psychology of habit* (pp. 91–109). Cham: Springer.

Rhodes, R. E., Spence, J. C., Berry, T., Deshpande, S., Faulkner, G., Latimer-Cheung, A., … & Tremblay, M. (2016). Understanding action control of parent support behavior for child physical activity. *Health Psychology, 35*, 131–140. https://doi.org/10.1037/hea0000233

Rhodes, R. E., & Yao, C. (2015). Models accounting for intention-behavior discordance in the physical activity domain: A user's guide, content overview, and review of current evidence. *International Journal of Behavioral Nutrition and Physical Activity, 12*(9), 1–15. https://doi.org/10.1186/s12966-015-0168-6

Rice, T. (2013). The behavioral economics of health and health care. *Annual Review of Public Health, 34*, 431–447. https://doi.org/10.1146/annurev-publhealth-031912-114353

Richeson, J. A., & Shelton, J. N. (2003). When prejudice does not pay: Effects of interracial contact on executive function. *Psychological Science, 14*, 287–290. https://doi.org/10.1111/1467–9280.03437

Richter, M., Gendolla, G. H. E., & Wright, R. A. (2016). Three decades of research on motivational intensity theory: What we have learned about effort and what we still don't know. In A. J. Elliot (Ed.), *Advances in motivation science* (Vol. 3, pp. 149–186). Cambridge, MA: Elsevier Academic Press. https://doi.org/10.1016/bs.adms.2016.02.001

Rise, J., Sheeran, P., & Hukkelberg, S. (2010). The role of self-identity in the theory of planned behavior: A meta-analysis. *Journal of Applied Social Psychology, 40*, 1085–1105.

Ritchie, H., & Roser, M. (2020). Mental health. https://ourworldindata.org/mental-health

Ritz, H., Frömer, R., & Shenhav, A. (2020). Bridging motor and cognitive control: It's about time! *Trends in Cognitive Sciences, 24*(1), 6–8. https://doi.org/10.1016/j.tics.2019.11.005

Robazza, C., Bertollo, M., Filho, E., Hanin, Y., & Bortoli, L. (2016). Perceived control and hedonic tone dynamics during performance in elite shooters. *Research Quarterly for Exercise and Sport, 87*, 284–294. https://doi.org/10.1080/02701367.2016.1185081

Robbins, B. D., & Parlavecchio, H. (2006). The unwanted exposure of the self: A phenomenological study of embarrassment. *Humanistic Psychologist, 34*(4), 321–345. https://doi.org/10.1207/s15473333thp3404_3

Roberto, C. A., & Kawachi, I. (2016). An introduction to behavioral economics and public health. In C. A. Roberto & I. Kawachi (Eds.), *Behavioral economics and public health* (pp. 1–26). New York: Oxford University Press. https://doi.org/10.1093/med/9780199398331.003.0001

Roberts, G. C., & Nerstad, C. G. L. (2020). Achievement goal theory in sport and physical activity. In D. Hackfort & R. J., Schinke (Eds.), *The Routledge international encyclopedia of sport and exercise psychology* (pp. XX–XX). Abingdon: Routledge.

Roberts, G. C., & Pascuzzi, D. (1979). Causal attributions in sport: Some theoretical implications. *Journal of Sport Psychology, 1*(3), 203–211.

Roberts, G. C., & Treasure, D. C. (2012). *Advances in motivation in sport and exercise.* Champaign, IL: Human Kinetics.

Robertson, C. V., & Marino, F. E. (2015). Prefrontal and motor cortex EEG responses and their relationship to ventilatory thresholds during exhaustive incremental exercise. *European Journal of Applied Physiology, 115*, 1939–1948. https://doi.org/10.1007/s00421-015-3177-x

Robinson, S. A., Bisson, A. N., Hughes, M. L., Ebert, J., & Lachman, M. E. (2019). Time for change: Using implementation intentions to promote physical activity in a randomized pilot trial. *Psychology & Health, 34*(2), 232–254.

Rodgers, W. M., Selzler, A. M., Haennel, R. G., Holm, S., Wong, E. Y., & Stickland, M. K. (2014). An experimental assessment of the influence of exercise versus social implementation intentions on physical activity during and following pulmonary rehabilitation. *Journal of Behavioral Medicine, 37*(3), 480–490. https://doi.org/10.1007/s10865-013-9503-z

Rodrigues, A. M., O'Brien, N., French, D. P., Glidewell, L., & Sniehotta, F. F. (2015). The question-behavior effect: Genuine effect or spurious phenomenon? A systematic review of randomized controlled trials with meta-analyses. *Health Psychology, 34*(1), 61–78. https://doi.org/10.1037/hea0000104

Roelands, B., De Pauw, K., & Meeusen, R. (2015). Neurophysiological effects of exercise in the heat. *Scandinavian Journal of Medicine and Science in Sports, 25*, 65–78. https://doi.org/10.1111/sms.12350

Roelands, B., Goekint, M., Heyman, E., Piacentini, M. F., Watson, P., Hasegawa, H., … & Meeusen, R. (2008). Acute norepinephrine reuptake inhibition decreases performance in normal and high ambient temperature. *Journal of Applied Physiology, 105*, 206–212. https://doi.org/10.1152/japplphysiol.90509.2008

Roelands, B., Hasegawa, H., Watson, P., Piacentini, M. F., Buyse, L., De Schutter, G., & Meeusen, R. R. (2008). The effects of acute dopamine reuptake inhibition on performance. *Medicine and Science in Sports and Exercise, 40*, 879. https://doi.org/10.1249/MSS.0b013e3181659c4d

Rogers, R. W. (1975). A protection motivation theory of fear appeals and attitude change. *The Journal of Psychology, 91*(1), 93–114. https://doi.org/10.1080/00223980.1975.9915803

Rogers, R. W. (1983). Cognitive and physiological processes in fear appeals and attitude change: A revised theory of protection motivation. In J. T. Cacioppo & R. E. Petty (Eds.), *Social psychophysiology: A sourcebook* (pp. 153–176). New York: Guilford Press.

Rolls, E. T. (2007). The affective neuroscience of consciousness: Higher-order syntactic thoughts, dual routes to emotion and action, and consciousness. In P. D. Zelazo, M. Moscovitch, & E. Thompson (Eds.), *The Cambridge handbook of consciousness* (pp. 831–859). New York: Cambridge University Press. https://doi.org/10.1017/CBO9780511816789.030

Roloff, Z. A., Dicks, N. D., Krynski, L. M., Hartman, M. E., Ekkekakis, P., & Pettitt, R. W. (2020). Ratings of affective valence closely track changes in oxygen uptake: Application to high-intensity interval exercise. *Performance Enhancement & Health*, 100158. https://doi.org/10.1016/j.peh.2020.100158

Romain, A. J., Bortolon, C., Gourlan, M., Carayol, M., Decker, E., Lareyre, O., Ninot, G., Boiché, J., & Bernard, P. (2018). Matched or nonmatched interventions based on the transtheoretical model to promote physical activity. A meta-analysis of randomized controlled trials. *Journal of Sport and Health Science, 7*, 50–57.

Rooks, C. R., Thom, N. J., McCully, K. K., & Dishman, R. K. (2010). Effects of incremental exercise on cerebral oxygenation measured by near-infrared spectroscopy: A systematic review. *Progress in Neurobiology, 92*, 134–150. https://doi.org/10.1016/j.pneurobio.2010.06.002

Rosenstock, I. M. (1974a). Historical origins of the health belief model. *Health Education Monographs, 2*(4), 328–335.

Rosenstock, I. M. (1974b). The health belief model and preventive health behavior. *Health Education Monographs, 2*(4), 354–386. https://doi.org/10.1177/109019817400200405

Rothman, A. J., Klein, W. M. P., & Sheeran, P. (2020). Moving from theoretical principles to intervention strategies: Applying the experimental medicine approach. In M. S. Hagger, L. D. Cameron, K. Hamilton, N. Hankonen & T. Lintunen (Eds.), *The handbook of behavior change* (pp. 285–299). New York: Cambridge University Press. https://doi.org/10.1017/97811086773180.020

Roussey, G., Gruet, M., Vercruyssen, F., Louis, J., Vallier, J.-M., & Bernard, T. (2018). Interactions between perceived exertion and thermal perception in the heat in endurance athletes. *Journal of Thermal Biology, 76*, 68–76. https://doi.org/10.1016/j.jtherbio.2018.07.006

Royer, H., Stehr, M., & Sydnor, J. (2015). Incentives, commitments, and habit formation in exercise: Evidence from a field experiment with workers at a fortune-500 company. *American Economic Journal: Applied Economics*, 7(3), 51–84.

Rupp, T., & Perrey, S. (2008). Prefrontal cortex oxygenation and neuromuscular responses to exhaustive exercise. *European Journal of Applied Physiology, 102*, 153–163. https://doi.org/10.1007/s00421-007-0568-7

Russell, J. A. (2003). Core affect and the psychological construction of emotion. *Psychological Review, 110*(1), 145–172. https://doi.org/10.1037/0033-295X.110.1.145

Russell, S., Jenkins, D., Rynne, S., Halson, S. L., & Kelly, V. (2019). What is mental fatigue in elite sport? Perceptions from athletes and staff. *European Journal of Sport Science, 19*, 1367–1376. https://doi.org/10.1080/17461391.2019.1618397

Russell, S., Jenkins, D., Smith, M., Halson, S., & Kelly, V. (2019). The application of mental fatigue research to elite team sport performance: New perspectives. *Journal of Science and Medicine in Sport, 22*, 723–728. https://doi.org/10.1016/j.jsams.2018.12.008

Ryan, R. M., & Brown, K. W. (2003). Why we don't need self-esteem: On fundamental needs, contingent love, and mindfulness. *Psychological Inquiry, 14*(1), 71–76.

Ryan, R. M., & Deci, E. L. (2000). Self-determination theory and the facilitation of intrinsic motivation, social development, and well-being. *American Psychologist, 55*(1), 68–78. https://doi.org/10.1037/0003-066X.55.1.68

Ryan, R. M., & Deci, E. L. (2017). *Self-determination theory: Basic psychological needs in motivation, development, and wellness.* New York: Guilford Press.

Sabiston, C. M., Brunet, J., Kowalski, K. C., Wilson, P. M., Mack, D. E., & Crocker, P. R. (2010). The role of body-related self-conscious emotions in motivating women's physical activity. *Journal of Sport and Exercise Psychology, 32*(4), 417–437. https://doi.org/10.1123/jsep.32.4.417

Sabiston, C. M., Pila, E., Crocker, P. R. E., Mack, D. E., Wilson, P. M., Brunet, J., & Kowalski, K. C. (2020). Changes in body-related self-conscious emotions over time among youth female athletes. *Body Image, 32*, 24–33. https://doi.org/10.1016/j.bodyim.2019.11.001

Sabiston, C. M., Pila, E., & Gilchrist, J. (2020). Self-conscious emotions in sport and exercise. In R. E. Eklund & G. Tenenbaum (Eds.), *Handbook of sport psychology* (pp. 299–319). New York: Wiley.

Sabiston, C. M., Pila, E., PinsonnaultBilodeau, G., & Cox, A. E. (2014). Social physique anxiety experiences in physical activity: A comprehensive synthesis of research studies focused on measurement, theory, and predictors and outcomes. *International Review of Sport and Exercise Psychology*, 7(1), 158–183. https://doi.org/10.1080/1750984X.2014.904392

Sabiston, C. M., Pila, E., Vani, M., & Thogersen-Ntoumani, C. (2019). Body image, physical activity, and sport: A scoping review. *Psychology of Sport and Exercise, 42*, 48–57. https://doi.org/10.1016/j.psychsport.2018.12.010

Sabiston, C. M., Sedgwick, W. A., Crocker, P. R. E., Kowalski, K. C., & Mack, D. E. (2007). Social physique anxiety in adolescence. *Journal of Adolescent Research*, *22*(1), 78–101. https://doi.org/10.1177/0743558406294628

Salam, H., Marcora, S. M., & Hopker, J. G. (2018). The effect of mental fatigue on critical power during cycling exercise. *European Journal of Applied Physiology*, *118*, 85–92. https://doi.org/10.1007/s00421-017-3747-1

Salamone, J. D., Correa, M., Ferrigno, S., Yang, J. H., Rotolo, R. A., & Presby, R. E. (2018). The psychopharmacology of effort-related decision making: dopamine, adenosine, and insights into the neurochemistry of motivation. *Pharmacological Reviews*, *70*, 747–762. https://doi.org/10.1124/pr.117.015107

Salamone, J. D., Correa, M., Yang, J.-H., Rotolo, R., & Presby, R. (2018). Dopamine, effort-based choice, and behavioral economics: Basic and translational research. *Frontiers in Behavioral Neuroscience*, *12*, 52. https://doi.org/10.3389/fnbeh.2018.00052

Sallis, J. F., Bull, F., Guthold, R., Heath, G. W., Inoue, S., Kelly, P., ... & Lancet Physical Activity Series 2 Executive Committee. (2016). Progress in physical activity over the Olympic quadrennium. *The Lancet*, *388*(10051), 1325–1336. https://doi.org/10.1016/S0140-6736(16)30581-5

Sallis, J. F., Cervero, R. B., Ascher, W., Henderson, K., Kraft, M. K., & Kerr, J. (2006). An ecological approach to creating active living communities. *Annual Review of Public Health*, *27*, 297–322.

Samuel, R. D., Englert, C., Zhang, Q., & Basevitch, I. (2018). Hi ref, are you in control? Self-control, ego-depletion, and performance in soccer referees. *Psychology of Sport and Exercise*, *38*, 167–175. https://doi.org/10.1016/j.psychsport.2018.06.009

Sansone, C., Sachau, D. A., & Weir, C. (1989). Effects of instruction on intrinsic interest: The importance of context. *Journal of Personality and Social Psychology*, *57*(5), 819–829. https://doi.org/10.1037/0022-3514.57.5.819

Santos-Lozano, A., Collado, P., Foster, C., Lucia, A., & Garatachea, N. (2014). Influence of sex and level on marathon pacing strategy. Insights from the New York City race. *International Journal of Sports Medicine*, *35*, 933–938. https://doi.org/10.1055/s-0034-1367048

Sarkar, M., & Fletcher, D. (2014). Psychological resilience in sport performers: a review of stressors and protective factors. *Journal of Sports Sciences*, *32*(15), 1419–1434.

Sarrazin, P., Vallerand, R., Guillet, E., Pelletier, L., & Cury, F. (2002). Motivation and dropout in female handballers: A 21-month prospective study. *European Journal of Social Psychology*, *32*(3), 395–418. https://doi.org/10.1002/ejsp.98

Sato, W., Kochiyama, T., Minemoto, K., Sawada, R., & Fushiki, T. (2019). Amygdala activation during unconscious visual processing of food. *Scientific Reports*, *9*(1), 7277. https://doi.org/10.1038/s41598-019-43733-2

Saunders, B., & Inzlicht, M. (2016). Vigour and fatigue: How variation in affect underlies effective self-control. In T. S. Braver (Ed.), *Motivation and cognitive control* (pp. 212–234). (Frontiers of Cognitive Psychology). London: Routledge. https://doi.org/10.4324/9781315656878

Schaefer, S., & Scornaienchi, D. (2020). Table tennis experts outperform novices in a demanding cognitive-motor dual-task situation. *Journal of Motor Behavior*, *52*, 204–213. https://doi.org/10.1080/00222895.2019.1602506

Schinkoeth, M., & Antoniewicz, F. (2017). Automatic evaluations and exercising: Systematic review and implications for future research. *Frontiers in Psychology*, *8*, 2103. https://doi.org/10.3389/fpsyg.2017.02103

Schinkoeth, M., Weymar, M., & Brand, R. (2019). Listening to the heart: Getting closer to the somatic core of affective valuation of exercise through heart rate variability analysis. *Psychology of Sport and Exercise*, *45*, 101541. https://doi.org/10.1016/j.psychsport.2019.101541

Schlam, T. R., Wilson, N. L., Shoda, Y., Mischel, W., & Ayduk, O. (2013). Preschoolers' delay of gratification predicts their body mass 30 years later. *The Journal of Pediatrics*, *162*, 90–93. https://doi.org/10.1016/j.jpeds.2012.06.049

Schmeichel, B. J., & Baumeister, R. F. (2010). Effortful attention control. In B. Bruya (Ed.), *Effortless attention: A new perspective in the cognitive science of attention and action* (pp. 29–49). Cambridge, MA: MIT Press. https://doi.org/10.7551/mitpress/9780262013840.003.0002

Schmeichel, B. J., Vohs, K. D., & Baumeister, R. F. (2003). Intellectual performance and ego depletion: Role of the self in logical reasoning and other information processing. *Journal of Personality and Social Psychology, 85*, 33–46. doi:10.1037/0022-3514.85.1.33

Schneider, W., & Shiffrin, R. M. (1977). Controlled and automatic human information processing: I. Detection, search, and attention. *Psychological Review, 84*, 1–66. https://doi.org/10.1037/0033-295X.84.1.1

Scholkmann, F., Kleiser, S., Metz, A. J., Zimmermann, R., Mata Pavia, J., Wolf, U., & Wolf, M. (2014). A review on continuous wave functional near-infrared spectroscopy and imaging instrumentation and methodology. *NeuroImage, 85*, 6–27. https://doi.org/10.1016/j.neuroimage.2013.05.004

Scholz, U., Berli, C., Lüscher, J., & Knoll, N. (2020). Dyadic behavior change interventions. In M. S. Hagger, L. D. Cameron, K. Hamilton, N. Hankonen & T. Lintunen (Eds.), *The handbook of behavior change* (pp. 632–648). New York: Cambridge University Press. https://doi.org/10.1017/97811086773180.043

Scholz, U., Sniehotta, F. F., Burkert, S., & Schwarzer, R. (2007). Increasing physical exercise levels: Age-specific benefits of planning. *Journal of Aging and Health, 19*(5), 851–866. https://doi.org/10.1177/0898264307305207

Schöndube, A., Bertrams, A., Sudeck, G., & Fuchs, R. (2017). Self-control strength and physical exercise: An ecological momentary assessment study. *Psychology of Sport and Exercise, 29*, 19–26. https://doi.org/10.1016/j.psychsport.2016.11.006

Schücker, L., & MacMahon, C. (2016). Working on a cognitive task does not influence performance in a physical fitness test. *Psychology of Sport and Exercise, 25*, 1–8. https://doi.org/10.1016/j.psychsport.2016.03.002

Schüz, B., Brick, C., Wilding, S., & Conner, M. (2020). Socioeconomic status moderates the effects of health cognitions on health behaviors within participants: Two multibehavior studies. *Annals of Behavioral Medicine, 54*, 36–48.

Schüz, B., Sniehotta, F. F., Wiedemann, A., & Seemann, R. (2006). Adherence to a daily flossing regimen in university students: Effects of planning when, where, how and what to do in the face of barriers. *Journal of Clinical Periodontology, 33*(9), 612–619. https://doi.org/10.1111/j.1600-051X.2006.00967.x

Schwabe, L., & Wolf, O. T. (2013). Stress and multiple memory systems: From 'thinking' to 'doing'. *Trends in Cognitive Sciences, 17*(2), 60–68. https://doi.org/10.1016/j.tics.2012.12.001

Schwarzer, R. (1992). Self-efficacy in the adoption and maintenance of health behaviours: Theoretical approaches and a new model. In R. Schwarzer (Ed.), *Self-efficacy: Thought control of action* (pp. 217–242). Washington, DC: Hemisphere.

Schwarzer, R. (2008). Modeling health behavior change: How to predict and modify the adoption and maintenance of health behaviors. *Applied Psychology, 57*, 1–29. https://doi.org/10.1111/j.1464–0597.2007.00325.x

Schwarzer, R., & Hamilton, K. (2020). Changing behavior using the health action process approach. In M. S. Hagger, L. D. Cameron, K. Hamilton, N. Hankonen, & T. Lintunen (Eds.), *Handbook of behavior change* (pp. 89–103). Cambridge: Cambridge University Press. https://doi.org/10.1017/97811086773180.007

Schwarzer, R., Lippke, S., & Luszczynska, A. (2011). Mechanisms of health behavior change in persons with chronic illness or disability: The Health Action Process Approach (HAPA). *Rehabilitation Psychology, 56*, 161–170. doi:10.1037/a0024509

Schweimer, J., & Hauber, W. (2006). Dopamine D1 receptors in the anterior cingulate cortex regulate effort-based decision making. *Learning & Memory, 13*, 777–782. https://doi.org/10.1101/lm.409306

Schweizer, K. (2002). Does impulsivity influence performance in reasoning? *Personality and Individual Differences, 33*(7), 1031–1043. https://doi.org/10.1016/S0191-8869(01)00209-4

Secher, N. H., Seifert, T., & Van Lieshout, J. J. (2008). Cerebral blood flow and metabolism during exercise: Implications for fatigue. *Journal of Applied Physiology, 104*, 306–314. https://doi.org/10.1152/japplphysiol.00853.2007

Seeley, E. A., & Gardner, W. L. (2003). The "selfless" and self-regulation: The role of chronic other-orientation in averting self-regulatory depletion. *Self and Identity, 2*, 103–117. https://doi.org/10.1080/15298860309034

Segar, M., Taber, J. M., Patrick, H., Thai, C. L., & Oh, A. (2017). Rethinking physical activity communication: Using focus groups to understand women's goals, values, and beliefs to improve health. *BMC Public Health, 17*, 462.

Segar, M. L., Eccles, J. S., & Richardson, C. R. (2011). Rebranding exercise: Closing the gap between values and behavior. *International Journal of Behavioral Nutrition and Physical Activity, 8*, 94. https://doi.org/10.1186/1479-5868-8-94

Seidel, O., Carius, D., Roediger, J., Rumpf, S., & Ragert, P. (2019). Changes in neurovascular coupling during cycling exercise measured by multi-distance fNIRS: A comparison between endurance athletes and physically active controls. *Experimental Brain Research, 237*, 2957–2972. https://doi.org/10.1007/s00221-019-05646-4

Serrano-Sanchez, J. A., Martí-Trujillo, S., Lera-Navarro, A., Dorado-García, C., González-Henríquez, J. J., & Sanchís-Moysi, J. (2011). Associations between screen time and physical activity among Spanish adolescents. *PloS ONE, 6*(9), e24453.

Shaabani, F., Naderi, A., Borella, E., & Calmeiro, L. (2020). Does a brief mindfulness intervention counteract the detrimental effects of ego depletion in basketball free throw under pressure? *Sport, Exercise, and Performance Psychology, 9*, 197–215. https://doi.org/10.1037/spy0000201

Shackman, A. J., Salomons, T. V., Slagter, H. A., Fox, A. S., Winter, J. J., & Davidson, R. J. (2011). The integration of negative affect, pain and cognitive control in the cingulate cortex. *Nature Reviews Neuroscience, 12*, 154–167. https://doi.org/10.1038/nrn2994

Shadmehr, R., Huang, H. J., & Ahmed, A. A. (2016). A representation of effort in decision-making and motor control. *Current Biology, 26*, 1929–1934. https://doi.org/10.1016/j.cub.2016.05.065

Sheeran, P. (2002). Intention – behavior relations: A conceptual and empirical review. *European Review of Social Psychology, 12*(1), 1–36. https://doi.org/10.1080/14792772143000003

Sheeran, P., & Abraham, C. (2003). Mediator of moderators: Temporal stability of intention and the intention-behavior relation. *Personality and Social Psychology Bulletin, 29*(2), 205–215. https://doi.org/10.1177/0146167202239046

Sheeran, P., Gollwitzer, P. M., & Bargh, J. A. (2013). Nonconscious processes and health. *Health Psychology, 32*(5), 460–473. https://doi.org/10.1037/a0029203

Sheeran, P., Klein, W. M. P., & Rothman, A. J. (2017). Health behavior change: Moving from observation to intervention. *Annual Review of Psychology, 68*(1), 573–600. https://doi.org/10.1146/annurev-psych-010416-044007

Sheeran, P., Orbell, S., & Trafimow, D. (1999). Does the temporal stability of behavioral intentions moderate intention-behavior and past behavior-future behavior relations? *Personality and Social Psychology Bulletin, 25*(6), 724–734. https://doi.org/10.1177/0146167299025006007

Sheeran, P., & Webb, T. L. (2016). The intention–behavior gap. *Social and Personality Psychology Compass, 10*(9), 503–518. https://doi.org/10.1111/spc3.12265

Sheeran, P., Webb, T. L., & Gollwitzer, P. M. (2005). The interplay between goal intentions and implementation intentions. *Personality and Social Psychology Bulletin, 31*(1), 87–98. https://doi.org/10.1177/0146167204271308

Sheldon, K. M., & Elliot, A. J. (1999). Goal striving, need satisfaction, and longitudinal well-being: The self-concordance model. *Journal of Personality and Social Psychology, 76*(3), 482–497. https://doi.org/10.1037/0022-3514.76.3.482

Shenhav, A., Botvinick, M. M., & Cohen, J. D. (2013). The expected value of control: An integrative theory of anterior cingulate cortex function. *Neuron, 79*, 217–240. https://doi.org/10.1016/j.neuron.2013.07.007

Shenhav, A., Cohen, J. D., & Botvinick, M. M. (2016). Dorsal anterior cingulate cortex and the value of control. *Nature Neuroscience, 19*, 1286–1291. https://doi.org/10.1038/nn.4384

Shenhav, A., Musslick, S., Lieder, F., Kool, W., Griffiths, T. L., Cohen, J. D., & Botvinick, M. M. (2017). Toward a rational and mechanistic account of mental effort. *Annual Review of Neuroscience, 40*, 99–124. https://doi.org/10.1146/annurev-neuro-072116-031526

Shepard, G. J., Banks, A. J., & Ryan, W. G. (2003). Ex-professional association footballers have an increased prevalence of osteoarthritis of the hip compared with age matched controls despite not having sustained notable hip injuries. *British Journal of Sports Medicine, 37*(1), 80–81.

Sherman, D. K., & Cohen, G. L. (2006). The psychology of self-defense: Self-affirmation theory. In M. P. Zanna (Ed.), *Advances in experimental social psychology* (Vol. 38, pp. 183–242). Cambridge, MA: Elsevier Academic Press. https://doi.org/10.1016/S0065-2601(06)38004-5

Sherrington, C., Tiedemann, A., Fairhall, N., Close, J. C., & Lord, S. R. (2011). Exercise to prevent falls in older adults: An updated meta-analysis and best practice recommendations. *New South Wales Public Health Bulletin, 22*, 78–83. https://doi.org/10.1071/NB10056

Shin, M., Kim, Y., & Park, S. (2019). Effects of state anxiety and ego depletion on performance change in golf putting: A hierarchical linear model application. *Perceptual and Motor Skills, 126*, 904–921. https://doi.org/10.1177/0031512519856970

Shiv, B., & Fedorikhin, A. (1999). Heart and mind in conflict: The interplay of affect and cognition in consumer decision making. *Journal of Consumer Research, 26*(3), 278–292. https://doi.org/10.1086/209563

Shiv, B., & Fedorikhin, A. (2002). Spontaneous versus controlled influences of stimulus-based affect on choice behavior. *Organizational Behavior and Human Decision Processes, 87*(2), 342–370. https://doi.org/10.1006/obhd.2001.2977

Shiv, B., Fedorikhin, A., & Nowlis, S. M. (2005). Interplay of the heart and the mind in decision-making. In S. Ratneshwar & D. G. Mick (Eds.), *Inside consumption: Consumer motives, goals, and desires* (pp. 166–184). New York: Routledge. https://doi.org/10.4324/9780203481295-15

Shortz, A. E., & Mehta, R. K. (2017). Cognitive challenges, aging, and neuromuscular fatigue. *Physiology & Behavior, 170*, 19–26. https://doi.org/10.1016/j.physbeh.2016.11.034

Shortz, A. E., Pickens, A., Zheng, Q., & Mehta, R. K. (2015). The effect of cognitive fatigue on prefrontal cortex correlates of neuromuscular fatigue in older women. *Journal of NeuroEngineering and Rehabilitation, 12*, 115. https://doi.org/10.1186/s12984-015-0108-3

Shrestha, N., Kukkonen-Harjula, K. T., Verbeek, J. H., Ijaz, S., Hermans, V., & Pedisic, Z. (2018). Workplace interventions for reducing sitting at work. *The Cochrane Database of Systematic Reviews, 6*, CD010912.

Shulman, E. P., Smith, A. R., Silva, K., Icenogle, G., Duell, N., Chein, J., & Steinberg, L. (2016). The dual systems model: Review, reappraisal, and reaffirmation. *Developmental Cognitive Neuroscience, 17*, 103–117. https://doi.org/10.1016/j.dcn.2015.12.010

Shuval, K., Leonard, T., Drope, J., Katz, D. L., Patel, A. V., Maitin-Shepard, M., Amir, O., & Grinstein, A. (2017). Physical activity counseling in primary care: Insights from public health and behavioral economics. *CA: A Cancer Journal for Clinicians, 67*, 233–244.

Silva M. N., Vieira, P. N., Coutinho, S. R., Minderico, C. S., Matos, M. G., Sardinha, L. B., & Teixeira, P. J. (2010). Using self-determination theory to promote physical activity and weight control: A randomized controlled trial in women. *Journal of Behavioral Medicine, 33*, 110–122.

Silva, V., Dias, C., Corte-Real, N., & Fonseca, A. M. (2017). When is mental toughness 02 needed in judo? Perceptions of athletes and coaches with different levels of achievement. *Revista Portuguesa de Ciências do Desporto, 3*, 26–47. https://doi.org/10.5628/RPCD.17.03.26

Silva-Cavalcante, M. D., Couto, P. G., Azevedo, R. de A., Silva, R. G., Coelho, D. B., Lima-Silva, A. E., & Bertuzzi, R. (2018). Mental fatigue does not alter performance or neuromuscular fatigue development during self-paced exercise in recreationally trained cyclists. *European Journal of Applied Physiology, 118*, 2477–2487. https://doi.org/10.1007/s00421-018-3974-0

Silva-Júnior, F. L. e, Emanuel, P., Sousa, J., Silva, M., Teixeira, S., Pires, F. O., Machado, S., & Arias-Carrion, O. (2016). Prior acute mental exertion in exercise and sport. *Clinical Practice and Epidemiology in Mental Health*, *12*, 94–107. https://doi.org/10.2174/1745017901612010094

Simon, H. A. (1979). Rational decision making in business organizations. *The American Economic Review*, *69*, 493–513.

Simon, H. A. (1983). *Reason in human affairs*. Stanford, CA: Stanford University Press.

Simon, H. A. (1991). Mind as machine: The cognitive revolution in behavioral science. In R. Jessor (Ed.), *Perspectives on behavioral science: The Colorado lectures* (pp. 37–52). Boulder, CO: Westview.

Simon, H. A. (2000). Bounded rationality in social science: Today and tomorrow. *Mind and Society*, *1*(1), 25–39. https://doi.org/10.1007/BF02512227

Simonton, K. L., & Garn, A. C. (2020). Negative emotions as predictors of behavioral outcomes in middle school physical education. *European Physical Education Review*, *26*(4), 764–781. https://doi.org/10.1177/1356336X19879950

Sims, J., Scarborough, P., & Foster, C. (2015). The effectiveness of interventions on sustained childhood physical activity: A systematic review and meta-analysis of controlled studies. *PLoS ONE*, *10*(7), e0132935. https://doi.org/10.1371/journal.pone.0132935

Sirois, F. M., Molnar, D. S., & Hirsch, J. K. (2017). A meta-analytic and conceptual update on the associations between procrastination and multidimensional perfectionism. *European Journal of Personality*, *31*(2), 137–159.

Slater, A., & Tiggemann, M. (2011). Gender differences in adolescent sport participation, teasing, self-objecti fi cation and body image concerns. *Journal of Adolescence*, *34*(3), 455–463. https://doi.org/10.1016/j.adolescence.2010.06.007

Slater, A., & Tiggemann, M. (2012). Time since menarche and sport participation as predictors of self-objectification: A longitudinal study of adolescent girls. *Sex Roles*, *67*(9–10), 571–581.

Slimani, M., Znazen, H., Bragazzi, N. L., Zguira, M. S., & Tod, D. (2018). The effect of mental fatigue on cognitive and aerobic performance in adolescent active endurance athletes: Insights from a randomized counterbalanced, cross-over trial. *Journal of Clinical Medicine*, *7*, 510. https://doi.org/10.3390/jcm7120510

Sloman, S. A. (1996). The empirical case for two systems of reasoning. *Psychological Bulletin*, *119*(1), 3–22. https://doi.org/10.1037/00332909.119.1.3

Slovic, P., Finucane, M., Peters, E., & MacGregor, D. G. (2002a). Rational actors or rational fools: Implications of the affect heuristic for behavioral economics. *Journal of SocioEconomics*, *31*(4), 329–342. https://doi.org/10.1016/S10535357(02)001749

Slovic, P., Finucane, M., Peters, E., & MacGregor, D. G. (2002b). The affect heuristic. In T. Gilovich, D. Grifffin, & D. Kahneman (Eds.), *Heuristics and biases: The psychology of intuitive judgment* (pp. 397–420). New York: Cambridge University Press. https://doi.org/10.1017/CBO9780511808098.025

Slovic, P., Finucane, M. L., Peters, E., & MacGregor, D. G. (2007). The affect heuristic. *European Journal of Operational Research*, *177*, 1333–1352.

Small, D. M., Gregory, M. D., Mak, Y. E. E., Gitelman, D., Mesulam, M. M. M., & Parrish, T. (2003). Dissociation of neural representation of intensity and affective valuation in human gustation. *Neuron*, *39*(4), 701–711. https://doi.org/10.1016/S08966273(03)00467-7.

Smith, A. H. (2009). Distinguishing the holistic context of the inferiority-superiority striving. *Journal of Individual Psychology*, *65*(3), 241–263.

Smith, E. R., & DeCoster, J. (2000). Dual-process models in social and cognitive psychology: Conceptual integration and links to underlying memory systems. *Personality and Social Psychology Review*, *4*(2), 108–131. https://doi.org/10.1207/S15327957PSPR0402_01

Smith, M. M., Sherry, S. B., Rnic, K., Saklofske, D. H., Enns, M., & Gralnick, T. (2016). Are perfectionism dimensions vulnerability factors for depressive symptoms after controlling for neuroticism? A meta-analysis of 10 longitudinal studies. *European Journal of Personality*, *30*(2), 201–212.

Smith, M. M., Sherry, S. B., Chen, S., Saklofske, D. H., Mushquash, C., Flett, G. L., & Hewitt, P. L. (2018). The perniciousness of perfectionism: A meta-analytic review of the perfectionism–suicide relationship. *Journal of Personality*, *86*(3), 522–542.

Smith, M. M., Vidovic, V., Sherry, S. B., Stewart, S. H., & Saklofske, D. H. (2018). Are perfectionism dimensions risk factors for anxiety symptoms? A meta-analysis of 11 longitudinal studies. *Anxiety, Stress, & Coping, 31*(1), 4–20.

Smith, M. R., Chai, R., Nguyen, H. T., Marcora, S. M., & Coutts, A. J. (2019). Comparing the effects of three cognitive tasks on indicators of mental fatigue. *The Journal of Psychology, 153*, 759–783. https://doi.org/10.1080/00223980.2019.1611530

Smith, M. R., Coutts, A. J., Merlini, M., Deprez, D., Lenoir, M., & Marcora, S. M. (2016). Mental fatigue impairs soccer-specific physical and technical performance. *Medicine & Science in Sports & Exercise, 48*, 267–276. https://doi.org/10.1249/MSS.0000000000000762

Smith, M. R., Marcora, S. M., & Coutts, A. J. (2015). Mental fatigue impairs intermittent running performance. *Medicine and Science in Sports and Exercise, 47*, 1682–1690. https://doi.org/10.1249/MSS.0000000000000592

Smith, M. R., Thompson, C., Marcora, S. M., Skorski, S., Meyer, T., & Coutts, A. J. (2018). Mental fatigue and soccer: Current knowledge and future directions. *Sports Medicine, 48*, 1525–1532. https://doi.org/10.1007/s40279-018-0908-2

Smith, B., & Wightman, L. (in press). Promoting physical activity to disabled people: Messengers, messages, guidelines and communication formats. *Disability and Rehabilitation*. https://doi.org/10.1080/09638288.2019.1679896

Smith, M. R., Zeuwts, L., Lenoir, M., Hens, N., Jong, L. M. S. D., & Coutts, A. J. (2016). Mental fatigue impairs soccer-specific decision-making skill. *Journal of Sports Sciences, 34*, 1297–1304. https://doi.org/10.1080/02640414.2016.1156241

Smyth, B. (2018). Fast starters and slow finishers: A large-scale data analysis of pacing at the beginning and end of the marathon for recreational runners. *Journal of Sports Analytics, 4*, 229–242. https://doi.org/10.3233/JSA-170205

Sniehotta, F. F. (2009). Towards a theory of intentional behaviour change: Plans, planning, and self-regulation. *British Journal of Health Psychology, 14*, 261–273.

Sniehotta, F. F., Presseau, J., & Araújo-Soares, V. (2014). Time to retire the theory of planned behaviour [Editorial]. *Health Psychology Review, 8(1)*, 1–7. https://doi.org/10.1080/17437199.2013.869710

Sniehotta, F. F., Scholz, U., & Schwarzer, R. (2005). Bridging the intention–behaviour gap: Planning, self-efficacy, and action control in the adoption and maintenance of physical exercise. *Psychology & Health, 20*(2), 143–160. https://doi.org/10.1080/08870440512331317670

Soman, D. (2004). Framing, loss aversion, and mental accounting. In D. J. Koehler & N. Harvey (Eds.), *Blackwell handbook of judgment and decision making* (pp. 379–398). Hoboken, NJ: Blackwell Publishing.

Sonstroem R., & Harlow Lisa, J. L. (1994). Exercise and self-esteem : Validity of model expansion and exercise associations. *Jounal of Sport & Exercise Psychology, 16*(1), 29–42. https://doi.org/10.1123/jsep.16.1.29

Spear, J. H. (2007). Prominent schools or other active specialties? A fresh look at some trends in psychology. *Review of General Psychology, 11*(4), 363–380. https://doi.org/10.1037/10892680.11.4.363

Sperandei, S., Vierira, M. C., & Reis, A. C. (2016). Adherence to physical activity in an unsupervised setting: Explanatory variables for high attrition rates among fitness center members. *Journal of Science and Medicine in Sport, 19*, 916–920.

Squire, L. R. (2004). Memory systems of the brain: A brief history and current perspective. *Neurobiology of Learning and Memory, 82*(3), 171–177. https://doi.org/10.1016/j.nlm.2004.06.005

St Clair Gibson, A., Swart, J., & Tucker, R. (2018). The interaction of psychological and physiological homeostatic drives and role of general control principles in the regulation of physiological systems, exercise and the fatigue process – The integrative governor theory. *European Journal of Sport Science, 18*(1), 25–36. https://doi.org/10.1080/17461391.2017.1321688

Staiano, W., Bosio, A., Morree, H. M. d., Rampinini, E., & Marcora, S. (2018). The cardinal exercise stopper: Muscle fatigue, muscle pain or perception of effort? In S. Marcora & M. Sarkar (Eds.), *Sport and the brain: The science of preparing, enduring and winning, part C*. Cambridge, MA: Elsevier.

Staiano, W., Parkinson, J., & Marcora, S. (2012). Caffeine moderates the negative effect of mental fatigue on endurance exercise performance ICSEMIS, Glasgow. https://www.researchgate.net/publication/305688141_Caffeine_moderates_the_negative_effect_of_mental_fatigue_on_endurance_exercise_performance

Stanovich, K. E., & Toplak, M. E. (2012). Defining features versus incidental correlates of Type 1 and Type 2 processing. *Mind & Society, 11*, 3–12.

Stanwood, G. D., Washington, R. A., Shumsky, J. S., & Levitt, P. (2001). Prenatal cocaine exposure produces consistent developmental alterations in dopamine-rich regions of the cerebral cortex. *Neuroscience, 106*, 5–14. https://doi.org/10.1016/S0306-4522(01)00256-1

Statistica. (2020). America's Top New Year's Resolutions for 2020. https://www.statista.com/chart/20309/us-new-years-resolutions-2020/

Sterelny, K. (2007). Cognitive load and human decision, or, three ways of rolling the rock up hill. In P. Carruthers, S. Laurence, & S. Stich (Eds.), *The innate mind: Culture and cognition* (Vol. 2, pp. 217–233). Oxford: Oxford University Press. https://www.oxfordscholarship.com/view/10.1093/acprof:oso/9780195310139.001.0001/acprof-9780195310139-chapter-14

Sterling, M., Jull, G., & Wright, A. (2001). The effect of musculoskeletal pain on motor activity and control. *Journal of Pain, 2*(3), 135–145. https://doi.org/10.1054/jpai.2001.19951

Stets, A., Smith, S. L., & Helton, W. S. (2019). Dual-task interference between swimming and verbal memory. *Human Factors*, 18720819871743. https://doi.org/10.1177/0018720819871743

Stiglic, N., & Viner, R. M. (2019). Effects of screentime on the health and well-being of children and adolescents: A systematic review of reviews. *BMJ Open, 9*, e0223191.

Stocker, E., Englert, C., & Seiler, R. (2019). Self-control strength and mindfulness in physical exercise performance: Does a short mindfulness induction compensate for the detrimental ego depletion effect? *Journal of Applied Sport Psychology, 31*, 324–339. https://doi.org/10.1080/10413200.2018.1471754

Stocker, E., Seiler, R., Schmid, J., & Englert, C. (2020). Hold your strength! Motivation, attention, and emotion as potential psychological mediators between cognitive and physical self-control. *Sport, Exercise, and Performance Psychology, 9*, 167–182. https://doi.org/10.1037/spy0000173

Stoeber, J. (2011). The dual nature of perfectionism in sports: Relationships with emotion, motivation, and performance. *International Review of Sport and Exercise Psychology, 4*, 128–145.

Stoeber, J., & Gaudreau, P. (2017). The advantages of partialling perfectionistic strivings and perfectionistic concerns: Critical issues and recommendations. *Personality and Individual Differences, 104*, 379–386.

Stoeber, J., & Otto, K. (2006). Positive conceptions of perfectionism: Approaches, evidence, challenges. *Personality and Social Psychology Review, 10*, 295–319.

Stoeber, J., Otto, K., & Stoll, O. (2006). Multidimensional Inventory of Perfectionism in Sport (MIPS): English Version. School of Psychology, University of Kent. (Unpublished).

Stoeber, J., Uphill, M. A., & Hotham, S. (2009). Predicting race performance in triathlon: The role of perfectionism, achievement goals, and personal goal setting. *Journal of Sport & Exercise Psychology, 31*, 211–245.

Stoll, O., Lau, A., & Stoeber, J. (2008). Perfectionism and performance in a new basketball training task: Does striving for perfection enhance or undermine performance? *Psychology of Sport and Exercise, 9*, 620–629.

Stork, M. J., Graham, J. D., Bray, S. R., & Martin Ginis, K. A. (2017). Using self-reported and objective measures of self-control to predict exercise and academic behaviors among first-year university students. *Journal of Health Psychology*, 22, 1056–1066. https://doi.org/10.1177/1359105315623627

Strachan, S. M., Brawley, L. R., Spink, K. S., Sweet, S. N., & Perras, M. G. M. (2015). Self-regulatory efficacy's role in the relationship between exercise identity and perceptions of and actual exercise behaviour. *Psychology of Sport and Exercise, 18*, 53–59.

Strachan, S. M., Perras, M. G. M., Forneris, T., & Stadig, G. S. (2017). I'm an exerciser: Common conceptualisations of and variation in exercise identity meanings. *International Journal of Sport and Exercise Psychology, 15*, 321–336. https://psycnet.apa.org/doi/10.1080/1612197X.2015.1096292

Strack, F., & Deutsch, R. (2004). Reflective and impulsive determinants of social behavior. *Personality and Social Psychology Review*, *8*(3), 220–247. https://doi.org/10.1207/s15327957pspr0803_1

Strack, F., & Deutsch, R. (2015). The duality of everyday life: Dual-process and dual system models in social psychology. In M. Mikulincer, P. R. Shaver, E. Borgida, & J. A. Bargh (Eds.), *APA handbook of personality and social psychology* (Vol. 1, pp. 891–927). Washington, DC: American Psychological Association. https://doi.org/10.1037/14341-028

Strait, C. E., Blanchard, T. C., & Hayden, B. Y. (2014). Reward value comparison via mutual inhibition in ventromedial prefrontal cortex. *Neuron*, *82*, 1357–1366. https://doi.org/10.1016/j.neuron.2014.04.032

Strangman, G., Culver, J. P., Thompson, J. H., & Boas, D. A. (2002). A quantitative comparison of simultaneous BOLD fMRI and NIRS recordings during functional brain activation. *NeuroImage*, *17*, 719–731. https://doi.org/10.1006/nimg.2002.1227

Strath, S. J., Swartz, A. M., Bassett, D. R., O'Brien, L., King, G., & Ainsworth, B. E. (2000). Evaluation of heart rate as a method for assessing moderate intensity physical activity. *Medicine and Science in Sports and Exercise*, *32*, 465–470. https://doi.org/10.1097/00005768-200009001-00005

Strobach, T., Englert, C., Jekauc, D., & Pfeffer, I. (2020). Predicting adoption and maintenance of physical activity in the context of dual-process theories. *Performance Enhancement & Health*, *8*(1), 100162. https://doi.org/10.1016/j.peh.2020.100162

Stroop, J. R. (1935). Studies of interference in serial verbal reactions. *Journal of Experimental Psychology*, *18*, 643–662. https://doi.org/10.1037/h0054651

Stryker, S., & Burke, P. J. (2000). The past, present and future of an identity theory. *Social Psychology Quarterly*, *63*, 284–297.

Stuntz, C. P., Grosshans, M., Boghosian, R., Brendel, A., & Williamson, M. (2020). Exert more and feel better, not worse?: Examining links among changes in exertion, feelings of accomplishment, and feeling states. *Psychology of Sport and Exercise*, *48*, 101657.

Sullivan, A. N., & Lachman, M. E. (2017). Behavior change with fitness technology in sedentary adults: A review of the evidence for increasing physical activity. *Frontiers in Public Health*, *4*, 289. https://doi.org/10.3389/fpubh.2016.00289

Suls, J., Mogavero, J. N., Falzon, L., Pescatello, L. S., Hennessy, E. A., & Davidson, K. W. (2020). Health behaviour change in cardiovascular disease prevention and management: Meta-review of behaviour change techniques to affect self-regulation. *Health Psychology Review*, *14*(1), 43–65. https://doi.org/10.1080/17437199.2019.1691622

Sundgot-Borgen, J., & Torstveit, M. K. (2004). Prevalence of eating disorders in elite athletes is higher than in the general population. *Clinical Journal of Sport Medicine*, *14*(1), 25–32.

Sutton, S. (2008). How does the Health Action Process Approach (HAPA) bridge the intention–behavior gap? An examination of the model's causal structure. *Applied Psychology*, *57*(1), 66–74. https://doi.org/10.1111/j.1464-0597.2007.00326.x

Swick, D., & Jovanovic, J. (2002). Anterior cingulate cortex and the Stroop task: Neuropsychological evidence for topographic specificity. *Neuropsychologia*, *40*, 1240–1253. https://doi.org/10.1016/S0028-3932(01)00226-3

Symons Downs, D., & Hausenblas, H. A. (2005). Elicitation studies and the theory of planned behavior: A systematic review of exercise beliefs. *Psychology of Sport and Exercise*, *6*, 1–31.

Tamana, S. K., Ezeugwu, V., Chikuma, J., Lefebvre, D. L., Azad, M. B., Moraes, T. J., Subbarao, P., … & Mandhane, P. J. (2019) Screen-time is associated with inattention problems in preschoolers: Results from the CHILD birth cohort study. *PLoS ONE*, *14*(4), e0213995.

Tamminen, K. A., Palmateer, T. M., Denton, M., Sabiston, C., Crocker, P. R. E., Eys, M., & Smith, B. (2016). Exploring emotions as social phenomena among Canadian varsity athletes. *Psychology of Sport and Exercise*, *27*. https://doi.org/10.1016/j.psychsport.2016.07.010

Tangney, J. P., Baumeister, R. F., & Boone, A. L. (2004). High self-control predicts good adjustment, less pathology, better grades, and interpersonal success. *Journal of Personality*, *72*, 271–324. https://doi.org/10.1111/j.0022–3506.2004.00263.x

Tangney, J. P., Miller, R. S., Flicker, L., & Barlow, D. H. (1996). Are shame, guilt, and embarrassment distinct emotions? *Journal of Personality and Social Psychology, 70*, 1256–1269.

Tangney, J. P., & Tracy, J. L. (2012). Self-conscious emotions. In M. R. Leary & J. P. Tangney (Eds.), *Handbook of self and identity* (pp. 446–478). New York: Guilford Press.

Tashman, L. S., Tenenbaum, G., & Eklund, R. (2010). The effect of perceived stress on the relationship between perfectionism and burnout in coaches. *Anxiety, Stress & Coping: An International Journal, 23*(2), 195–212. https://doi.org/10.1080/10615800802629922

Tanna, S., Arbour-Nicitopoulos, K., Rhodes, R. E., & Bassett-Gunter, R. (2017). A pilot study exploring the use of a telephone-assisted planning intervention to promote parental support for physical activity among children and youth with disabilities. *Psychology of Sport and Exercise, 32*, 25–33. https://doi.org/10.1016/j.psychsport.2017.05.003

Taylor, I. M. (2015). The five self-determination mini-theories applied to sport. In S. S. Mellalieu & S. Hanton (Eds.), *Contemporary advances in sport psychology* (pp. 68–90). Abingdon: Routledge.

Taylor, I. M., Boat, R., & Murphy, S. L. (2018). Integrating theories of self-control and motivation to advance endurance performance. *International Review of Sport and Exercise Psychology*, 1–20. https://doi.org/10.1080/1750984X.2018.1480050

Taylor, I. M., Smith, K., & Hunte, R. (in press). Motivation processes during endurance performance. *Scandinavian Journal of Medicine & Science in Sports, 30*, 1769–1776. https://doi.org/10.1111/sms.13739

Taylor, J. L., & Gandevia, S. C. (2008). A comparison of central aspects of fatigue in submaximal and maximal voluntary contractions. *Journal of Applied Physiology, 104*, 542–550. https://doi.org/10.1152/japplphysiol.01053.2007

Tedesqui, R. A. B., & Young, B. W. (2017). Associations between self-control, practice, and skill level in sport expertise development. *Research Quarterly for Exercise and Sport, 88*, 108–113, doi:10.1080/02701367.2016.1267836

Teixeira, P. J., Carraça, E. V., Markland, D., Silva, M. N., & Ryan, R. M. (2012). Exercise, physical activity, and self-determination theory: A systematic review. *The International Journal of Behavioral Nutrition and Physical Activity, 9*, 78. https://doi.org/10.1186/1479-5868-9-78

Teixeira, P. J., Carraça, E. V., Marques, M. M., Rutter, H., Oppert, J. M., De Bourdeaudhuij, I., … & Brug, J. (2015). Successful behavior change in obesity interventions in adults: A systematic review of self-regulation mediators. *BMC Medicine*. https://doi.org/10.1186/s12916-015-0323-6

Thaler, R. H., Sunstein, C. R., & Balz, J. P. (2013). Choice architecture. In E. Shafir (Ed.), *The behavioral foundations of public policy* (pp. 428–439). Princeton, NJ: Princeton University Press.

The Telegraph. (2017). The most common New Year's resolutions – and how to stick to them. https://www.telegraph.co.uk/health-fitness/body/common-new-years-resolutions-stick/

Thøgersen-Ntoumani, C., Dodos, L., Chatzisarantis, N., & Ntoumanis N. (2017). A diary study of self-compassion, upward social comparisons, and body image-related outcomes. *Applied Psychology Health and Well Being, 9*(2), 242–258. https://doi.org/10.1111/aphw.12089

Thompson, J. K., Heinberg, L. J., Altabe, M., & Tantleff-Dunn, S. (1999). Exacting beauty: Theory, assessment, and treatment of body image disturbance. Washington, DC: American Psychological Association.

Thorndike, E. L. (1911). *Animal intelligence: Experimental studies*. New York: Macmillan. https://doi.org/10.5962/bhl.title.55072

Thurber, C., Dugas, L. R., Ocobock, C., Carlson, B., Speakman, J. R., & Pontzer, H. (2019). Extreme events reveal an alimentary limit on sustained maximal human energy expenditure. *Science Advances, 5*(6), eaaw0341. https://doi.org/10.1126/sciadv.aaw0341

Thürmer, J. L., Wieber, F., & Gollwitzer, P. M. (2017). Planning and performance in small groups: Collective implementation intentions enhance group goal striving. *Frontiers in Psychology, 8*, 603. https://doi.org/10.3389/fpsyg.2017.00603

Time Magazine. (2012). Top 10 commonly broken resolutions. http://www.time.com/time/specials/packages/article/0,28804,2040218_2040220_2040221,00.html

Toates, F. (2006). A model of the hierarchy of behaviour, cognition, and consciousness. *Consciousness and Cognition, 15*(1), 75–118. https://doi.org/10.1016/j.concog.2005.04.008

Toering, T., & Jordet, G. (2015). Self-control in professional soccer players. *Journal of Applied Sport Psychology, 27*, 335–350. https://doi.org/10.1080/10413200.2015.1010047

Toft, B. S., & Uhrenfeldt, L. (2015). The lived experiences of being physically active when morbidly obese: A qualitative systematic review. *International Journal of Qualitative Studies on Health and Well-Being*. https://doi.org/10.3402/qhw.v10.28577

Tomkinson, G. R., Lang, J. J., & Tremblay, M. S. (2019). Temporal trends in cardiorespiratory fitness of children and adolescents representing 19 high-income and upper middle-income countries between 1981 and 2014. *British Journal of Sports Medicine, 53*, 478–486.

Tooby, J., Cosmides, L., Sell, A., Lieberman, D., & Sznycer, D. (2008). Internal regulatory variables and the design of human motivation: A computational and evolutionary approach. In A. J. Elliot (Ed.), *Handbook of approach and avoidance motivation* (pp. 251–271). New York: Psychology Press.

Tracy, J. L., & Robins, R. W. (2004). Putting the self into self-conscious emotions: A theoretical model. *Psychological Inquiry*, (15), 103–125. https://doi.org/10.1207/s15327965pli1502

Tracy, J. L., & Robins, R. W. (2007). The psychological structure of pride: A tale of two facets. *Journal of Personality and Social Psychology, 92*, 506–525.

Triplett, N. (1898). The dynamogenic factors in pace-making and competition. *American Journal of Psychology, 9*, 507–533.

Troop, N. A. (2016). The effect of current and anticipated body pride and shame on dietary restraint and caloric intake. *Appetite*. https://doi.org/10.1016/j.appet.2015.09.039

Troop, N. A., & Redshaw, C. (2012). General shame and bodily shame in eating disorders: A 2.5-year longitudinal study. *European Eating Disorders Review, 20*(5), 373–378. https://doi.org/10.1002/erv.2160

Turner, C. E., Byblow, W. D., Stinear, C. M., & Gant, N. (2014). Carbohydrate in the mouth enhances activation of brain circuitry involved in motor performance and sensory perception. *Appetite, 80*, 212–219. https://doi.org/10.1016/j.appet.2014.05.020

Tyler, J. M., & Burns, K. C. (2008). After depletion: The replenishment of the self's regulatory resources. *Self and Identity, 7*, 305–321. https://doi.org/10.1080/15298860701799997

Tyler, J. M., & Burns, K. C. (2009). Triggering conservation of the self's regulatory resources. *Basic and Applied Social Psychology, 31*, 255–266. https://doi.org/10.1080/01973530903058490

Ufholz, K. E., & Harlow, L. L. (2017). Modeling multiple health behaviors and general health. *Preventive Medicine, 105*, 127–134. https://doi.org/10.1016/j.ypmed.2017.08.003

Ullsperger, M., Danielmeier, C., & Jocham, G. (2014). Neurophysiology of performance monitoring and adaptive behavior. *Physiological Reviews, 94*, 35–79. https://doi.org/10.1152/physrev.00041.2012

Vadillo, M. A., Gold, N., & Osman, M. (2016). The bitter truth about sugar and willpower: The limited evidential value of the glucose model of ego depletion. *Psychological Science, 27*, 1207–1214. doi:10.1177/0956797616654911

Vallerand, J., Rhodes, R. E., Walker, G. J., & Courneya, K. S. (2016). Understanding strength exercise intentions and behavior in hematologic cancer survivors: An analysis of the intention-behavior gap. *Journal of Cancer Survivorship, 10*, 144–147.

Vallerand, J. R., Rhodes, R. E., Walker, G. J., & Courneya, K. S. (2018). Feasibility and preliminary efficacy of an exercise telephone counselling intervention for hematologic cancer survivors: A phase II randomized controlled trial. *Journal of Cancer Survivorship, 12*, 357–370.

Vallerand, R. J., & Reid, G. (1984). On the causal effects of perceived competence on intrinsic motivation: A test of cognitive evaluation theory. *Journal of Sport Psychology, 6*(1), 94–102.

Van Cutsem, J., De Pauw, K., Buyse, L., Marcora, S. M., Meeusen, R., & Roelands, B. (2017). Effects of mental fatigue on endurance performance in the heat. *Medicine and Science in Sports and Exercise, 49*, 1677–1687. https://doi.org/10.1249/MSS.0000000000001263

Van Cutsem, J., De Pauw, K., Marcora, S., Meeusen, R., & Roelands, B. (2018). A caffeine-maltodextrin mouth rinse counters mental fatigue. *Psychopharmacology, 235*, 947–958. https://doi.org/10.1007/s00213-017-4809-0

Van Cutsem, J., De Pauw, K., Vandervaeren, C., Marcora, S., Meeusen, R., & Roelands, B. (2019). Mental fatigue impairs visuomotor response time in badminton players and controls. *Psychology of Sport and Exercise, 45*, 101579. https://doi.org/10.1016/j.psychsport.2019.101579

Van Cutsem, J., Marcora, S., De Pauw, K., Bailey, S., Meeusen, R., & Roelands, B. (2017). The effects of mental fatigue on physical performance: A systematic review. *Sports Medicine*, *47*, 1569–1588. https://doi.org/10.1007/s40279-016-0672-0

Van Cutsem, J., Roelands, B., Pluym, B., Tassignon, B., Verschueren, J. O., & Meeusen, R. (2020). Can creatine combat the mental fatigue-associated decrease in visuomotor skills? *Medicine and Science in Sports and Exercise*, *52*, 120–130. https://doi.org/10.1249/mss.0000000000002122

Van Yperen, N. W., Blaga, M., & Postmes, T. (2014). A meta-analysis of self-reported achievement goals and nonself-report performance across three achievement domains (work, sports, and education). *PloS One*, *9*(4), e93594. https://doi.org/10.1371/journal.pone.0093594

Vani, M. F., Pila, E., deJonge, M., Solomon-Krakus, S., & Sabiston, C. M. (2020). "Can you move your fat ass off the baseline?" Exploring the sport experiences of adolescent girls with body image concerns. *Qualitative Research in Sport and Exercise*. https://doi.org/10.1080/2159676X.2020.1771409

Vani, M. F., Pila, E., Willson, E., & Sabiston, C. M. (2020). Body-related embarrassment: The overlooked self-conscious emotion. *Body Image*. https://doi.org/10.1016/j.bodyim.2019.10.007

Vani, M. F., Willson, E., Pila, E., & Sabiston, C. M. (2018). Embarrassment in physical activity: The overlooked emotion. In *International Society of Behavioral Nutrition and Physical Activity Conference*. Hong Kong.

Vansteenkiste, M., & Ryan, R. M. (2013). On psychological growth and vulnerability: Basic psychological need satisfaction and need frustration as a unifying principle. *Journal of Psychotherapy Integration*, *23(3)*, 263–280. https://doi.org/10.1037/a0032359

Vartanian, L. R., Wharton, C. M., & Green, E. B. (2012). Appearance vs health motives for exercise and for weight loss. *Psychology of Sport & Exercise*, *13*, 251–256. https://doi.org/10.1016/j.psychsport.2011.12.005

Venema, T. A. G., Kroese, F. M., & De Ridder, D. T. D. (2018). I'm still standing: A longitudinal study on the effect of a default nudge. *Psychology & Health*, *33*(5), 669–681.

Veness, D., Patterson, S. D., Jeffries, O., & Waldron, M. (2017). The effects of mental fatigue on cricket-relevant performance among elite players. *Journal of Sports Sciences*, *35*, 2461–2467. https://doi.org/10.1080/02640414.2016.1273540

Venhorst, A., Micklewright, D., & Noakes, T. D. (2018). Towards a three-dimensional framework of centrally regulated and goal-directed exercise behaviour: A narrative review. *British Journal of Sports Medicine*, *52*(15), 957–966. https://doi.org/10.1136/bjsports-2016-096907

Verdejo-García, A., & Bechara, A. (2009). A somatic marker theory of addiction. *Neuropharmacology*, *56*(Suppl 1), 48–62. https://doi.org/10.1016/j.neuropharm.2008.07.035

Verhoeven, A. A., Adriaanse, M. A., De Ridder, D. T., De Vet, E., & Fennis, B. M. (2013). Less is more: The effect of multiple implementation intentions targeting unhealthy snacking habits. *European Journal of Social Psychology*, *43*(5), 344–354. https://doi.org/10.1002/ejsp.1963

Verhoeven, A. A., Adriaanse, M. A., de Vet, E., Fennis, B. M., & de Ridder, D. T. (2014). Identifying the 'if 'for 'if-then' plans: Combining implementation intentions with cue-monitoring targeting unhealthy snacking behaviour. *Psychology & Health*, *29*(12), 1476–1492. https://doi.org/10.1080/08870446.2014.950658

Verplanken, B., & Sui, J. (2019). Habit and identity: Behavioral, cognitive, affective, and motivational facets of an integrated self. *Frontiers in Psychology*, *10*, 1504. https://doi.org/10.3389/fpsyg.2019.01504

Vogt, T., Gassen, S., Wrede, S., Spielmann, J., Jedrusiak-Jung, M., Härtel, S., & Mayer, J. (2018). Football practice with youth players in the "Footbonaut". *German Journal of Exercise and Sport Research*, *48*, 341–348. https://doi.org/10.1007/s12662-018-0514-3

Vohs, K. D., Baumeister, R. F., & Ciarocco, N. J. (2005). Self-regulation and self-presentation: Regulatory resource depletion impairs impression management and effortful self-presentation depletes regulatory resources. *Journal of Personality and Social Psychology*, *88*, 632–657. https://doi.org/10.1037/0022-3514.88.4.632

Vrijkotte, S., Meeusen, R., Vandervaeren, C., Buyse, L., Cutsem, J. van, Pattyn, N., & Roelands, B. (2018). Mental fatigue and physical and cognitive performance during a 2-bout exercise test.

International Journal of Sports Physiology and Performance, 13, 510–516. https://doi.org/10.1123/ijspp.2016-0797

Wagstaff, C. R. (2014). Emotion regulation and sport performance. *Journal of Sport and Exercise Psychology, 36*, 401–412. https://doi.org/10.1123/jsep.2013–0257

Walker, A. E. (2007). Multiple chronic diseases and quality of life: Patterns emerging from a large national sample, Australia. *Chronic Illness, 3*, 202–218.

Walsh, M. L. (2000). Whole body fatigue and critical power. *Sports Medicine, 29*, 153–166. https://doi.org/10.2165/00007256-200029030-00002

Walsh, V. (2014). Is sport the brain's biggest challenge? *Current Biology, 24*, 859–60. https://doi.org/10.1016/j.cub.2014.08.003

Warburton, D. E., Nicol, C. W., & Bredin, S. S. (2006). Health benefits of physical activity: The evidence. *Canadian Medical Association Journal, 174*(6), 801–809. https://doi.org/10.1503/cmaj.051351

Warburton, D. E. R., & Bredin, S. S. D. (2017). Health benefits of physical activity: A systematic review of current systematic reviews. *Current Opinion in Cardiology, 32*, 541–556. doi: https://doi.org/10.1097/hco.0000000000000437

Warm, J. S., Parasuraman, R., & Matthews, G. (2008). Vigilance requires hard mental work and is stressful. *Human Factors, 50*, 433–441. https://doi.org/10.1518/001872008X312152

Wascher, E., Rasch, B., Sänger, J., Hoffmann, S., Schneider, D., Rinkenauer, G., ... & Gutberlet, I. (2014). Frontal theta activity reflects distinct aspects of mental fatigue. *Biological Psychology, 96*, 57–65. https://doi.org/10.1016/j.biopsycho.2013.11.010

Watson, P. J., Booker, C K., & Main, C J. (1997). Evidence for the role of psychological factors in abnormal paraspinal activity in patients with chronic low back pain. *Journal of Musculoskeletal Pain, 5*(4), 41–56. https://doi.org/10.1300/J094v05n04_05

Watts, T. W., Duncan, G. J., & Quan, H. (2018). Revisiting the marshmallow test: A conceptual replication investigating links between early delay of gratification and later outcomes. *Psychological Science, 29*, 1159–1177. doi:10.1177/0956797618761661

Weare, K. (2002). The contribution of education to health promotion. In: R. Bunton, & G. Macdonald (Eds.), *Health promotion: Disciplines, diversity, and developments* (2nd ed., pp. 102–125). New York: Routledge. https://doi.org/10.4324/9780203986851-13

Webb, T. L., Christian, J., & Armitage, C. J. (2007). Helping students turn up for class: Does personality moderate the effectiveness of an implementation intention intervention? *Learning and Individual Differences, 17*(4), 316–327. https://doi.org/10.1016/j.lindif.2007.03.001

Webb, T. L., & Sheeran, P. (2003). Can implementation intentions help to overcome ego-depletion? *Journal of Experimental Social Psychology, 39*, 279–286. https://doi.org/10.1016/S0022–1031(02)00527-9

Webb, T. L., & Sheeran, P. (2004). Integrating concepts from goal theories to understand the achievement of personal goals. *European Journal of Social Psychology, 35*(1), 69–96. https://doi.org/10.1002/ejsp.233

Webb, T. L., & Sheeran, P. (2006). Does changing behavioral intentions engender behavior change? A meta-analysis of the experimental evidence. *Psychological Bulletin, 132*(2), 249–268. https://doi.org/10.1037/0033-2909.132.2.249

Webb, T. L., & Sheeran, P. (2008). Mechanisms of implementation intention effects: The role of goal intentions, self-efficacy, and accessibility of plan components. *British Journal of Social Psychology, 47*(3), 373–395. https://doi.org/10.1348/014466607X267010

Webb, T. L., Sheeran, P., & Luszczynska, A. (2009). Planning to break unwanted habits: Habit strength moderates implementation intention effects on behaviour change. *British Journal of Social Psychology, 48*(3), 507–523. https://doi.org/10.1348/014466608X370591

Weinberg, R. S., Gould, D., & Jackson, A. (1979). Expectations and performance: An empirical test of Bandura's self-efficacy theory. *Journal of Sport Psychology, 1(4)*, 320–331.

Weiner, B. (1974). *Achievement motivation and attribution theory.* Morristown, NJ: General Learning Press.

Weinstein, N. D. (1988). The precaution adoption process. *Health Psychology, 7*, 355–386.

Weinstein, N. D. (1993). Testing four competing theories of health-protective behavior. *Health Psychology, 12*(4), 324–333. https://doi.org/10.1037/0278-6133.12.4.324

Werner K. M., & Milyavskaya, M. (2019). Motivation and self-regulation: The role of want-to motivation in the processes underlying self-regulation and self-control. *Social and Personality Psychology Compass, 13*(1), e12425. https://doi.org/10.1111/spc3.12425

Werner, K. M., Milyavskaya, M., Foxen-Craft, E., & Koestner, R. (2016). Some goals just feel easier: Self-concordance leads to goal progress through subjective ease, not effort. *Personality and Individual Differences, 96*, 237–242. https://doi.org/10.1016/j.paid.2016.03.002

West, R. (2009). The multiple facets of cigarette addiction and what the mean for encouraging and helping smokers to stop. *Journal of Chronic Obstructive Pulmonary Disease, 6*, 277–283.

Westbrook, A., & Braver, T. S. (2015). Cognitive effort: A neuroeconomic approach. *Cognitive, Affective, & Behavioral Neuroscience, 15*, 395–415. https://doi.org/10.3758/s13415-015-0334-y

White, N. M., Packard, M. G., & McDonald, R. J. (2013). Dissociation of memory systems: The story unfolds. *Behavioral Neuroscience, 127*(6), 813–834. https://doi.org/10.1037/a0034859

Whitehead, A. E., Jones, H. S., Williams, E. L., Rowley, C., Quayle, L., Marchant, D., & Polman, R. C. (2018). Investigating the relationship between cognitions, pacing strategies and performance in 16.1 km cycling time trials using a think aloud protocol. *Psychology of Sport and Exercise, 34*, 95–109. https://doi.org/10.1016/j.psychsport.2017.10.001

Wieber, F., Thürmer, J. L., & Gollwitzer, P. M. (2013). Intentional action control in individuals and groups. *Acting Intentionally and Its Limits: Individuals, Groups, Institutions*, 133–162. https://doi.org/10.1515/9783110284461.133

Wiedemann, A. U., Lippke, S., & Schwarzer, R. (2012). Multiple plans and memory performance: Results of a randomized controlled trial targeting fruit and vegetable intake. *Journal of Behavioral Medicine, 35*(4), 387–392. https://doi.org/10.1007/s10865-011-9364-2

Wienert, J., Kuhlmann, T., Storm, V., Reinwand, D., & Lippke, S. (2019). Latent user groups of an eHealth physical activity behaviour change intervention for people interested in reducing their cardiovascular risk. *Research in Sports Medicine, 27*, 34–49.

Wilding, S., Conner, M., Sandberg, T., Prestwich, A., Lawton, R., Wood, C., Miles, E., Godin, G., & Sheeran, P. (2016). The question-behaviour effect: A theoretical and methodological review and meta-analysis. *European Review of Social Psychology, 27*(1), 196–230. https://doi.org/10.1080/10463283.2016.1245940

Williams, D. M., & Bohlen, L. C. (2019). Motivation for exercise: Reflective desire versus hedonic dread. In M. H. Anshel (Ed.), *APA handbook of sport and exercise psychology* (Vol. 2, pp. 363–385). Washington, DC: American Psychological Association. https://doi.org/10.1037/0000124-019

Williams, D. M., Dunsiger, S., Emerson, J. A., Gwaltney, C. J., Monti, P. M., & Miranda, R. Jr. (2016). Self-paced exercise, affective response, and exercise adherence: A preliminary investigation using ecological momentary assessment. *Journal of Sport and Exercise Psychology, 38*, 282–291.

Williams, D. M., Dunsiger, S., Miranda, R. Jr., Gwaltney, C. J., Emerson, J. A., Monti, P. M., & Parisi, A. F. (2015). Recommending self-paced exercise among overweight and obese adults: A randomized controlled trial. *Annals of Behavioral Medicine, 49*(2), 280–285.

Williams, D. M., & Evans, D. R. (2014). Current emotion research in health behavior science. *Emotion Review, 6*(3), 277–287. https://doi.org/10.1177/1754073914523052

Williams, D. M., Rhodes, R. E., & Conner, M. T. (2019). Conceptualizing and intervening on affective determinants of health behaviour. *Psychology & Health, 34*, 1267–1281.

Williams, K., Steptoe, A., & Wardle, J. (2013). Is a cancer diagnosis a trigger for health behaviour change? Findings from a prospective, population-based study. *British Journal of Cancer, 108*(11), 2407–2412. https://doi.org/10.1038/bjc.2013.254

Williamson, C., Baker, G., Mutrie, N., Niven, A., & Kelly, P. (2020). Get the message? A scoping review of physical activity messaging. *International Journal of Behavioral Nutrition and Physical Activity, 17*, 51. https://doi.org/10.1186/s12966-020-00954-3

Williamson, J. W., McColl, R., Mathews, D., Mitchell, J. H., Raven, P. B., & Morgan, W. P. (2001). Hypnotic manipulation of effort sense during dynamic exercise: Cardiovascular responses and brain activation. *Journal of Applied Physiology, 90*, 1392–1399. https://doi.org/10.1152/jappl.2001.90.4.1392

Williamson, J. W., McColl, R., Mathews, D., Mitchell, J. H., Raven, P. B., & Morgan, W. P. (2002). Brain activation by central command during actual and imagined handgrip under hypnosis. *Journal of Applied Physiology, 92*, 1317–1324. https://doi.org/10.1152/japplphysiol.00939.2001

Wilson, T. E., Hennessy, E. A., Falzon, L., Boyd, R., Kronish, I. M., & Birk, J. L. (2020). Effectiveness of interventions targeting self-regulation to improve adherence to chronic disease medications: A meta-review of meta-analyses. *Health Psychology Review, 14*(1), 66–85. https://doi.org/10.1080/17437199.2019.1706615

Wilson, M. R., Vine, S. J., & Wood, G. (2009). The influence of anxiety on visual attentional control in basketball free throw shooting. *Journal of Sport and Exercise Psychology, 31*, 152–168. doi:10.1123/jsep.31.2.152

Wilmore, J. H., Costill, D. L., & Kenney, W. L. (2008). *Physiology of sport and exercise* (4th ed.). Champaign, IL: Human kinetics.

Wingfield, G., Marino, F., & Skein, M. (2018). The influence of knowledge of performance endpoint on pacing strategies, perception of effort, and neural activity during 30-km cycling time trials. *Physiological Reports, 6*, e13892. https://doi.org/10.14814/phy2.13892

Winkielman, P., & Berridge, K. C. (2004). Unconscious emotion. *Current Directions in Psychological Science, 13*(3), 120–123. https://doi.org/10.1111/j.09637214.2004.00288.x

Winkielman, P., Berridge, K. C., & Wilbarger, J. L. (2005). Unconscious affective reactions to masked happy versus angry faces influence consumption behavior and judgments of value. *Personality and Social Psychology Bulletin, 31*(1), 121–135. https://doi.org/10.1177/0146167204271309

Wirz, L., Bogdanov, M., & Schwabe, L. (2018). Habits under stress: Mechanistic insights across different types of learning. *Current Opinion in Behavioral Sciences, 20*, 9–16. https://doi.org/10.1016/j.cobeha.2017.08.009

Witte, E. H., & Zenker, F. (2017). Extending a multilab preregistered replication of the ego-depletion effect to a research program. *Basic and Applied Social Psychology, 39*, 74–80. https://doi.org/10.1080/01973533.2016.1269286

Witte, K. (1992). Putting the fear back into fear appeals: The extended parallel process model. *Communications Monographs, 59*(4), 329–349.

Wolff, W. (2017). Funktionelle Nahinfrarotspektroskopie in der sportpsychologischen Forschung. *Zeitschrift für Sportpsychologie, 24*, 17–28. https://doi.org/10.1026/1612-5010/a000184

Wolff, W., Baumann, L., & Englert, C. (2018). Self-reports from behind the scenes: Questionable research practices and rates of replication in ego depletion research. *PLoS One, 13*(6), e0199554. https://doi.org/10.1371/journal.pone.0199554

Wolff, W., Bertrams, A., & Schüler, J. (2019). Trait self-control discriminates between youth football players selected and not selected for the German talent program: A Bayesian analysis. *Frontiers in Psychology, 10*. https://doi.org/10.3389/fpsyg.2019.02203

Wolff, W., Bieleke, M., Hirsch, A., Wienbruch, C., Gollwitzer, P. M., & Schüler, J. (2018). Increase in prefrontal cortex oxygenation during static muscular endurance performance is modulated by self-regulation strategies. *Scientific Reports, 8*, 15756. https://doi.org/10.1038/s41598-018-34009-2

Wolff, W., Bieleke, M., & Schüler, J. (2019). Goal striving and endurance performance. In C. Meijen (Ed.), *Endurance performance in sport: Psychological theory and intervention* (pp. 125–137). Abingdon & New York: Routledge.

Wolff, W., & Martarelli, C. (2020). Bored into depletion? Towards a tentative integration of perceived self-control exertion and boredom as guiding signals for goal-directed behavior. *Perspectives on Psychological Science, 15*(5), 1272–1283. https://doi.org/10.1177/1745691620921394

Wolff, W., Martarelli, C., Schüler, J., & Bieleke, M. (2020). High boredom proneness and low trait self-control impair adherence to social distancing guidelines during the COVID-19 pandemic. *International Journal of Environmental Research and Public Health, 17*. https://doi.org/10.31234/osf.io/jcf95

Wolff, W., Schüler, J., Hofstetter, J., Baumann, L., Wolf, L., & Dettmers, C. (2019). Trait self-control outperforms trait fatigue in predicting MS patients' cortical and perceptual responses to an exhaustive task. *Neural Plasticity*, 2019, 8527203. https://doi.org/10.1155/2019/8527203

Wolff, W., Sieber, V., Bieleke, M., & Englert, C. (2019). Task duration and task order do not matter: No effect on self-control performance. *Psychological Research*. https://doi.org/10.1007/s00426-019-01230-1

Wolff, W., Thürmer, J. L., Stadler, K.-M., & Schüler, J. (2019). Ready, set, go: Cortical hemodynamics during self-controlled sprint starts. *Psychology of Sport and Exercise*, *41*, 21–28. https://doi.org/10.1016/j.psychsport.2018.11.002

Woodman, T., & Hemmings, S. (2008). Body image self-discrepancies and affect: Exploring the feared body self. *Self and Identity*, 7(4), 413–429. https://doi.org/10.1080/15298860701800225

Woolley, K., & Fishbach, A. (2016). For the fun of it: Harnessing immediate rewards to increase persistence in long-term goals. *Journal of Consumer Research*, *42*(6), 952–966.

Woolley, K., & Fishbach, A. (2017). Immediate rewards predict adherence to long-term goals. *Personality and Social Psychology Bulletin*, *43*(2), 151–162. https://doi.org/10.1177/0146167216676480

World Health Organization. (2010). Global recommendations on physical activity for health. Retrieved from https://www.who.int/dietphysicalactivity/global-PA-recs-2010.pdf

World Health Organization. (2016). Prevalence of insufficient physical activity. Global health observatory data. Retrieved from https://www.who.int/gho/ncd/risk_factors/physical_activity_text/en/

World Health Organization. (2018). Fact Sheet – The top 10 causes of death. https://www.who.int/en/news-room/fact-sheets/detail/the-top-10-causes-of-death

Wright, R. A. (2008). Refining the prediction of effort: Brehm's distinction between potential motivation and motivation intensity. Social *and Personality Psychology Compass*, *2*, 682–701. https://doi.org/10.1111/j.1751-9004.2008.00093.x

Wright, R. A., Mlynski, C., & Carbajal, I. (2019). Outsiders' thoughts on generating self-regulatory-depletion (fatigue) effects in limited-resource experiments. *Perspectives on Psychological Science*, *14*, 469–480. https://doi.org/10.1177/1745691618815654

Wrosch, C., Scheier, M. F., & Miller, G. E. (2013). Goal adjustment capacities, subjective well-being, and physical health. *Social and Personality Psychology Compass*, 7(12), 847–860.

Wrosch, C., Scheier, M. F., Miller, G. E., Schulz, R., & Carver, C. S. (2003). Adaptive self-regulation of unattainable goals: Goal disengagement, goal reengagement, and subjective well-being. *Personality and Social Psychology Bulletin*, *29*(12), 1494–1508. https://doi.org/10.1177/0146167203256921

Wundt, W. (1907). *Outlines of psychology*. Leipzig, Germany: Wilhelm Engelmann.Young, M. D., Plotnikoff, R. C., Collins, C., Callister, R., & Morgan, P. J. (2014). Social cognitive theory and physical activity: A systematic review and meta-analysis. *Obesity Reviews*, *12*, 983–995.

Xu, X., Demos, K. E., Leahey, T. M., Hart, C. N., Trautvetter, J., Coward, P., Middleton, K. R., & Wing, R. R. (2014). Failure to replicate depletion of self-control. *PLOS ONE*, *9*, e109950. https://doi.org/10.1371/journal.pone.0109950

Yang, J., Park, K., & Shin, M. (2019). Effects of ego-depletion and state anxiety on performance changes in dart-throwing tasks: A latent curve model approach. *Frontiers in Psychology*, *10*, 2027. https://doi.org/10.3389/fpsyg.2019.02027

Yordy, G. A., & Lent, R. W. (1993). Predicting aerobic exercise participation: Social cognitive, reasoned action, and planned behavior models. *Journal of Sport and Exercise Psychology*, *15*(4), 363–374. https://doi.org/10.1123/jsep.15.4.363

Yusainy, C., & Lawrence, C. (2015). Brief mindfulness induction could reduce aggression after depletion. *Consciousness and Cognition*, *33*, 125–134. https://doi.org/10.1016/j.concog.2014.12.008

Zajonc, R. B. (1980). Feeling and thinking: Preferences need no inferences. *American Psychologist*, *35*(2), 151–175. https://doi.org/10.1037/0003066X.35.2.151

Zajonc, R. B. (1984). On the primacy of affect. *American Psychologist*, *39*(2), 117–123. https://doi.org/10.1037/0003066X.39.2.117

Zajonc, R. B., & Markus, H. (1982). Affective and cognitive factors in preferences. *Journal of Consumer Research*, *9*(2), 123–131. https://doi.org/10.1086/208905

Zemack-Rugar, Y., Corus, C., & Brinberg, D. (2010). The "What the Hell Effect" scale: Measuring post-failure sequential self-control and choice tendencies. In M. C. Campbell, J. Inman, & R.

Pieters (Eds.), *NA – Advances in consumer research* (Vol. 37, pp. 143–145). Duluth, MN: Association for Consumer Research.

Zenko, Z., & Ekkekakis, P. (2019a). Internal consistency and validity of measures of automatic exercise associations. *Psychology of Sport and Exercise, 43*, 4–15. https://doi.org/10.1016/j.psychsport.2018.12.005

Zenko, Z, & Ekkekakis, P. (2019b). Critical review of measurement practices in the study of automatic associations of sedentary behavior, physical activity, and exercise. *Journal of Sport and Exercise Psychology, 41*, 271–288.

Zenko, Z., Ekkekakis, P., & Ariely, D. (2016). Can you have your vigorous exercise and enjoy it too? Ramping intensity down increases postexercise, remembered, and forecasted pleasure. *Journal of Sport and Exercise Psychology, 38*, 149–159.

Zenko, Z., Ekkekakis, P., & Kavetsos, G. (2016). Changing minds: Bounded rationality and heuristic processes in exercise-related judgments and choices. *Sport, Exercise, and Performance Psychology, 5*(4), 337–351. https://doi.org/10.1037/spy0000069

Zenko, Z., Willis, E. A., & White, D. A. (2019). Proportion of adults meeting the 2018 physical activity guidelines for Americans according to accelerometers. *Frontiers in Public Health, 7*, 135.

Zering, J. C., Brown, D. M. Y., Graham, J. D., & Bray, S. R. (2017). Cognitive control exertion leads to reductions in peak power output and as well as increased perceived exertion on a graded exercise test to exhaustion. *Journal of Sports Sciences, 35*, 1799–1807. https://doi.org/10.1080/02640414.2016.1237777

Zhang, C. Q., Zhang, R., Schwarzer, R., & Hagger, M. S. (2019). A meta-analysis of the health action process approach. *Health Psychology, 38*, 623–637.

Ziegelmann, J. P., Lippke, S., & Schwarzer, R. (2006). Adoption and maintenance of physical activity: Planning interventions in young, middle-aged, and older adults. *Psychology & Health, 21*(2), 145–163. https://doi.org/10.1080/14768320500018891

Zimmerman, F. J. (2009). Using behavioral economics to promote physical activity. *Preventive Medicine, 49*, 289–291.

Zorrilla, E. P., & Koob, G. F. (2013). Amygdalostriatal projections in the neurocircuitry for motivation: A neuroanatomical thread through the career of Ann Kelley. *Neuroscience and Biobehavioral Reviews, 37*(9, Part A), 1932–1945. https://doi.org/10.1016/j.neubiorev.2012.11.019

Zubala, A., MacGillivray, S., Frost, H., Kroll, T., Skelton, D. A., Gavine, A., Gray, N. M., Toma, M., & Morris, J. (2017). Promotion of physical activity interventions for community dwelling older adults: A systematic review of reviews. *PLoS ONE, 12*(7), e0180902. https://doi.org/10.1371/journal.pone.0180902

INDEX

Note: **Bold** page numbers refer to tables; *italic* page numbers refer to figures and page numbers followed by "n" denote endnotes.

For Product Safety Concerns and Information please contact our EU
representative GPSR@taylorandfrancis.com
Taylor & Francis Verlag GmbH, Kaufingerstraße 24, 80331 München, Germany

www.ingramcontent.com/pod-product-compliance
Ingram Content Group UK Ltd.
Pitfield, Milton Keynes, MK11 3LW, UK
UKHW050759180926
475701UK00008B/1130

* 9 7 8 0 3 6 7 4 3 3 1 4 7 *